Improving Healthcare Quality and Cost with Six Sigma

FT Press

FINANCIAL TIMES

In an increasingly competitive world, it is quality
of thinking that gives an edge—an idea that opens new
doors, a technique that solves a problem, or an insight
that simply helps make sense of it all.

We work with leading authors in the various arenas
of business and finance to bring cutting-edge thinking
and best-learning practices to a global market.

It is our goal to create world-class print publications
and electronic products that give readers
knowledge and understanding that can then be
applied, whether studying or at work.

To find out more about our business
products, you can visit us at www.ftpress.com.

IMPROVING HEALTHCARE QUALITY AND COST WITH SIX SIGMA

DR. BRETT E. TRUSKO
CAROLYN PEXTON
DR. H. JAMES HARRINGTON
PRAVEEN GUPTA

An Imprint of PEARSON EDUCATION

Upper Saddle River, NJ • New York • London
San Francisco • Toronto • Sydney • Tokyo • Singapore
Hong Kong • Cape Town • Madrid • Paris • Milan
Munich • Amsterdam

Vice President, Publisher: Tim Moore
Executive Editor: Jim Boyd
Editorial Assistant: Pamela Boland
Associate Editor-in-Chief and Director of Marketing: Amy Neidlinger
Publicist: Amy Fandrei
Marketing Coordinator: Megan Colvin
Cover Designer: Alan Clements
Managing Editor: Gina Kanouse
Senior Project Editor: Lori Lyons
Copy Editor: Lisa Thibault
Indexer: WordWise Publishing Services
Compositor: Nonie Ratcliff
Proofreader: Linda K. Seifert
Manufacturing Buyer: Dan Uhrig

© 2007 by Pearson Education, Inc.
Publishing as FT Press
Upper Saddle River, New Jersey 07458

**FT Press offers excellent discounts on this book when ordered in quantity for bulk purchases or special sales.
For more information, please contact U.S. Corporate and Government Sales, 1-800-382-3419,
corpsales@pearsontechgroup.com. For sales outside the U.S., please contact International Sales at
international@pearsoned.com.**

Company and product names mentioned herein are the trademarks or registered trademarks of their respective owners.

MINITAB® and all other trademarks and logos for the Company's products and services are the exclusive property of
Minitab Inc. All other marks referenced remain the property of their respective owners. See minitab.com for more infor-
mation. Portions of the input and output contained in this publication/book are printed with permission of Minitab Inc.
All material remains the exclusive property and copyright of Minitab Inc. All rights reserved.

Printed in the United States of America

ISBN-10: 0-13-261867-2
ISBN-13: 978-0-13-261867-0

This product is printed digitally on demand. This book is the paperback version of an original hardcover book.

Pearson Education LTD.
Pearson Education Australia PTY, Limited.
Pearson Education Singapore, Pte. Ltd.
Pearson Education North Asia, Ltd.
Pearson Education Canada, Ltd.
Pearson Educatio[ac]n de Mexico, S.A. de C.V.
Pearson Education—Japan
Pearson Education Malaysia, Pte. Ltd.

Library of Congress Cataloging-in-Publication Data is on file.

DEDICATION

To my incredibly encouraging wife, Kirsten; my children, Nikolas, Dominick,
and Treyton; my parents, Jerry and Faye Truskowski, for the obvious reasons;
and my wife's parents, Jack and Bonnie Barthel, who have never suggested
(that I know of) that their daughter find a "non-writing" husband.
All of whom prove that even to a Six Sigma practitioner, a special cause
once in a while isn't always bad.
—Brett Trusko

To my family for their love, support, and patience. Special thanks and
appreciation to my husband Craig, my son Kenny and daughter Laurie,
and to my parents, Allen and Muriel Gove.
—Carolyn Pexton

To the many people who have and will die because their healthcare
provider did not use the Six Sigma approaches.
—Dr. H. James Harrington

To my friends and family doctors, including Dr. Robert Weber,
Vinod Motiyani, John Saran, Michael Koehne, Diane Metrick,
John Saniat, Nandini Upadhayay, and Bob Manam.
—Praveen Gupta

CONTENTS

Acknowledgments

Dr. Brett E. Trusko: I would like to acknowledge all my clients and professional contacts—too numerous to mention, but each and every one critically important.

Carolyn Pexton: While we cannot possibly list everyone who has played a role in bringing Six Sigma to healthcare, the authors would like to gratefully acknowledge some of the many practitioners and pioneers who have generously offered their expertise, leadership, and commitment to excellence along the way:

Frank Alvarez, Heather Anderson, Jay Anderson, Sandra Bacon, Elaine Banzhaf, Kathleen Bradley, Jason Broad, Jean Cherry, Alan Cooper, Mary Reich Cooper, Mary Cramer, Edward Craven, Glenn Crotty, Chuck DeBusk, Tom Decker, Chris Desmarais, John Desmarais, John DeVries, Maureen Donahue, Adrienne Elberfeld, Shari Eschete, Barbara Feldman, Glenn Fosdick, Kathleen Gallo, Andy Ganti, Cindy Garza, Tomas Gonzalez, Bonnie Gorges, Dave Green, Ben Hahlen, Roger Hoerl, Blake Hubbard, David Ingraham, John Kalb, David Keefe, Joe Kent, Eleanor Killam, Tracy Kirkconnell, Janice Kishner, Matthew Krathwohl, Beth Lanham, Jason Lebsack, Lisa Lopez, Karen Matijak, Jack McDaniel, Susan McGann, Mara Migliazza, Ben Miles, Donald Miller, Rich Miller, Bev Moncy, Charlie Morris, Robert Morrow, Carol Mullin, Nan Nelson, Gary Norman, Nick Nauman, Monte Parker, Shauna Pearce, Frank Pietrantoni, Nancy Pratt, Darcy Prejeant, Irma Pye, Art Rangel, Lou Rhodes, Nancy Riebling, Nancy Roberts, Heath Rushing, Deborah L. Smith, Sondra Smith, Todd Sperl, Jim Springfield, Rich Stahl, Greg Stock, Hylton Surrett, Carolyn Sweetapple, Jim Swindler, Michael Toomey, Barbara Truskoski, James Tucci, Kevin Tuttle, Mary Ellen Uphoff, Mark Van Kooy, Matiana Vela, Jennifer Volland, Lory Wallach, Scott Ward, Marie Weissman, David Yarbro, Lois Yingling, Deborah P. Young, Michael Zia, Robert Zisman.

Special thanks to Chuck DeBusk for taking his valuable time to review and provide feedback during the content development process. Thanks also to Mike Cyger, president of iSixSigma, for establishing a special networking and education portal for Six Sigma and Lean practitioners in healthcare (www.healthcare.isixsigma.com).

Dr. H. James Harrington: I would like thank Dr. Tom McNellis for his insight into the use of Six Sigma in the healthcare operations and thank Candy Rogers for typing the manuscript and proofreading the many drafts.

Praveen Gupta: Thanks to my coauthors for memorable teamwork, family members for support, and colleagues and friends for ideas. I would like to especially acknowledge my in-laws—Mummy, Papa, Alka, Seema, Navita, and Arun—for their unquestionable support that encourages me to pursue my interests in writing, including this one. My heartfelt thanks go to my wife, Archana, for instilling healthy habits in our family. The best healthcare begins at home.

Thanks also to the team at Pearson for their guidance and support throughout the project: Jim Boyd, Amy Neidlinger, Amy Fandrei, Alan Clements, Lori Lyons, Lisa Thibault, Nonie Ratcliff, and Linda Seifert.

ABOUT THE AUTHORS

Dr. Brett E. Trusko is a Biomedical Informatics and Healthcare Quality Researcher at the Mayo Clinic College of Medicine, where he studies healthcare quality issues. He is a frequent keynote speaker as both a healthcare quality professional and a healthcare futurist. He has written several hundred articles on issues related to improving healthcare quality. In addition, he works with organizations to apply innovative thinking to their Six Sigma initiatives. A Master Six Sigma Black Belt, Dr. Trusko's background includes Board Member, US Health Information Technology Standards Panel, 10 years of clinical experience, and 20 years of consulting with several large multinational consulting firms. He spent several years working closely with the late Russell Coile, Jr. as a healthcare futurist. Dr. Trusko can be reached at brett.trusko@gmail.com.

Carolyn Pexton has more than 20 years' experience in communications and healthcare, and is currently serving as the director of communications for Performance Solutions at GE Healthcare. In this role, she works closely with healthcare customers and manages public relations, marketing communications, and internal communications for the Performance Solutions team. Pexton is Six Sigma Green Belt-certified, and has presented and published extensively on a variety of topics including Lean Six Sigma and change management within the healthcare industry. Carolyn can be reached at carolyn.pexton@med.ge.com.

Dr. H. James Harrington is one of only five Grand Master Six Sigma Black Belts worldwide. He has published more than 25 books related to performance improvement. In the book *Tech Trending*, Dr. Harrington was referred to as "the quintessential tech trender." *The New York Times* referred to him as having a "...knack for synthesis and an open mind about packaging his knowledge and experience in new ways—characteristics that may matter more as prerequisites for new-economy success than technical wizardry..." He wrote the book from which other consultants work. Not only has Dr. Harrington been honored with many national and international awards, he has also had four quality awards named after him. Former President Bill Clinton commissioned Dr. Harrington as an ambassador for Good Will. Dr. Harrington can be reached at hjh@harrington-institute.com

Praveen Gupta, President of Accelper Consulting, has more than 25 years of experience in business performance improvement. Praveen worked with the inventor while developing the Six Sigma methodology in the late eighties. Praveen has authored several books, including *Six Sigma Business Scorecard* and *Business Innovation*. A Master Six Sigma Black Belt, Praveen currently consults with organizations looking for sustained profitable growth through excellence and innovation. Praveen can be reached at praveen@accelper.com.

FOREWORD

Through all of human history, health caregivers have been respected individuals in society. Now with the Internet, consumerism, the Baby Boomers aging, risk adjustment, outcomes measurement, and quality metrics, blind trust in clinicians has begun to erode.

The "Crossing the Quality Chasm" reports (Committee on Quality of Healthcare in America, 2001) by the Institute of Medicine over the past decade have identified the stark reality of errors in the healthcare system—more than 98,000 preventable deaths each year. Although the exact number is disputed, one life lost to error is one too many.

Many in academia, clinical practice, and government have suggested that use of information technology in healthcare is the answer to error reduction. However, information technology by itself can have only a limited impact, unless the information is used for deliberate improvement in healthcare practices. Despite the evidence that IT improves care, basic electronic information about patients remains out of reach for most clinicians.

The rising cost of healthcare and sustained poor quality mandates deployment of better practices and continual improvement in healthcare operations at a much faster rate than historically achieved. There have been many attempts to improve quality in healthcare, but most have been based on management fads and have been unsustainable. Six Sigma methodologies have been deployed successfully in the industrial sector. I believe the healthcare industry can realize similar benefits using Six Sigma. Many healthcare organizations have already benefited from Six Sigma deployment.

The *Improving Healthcare Quality* book offers help. The four coauthors of the book, experts in the excellence, process quality. and healthcare fields, have collaborated nicely to offer a customized approach to implementing Six Sigma in the healthcare industry. The book is very well organized and contains actual cases for ease of learning and application.

I believe *Improving Healthcare Quality* is the most comprehensive book for applying an improvement methodology in healthcare to improve both quality and cost. It is time healthcare professionals—administrators, physicians, and support staff—learn about reputed improvement methodologies and commit to improve healthcare services to clients. We have committed our lives to serve people; we must recommit our abilities to do our best. *Improving Healthcare Quality* will be a vital tool that will enable us to do our best.

I have enjoyed reading the book, and expect the same for you, the reader. I am confident that trust in clinicians and confidence in the healthcare system will markedly increase.

John D. Halamka, MD
Harvard Medical School

INTRODUCTION

This book is an introduction to quality methods, Six Sigma, and healthcare. No doubt, if you purchase this book you are concerned about the quality issue and the future of healthcare. You have probably tried TQM (Total Quality Management), CQI (Continuous/Clinical Quality Improvement), and a number of other approaches to improving quality in your organization. We too have thought about this long and hard throughout the years as consultants, speakers, and writers in the healthcare field. You might be familiar with Dr. Brett Trusko's work as a futurist who collaborated with the late Russell Coile Jr. Little did he know some 20 years ago that most of our work in healthcare would boil down to quality issues. We have spoken and written about quality, organizational development, motivation, teamwork, information technology, and finance in healthcare with a Pollyanna perspective that with enough caring and hard work we can solve the problems of healthcare. Only recently did we really begin to understand that all these issues were reflective of a dysfunctional system that works against excellence in healthcare.

For example, our healthcare system in the U.S. systematically rewards heroics and intervention while penalizing planning, quality, management, and effectiveness. For years we have reimbursed providers based upon costs while efficiency has generally resulted in lower reimbursements. In our capitalist economy, we usually find that the best provider of a good or service is the one that is the most efficient, not the least. But this is precisely how we handle healthcare in the U.S. The more healthcare resources we consume as providers of healthcare, the more reimbursements we receive. How would we feel about paying a mechanic more for replacing parts that our car doesn't even need? How about rewarding grocery stores for finding the most expensive method of shipping groceries to the store?

Of course, healthcare providers aren't mechanics, and hospitals aren't grocery stores. Hospitals are hospitals and physicians are physicians. Healthcare is generally an imprecise science. However, using the excuse of an imprecise science as a reason not to improve healthcare is irresponsible. In fact, healthcare is an imprecise science, but at the same time there is much in healthcare that can and should be improved.

The authors have worked in healthcare for more than 60 years. We have been unit secretaries, surgical scrub technicians, and administrators. We have seen healthcare finances from the inside out and worked in the clinical setting. Healthcare is not an easy business. Healthcare professionals are some of the most dedicated and caring people on earth. When publications such as the May 1, 2006, edition of *Time* magazine (Gibbs, 2006) and morning news shows like *The Today Show* and others prominently feature stories about how to protect yourself from medical errors in a hospital, we would expect to see more healthcare professionals expressing outrage against the system. Dedicated, caring professionals are and should be outraged at the shallow investigative reporting. But the fact is that healthcare professionals usually don't have a very good defense against attacks, because in most cases, they don't really know what happened. They don't know what happened because they don't understand their processes, and they don't understand their processes because the processes tend to be complicated and fluid.

As professionals who have worked in healthcare for so many years, we the authors can personally vouch for the fact that most healthcare providers strive for delivery excellence. These providers have witnessed miracles, such as the snaking of wires from the leg to the brain to clear a clot and save a life. They have seen two-pound premature babies live, and people on the verge of death brought back to living. Miracles of excellence happen constantly in the healthcare provider's world. And when errors occur, healthcare professionals grieve. There may be no other profession or industry that is more driven by a desire for excellence in the world. Unfortunately, processes and systems created by misaligned incentives sometimes make it difficult to provide excellence. This is where discussion of Six Sigma really begins.

Six Sigma is an approach to quality that should appeal to healthcare professionals intrinsically. It is based on improving processes and procedures, based on evidence. One of our authors has a bachelor's degree in biology, two have degrees in engineering, and others have diplomas in business. Dr. Trusko stated in one of our early writers meetings that when he first heard of Six Sigma years ago, it was like coming home. Of course, running a business requires making decisions based upon facts and not just intuition or politics. Unfortunately, this is exactly the way most healthcare provider institutions are run. Now throw into the mix the politics of government funding and insurance companies, and it's no wonder we accomplish anything with healthcare. Not that governments and insurance companies are not trying to do the right thing; in fact, the motivation is based on doing the most good for the most people. Healthcare providers, in a relatively weak bargaining position due to the cottage nature of the industry, generally have to work within the system that the government and the insurance industry have created. But there are things that healthcare providers can do to increase efficiency, reduce malpractice costs, and increase profits. Even in a system that rewards resource utilization, having an intimate understanding of your business, your processes, and the influence you have on outcomes allows the healthcare provider to maximize its revenue while minimizing the anguish of medical mistakes.

THE NEED FOR CUTTING COSTS AND IMPROVING QUALITY IN HEALTHCARE

TRENDS IN THE HEALTHCARE INDUSTRY

SECTIONS

The Quality Crisis in Healthcare
Demographics: Financial, Political, Social, and Technological
The Cost of Healthcare and Six Sigma
Healthcare Quality and Error Reduction
Conclusion

Healthcare is preparing to go into hyper-change. Just as the computer and the Internet have enabled "telework," home shopping, and a permanent change in the recording industry's distribution strategy, so will healthcare be affected in the next 10 years.

Events that are unfolding and are leading the change in healthcare are threefold:

- Evolution in the healthcare IT industry

- Introduction of HSA/CDHC and consumerism in healthcare

- Recognition of medical errors as a serious issue in healthcare

This book is not about the evolution of the healthcare IT industry, nor is it about consumerism in healthcare. It is, however, about medical errors, and the counterpoint of the issue, healthcare excellence—specifically, healthcare excellence that can be achieved through Six Sigma.

Trends in healthcare have been evolving in the direction of the customer since the advent of the Internet. One of the first popular search topics was healthcare, and it continues today. We have coined the phrase, "The Wired Retired" just to describe those aging baby boomers who have helped fuel the most rapid adoption of a technology in the history of the world. These boomers, wired retired, and even the young have not accepted the status quo of healthcare as it has been delivered since the dawn of the medicine man.

This education of the healthcare consumer has, for better or worse, led to the start of a healthcare consumer revolution, which logically leads to the recognition of quality and medical mistakes. This chapter describes some of these trends and how they lead us to Six Sigma.

THE QUALITY CRISIS IN HEALTHCARE

"Hospital Apologizes for Surgical Mistake," *The New York Times,* January 19, 2003, by the Associated Press. Linda McDougal, 46, underwent a double mastectomy after being advised by her surgeon that she had an aggressive form of cancer. Two days after the surgery, she was informed that the lab at United Hospital in St. Paul, MN, had switched her lab results with another patient and that Ms. McDougal in fact had never had cancer. Ms. McDougal has been fighting several infections and will undergo reconstructive surgery before she decides whether to sue for malpractice.

Medical errors became a national issue in 1999, when the Institute of Medicine issued a highly published report stating that medical errors in the United States contribute to more than 1 million injuries and up to 98,000 deaths annually. A study by Thomas, Studdert, et al.[1] in *Inquiry* of 14,732 randomly selected 1,992 discharges from 28 hospitals found that medical errors cost an average of more than $65,000 per incident.

The most common medical errors are

- Sepsis infections, which result in a 22 percent higher risk of death and add an additional cost of $57,727 to the hospital stay and 11 extra days of hospitalization
- Surgical wounds, which result in a 10 percent higher risk of death and add an average additional cost of $40,323, plus more extra days of hospitalization
- Medical objects accidentally left in patients
- Adverse drug reactions (wrong or incorrect quantity of a drug given to the patient)

A study published in the *Journal of the American Medical Association* indicated that medical injuries in U.S. hospitals in 2000 led to about 32,600 deaths and at least 2.4 million extra days of patient hospitalization, with an additional cost to the U.S. healthcare system of about $9.3 billion. This is considerably lower than the 1999 study on medical errors reported by the Institute of Medicine that stated up to 98,000 deaths were caused by medical errors. In fact, it doesn't matter what the correct number actually is—even one lost life is one too many!

Although much of the information presented so far relates to the U.S. healthcare system, it is arguably one of the best in the world, and its error rate is probably below average. In some developed countries, one would assume the healthcare error rate is many times worse than in the U.S. The developing countries error rate is even much higher.

In an article recently published in the *International Journal of Health Care Quality Assurance*, Jim Harrington and Brett Trusko wrote that you are probably safer traveling in Saudi Arabia than lying in bed at your local hospital. In 2003, the best estimates are that only approximately 613 people were killed by terrorists. Our assessment when we wrote the article in 2005 was that by far, healthcare and government (confirmed by the handling of the Hurricane Katrina response) are the two major industries that have the biggest opportunity for improvement in process and quality.

Unfortunately, and even today with all of the coverage around healthcare related to Health Savings Accounts (HSAs), it seems that American consumers care less about the number of people killed due to medical errors than they care about other industry errors such as e-coli, mad cow disease, and airline accidents. As a case in point, let's examine the response to the Firestone/Ford rollover case a few years back. At worst, the problem killed a few dozen people, but it was highlighted on television and in newspapers, and at several times the Federal Government felt obligated to step into the debate. As a result of the bad publicity, Firestone and Ford stock fell. However, the truth is that you are also safer driving your car (with the defective tires) than you are lying in a hospital bed.

Simply put, healthcare needs to be reinvented. Some statistics related to the healthcare quality crisis in America include

- By extrapolating the deaths attributable to healthcare errors in the United States to the global population, we estimate that somewhere between 1.5 million and 2.2 million people die annually as a result of healthcare errors. The low-end estimates of a global pandemic related to bird flu are smaller than those of medical mistakes.[2] However, more money is spent to protect the world from bird flu than medical errors (understanding that the potential deaths from bird flu would outnumber those from errors by many thousands if the direst of predictions come true).

- According to the Centers for Disease Control, 1 person dies every 8 minutes as a result of nosocomial infection, 95 percent of which are preventable (CDC).

- Hospitals with an "atmosphere of mistrust" have a death rate 58 percent higher than average.[3]

- Some 2 million patients per year contract an infection in the U.S. while hospitalized for other conditions, and 88,000 die as a direct or indirect result. This adds an extra healthcare cost of $5 billion.[4]

- In the U.S., healthcare accounts for 15 percent of the GDP and, according to Uwe Reinhardt, a noted health policy expert and economist at Princeton University, that number is expected to be 20 percent of the GDP by 2013.[5]

- According to the Corporate Research Group, healthcare premiums rose only a modest 9 percent in 2005. Historically speaking, this is a small increase. Recent studies suggest that that amount is more in the last couple of years.

- U.S. national healthcare spending is $1.7 trillion.

- Approximately 46.6 million people in the U.S. do not have healthcare insurance.

- The first group of baby boomers is now retiring. This represents some 77 million people entering a time of life when healthcare consumption begins to rise.

- U.S. healthcare consumers pay the highest prices in the world for drugs, therapists, medical diagnostics, and treatment technologies, effectively subsidizing both healthcare research and development and treatment in other industrialized nations, as well as developing countries.

- Patients are uninformed about the quality of service and acceptable standard of care they will receive. This is largely in part due to poor information technologies in the United States. This issue is being addressed with approximately $100 million given to the Healthcare Technology office, which is only a fraction of what has been spent on the Iraq war, Homeland Security, and more importantly, other countries on their healthcare IT infrastructure.

- Geographic location is a significant variable in the quality of care a patient receives because higher quality doctors tend to be attracted to urban locations.

- It takes 15 to 20 years for evidence to be integrated into clinical care.

- Few healthcare facilities are ISO 9000 certified.

- Healthcare fraud and abuse are estimated to cost between $50 and $75 billion per year.

- Performance metrics in healthcare are virtually nonexistent, and there is strong resistance due to nonconformity of processes, regional differences in the way healthcare is practiced, and the fear of loss of business or litigation based on poor performance against metrics. Unfortunately, it is the understanding and communication of this information that helps to solve other problems.

- Indications are that physicians incorporate the latest medical evidence into their treatment decisions only 50 percent of the time, preferring to practice what they are comfortable with.

- Healthcare costs are contributing to the move of jobs off-shore (a tax on employment) with the latest reports attributing $1,200 of the cost of a new American-made car to healthcare premiums.

- According to the World Health Organization, administrative costs account for 15 percent of the healthcare premium dollar, and some studies suggest as much as 25 percent.

- We estimate that 30–40 percent of the cost of waste in the healthcare system is caused by medical inefficiencies and resultant errors.

- According to the Kaiser Family Foundation, the uninsured are about three times as likely as the insured to postpone seeking care, fail to get needed care, leave prescriptions unfilled, or skip recommended treatment. And many end up disabled—or die—because of these delays.
- The U.S. is the only developed country where healthcare is not run by the government.
- Total Quality Management (TQM) and Continuous Quality Improvement (CQI) were at best poorly implemented in most healthcare organizations in the 1980s and '90s.
- There is a critical shortage of nurses.
- The U.S. Government estimates that it can save $140 billion per year through improved patient care and the elimination of redundant tests.
- According to the Institute of Medicine, a total of 2 percent of hospital patients experience an adverse drug reaction, resulting in increased length of stay and $4,700 added in needless expense. This accounts for 2.5 percent of the typical hospital's budget.
- The healthcare error rate is approximately 6,210 errors per million opportunities (3.8 sigma), and for some, treatment activities run as high as a 1 sigma. Compare this with the manufacturing Six Sigma standard of 3.4 errors per opportunity for all processes.
- A patient improves faster at home by 10 to 60 percent than in a healthcare facility.
- In 2002, 13 percent of hospitals reported that they used EHRs (Electronic Health Records) (HIMSS, 2002). Physician office EHR use rates reported in 2002 ranged from 14 percent to a possible high of 28 percent, but there is almost no integration between systems, which is where the real value lies.
- About 20 percent of U.S. products and services' extra cost is caused by the legal system.
- In Canada, medical errors account for 9,000 to 24,000 deaths per year.
- One in four babies born vaginally suffers injury.
- One hip is fractured out of every 1,124 hospitalized seniors.
- Adverse events occurred in 7.5 percent of medical or surgical admissions, 37 percent of which are deemed preventable.
- Australia's adverse event rate is 16.6 percent (the Quality in Australian Healthcare Study Report).
- The U.K.'s adverse event rate is about 10 percent (UK Department of Health).
- Europe's adverse event rate is about 10 percent (European Working Party on Health).
- In the U.K., the average waiting time to get into a hospital is 9 months after the doctor recommends an operation. The government is trying to improve this to 18 weeks.

If this isn't enough to make you stand up and pay attention, then this book isn't for you.

DEMOGRAPHICS: FINANCIAL, POLITICAL, SOCIAL, AND TECHNOLOGICAL

The U.S., and in many respects, the global healthcare system, is in a period of tremendous change. After a prolonged period of technological innovation in the delivery of clinical care and medical advances, the realization has finally hit that delivery of quality healthcare might mean a little more than the latest scanning technology.

Changes in demographics, the political environment, social perceptions of healthcare quality, and information technology have the potential to dramatically change the face of healthcare. The population in the industrialized countries is (on the average) aging, creating issues of financing even more expensive technologies. Because the majority of healthcare in both the United States and the world is financed by the government, political questions related to healthcare delivery have been moving slowly to center stage and is anticipated to be the major focus of many elections in the coming years. Societal norms and values with questions about the quality of life have prompted discussions related to the ability to maintain life regardless of the perceived quality of that life.

While all of these issues will be played out over the next several years, there is a common theme related to the health of not just the U.S. population, but that of a global community—and that is the value and the quality of the healthcare delivered, not just the quantity.

Improved value and quality, which I will refer to as *efficient healthcare*, allows us to address directly or indirectly many of the problems we face in relation to the trends described earlier in this chapter. Efficient healthcare allows us to address the increased needs of a changing demographic in a fair and equitable manner, whether that be the aging of the industrialized world, the changing face of poverty, the uninsured, or the limitations on a government in a publicly financed healthcare system. Efficient healthcare assures us that the financing for healthcare isn't wasted or otherwise expropriated in fraudulent billing schemes or through administrative costs, estimated to be approximately 31 percent of the cost of healthcare in the United States (or approximately $300 billion) in 1999.[6] Granted, much of this is due to bureaucratic and regulatory requirements, but a great deal is also due to the requirements of defensive medicine and issues of quality, especially related to medical mistakes. In a major study by Brennan[7], more than 30,000 patients admitted to 51 hospitals in the State of New York were studied with the finding that adverse events, defined as "injuries resulting from the care process," occurred in 3.7 percent of all patients who were hospitalized. Of the 3.7 percent, 27.5 percent of events were judged to be caused by negligence. Death was associated with 13.6 percent of the occurrences with "a substantial amount of injury to patients from medical management, and many injuries are a result of substandard care." A similar study by Thomas, et al.[8] consisted of 15,000 discharges from Colorado and Utah hospitals, finding that 2.9 percent experienced an adverse event, and 32.6 percent in Utah and 27.4 percent in Colorado led to a death rate of 8.8 percent in the population suffering adverse events. The data from these two studies contributed to the now famous estimate in 1997 by the Institute of Medicine[9] that 44,000 to 98,000 Americans died annually due to negligent care. While the IOM asked for a 50 percent reduction in medical errors in five years, in that initial report the best they could say in 2005 was that we "have a vision in place."[10]

Although the 2004 presidential election held promise for a national debate on healthcare, the war in Iraq and issues of terrorism overshadowed the discussion (which is interesting given the cost of healthcare and the fact that the number of people who perished in the attacks on the World Trade Center is equal to the number that perish every three days due to medical mistakes). As the nation once again finds its footing, and job losses attributable to the high cost of healthcare are addressed, there promises to be interesting debates in the political arena.

Societal questions remain the great unknown of healthcare quality. Attitudes about healthcare quality are bound to change as society assesses healthcare issues, especially in light of the fact that more and more Americans and citizens of the industrialized world will be faced with difficult decisions regarding the healthcare of their ever-aging parents and friends. Will quality take the place of quantity, or will society demand greater quantity, regardless of the quality? Most likely, there will be greater demands for both quality and quantity, with the likely outcome being greater quality and less quantity.

Technologically speaking, information will be the key to the kingdom of healthcare quality. The 2001 IOM report made ten recommendations, seven of which are dependent on improvements in IT. Worldwide healthcare IT improvements have become a priority with major initiatives in the U.K., Australia, and Canada, to name a few. The United States even appointed a healthcare IT czar. IT improvements are dependent on standards, agreements, and legal modifications centered on the medical record. Dramatic efforts are taking place at the time of this writing, and we anticipate that high quality information in healthcare will become more available within the next five years, creating the opportunity to lay the groundwork for quality efforts today.

Demographics

The single greatest driving force in healthcare is the aging of baby boomers. This population is roughly defined as individuals between the ages of 45 and 62 in 2006. Without a doubt, the aging of the industrialized world and the resultant increase in healthcare consumption throughout the next 40 years will present challenges to governments and societies that have never been seen before. According to actuaries at the Centers for Medicare and Medicaid Services (CMS), people age 65 and older spent $11,089 for personal healthcare goods and services in 1999, while those under 65 spent only $2,793 per capita, with the average person in the United States spending $3,834 per year. As a percent of total healthcare spending, that over-65 population, which is currently approximately 13 percent of the population, represents 36 percent of total healthcare dollars spent. Or stated another way, the $387 billion dollars spent on the over-65 group is quadruple of that spent on the under-65.[11]

Taken as a purely futuristic exercise, we can extrapolate forward that given the estimated percent of those older than 65 expected in the year 2019 to move from an estimated 12.5 percent of the population in 1999 to 15.7 percent of the population in 2019 and to 21.3 percent in 2049 will consume more than half the money spent on healthcare. Regardless of quality improvement efforts, the percentages will remain very high and continue to go higher over time. The most severe implication of this is that healthcare for the elderly is paid in large part by the government (46 percent Medicare and 15 percent Medicaid). If all we consider is the total cost outlay to a government that is already struggling financially, then it is clear to see that Health and Human Services will soon begin to demand value for the healthcare dollars it spends.

Older people consume more healthcare than younger people. Given the shift in the population in the United States, this means that we may see an inflation-adjusted increase (held constant in today's dollars) in healthcare expenses of greater than \$3.2 trillion almost entirely accounted for by the aging population and healthcare inflation (at 10 percent annually). Additionally, the aging baby boomers do not have as many younger people contributing to the Medicare system, which conceivably could lead to several outcomes, including greater borrowing by the government, higher taxes to pay for healthcare for the retired, or in all likelihood reduction in services to the elderly.

Because none of these alternatives is desirable (and perhaps not possible), we have another option: to improve the quality of healthcare dramatically during the next five to ten years, aimed at reducing the costs of healthcare to the entire population, and potentially aim for an actual inflation-adjusted decrease in the cost of healthcare. Quality initiatives can aid in the overall plan to improve quality and reduce costs.

The aging population will lead to a number of other changes in the healthcare system, such as a shift in the spending patterns of healthcare beneficiaries. Not only will the costs go up as older Americans change their spending patterns, but the mix of expenses will change. For example, it is anticipated that as older women move beyond menopause, there will be a large jump in heart disease among females—a condition that is largely ignored in the female population today and, consequently, ignored in general.

Along with shifts in spending patterns, the federal government will find that federal budget allocations will become more and more difficult as healthcare takes an increasing amount of the pie. Current account deficits in the industrial nations of the world will become larger and create real choices between caring for the population and other priorities of the federal government. Given that there is no viable choice to make between healthcare and the rest of the "rest" of the governments' priorities, the only choice is to bring the cost of healthcare down, either artificially through reduced reimbursements (not a realistic alternative), allocations (another difficult choice), or by improving the quality of healthcare to the point where costs are actually decreasing.

One of the great taxes that few know they pay is collected through the government paying for healthcare at a rate below the cost of healthcare, effectively passing that cost on to individuals who are insured or creating a "healthcare tax" that the average individual isn't aware they pay. The fact is that we already have a form of socialized medicine—it just isn't universal coverage.

A potential bright side to the aging demographic is the shift in occupations that will become available to American workers. The baby boomers are the wealthiest population in the history of the world. After retirement and throughout the next 40 years, there will be unlocked wealth on a scale never seen before in history. This wealth will be available to a smaller population, potentially creating incredible opportunities for enterprising individuals who can deliver healthcare and personal services cheaper, better, and faster.

Other Demographic Considerations

Other drivers of healthcare change are related to structural changes in society, such as the rise of immigrants, money in the hands of females, and perhaps most importantly a term used more and more often these days—consumer centric healthcare.

Females

Females in the United States are the primary purchasers of healthcare. It is an unfortunate fact of the U.S. healthcare system that most healthcare delivery is focused on men, a fact that many healthcare providers are beginning to recognize and address. Couple this with the fact that the aging demographic is not only aging, but is living longer, and many of those living longer are females. In fact, the current population of baby boomers will live longer than any generation in the history of the world. Not only will they live longer, they will have problems that we never before envisioned. It is likely that the older female population in 50 years will be higher than today, and also bestowed with the power to change the way healthcare is delivered.

Obesity

In many parts of the world, particularly in industrialized nations, the average weight of the population in steadily increasing. Of particular concern is the increased rate of childhood obesity (or clinically overweight children), which by some estimates applies to almost a third of the population in some countries. Yes, you may want to read that again—according to www.earthtimes. org, fully a third of the children in the U.K. are obese. And what we know about obesity is that people who are heavy generally are sicker than the non-obese person, and that the heavier a person, the less likely they will be to get well once they are sick. Illnesses that strike the obese are diabetes, heart disease, and many related bone and joint diseases.

Racial Diversity

Racial diversification in most developing countries is increasing due to falling fertility rates. While many deny the need, a generally large population of older citizens requires a support infrastructure that is no longer available after the fertility rates drop. This failure to replace the population demands that the society accept ever larger numbers of immigrants from "younger" countries to fill much needed areas in services, manual labor, and healthcare.

Racial diversity creates problems for quality in a healthcare system, where communication is critical to a patient's health. Anyone who has had a very young, sick child can attest to the frustration of knowing that he or she is ill but not able to communicate just what it is that hurts or where it hurts. Racial differences also create a paradigm of standards. For example, an immigrant who has endured extreme hunger might answer differently than a Native American when asked if they are hungry, because the paradigm of hunger would be so different from one population to the next.

So, from the perspective of quality of care, racial diversity can significantly increase the risk to the patient who is of a different ethnic background than that of the caregiver.

Fertility Rates and Racial Diversity

Immigrants influence fertility data in two ways:

- First, regardless of their countries of origin, they tend to have higher fertility rates than do native-born people.

- Second, immigrants are concentrated in the 20- to 39-year-old age group, which is also the prime period of family formation.

Under conditions of low fertility—such as has characterized the U.S. population in the past 30 years—immigration becomes especially important. For example, although Washington State is not one of the major destinations for immigrants, in 1998 about 19 percent of residents giving birth were foreign-born. Long-standing fertility differences between racial and ethnic groups contribute to increasing population diversity.[12]

Worker Shortage

The government's latest projection is that we would need 5.3 to 10 million new healthcare workers by 2010. As the demand for workers increases based on lower fertility rates and an aging population, many see an impending worker shortage in the industrialized world. This shortage may be the largest determinant of how quickly we move to the world of George Jetson (*The Jetsons* being a 1960s cartoon depicting life in the future where robots are in every household and George's idea of a hard day's work is "punching buttons all day"). With a worker shortage, labor becomes expensive, and in a utopian scenario we learn how to be more efficient with our production and services. In some respects, the high cost of labor in certain parts of the world has permanently changed the complexion of the GNP, while areas of the world where labor is less expensive have been able to erode much of the middle class in some countries.

To see how this labor shortage might affect healthcare, we can take the formula:

Demand for workers = Private consumption + Public consumption

As the demand for labor increases with the needs of an older population, the labor market will driven by private consumption, such as hospitals, personal trainers, and grocery store clerks, and through the public consumption of Medicare clerks and government agencies dedicated to an ever-rising population. Of course, because there potentially will be fewer workers, we will find that just as the demand for healthcare professionals and the supporting infrastructure increases, we will have a decreasing number of individuals in the labor pool. This will potentially drive up the price of healthcare and compound the problems of healthcare finance as outlined earlier.

Employment opportunities will generally come in the service sector in the form of nurses' aides, home care aides, and general support for the elderly (such as housekeeping, maintenance, and so forth). Many of these occupations tend to be labor-intensive but require skills beyond those of the average individual walking off the street. In some respects, even the housekeeper is semi-specialized because the procedures for cleaning and servicing patient rooms and common areas are likely to increase as healthcare providers try to get a better handle on infections in the future.

Supply of Workers

Unfortunately for the human resources department in the healthcare industry, the United States has been experiencing a birth rate that is just below the population replacement rate. Therefore, the population in the U.S., without immigration, is going down. This phenomenon is particularly acute in places like Italy and Japan, where birth rates have fallen off significantly during the last 20 years. In the United States—a nation of immigrants—this means that we have a chance to allow young immigrants to enter the country and fill the worker shortage. In countries like Japan, where attitudes toward non-Japanese immigrants are more negative, there will need to be major changes to accommodate the healthcare needs of an aging population.

In some respects, there is a macabre bright spot in all this. Savings rates in the United States are actually negative. This means that people who previously thought they would retire early may find themselves working many years beyond the age they thought they would retire. This necessity to work is also a potential labor source for the future. The elderly already serve as volunteers in most hospitals, so why not paid employees? Given the laws of supply and demand, these lesser skilled healthcare jobs may pay a living wage in the future.

Therefore, predictions of widespread worker shortages as a result of baby boomers retiring are overstated. Many baby boomers will continue working past the age of 65. Some will work because they do not have enough resources to comfortably retire. This may be because they did not plan well, or because downsizing, outsourcing, or divorce put a hole in their best-laid plans. Others will continue to work, or create new careers after retiring from their primary career. Why? Because they cannot imagine a life without contributing something, and cannot imagine a life without the stimulation a working environment provides. With general advances in medicine, it is likely that healthy seniors will work abbreviated schedules and stay active and vital.

Outsourcing

The outsourcing trend will continue. We have a global market for labor. Any skill that can be taught and that goes into any product or service which can be exported will be exported—both the labor and the product. Outsourced jobs will not come back to this country. This means that the projected labor shortage may not be as large as predicted, either. This also will mean that our labor needs to be incredibly productive, and sometimes older workers are just that.

Consumer-Centric Healthcare

Take all the above demographic changes and throw in the Internet. Some studies suggest that when a customer/patient is experiencing a healthcare incident in their life, they may spend up to 50 percent of the time on the Internet. This unheralded access to healthcare information, coupled with the emergence of Health Savings Accounts, promises to create unique challenges for the healthcare provider in the future.

Financial

Income inequality, or *relative income*, is when the median (half earn more and half earn less) is different than the relative income. In 1969, 18 percent of people earned low relative incomes and 15 percent had high relative incomes. Although a comprehensive report of current relative income awaits analysis of the 2000 census data, numerous surveys suggest that income disparity continued to increase during the 1990s. One survey found that in 1973, average income for the wealthiest fifth of households was $83,000; by 1994, it had soared to $105,000 (in adjusted dollars). For the poorest fifth of households, average income dropped from $8,100 to $7,800.[13]

This inequality of income points to the potential for many more elderly to fall into the charity care category. As more charity care is required, costs shift from those who pay to those who can't. We have recently witnessed a minor backlash against the increasing costs of healthcare, especially considering the public perception that quality is falling dramatically, notably in the United States. Healthcare providers have an advantage that many industries do not have in that when healthcare is needed, it must be purchased. The healthcare industry also has the curse that people generally view healthcare as a right and many do not feel obligated to pay their hospital bills, such as choosing to pay their credit cards before they pay their hospital bills.

The terms *costs* and *expenditures* often are used interchangeably. They are, however, conceptually different. Costs reflect the resources devoted to healthcare that are not available to produce other goods and services. Expenditures are what are paid for health services by purchasers or what is received by providers. The two differ when the payment (expenditure) is greater—or less—than the resources (costs) that go into providing the services. As we dedicate more and more costs to the healthcare system, this means that we have fewer and fewer resources to apply to other problems such as energy independence, the poor, and education. From this perspective alone, the healthcare community has an obligation to deliver healthcare in the most efficient and effective manner possible.

The Pluralistic Healthcare Insurance System

Private insurance coverage dominates the U.S. healthcare system. Most Americans under the age of 65 receive their health insurance benefits through their employer or the employer of their parent or spouse. About 65 percent of Americans fewer than 65 have private insurance, including both group and individual coverage. Most of the remainder are either uninsured or covered by Medicaid. About 4.5 percent (10.5 million) of those under 65 are covered by individual health insurance plans (GAO, 1996), including the self-employed, those not in the labor force, those working for employers who do not offer coverage along with their dependents, early retirees, those who lose their jobs and have exhausted or are not eligible for continued benefits, and dependents of these individuals.

Medicaid covers about 36 million low-income and needy individuals nationally and serves a heterogeneous mix of individuals with diverse needs. Medicare covers 37 million elderly and disabled individuals, as well as those with permanent kidney failure.

This leaves approximately 40 million uninsured individuals in the United States. As previously discussed, these individuals either do not receive healthcare, depend on others to pay for them, or actually pay their own bills. Regardless of exact numbers or how the bills are paid, there are a significant number of individuals who live day-to-day on the brink of either a financial or healthcare disaster—financial for obvious reasons, and healthcare because preventative medicine, prenatal care, and medical conditions are not done, performed, or treated.

Political

The politics of healthcare are complicated. In the early 1990s, the Clinton Administration introduced a bold plan for "fixing" healthcare. The plan never got off the ground because of a combination of the following:

- An insurance industry with a lot to lose
- A "free enterprise" democracy who views "socialized medicine" with skepticism
- A community of practitioners who see socialized medicine as a path to poor quality, long waits, and rationing

This book is not about having an opinion on healthcare policy and politics. It is about pointing out the very real fact that healthcare quality and costs is a major driving force behind political efforts to change the way healthcare is paid for. Politicians see the world's most expensive healthcare with marginal or at least debatable quality. Conventional wisdom basically tells us that the more we spend, the higher the quality. We believe that more expensive cars are generally of higher quality, more expensive food is of higher quality, and more expensive clothes are of higher quality, so this should also hold true for healthcare. Unfortunately, there appears to be little correlation between the cost of healthcare and the quality. In fact, quality luminaries point out that quality is cheap. Higher quality means cheaper healthcare! There does appear to be a lot of factors that affect quality, including defensive medicine, government policy, insurance, socioeconomic profiles of patients, and numerous other factors.

Going back to the Clinton plan of the early '90s, at the time of this book's writing several initiatives in many states are introducing significant changes in healthcare reimbursement and even a little-noticed move by the U.S. Office of Personnel Management to require preferred provider organizations (PPOs) and other fee-for-service plans to collect and report quality performance measures. It will remain to be seen whether anything meaningful will come from any of the state plans or the numerous efforts to require quality data—but the tide is swelling for changes in healthcare generally motivated by the failure of the industry to address its own problems.

Social

Social factors that are motivating a move to quality in healthcare include the increasing number of uninsured, the impact of wellness, and the divergence of aging and disease.

The growing number of uninsured has begun to affect our society as well as our economy. Individuals who are insured are beginning to see the uninsured, right or wrong, as free riders to the system. Most of the insured will not argue that healthcare should not be denied to anyone, but for the first time we may be seeing a change in attitude from the general population. Not an attitudinal change related to distain or anger against the uninsured, but one of concern for the failure of a system that leaves so many people vulnerable.

Another unknown social phenomenon is the impact of wellness. Although we see increasing obesity in the United States and worldwide, we also see the healthier becoming more healthy. Still unknown is the long-term effects of a great number of people who are getting better healthcare and exercising more than any other generation in history. We assume that these later-in-life athletes will develop more long-term injuries to knees and joints but a reduction in conditions related to a sedentary lifestyle, such as diabetes and heart disease. These late-life athletes are understandably concerned about themselves having to supplement those less concerned with their health. Perhaps more so than any other time in the past, we see growing discrimination against the overweight and unhealthy.

Another interesting phenomenon appears to be a divergence of aging and disease. In the past, disease was directly related to age. While this is still generally the case, with the advent of science, new medicines, and better approaches to chronic disease, aging need not be a recipe for disease. Instead, lifestyle, preventative medicine, and improved medical management may significantly affect this paradigm.

Technological

Technology by itself may be the single most important factor affecting healthcare in the future. David Brailer recently resigned as the healthcare IP czar for the United States. Upon his resignation, he noted that his interest in the job was related primarily to improving the quality of medicine in the United States rather than improving technology. In fact, it is impossible to improve quality without improving information. As you will see later in this book, Six Sigma and other quality approaches rely heavily on information to improve processes and quality.

Additionally, technology allows for healthcare breakthroughs and has created the conditions and opportunities for healthcare in the United States to be the best in the world. Given the right circumstances, we have more space-age technology available to us as patients in the United States than anywhere else in the world. Unfortunately, even the best technology utilized in an ineffective way does not necessarily improve quality.

In the long term, technology is the absolute dominant driver in healthcare spending—and thus, employment. Technology accounts for more than half of the growth in healthcare spending per capita over time, and it does so by offering new treatments and diagnostic procedures. Late-life athletes who have trouble with their knees now receive minimally invasive surgery that was unavailable 15 or 20 years ago. Medical care is offering more than it did before, people benefit from it, but it costs more money; however, whether costs are contained or not, it's inevitable that healthcare is going to become a more important source of jobs over time. And that is happening around the world as well as in this country.[14]

The problem with healthcare technology is that one hour of care in the emergency room means one hour of paperwork. It's not a good way to keep content those people who went into the care professions. The U.S. government, as well as several other governments around the world, is aggressively moving on the problems related to healthcare paperwork, lack of IT, and the standardization and digitization of medical records.

THE COST OF HEALTHCARE AND SIX SIGMA

The cost of healthcare is a reflection of a number of phenomenon, including a cost-shifting effect from uninsured and "underpayers" (governmental payers such as Medicaid and Medicare that pay essentially cost), increases in infrastructure and medication costs, as well as increased labor and supplies. But all things remaining equal (everyone has to pay higher prices for fuel, for example), the increased costs for healthcare boil down to a few significant issues—a downward spiral, if you will, of healthcare quality erosion (see Figure 1.1).

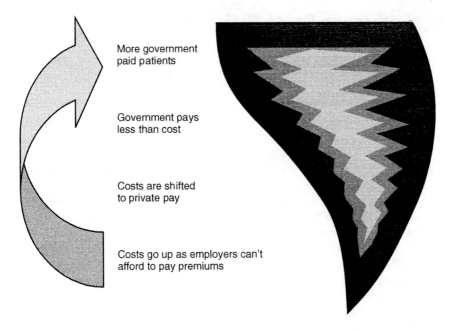

More government
paid patients

Government pays
less than cost

Costs are shifted
to private pay

Costs go up as employers can't
afford to pay premiums

FIGURE 1.1   The cost spiral in healthcare.

The components of the spiral start with the uninsured and governmental programs that pay less than the cost of healthcare. This forces the shifting of cost and those who pay, including private payers and insurance plans. During the 1990s, in an effort to control costs the system created *managed care*. The bottom line in managed care is for an insurance company to contract with a healthcare provider to provide care for a fixed cost. This arrangement effectively removes one source of cost shifting—meaning, traditional health insurance plans and private payers were absorbing increasing costs. At the same time, federal and state governments found that budgets were increasingly running at deficits. Cost-cutting measures by those governments in many cases went to social programs such as Medicaid and Medicare. This reduction put more pressure on insurers and private payers, which continued the spiral.

Today, major employers throughout the United States blame the cost of healthcare for losing a competitive edge in world markets. In fact, many employers have moved operations to places such as Canada, where healthcare is provided by the government. Some estimates in the car industry place the cost of healthcare at 15 percent of the price of a new automobile. Faced with global competition and an ever-frustrated electorate, politicians are beginning to act. Unfortunately, most of the action is not related to increasing the quality of healthcare but to reducing the cost. The understanding that high quality is actually cheaper than low quality has not been recognized. These concepts—reduce costs and improve quality from a Six Sigma perspective—are complementary, not competing. Increased quality leads to lower costs —most importantly in healthcare—and improved experience and outcome for the patient.

HEALTHCARE QUALITY AND ERROR REDUCTION

Errors are difficult to measure—not only because of inadequate reporting and varied definitions, but also because most errors are not a single act but a chain of events. For example, prescribing the wrong dose of a drug may be counted as a single error and given a single name, such as a "prescription error," but the physician's prescribing error may have occurred because the medical record contained an incorrect body weight or because a laboratory report was missing. Researchers and administrators ignore the complexity and systems that can produce skewed statistics and propagate imprecise notions about the anatomy, causes, and consequences of errors. A better way to address medical errors would be to develop a cascading model that can be addressed by the Six Sigma approach to process evaluation.

In other words, in a process management environment that Six Sigma promotes, we are not simply looking for the cause of an error for the error's sake; we are instead looking for a total understanding of the process that led up to the error. As many of us have discovered, very seldom do we find anything in this world that is actually black and white—and the same is true of medical errors. Many times the error is caused by a single small and seemingly insignificant error or process breakdown that cascades into something much larger. As an example, consider a lab slip that travels from the unit secretary to the lab, and back to the patient's room. How many opportunities might that slip have had to pick up a bacterial agent in route? Then consider that the slip is dropped in the hallway and picked up by a nurse who then comes in contact with another patient and now cross-infects another patient. It's a seemingly minor incident and, given the frequency of handwashing, it's probably not in your healthcare organization.

This is apparently not the case in Pennsylvania where the Pennsylvania Health Care Cost Containment Council reported in March 2006 that hospitals in Pennsylvania alone reported 13,711 infections during the first nine months of 2005 compared with 11,688 for all of 2004. The infections were associated with an additional 1,456 deaths, 227,000 extra hospital days, and an added $52,600 to treat every patient. As the old saying goes, for lack of a nail, the battle was lost…. Perhaps the saying should be revised to say that for lack of a lab information system, the patient died. Of course, it is irresponsible to suggest that any of these infections were caused by the lack of a lab order information system—but is it any less irresponsible than not finding out why these infections were caused in the first place. To fail to understand the process and the opportunities for "errors" is perhaps the most irresponsible part of the equation.

Why It's Difficult to Deal with Healthcare Errors

If you as the reader are looking for some great insight into why we fail to act aggressively in regards to healthcare errors, the debate has been discussed without resolve for years—defensive medicine.

Defensive medicine merely means that in a litigious society, we order extra tests and don't really pursue the cause of errors as aggressively as we might if it weren't financially devastating to be found guilty of making an error—an error that in most cases could have been avoided had the process been designed so as to eliminate or at least mitigate the opportunity for error.

Consider the multiple stories of hospital operating rooms that amputated the incorrect limb on patients. The best advice I have read on dealing with this blatant process breakdown is for patients themselves to write in permanent ink on the affected limb "amputate this one" and "don't amputate this one" on the other limb. Granted, an amusing story for the press, but a tragic reflection on our healthcare providers when they can't get something as simple as amputating the correct limb right. An even better question is why the patient is advised to do the labeling themselves? It seems to me that we could have figured this one out ourselves years ago. Labeling a limb is a low-tech solution to a catastrophic problem that easily could have been generated by an astute Six Sigma quality team.

CONCLUSION

Everything in today's healthcare world is pointing to increased costs and lower quality in healthcare. Efforts are being made by the federal government to promote healthcare technology as a shortcut to quality, but as we have seen in the examples, IT is a tool of quality and not quality itself. Patient families and healthcare professionals will still forget to wash their hands, paper will continue to move around the organization, and we will continue to see the incorrect limbs amputated. Only by applying true quality techniques such as Six Sigma to our processes (patient care and administrative) can we begin to proactively address the quality problems in healthcare.

Additionally, and perhaps most importantly, adopting Six Sigma allows the healthcare organization to proactively address process breakdowns before they become life-threatening errors. As you will see in this book, the application of Six Sigma in healthcare is a natural approach to solving many of the problems healthcare faces. The methodology seeks to improve customer satisfaction, reduce cycle times, reduce costs, and improve quality. Six Sigma is different from other efforts in the past since the focus of the improvement is always the patient or other customer. We will talk about why customer satisfaction through reduced variability leads to higher quality and, contrary to popular belief, higher quality is always the low-cost alternative.

ENDNOTES

1. Thomas, EJ, Studdert, DM et al. "Costs of Medical Injuries in Utah and Colorado." *Inquiry*, 1999 Fall; 36(3):255-64.

2. James, Michael. "How many people could the bird flu kill?" CBS News ,Online Edition, September 30, 2005.

3. http://www.cdc.gov/ncidod/eid/vol4no3/weinstein.htm

4. Ibid.

5. Beck, Ellen. "Analysis: What's ailing U.S. healthcare?" United Press International, June 21, 2004.

6   Woolhandler, Steffie, Campbell, T. and Himmelstein, D. "Health care administration in the United States and Canada: Micromanagement, macro costs." *International Journal of Health Services*, 2004. 34, 1: 65-7.

7   Brennan TA, Leape LL, Laird NM, et al. "Incidence of adverse events and negligence in hospitalized patients: Results of the Harvard Medical Practice Study I." *New England Journal of Medicine*, 1991. 324: 370-376.

8   Thomas EJ, Studdert DM, Burstin HR, et al. "Incidence and types of adverse events and negligent care in Utah and Colorado." *Medical Care 2000*; 38: 261-271.

9   Institute of Medicine, *Crossing the Quality Chasm; A New Health System for the 21st Century.* Washington, DC: National Academy Press, 2001.

10   Institute of Medicine, Fall 2005 Report.

11   Keehan, SP, Lazenby, HC, et al. "Age estimates in the National Accounts," Healthcare Finance Review/Web Exclusive. December 2, 2004, Volume 1, Number 1.

12   Hale, Christiane. "Demographic Trends Influencing Public Health Practice," *Washington Public Health*, Fall 2000.

13   Ibid.

14   Brown, Nell Porter, *Harvard Magazine*, September-October 2003, Quoting Paul Ginsburg.

EXCELLENCE (BENCHMARKS) AND IMPROVEMENT CHALLENGES IN HEALTHCARE SYSTEM

SECTIONS

How Do We Define Quality?
Cost and Quality
Why Is Excellence So Hard?
Conclusions

Excellence is sometimes a confusing word. In healthcare it can mean error-free delivery of care. It can mean delivering what customers want in a consistent manner. It can mean error-free bills, medical records, or other reporting mechanisms, or it can mean all of the above. Excellence in healthcare means that the healthcare provider does everything at a level above customer expectations. Customers expect a lot today, and by all indications, even more tomorrow. Part of Six Sigma involves understanding what excellence is to your customer and delivering it consistently over time.

HOW DO WE DEFINE QUALITY?

From the healthcare perspective, the concept of *elimination of defects* of Six Sigma is equivalent to reducing errors and healthcare. It goes without saying that what's good for patients (reduction in errors) is also good for medical professionals and the larger society.

As you most likely already know, Six Sigma is a management methodology that aims to reduce errors or defects from whatever their present level to a Six Sigma standard of 3.4 per million opportunities.

In the business world, Six Sigma is what is known as a "hot topic" today. Many of the world's leading manufacturers' high tech and service companies have adopted Six Sigma in the last several years. Additionally, a growing number of hospitals are also adopting Six Sigma or its alternative version "Lean."

Beyond the stated goal of Six Sigma is error reduction. Anyone even casually involved in healthcare understands the linkage between error reduction and the reduction of costs. For example, we know that almost 100,000 people are killed by healthcare errors in the U.S. each year. Attached to every death is the process of identifying and or correcting the error, not to mention the added cost of treating those patients when the error did not immediately kill the patient.

For discussion purposes, let's distinguish between seven possible error types in healthcare:

- **Patient-to-patient errors**. Includes such things as accidentally overdosing, not following doctor's orders, not understanding orders, accidents caused by dementia and other issues related to patients hurting themselves by their own action or failure of action. In many respects, patient-to-patient errors might be the most difficult to address, although better training, instructions, documentation and follow-up might be possible solutions to these errors.

- **Professional judgment errors**. Occur when a medical professional fails to correctly diagnose, makes a poor judgment call, or perhaps errs due to being too tired or inattentive. Errors of judgment might be slightly easier to deal with than patient-to-patient errors only because professionals, who are also employees and otherwise have an incentive to perform an error-free fashion, might accept personal training, modification of procedures, and/or other approaches to creating an error-free, Poka-yoke, approach to healthcare delivery. After all, it's in the best interests of healthcare professionals not to commit errors rather than deal with errors after the fact.

- **Process inadequacy**. Results from the silos, fiefdoms, and competition. In healthcare, almost more than anywhere else, the continuity of care throughout the organization is critical to the patient's well being. Errors occur in a disproportionate amount when handoffs between professionals, shifts, departments, disciplines (surgical to medical, for example), and facilities (hospital to hospital, physician to hospital, hospital to physician) occur. Additionally, as many process professionals understand, there is almost always rework inside a process. In the healthcare setting, this might reveal itself in something as minor as incorrectly measuring vital signs. From the process perspective, a failure to recognize and react to changes in a patient's condition would be a process failure. Additionally, handoffs from one department to another without a full and adequate information set for a shift change might be a process error.

- **Legal and regulatory imposed errors**. Might be caused by outside organizations and agencies in a misguided attempt to protect patients. With all due respect to attorneys and legislators, legislating the practice of medicine can sometimes create opportunities for error. An example of legislated opportunity for error might include certificate of need states where the number, type, and location of hospital resources are allocated by a board rather than by the demands of the market. These errors are fewer than others but potentially the most difficult to address.

- **Errors by incentive**. Incentives, more than anything else, motivate the practice of medicine. In these days of reduced reimbursement, increased paperwork, and overall higher costs of being in the healthcare business, incentives play a greater role in how medicine is practiced than ever before. For example, as malpractice suits increase, more money is spent on protecting oneself than in the interest of the patient. Alternatively, if a physician is more highly paid for performing surgical procedures and prevention, decisions regarding the care of a patient might be influenced, all things being equal, in favor of the invasive procedure. And that's why recent example of errors by incentives might be traced back to practice patterns in regards to increased numbers of cesarean sections in certain parts of the country. There has been speculation that in markets where malpractice related to childbirth has created a defensive response by many OB/GYN physicians, it is preferable for the physicians to protect themselves at a greater risk to the patient (assuming, perhaps wrongly, a greater risk due to surgery than natural childbirth).

- **Business, policy, and strategy errors**. As seen on TV, hospital administration is perceived to make business decisions detrimental to the well being of the patient. While this is mostly high drama, there is some degree of truth when business decisions affect patients. Once again, medical professionals are a highly dedicated group of individuals. Unfortunately, in the complex world of healthcare today, decisions are sometimes made that may in fact detrimentally affect a patient or group of patients. Also in this complex world, communications by frontline healthcare providers are sometimes not communicated well or not heard by the policymakers. When this happens, everyone loses. Six Sigma creates conditions for these communications to improve. With improved communications comes a better understanding by administrators of the needs of the frontline staff.

- **Inequality Errors**. Result from the traditional training of physicians. While historically physicians have been seen as the captain of the ship, in more recent times physicians have lost some of their influence and power. Traditionally, when the physician gave an order, the nurse did whatever the physician demanded without question. While much of this inequality has disappeared in the modern healthcare facility, there are still many "old school" physicians who demand deference by nurses and other medical professionals. One nursing school professor that I spoke with pointed out that modern nursing training stresses the absolute necessity of questioning orders by physicians that might lead to a medical error. Unfortunately, much of the physicians' training necessitates a strong personality and confidence that might intimidate some nurses and paraprofessionals. The difficulty lies in the competing means of confidence and collegiality within the healthcare team. In some respects, this category of errors might seem to be a subcategory of process but in the quality between professionals is a subcategory which is important enough that it should be recognized independently.

The promise of Six Sigma is that, done correctly, communications are improved, changes are managed, problems are detected and solved, and systems are put in place to detect errors in the future.

The roots of Six Sigma are not new to healthcare organizations. Anyone who has worked in healthcare for very long has seen attempts at TQM, CQI, kaizen, continuous learning, leadership development, and any number of other attempts to improve healthcare delivery. How we combine them into a Six Sigma methodology is the new and exciting opportunity.

COST AND QUALITY

In considering Six Sigma, it helps to back up and examine the relationship of cost to quality. Conventional thought has it that quality is expensive. Taken in the context of straight cost of quality, this may in fact be true; however, it is not. The question that one should be asking is on the flip side of the coin—what is the "cost" of "poor quality?" The *cost of poor quality* is generally defined as those costs that are generated as a result of delivering defective products or services, the most glaring in healthcare being the cost of malpractice. When one considers more than just the premiums paid, costs such as ruined careers, time spent defending the organization, ruined reputations, and lowered morale, not to mention the personal cost to the patient and their family, the cost of errors resulting in malpractice are much greater than those reflected in premiums. In a less extreme situation, these costs include the cost required to fulfill the gap between the desired and the actual quality of healthcare delivery. It also includes the cost of lost opportunity due to the loss of resources used in correcting the error or defect. This cost includes labor costs, rework cost, disposition costs, and material costs that have been added to the service up to the point of failure. This does not even include the cost of detection, prevention, and quality assurance, and perhaps most damaging of all to the healthcare—trust of the patient and their family.

A traditional description of the cost for quality generally covers the following:

- The cost of labor to fix an error (How much does it cost for the phlebotomist to redraw a sample when the first one was contaminated?)

- The cost of extra supplies used (How much does it cost to resterilize a surgical pack that was inadvertently opened?)

- The cost of extra utilities (What does it cost to keep two half-full surgical units open because of a scheduling error, instead of combining them and closing one for the night?)

- The cost of a lost opportunity (How could we use the cash otherwise tied up in pharmacy or supply inventories?)

- Loss of revenue (How much patient revenue is lost when our emergency room is full due to a discharge hold-up on the floors and we have to turn back patients?)

- Potential loss of market share (How many patients and qualified medical professionals will not be associated with our facility due to known quality issues or poor reputation?)

- The lower service level to patients (Can we be truly customer-focused if we expend energy and resources on mistakes?)

In short, when looking at Six Sigma from the perspective of the cost of poor quality, it becomes readily apparent that looking at quality from a direct cost perspective in many cases doesn't justify the expense. When looking at the larger picture, including the cost of poor quality, there are many more considerations to including a return on investment calculation.

One other perspective on Six Sigma is the Baldrige National Quality Program healthcare criteria. No doubt if you are considering Six Sigma in your healthcare organization, you are aware of this program. If you are not, the program criteria for equality organization are as follows:

- Visionary leadership
- Patient-focused excellence
- Organizational and personal learning
- Value staff and partners
- Agility
- Focus on the future
- Manage for innovation
- Manage by fact
- Public responsibility and community health
- Focus on results and creating value
- Systems perspective

Six Sigma allows an organization aspiring to be high performance, in Baldrige terms, address patient focus, agility, management by fact, and focus on results and systems perspective to be addressed in a single program. In a particularly entrepreneurial organization, a Six Sigma methodology may actually allow the organization to work on all the requirements of the Baldrige criteria, and in fact past winners have been "Six Sigma" organizations. Later in this book as we explain Six Sigma in greater detail, it will become apparent that visionary leadership, a focus on patient, organizational and personal learning, valuing staff and partners, agility, focus on the future, managing for innovation, managing by fact, public responsibility and community health, focus on results in creating value, and systems perspective are all an integral part of a Six Sigma program. Therefore, if you are exploring Six Sigma as a path to a Baldrige award and considering Six Sigma as the enabler, you have a good chance of success.

WHY IS EXCELLENCE SO HARD?

Excellence is difficult in every organization. Forces inside and outside the organization make quality efforts difficult to implement. A short-term orientation resulting from stockholders and annual bonus plans push managers into making decisions for the short term while excellence requires long-term thinking. In our personal lives, we understand the value of long-term think-ing. We get a college education, we save for retirement, we invest in our children, and we make many other investment decisions throughout our lives. But we don't own our hospital and many of us don't own our practice.

Practice Patterns

As the term implies, *practice patterns* reflect both patterns and practice. Physicians trained at one medical school versus another typically learn different standards of care. This is not to indict anyone for practicing better or worse medicine, just different. Because quality relies on standardization of processes and physicians, in practice, apply different methodologies than their colleagues, standardizing on a best practice is difficult.

Therefore, if one were to take two different physicians performing the same procedure, we would see that process is very different. An example of this is the non-standardization of surgical packs between one physician and another. Someone who hasn't spent much time in the operating suite would assume that one open heart surgery is performed in exactly the same way as another open heart surgery. But many hospitals found that they could achieve excellence in coronary artery bypass surgery by, among other things, standardizing procedures and surgical packs.

Not Invented Here

A significant impediment to healthcare excellence, that is familiar to many, is the phenom-enon of *not invented here*. The not-invented-here problem in healthcare is due to the cottage industry orientation (and history) of most healthcare providers. Physicians still tend to prac-tice individually or in small groups, and many hospitals are still an important part of their community—their boards are local, their patients are local, and therefore communities still view their hospitals as personal and attract a paternalistic and the oftentimes nonqualified board of directors.

Not invented here leads to the protection of inefficiencies of processes, people, and finan-cial practices in the organization. Not invented here means that the organization is generally closed-minded in considering new, unique, or otherwise groundbreaking changes in the way they do business. There are several factors which contribute to this attitude. Some of those factors include administrators who would never work in another location or facility, longtime medical staff such as registered nurses who are offered little continuing professional education and gen-erally work for the same facility for a much longer tenure than other similar businesses. We have even witnessed a senior financial executive, who was fired from one hospital for suspect finan-cial dealings, being hired by the organization "down the street" six months later. The hiring organization was fully aware of the financial improprieties, but for some reason chose to hire the local financial executive rather than bring someone in from outside the community.

Healthcare results should be consistent from one state to another. Yet the rate of nursing home residents who are physically restrained is almost 10 times higher in the lowest performing state as in the highest. Likewise, while 91% of women receive prenatal care in the first trimester in the leading state, only 69% do in the trailing state.[1]

Defensive Medicine

Perhaps most mentioned as a problem with healthcare is the issue of defensive medicine. *Defensive medicine* occurs as a response to lawsuits and the risk of losing a license and perhaps a livelihood. Some attribute the high cost of healthcare in large part to the practice of defensive medicine. When a physician or hospital is in fear of being sued on a regular basis, they tend to order more tests and create more redundancy and documents for more than what is generally necessary. Defensive medicine is the driving force behind continuing discussions of tort reform as related to U.S. healthcare.

Because the path to quality generally means that we evaluate processes where there are too many tests, too much redundancy, and too much documentation (to name a few process improvement tools), defensive medicine works exactly opposite to quality. Yes, we need state this again; *defensive medicine is not quality medicine.* Quality medicine is doing the right things to the right people in the right place at the right time in an efficient and cost-effective manner.

Failure to Invest in Information Technology

Healthcare has always been a large investor in technology. However, this technology generally provides no information beyond the CAT scan, x-ray, catheterization, lab test, and so on. Once again, it is important to restate that while the modern healthcare organization is thought of as one of the most high tech places in the world, this technology is related almost entirely to the clinical aspects of healthcare. Quality necessitates information that allows us to make better decisions about processes in which clinical technology is used. The hospital and physician use this technology to make decisions about what to do with that clinical information and how to leverage it to avoid medical errors. Diagnosing the disease and improving a process are two entirely different animals.

Up until recently, healthcare has been known to be one of the lowest investing industries in IT at an annual percentage rate of approximately 3.5 percent. Only recently has this percentage increased to something like 4.5 percent. Most other industries similar to healthcare invest in IT at a rate closer to 9 to 10 percent. Given the tremendous need for IT in the healthcare environment, is it any wonder that healthcare is one of the poorest quality industries in the world? One need only look at the typical patient chart stuffed full of papers to understand the amount of information gathered during a typical patient stay. Also, in looking at one of these charts, one would notice that the chart only includes the current admission and does not capture information from previous visits, visits to the doctor's office, and especially visits to other hospitals. This lack of information leads to the same tests being done multiple times, failure to recognize preexisting conditions, and a multitude of other potentially life-threatening conditions that are unknown to the medical professional. Add to this the fact that most patients barely know anything about their healthcare status, and one can understand why excellence in healthcare is so difficult to achieve.

Relatively Poor Salaries

Early in his career, Dr. Trusko spent several years as a hospital administrator. One of the reasons that many other professionals (including him) leave healthcare is the relative low salaries compared to similar professions in the "real world". In real dollars, healthcare professionals make approximately two-thirds what a similarly skilled professional outside the healthcare industry is able to command. Healthcare administration publications often discuss the impending physician and nurse shortage and how to deal with it. One way, of course, is to make the job more palatable by examining work schedules, duties, and the generally difficult nature of the job of providing healthcare. Another factor affecting the nursing shortage is that nurses find that their skills are easily transferable into non-nursing careers—ones that pay much better than the hospital or physician's office.

Granted, most highly qualified medical professionals are looking for something much more meaningful than money. However, there is also the large number of healthcare professionals who might not be qualified outside of healthcare. While it may not be too popular an idea that there are two types of people who work in healthcare, it's a fact that the two types do exist: the highly talented dedicated professional and individuals who don't have the skills to compete in the real world. We like to think that the majority of these people are from the former group but have worked with the latter.

Creating excellence in healthcare means employing excellent people. With the current financial state of healthcare in the U.S. (most hospitals lose money), healthcare is forced to hire people with lesser skills who work for a lower wage. Only by taking a collective look inside ourselves as a country in deciding to find ways to make a healthcare career more lucrative will we be able to attract and retain individuals of the caliber necessary to assure that our healthcare system is the most excellent in the world.

Incentives for Inefficiency

The design of the American healthcare reimbursement system is also an impediment to excellence. Generally speaking, healthcare reimbursement is a cost-based system. We, as healthcare professionals, are not motivated through incentive to make and keep people healthy because we're paid for treating sick people, not people who are well. We receive little or no reimbursement for treating eating disorders, and the best we can do for an overweight patient is to inform them that they are obese and should lose some weight. We're paid quite well for open heart surgery but not for referring a patient to the gym. These lack of incentives compound poor health over the years as we ignore our health by only treating our sickness.

From the cost perspective, our federal programs reimburse us almost exclusively based upon how much we spend. Because we are paid for spending, there is a tendency to avoid reducing the cost of a procedure because it results in a reduction of payment from the government. There are always exceptions to these rules, but as a generalization we're not motivated through incentive to improve the delivery of care quality, much to the chagrin of most healthcare professionals who would prefer to practice medicine in a safe, efficient, and effective manner.

Benchmarks

Benchmarking in healthcare can be the easiest and most difficult benchmarking of any industry we know of. While healthcare models have many examples outside of healthcare, they also have so many exceptions that the typical healthcare professional fails to see the opportunity. Some examples of potential benchmarking opportunities in healthcare include:

- **Hotels**. Here excellence and customer service has been taken to a whole new level. When I check into my favorite hotel chain, the staff knows what kind of bed I like, what newspaper I like to read, and even the type of pillows I prefer. Now one can argue that healthcare is not like the hotel business; however, it seems to many people that healthcare is exactly like a hotel. One checks in and is shown to the room and stays there for multiple nights. One advantage hospitals have is that they aren't expected to drop everything to deliver room service or shine a pair of shoes. Perhaps, though, hospitals could learn something from hotels—things like customer service, putting the customer first, giving the patient what they want and expect, and doing it for less money than the hospital currently does. Yes, hospitals must follow special rules that make the overhead of doing business in healthcare much more expensive than a hotel. This is acknowledged as an impediment to excellence. But we know that there are many things that we do that we could benchmark against at a hotel.

- **Restaurants**. In our experience we have yet to find a cafeteria at a hospital with food that's healthy, tastes good, and would compete in any way with a restaurant. Jokes about hospital food have been around as long as hospitals. It seems rather obvious, but the quality of food and eating experience might actually help a patient to get better sooner rather than later. Additionally, in the hospital cafeteria, one would expect there to be a healthier menu than even the best health-food restaurant. In fact, most hospital cafeteria food is barely as good as the most infamous of fast-food restaurants, and many have McDonald's physically located in their buildings. The combination of unhealthy, flavorless food allows you to see the opportunity for benchmarking against restaurants.

CONCLUSIONS

The challenges to healthcare excellence are many and difficult to deal with. There are the problems of structure, personalities, patients, and providers. The way we pay for healthcare is under siege as the price of healthcare continues to rise at double digits almost every year with very few exceptions. As Carolyn Clancy states "The state of healthcare quality in America today is stubbornly short of where we want it to be, agonizingly short of where we know it should be, and slow and sporadic in making improvement."[1]

Many, if not most of the problems we face in healthcare are out of our control as individual healthcare practitioners, and even as powerful organizations. But there are many things we can change.

We can listen to the voice of the customer and work toward a consumer- and family-centric orientation that takes into account the needs of the customer and their family to create a partnership. In a partnership model, everyone has a vested interest in improving care. In a model where there are clearly persons in superior and inferior positions, communication can't take place. And when communication doesn't take place, the patient suffers.

We can challenge the way we practice medicine and stop accepting variation as the status quo. Although every patient may be different, the delivery of medicine is more homogeneous than not. Best practices are universal, and it is generally accepted that if we can achieve excellence in one state or community, then we should be able to achieve it in all states or communities. There is no reason for a population, such as African Americans, to receive worse care than whites.

The Quality Challenge as stated by Clancy (2005) consists of the five C's:

- **Candor**. We must accept that improvement is needed. For every patient who believes that their physician is the best in the field, there must also be a recognition that there is someone who is the worst in the field. These practitioners must be helped; through the use of Six Sigma, it is possible to identify and intervene where necessary.

- **Comparison**. Six Sigma allows us to develop and monitor the standard to which clinicians, administration, and others involved in healthcare can compare themselves, their facilities, and their patients. Patients should be able to have access to information about providers and their outcomes and should be allowed to make choices based on those outcomes. This information will become available, and providers must make the decision now do have good and accurate information for healthcare consumers.

- **Consequences**. Many providers believe that a program such as Six Sigma can expose shortcomings in the delivery of care. The practice of Six Sigma in a collegial and open manner will expose poor performance but also expose some standard procedures in administration and patient care. The culture of Six Sigma should not be a witch hunt, but a collaborative effort to improve the quality of healthcare.

- **Courage**. Six Sigma is happening in some of the best healthcare facilities in the country. Individuals within these facilities are innovating and working hard to improve healthcare and the processes that make it work. Contrary to what the nightly news magazines might make customers believe, there are great things happening in healthcare. Unfortunately, there are still too many stories of healthcare gone wrong, and these stories sell ad space.

- **Cooperation**. A basic premise of Six Sigma is breaking down silos—generally between executives in the healthcare organization. In the case of healthcare, this definition can mean so much more. By gaining the trust and understanding that Six Sigma helps to foster, all constituencies can benefit.

ENDNOTES

1. Clancy, Carolyn M. et al. "The quality challenge." *American Journal of Medical Quality.* V. 20, No 4, July/August 2005, p219.

APPLICABILITY OF SIX SIGMA IN HEALTHCARE ORGANIZATIONS

SECTIONS

A Brief Explanation of Six Sigma
Why Do You Need Six Sigma?
Quality
Six Sigma Applied to Healthcare
Six Sigma at Work in Healthcare
Different Views of Healthcare Quality
Conclusions
Endnotes

We hope by now we have presented you with enough information about healthcare systems around the world that you will agree that they need to be reformed. We need to start measuring our healthcare failures in deaths per million, not deaths per "hundreds or even deaths per thousands." Even deaths per million is not good enough in the healthcare system. The required standard should be measured in the deaths per billion and errors per million. This is where proven, preventative approaches—such as Total Improvement Management, Six Sigma, and Lean—can provide real benefit to the healthcare system. Both of these two approaches have been refined as they were used in other industries, and they are now ready to advance the healthcare industry into a new, higher level of customer satisfaction and performance.

Studies indicate that the services industries have an average sigma level of between 2.0 to 2.5; that's an error rate of 159,000 to 208,000 per million opportunities. But many of the healthcare activities perform much worse. For example, the process for treating depression is estimated to be running at the 2 sigma level or 308,538 errors per million opportunities.

Although process capability techniques have been used extensively in manufacturing for more than 50 years, a major breakthrough occurred when Motorola applied them to its business support functions as a logical extension of its manufacturing quality initiatives. The results were improvements of ten times to a hundred times in Motorola's business processes in as short a period as two years. When Motorola won the Malcolm Baldrige Award in 1988, it credited the Six Sigma program as the primary driver of its improvement. During the first part of the 1990s, the Six Sigma program continued in Motorola and spread slowly into other organizations. But in the mid-1990s, GE latched onto the concepts and committed millions of dollars to implementing the program throughout the entire organization. GE's program expanded from 200 projects in 1995 to 6,000 projects in 1997, which resulted in more than $320 million in savings, all directly attributed to this Six Sigma program. In 1998, GE estimated that its savings were about $750 million.

Notable healthcare Six Sigma projects include North Shore-Long Island Jewish Health System, Memorial Hospital and Health, of Marlton NJ, McLeod Regional Medical Center, Froedtert Memorial, New York Presbyterian, Vytra Health Plans, several Blue Cross and Blue Shield Plans, MD Anderson Cancer Center, Thibodaux Regional Hospital, University of New Hampshire, Commonwealth Health Corporation, Charleston Area Medical Center, Mount Carmel Health System and Bon Secours National Health System, just to name a few (see case studies chapters).

Six Sigma projects are defined as projects designed to reduce error rates to a maximum of 3.44 errors per million exposures (or "opportunities") through the use of statistical analysis techniques, problem solving, and quality principles. The typical healthcare organization has error rates in excess of between 2,700 and 45,500 (3 and 2 sigma) errors per million opportunities. Individuals, departments, projects, functions, plants, or entire organizations can use the Six Sigma approach.

More important than the specific measurement of error rates (because healthcare is about people as well as process) is the methodology behind Six Sigma. The Six Sigma process forces hospitals to measure those things that are important to the business of healthcare, things like quality, mortality, customer satisfaction, and employee satisfaction. If a hospital says that it is a patient-focused organization, what does that mean? And if the organization claims to be patient-centered (or focused), then how does it measure "patient focused?" If the hospital says it can't measure that, then it is it really important to them? Most organizations limit their measurement mechanisms to traditional accounting measurements, such as income and expenses, but medical mistakes are typically not measured and are generally underreported due to malpractice and the tendency to penalize and terminate individuals who report errors. (After all, one critical error can lead to the revocation of a practitioner's license.) Under a Six Sigma methodology, the hospital will find ways to measure what is important to them by tracing and analyzing the things they value the most as they relate to the internal or external customer's needs. Organizations that can't measure what they say they value don't really value what they profess to value. And if they can't measure it, they can't improve it!

While many healthcare organizations have attempted process improvement throughout the last 20 years, most have ended in disappointment. The discipline of the Six Sigma approach to quality through process improvement (as apposed to isolated quality attempts—such as inspection and post-mortem review of errors) is potentially the industry's best opportunity to address lingering issues of quality and the resultant real costs that are added to any system when poor quality is the rule, rather than the exception.

> "When you can measure what you are speaking about, and express it in numbers, you know something about it; but when you cannot measure it, when you can not express it in numbers, your knowledge is of a meager and unsatisfactory kind. It may be the beginning of knowledge, but you have scarcely, in your thoughts, advanced to the stage of science."
>
> —William Thomson, Lord Kelvin (1824–1907)

A BRIEF EXPLANATION OF SIX SIGMA

An ever-growing number of healthcare organizations are using Six Sigma to improve processes, from admitting to discharge and all the administrative and clinical processes in between. This adoption is driven by several factors including the need to improve the organization's bottom line, eliminate medical errors, and position themselves for an imminent global consumer-centered healthcare revolution. Healthcare providers once enjoyed a respect by their customers that few institutions in the world enjoy. Then came continuous years of double-digit cost increases capped off by the Institute of Health report indicating that medical errors kill approximately 98,000 people per year in the United States. These mistakes can range from prescription errors to a failure to wash hands. Many healthcare consumers began to question why increasing costs did not equate to improved quality. Accordingly, the healthcare industry finds itself at a crossroads—to continue on the current path, which would lead to disaster, and or the other road, leading to potential redemption. Many organizations thankfully have chosen a path of redemption: Six Sigma.

A brief history of Six Sigma is helpful to a healthcare entity considering a Six Sigma initiative. The earliest quality initiatives were based on 100 percent inspection, a concept that would be impossible in a service-oriented environment such as healthcare. Because this was expensive and time-consuming, sampling plans were developed to define acceptable defect levels. Then in the 1970s, quality guru Phil Crosby established a program called *zero defects*. This program was an inspirational way of explaining to employees the notion that everything should be done right the first time, that there should be no failures or defects in the work output. In the healthcare world, a defect can be as benign as an unpaid bill or as serious as a medication error causing the death of a patient. Probably more critical than in any other industry, zero defects should be the order of the day in a patient encounter.

The zero defects concept was somewhat controversial because some quality experts felt it mainly focused on meeting internal design specifications. It did not focus on customer requirements or on continuous improvement. Many quality professionals disagreed with the concept because they believed that it was impossible to have zero defects all the time. These process-oriented professionals felt that process capability requirements were a better way of defining acceptable performance. But the U.S. government quickly embraced this concept, and it became the "in" thing to do for a number of years.

In the 1970s and early 1980s, organizations such as IBM released requirements that their process capabilities (C_{pk}) must reach a 1.40 level, or an acceptable corrective action plan needed to be in place before products could be shipped to their customers. IBM's technical report entitled "Process Qualification—Manufacturing Insurance Policy"[1] required that a process "plus or minus 4 sigma limit" must fall within the specification limit when the following are considered:

- Accuracy
- Precision
- Repeatability/reproducibility
- Variation/stability
- Linearity, or resolution
- Sensitivity
- Variation between similar pieces of equipment used for the same purpose

In the mid 1980s, Motorola's president directed that all processes should have a tenfold improvement within a five-year period. This called for radical changes in the way processes within Motorola functioned, thus the creation of Six Sigma. This program set an objective for all processes to statistically perform at an error rate no greater than 3.4 errors per million opportunities. The real breakthrough in Motorola's Six Sigma approach was that the Six Sigma concept was applied to all processes, not just the manufacturing processes. (Obviously, in hindsight, was the fact that general systems theory creates a relationship between nearly all the processes in an organization.)

To calculate the process performance, samples of the output were plotted on a histogram, and the standard deviation was calculated. Once the standard deviation and mean were calculated, it was easy to compare the Six Sigma calculated performance limit to the specifications and/or requirements, if the organization has defined its requirements for each process and each activity within the process. Of course, this was not the case for most non-production activities. As a result, organizations that undertake a Six Sigma program are forced into a major upgrading of their internal requirements and measurement system.

Once the process variation and mean performance are compared to the requirements, most processes fail to meet the Six Sigma requirements. Many non-production processes fail to even meet a ±3 sigma performance level (3 defects per 1,000, or 3,000 per million). To place this in context, a routine appendectomy might consist of 200 to 300 opportunities for error (hand and room washing, instrument sterilization, scheduling, pharmaceuticals, skills of surgeon, and so on), most non-critical, but many fatal. The non-critical are the most common and result in "nickel and diming" up the cost of care, while the well-publicized critical errors might result in malpractice or expensive corrective action, such as repeat procedures or infection, or death of the patient, each of which is extremely expensive to organizations in reputation and in dollars. In a fast-paced and variable environment, such as a hospital emergency room, one might expect dramatic fluctuations in the sigma performance level, but typically the deviations from the mean are not much greater than that found in an accounting office. This is true because the defects built into the system are generally consistent across time.

Six Sigma quality became popular immediately following Motorola winning the Baldrige Award in 1988. The information package that Motorola distributed to explain their winning stated:

> "To accomplish its quality and total customer satisfaction goals, Motorola concentrates on several key operational initiatives. At the top of the list is Six Sigma Quality, a statistical measure of variation from a desired result. In concrete terms, Six Sigma translates into a target of no more than 3.4 defects per million products, customer services included. At the manufacturing end, this requires designs that accommodate reasonable variation in component parts but production processes that yield consistently uniform final products. Motorola employees record the defects found in every function of the business, and statistical technologies are increasingly made part of each and every employee's job."

Although Motorola called its program Six Sigma, Motorola only required that Six Sigma be applied to one point in time ($C_p = 2$) and allowed the process to perform at lower levels when the process drift is considered (C_{pk}). Table 3.1 relates the various levels of sigma to defects per thousand and per million.

TABLE 3.1 Quality Levels and Corresponding Number of Defects

Quality Level	Defects Per 1,000 Opportunities	Defects Per Million Opportunities
1 sigma	317	317,310
2 sigma	45	45,500
3 sigma	2.7	2,700
3.5 sigma	0.465	465
4 sigma	0.063	63
4.5 sigma	0.0068	6.8
5 sigma	0.00057	0.57
6 sigma	0.000002	0.002

Note that our calculation differs from the 3.4 per million as defined by Motorola because we take into account the shift of process average.

Regardless of the specific measurement methodology used, a low sigma can result in consequences not traditionally identified in the normal course of business. For example, utilizing our Six Sigma measurement in the context of power company outages or misspelled words in a library, we see the data shown in Table 3.2.

TABLE 3.2   Defect Rate Versus Sigma Level for Power Outages and Misspelled Words

Sigma Level	Defect Rate (ppm)	Duration of Power Outages Per Month	Number of Misspelled Words
1	317,400	228.5 hours	159 per page
2	45,600	32.8 hours	23 per page
3	2,700	1.94 hours	1.35 per page
4	63	2.72 minutes	1 per 31 page
5	0.57	1.48 seconds	1 per several books
6	0.002	0.005 seconds	1 per small library
7	0.000003	0.00001 seconds	1 per large library

Although .002 errors per million fuses, bolts, screws, nuts, garden hoses, or brooms may not be an aggressive target, when you start to apply the same requirements to management decisions, drawings, books, letters, sales contracts, meals served, auto repairs, medical operations, sales calls, or lines of codes, it turns out to be a very aggressive target. This is particularly true in any type of service activity in which quality cannot be inspected or tested.

The Six Sigma program is not just a new performance standard because the new performance standard cannot be met if the organization does the same old thing the same old way. It is for this reason that Motorola calls its program the "Six Sigma Quality Program." It drove a major improvement effort that radiated through the organization. Motorola's Six Sigma quality program is shown in Figure 3.1.

You will note that the Six Sigma quality program is divided into four major quadrants:

- Improvement process
- Quality initiatives
- Quality measurements
- Improvement tools

To help with the implementation of the Six Sigma quality program, Motorola formed the Six Sigma Research Center to develop a set of reference books known as the Encyclopedia of Six Sigma. This encyclopedia consists of three main parts:

- A collection of statistical tools
- Application case studies
- Descriptive, specific optimization methods

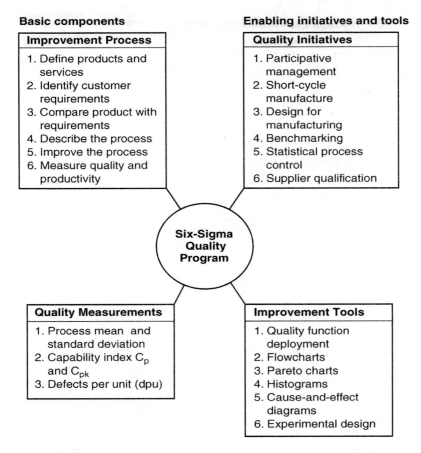

Basic components

Enabling initiatives and tools

Improvement Process
1. Define products and services
2. Identify customer requirements
3. Compare product with requirements
4. Describe the process
5. Improve the process
6. Measure quality and productivity

Quality Initiatives
1. Participative management
2. Short-cycle manufacture
3. Design for manufacturing
4. Benchmarking
5. Statistical process control
6. Supplier qualification

Six-Sigma Quality Program

Quality Measurements
1. Process mean and standard deviation
2. Capability index C_p and C_{pk}
3. Defects per unit (dpu)

Improvement Tools
1. Quality function deployment
2. Flowcharts
3. Pareto charts
4. Histograms
5. Cause-and-effect diagrams
6. Experimental design

FIGURE 3.1 Six Sigma quality program

Motorola established an innovative recognition system, called the *Black Belt program*, to support the Six Sigma quality program. Individuals progress through various levels that were designated as:

- **Green Belts**. Individuals who have completed the training.
- **Black Belts**. Individuals highly competent to serve as the on-site consultants for applications of Six Sigma methodologies.
- **Master Black Belts**. Individuals who have mastered the Six Sigma process and are capable of teaching the process to others.

The following is a ten-step process to achieve Six Sigma in a clinically intensive process:

1. **Identify Your Products**. What is the service or product that you are producing? In the case of an operating suite, it might be technically superior procedures.

2. **Identify Customer Requirements**. What is the customer's perception of error-free products or service? The response might be any adverse condition that would be deemed a medical mistake.

3. **Diagnose the Frequency and Source of Errors**. What is the source of errors? In an emergency department, errors could come from any number of places including supply carts or ineffective ambulance routing leading to overcrowded waiting rooms.

4. **Design the Process**. How can the process enablers be put together to provide a best-value solution? In said emergency room, perhaps some mechanisms can avoid the overcrowding.

5. **Develop a Simulation Model**. This model is used to project the process" performance characteristics and determine if the process will meet the customer's error-free needs. Try a new scheduling system.

6. **Error-Proof the Process**. How can the process be changed to eliminate potential errors? In the operating suite, this might include new flow of personnel or redesigned procedure packs. In a billing department, this might include correction of mistakes by the admitting department.

7. **Install Internal and External Control Points and Measurements**. How can you detect trends before they become errors? In the case of the billing department, one might institute reporting of missing information or unsigned discharge orders before they reach final billing. In the case of the emergency room, correctly stocked supply carts might eliminate trips to and from Central Supply.

8. **Install New Process**es. How do you get the users to embrace the new process? (A pilot installation often is required. In any case, an early change management intervention is advised as is input by those affected.)
   - Certify each step or activity in the process
   - Qualify the total process as a single item

9. **Measure Performance**. Does the process meet the Six Sigma requirements? If not, how does the process need to be adjusted to do so?

10. **Continuously Improve**. How can the process" effectiveness, efficiency, and adaptability be improved?

To meet the very challenging quality requirements associated with Six Sigma, an organization has only three options: Reduce the process variability, center the mean of the population, or open the acceptable performance limit.

The first approach should always be to focus on centering the process mean and reducing the process breadth. Motorola's research institute recommends the following six steps [2]:

1. Identify the product characteristics that are critical to satisfying both the physical and functional requirements of the customer and the requirements of relevant regulatory agencies. This might mean that patients who come into your facility for a series of tests will have all of them performed on a single day rather than over an extended period.

2. Determine the specific product elements that contribute to achieving these critical characteristics. What does your organization do to streamline the process for the patient or coordinate appointments?

3. According to product elements, determine the process step or process choice that controls each critical characteristic. Is your organization designed to serve the staff, the equipment, the patient, or none of the above?

4. Determine a nominal design value and the maximum (real) allowable tolerance for each critical characteristic, which still guarantees successful required performance. How would you have to change the scheduling process to achieve the Six Sigma goals?

5. Determine the capability for parts and process elements that control critical characteristics. In the example of scheduling appointments in the same visit, is the limitation in IT systems, in physical layout of the plant, or is it rooted in outmoded processes?

6. If C_p is not = 2 (C_{pk} = 1.5), then change the design of the process to achieve C_p = 2 (or institute process control measures which will narrow process capability sufficiently to achieve C_p = 2). Note: C_{pk} is the process capability index and is referenced later in the book.

To make Six Sigma more personal, consider the case of a physician who performs more than 1,000 surgical procedures (1,000 opportunities for error per case) with no more than 1 mistake. Certainly, this is very challenging based upon normal performance levels. It requires a radical new design to the way the operating room functions.

A number of points need to be considered when you are using the Six Sigma process:

- Six Sigma works well where there are high production rates of the same or very similar parts. In other words, many organizations have tackled CABG (Coronary Artery Bypass Graft) since it fits the above requirement well.

- Six Sigma is very difficult to obtain in areas like administration, sales, personnel, and so on where results are difficult to measure and are unique from one incident to another.

- It is extremely difficult for management to perform at the Six Sigma level due to the high degree of variation in the "process" of managing.

- Six Sigma works well when variables data can be collected, but not so well when attributes data are used.

- It is based upon the use of normal distribution, not abnormal or skewed distributions.

Motorola defined a list of tools required to support the Six Sigma program. They are grouped into three categories: design, process, and material. These tools are easily adaptable to healthcare if you consider them from a slightly different perspective:

- **Design Tools (or "Design of Care")**
  - Design to standard parts/materials
  - Design to standard processes
  - Design to known capabilities
  - Design for assembly
  - Design for simplicity
  - Design for robustness
- **Process Tools (or "Process in Healthcare")**
  - Short cycle manufacturing
  - Process characterization
  - Process standardization
  - Process optimization
  - Statistical process control
- **Material Tools (or "Central/Sterile Supply Optimization")**
  - Parts standardization
  - Supplier SPC (Statistical Process Control)
  - Supplier certification
  - Material requirements planning

WHY DO YOU NEED SIX SIGMA?

Assume that a typical surgical procedure contains 1,200 processing steps (not unusual because the typical healthcare organization has approximately 20,000 individual processes). If each step has a short-term 4 sigma capability, the throughput yield would be (RT is rolled throughput yield):

$$Y_{RT} = 0.999968^{(1200)} = 96.24\%$$

If you consider over a period of time, the process drifts away from the nominal as much as 1.5 sigma, the yield at each step would be degraded to .9938 and the throughput yield would be:

$$Y_{RT} = 0.9938^{(1200)} = 0.05\%$$

In other words, you have near zero possibility of completing a surgical procedure without committing an error. This is assuming that all the steps are in series with each other. Table 3.3 provides you with a breakdown of this concept based upon the number of steps in the process, and various sigma limits, assuming a 1.5 sigma shift.

TABLE 3.3 Throughput Yield Versus the Number of Process Steps and Processes

Number of Process Steps	3	4	5	6
1	93.32%	99.379%	99.9767%	99.9996%
2	87.09	98.76	99.95	99.99932
5	70.77	96.93	99.88	99.9983
10	50.09	93.96	99.77	99.9966
50	3.15	73.24	98.84	99.98
100	0.10	53.64	97.70	99.966
500	0	4.44	89.02	99.83
1000	0	0.2	79.24	99.66
2000	0	0	62.75	99.32

QUALITY

By applying Six Sigma principles, it is relatively easy to reduce current error rates, and a 50 percent reduction in errors in a 3 sigma healthcare organization cannot only lead to greater customer satisfaction, but large reductions in claims related to medical mistakes. The following sections describe some examples.

GE

Jack Welch launched the Six Sigma program at GE with 200 projects in 1995. In 1996, it increased to 3,000 projects. It expanded to 6,000 projects in 1997. The target for the Six Sigma program was to save $150 million in productivity gains and profits. The actual 1997 savings was $320 million, more than double the goal. In 1998, net savings were estimated to be about $750 million.

Some people within GE were concerned because they believed Six Sigma will cause bureaucracy to increase. Welch's reply to this concern was, "I don't give a damn if we get a little bureaucracy as long as we get the results."

William Woodburn, head of GE's industrial diamonds business, reports that in four years the operation's returns on investment increased fourfold and, at the same time, the cost structure was cut in half. He gives the Six Sigma program credit for much of the improvement. To get the improvements, he had to cut more than a third of the workforce, which included more than 50 percent of the salaried staff.[3]

Allied Signal

Lawrence A. Bossidy, former GE Vice Chairman, started the Six Sigma program at Allied Signal Inc. when he was CEO in 1991. The increased productivity and profit got Jack Welch's attention. At this time, GE was running at a 3 to 4 sigma level. The gap between 4 sigma and Six Sigma at GE was costing GE between $8 and $12 billion a year.

> "There is one rule for Industrialists and that is: Make the best quality of goods possible at the lowest cost possible, paying the highest wages possible."
>
> —Henry Ford (1863–1947)

> "I'm surprised we didn't come up with this a few decades ago. For a hospital like ours, questioning and second-guessing is common."
>
> —Dr. George Kerlakean, Good Samaritan Hospital

SIX SIGMA APPLIED TO HEALTHCARE

The Six Sigma approach is in its infancy in the healthcare industry. It has been applied to some extent to refine some hospitals' business processes using reengineering or process redesign methodologies. Monica Berry, president of the American Society for Healthcare Risk Management, stated, "If we look at quality as it has been implemented in the past, we won't be successful in reducing patient errors."

Most healthcare providers have put in place some type of Total Quality Management (TQM) or Continuous Quality Improvement (CQI) program. A Six Sigma project does not endanger these programs. In fact, it will enhance them as it builds on their strengths and puts additional focus on the measurement system.

The TQM programs focuses on defining the voice of both internal and external customers, Process Control, Process Redesign, Problem Solving (PDCA), teams and the need for objective data, total organizational involvement, and reporting in order to improve the processes.

The Continuous Quality Improvement model was defined in 1987 in the American Society for Quality book, *The Improvement Process*.[4] It defines the continuous improvement process in the following 10 building blocks.

1. Obtain top management's commitment.
2. Establish an improvement steering council.
3. Obtain total management participation.
4. Secure team participation.
5. Obtain individual involvement.

6. Establish system improvement teams (process control teams).

7. Develop supplier involvement activities.

8. Establish a systems assurance audit activity.

9. Develop and implement short-range and long-range improvement plans, and implement short-range strategy that will eliminate and prevent errors.

10. Establish recognition and reward systems that reinforce desired behaviors.

The system approach required cross-functional teams to be formed to work on process problems. For example, to reduce medication errors in a hospital required a team made up of delivering nurses, ordering physicians, dispensing pharmacists, and medication suppliers, all working together. At Stanford Hospital, they formed 11 cross-departmental teams. For example, the Cardiac Surgery team was made up of the following members:

- Physician champion/Co-Leader
- Department manager/Co-Leader
- Clinical specialists
- Pharmacists
- Social workers
- Case managers
- Respiratory therapists
- Managers from all the process departments
- Clinical financial analysts
- A consultant

The measurement system for the CQI approach was called "Poor Quality Cost," as defined in ASQC's improvement in reduction in the cost of the following:

- Prevention cost
- Appraisal cost
- Internal error cost
- External error cost
- Test Equipment cost
- Customer-incurred cost (resulting from errors)
- Customer-dissatisfaction cost
- Loss-of-reputation cost
- Last opportunity cost

Note that in the 1980s, the CQI approach was directed at reducing cost caused by errors. This changed in the 1990s as cycle time became as important in many cases, sometimes more important than cost.

The problem-analysis cycle was called "The Opportunity Cycle" and consisted of five phases:

- Phase 1 - Problem Selection
- Phase 2 - Root cause Analysis
- Phase 3 - Correction
- Phase 4 - Measurement
- Phase 5 - Prevention

Many organizations just stayed with the old, proven Shewhart (or Deming) cycle because it was simpler. It consists of the following:

- **Plan**. What to identify or accomplish.
- **Do**. Initiate the strategy or plan.
- **Check**. Evaluate the outcome of the strategy or plan.
- **Act**. What have we ascertained?

Shewhart worked for the Western Electric Company, a manufacturer of telephone hardware for Bell Telephone, from 1918 until 1924. Bell Telephone's engineers had a need to reduce the frequency of failures and repairs. In 1924, Shewhart framed the problem in terms of "assignable-cause" and "chance-cause" variation and introduced the use of the "control chart" as a tool for distinguishing between the two. Bringing a production process into a state of "statistical control," where the only variation is chance-cause, was necessary to manage the process economically.

Shewhart worked to advance this thinking for Bell Telephone Laboratories and their foundation in 1925, until his retirement in 1956.

Shewhart's charts were adopted by the American Society for Testing and Materials (ASTM) in 1933. The charts were used to improve production during World War II in the form of American war standards Z1.1, Z1.2, and Z1.3. W. Edwards Deming championed Shewhart's methods, working as a consultant to Japanese industries from 1950 to 1990.[5]

Another quality model sometimes used in healthcare was developed by a well-known physician, Dr. Avedis Donabedian.

Dr. Avedis Donabedian was widely recognized for his structure-process-outcome formulation for quality assessment activities. This model has set the framework for most contemporary quality measurement and improvement activities. His professional work focused on the systemization of knowledge throughout healthcare organizations, especially with respect to quality assessment and monitoring. His contributions include six books and many other publications.[6]

The Donabedian model developed in the 1980s focused on three domains:

- Structure
- Process
- Outcome

You will note that all three approaches have a focus on processes such as the following:

- Pharmaceutical care
- Diagnostic testing
- Accurate drug administration
- Registration
- Billing
- Appointment scheduling

It is easy to see that the Six Sigma approach should blend easily with your present quality system and improve upon it. It is a normal addition to your current system to help update it with the best and latest proven technology.

SIX SIGMA AT WORK IN HEALTHCARE

Some healthcare units are running pilot Six Sigma projects, and the results are very encouraging. Typical improvements are

- Reduced length of stay
- Improved customer satisfaction
- Reduced time to enter the healthcare unit
- Reduced inventory
- Increased efficiency in the billing system

Typical Six Sigma activities include the following:

- Charleston Area Medical Center applied Six Sigma to its supply chain management for surgical supplies saving $1 million.
- Virtual Health focused on its congestive heart failure patients and reduced variation leading to shorter length of time to recover.
- Scottsdale Healthcare applied Six Sigma approaches to the emergency room process and reduced the time required to transfer a patient to an in-patient hospital bed, increasing profits by $1.6 million per year.

"We do this project so that our staff learns and achieves results by proactively participating in the Six Sigma process. The result (decline) in registered nurse overtime alone was 65 percent over one year."

—Douglas Sears, Bon Secours Health Systems

"The results were a reduced average ventilators length of stay of 25 percent and reduction of defects per million opportunities by 12 percent for annualized savings of $450,000."

—Sarah Davis, Director of Nursing, Sentara

- One of the Stanford Hospital and Clinics' Six Sigma teams directed the Coronary Artery Bypass Graft (CABG) Surgery process. The results were outstanding:
  - Annual savings of $15 million (U.S.)
  - The mortality rate dropped from 7.1 percent to 3.7 percent for all CABG procedures
  - Costs were reduced by 40 percent
  - Intensive care time was reduced by 8 hours
  - Intubation time was reduced from 12–16 hours to 4–6 hours
- Theresa Garrison reports that at St. Louis Hospital, they were able to reduce infections by 65 percent.
- Hospital with good team spirit and nurses with authority to act on their own in case of sudden problems had 59 percent lower than average death rates.
- Stanford Hospital and Clinic saved $25 million per year from standardized purchasing and other process improvements.

Six Sigma will help in many ways. It is not just a problem-solving tool; it is also an information gathering and analysis tool. There is a huge information gap. The present data systems in most hospitals are poor at best. Therefore, doing any Six Sigma project in the typical healthcare setting can prove to be difficult and time consuming.

Because the typical healthcare project requires more manual information gathering (observations, stop-watch exercises, walk-through) than the average manufacturing organization we often find that this is the true "moment of truth" for the healthcare organization. For example, if one wants to track the time it takes to go through the admissions process in the typical hospital, the Six Sigma practitioner will likely find that the information isn't available or is only available without the granularity that is necessary to create a sound hypothesis. Because data collection can be expensive and time consuming and there are so many information voids in the typical healthcare organization, many give up the Six Sigma effort at this point (or the effort languishes in a near-completion state).

At this point, the enlightened organization redoubles its efforts to capture valuable information for the current and future studies (as well as SPC). While we do not know the actual number of times Six Sigma efforts are abandoned at this critical state, we have seen it happen far too many times and, just as the road to the Ph.D. is strewn with unfinished dissertations, so is the road to the Black Belt. This is one of the most important reasons for following the implementation guidelines from later in this book to a tee, as well as finding a champion or MBB who has not only been a part of a Six Sigma program, but one who has actually started a program and has executive presence and strong leadership skills.

Vicky Gregg from Blue Cross Blue Shield of Tennessee, when he was discussing the quality and quality of outcome information that was available to the customers, stated, "If you think about it as the equivalent of a manufacturer not having the system and information flow to understand and measure quality, that's pretty scary." The Six Sigma approach to data collection analysis can help with this problem along with electronic record keeping.

Six Sigma also attacks the basic problem that all hospitals have: the variation in the way things are done. For example, a simple urinary tract infection without any complications can be treated in 135 different ways. Which process provides the best overall value? No one knows or everyone would be using it.

Training is a key part of preparing the organization for Six Sigma. The following is the minimum Six Sigma training required by job assignment based upon ASQ (American Society for Quality) recommendations:

- Executive: one day overview
- Upper Management Champions: 5 days
- Six Sigma Green Belt: 10 days on Six Sigma concepts
- Six Sigma Black Belt: 20 days during a 4-month period

Most organizations do all of the above in half the time and will heavily focus the training on field experience and improvement projects.

DIFFERENT VIEWS OF HEALTHCARE QUALITY

One of the problems that slow down quality in healthcare is the many different views of what quality is. For example,

- The paying organization views quality as a measure of the value associated with the delivered care.

- The physician/nurse views quality as making the right diagnosis, prescribing the right medicine, and employing the right procedure to make the patient better. It's doing the right job from a scientific point of view.

- The patients view quality as the perceived services, such as: Are the employees gracious? Do they appear to be competent? Are they receiving timely care? Is the hospital a good environment?

- The healthcare managers view quality as the appropriateness of care. Quality in healthcare is the evaluation of the appropriateness of treatment.

When we develop the healthcare system, all four views of quality must be designed into the system.

CONCLUSIONS

Many other non-healthcare organizations have embraced the Six Sigma concepts. Among them are IBM, Texas Instruments, Defense System Electronics Group (DSEG), and GE. While the implementation of Six Sigma in a healthcare-provider setting is in its early stages, some of the top healthcare organizations in the world are interested in the possibilities. Most quality-focused organizations performed at the 4 sigma level at the beginning of the 1990s. As of this date, we know of no organization that is performing all of its measurements to the Six Sigma requirements. Our experience indicates that Six Sigma and the related methodologies are not implemented without difficulties.

G. Don Taylor and John R. English, in their paper entitled "A Benchmarking Framework for Quality Improvement,"[7] point out the five following problems related to the Six Sigma methodology:

- Determining how to measure defects
- Applying Six Sigma in non-traditional settings
- Determining whether to relax specifications or to reduce the normal variability of the product
- The use of restrictive assumptions
- The determination of appropriate tools to use to achieve Six Sigma goals

Motorola, on the other hand, reports the following results (in a manufacturing environment):

- Improved yields and lower than expected fallout during manufacturing (this could equate to less use of supplies or less errors)
- Better productivity
- Higher performance
- Improved MTTF (Mean Time To Failure)
- Lower manufacturing cost (or lower costs per procedure, patient, and so on)
- Improved customer satisfaction

GE has embraced the Six Sigma concept in order to drive its future quality improvement activities. GE's Six Sigma program is the largest quality initiative ever mounted in the U.S. They call their design for Six Sigma *DMADV*, which stands for:

- **Define**. Define the process, product or service that will be improved. Define the customer's view of error-free performance.
- **Measure**. Evaluate the current item's performance.
- **Analyze**. Define best practices, benchmarks, and enablers.
- **Design**. Develop a best-value future-state solution.
- **Verify**. Measure the new item to ensure it meets the requirements documented in the define stage and the Six Sigma requirements.

As an example, the following are a few of the tools and techniques used by GE in support of Six Sigma:

Quality Function Deployment	Cost/Benefit Analysis	Pareto Charts
Organizational Change Management	Business Process Improvement	Process Capability
Value-Added Analysis	Shareholder Analysis	Scatter Diagrams
Charting (Pie, Bar, etc.)	Prioritization Matrix	Histogram
Root Cause Analysis	Problem Cycle	The 5 W's
Critical Source Factors	Surveys	Benchmarking
Classification of Solution Criteria	Focus Groups	Gap Analysis
Activity-Based Costing	Process Frame (boxing)	SPC
Regression Analysis	Visioning	Affinity Diagrams
Design of Experiments	Gantt Chart	Process Analysis
Cause-and-Effect Analysis	Project Management	Stratification

Force-Field Analysis	Common/Special Causes	Work-Out
Cycle Time/Work Flow analysis	Moments of Truth	Value Analysis
Quantifying Opportunities	Resistance Analysis	Brainstorming
"Should-Be" Process Maps	Behavior Conditioning	Mind Mapping
Work Breakdown Structure	Risk Assessment	Charters
Continuous Improvement	Standardization	Measurement Plan

It is very important to point out that one of the most used tools in Total Six Sigma is Business Process Improvement (BPI). The three major methodologies that are included in BPI include the following:

BPI - most used tool in 6 sigma (handwritten annotation)

- Process redesign
- Process reengineering
- Process benchmarking

All three require that a very effective change management project is used in conjunction or the possibility of failure runs very high.

Hammer and Champy in their book, *Reengineering the Corporation*, reported, "Some 50 to 70 percent of reengineering attempts fail to deliver the intended dramatic results."[8]

Six Sigma Potential in Healthcare

So, where can a healthcare organization find Six Sigma opportunities? It's clear in manufacturing where opportunities lie, but in the healthcare space we are talking about service, we are talking about mass customization, and we are talking about customer/patient lives.

In fact, there are almost limitless opportunities in healthcare. Most Six Sigma practitioners find that services in general, and healthcare in particular, are some of the most fertile ground available. These opportunities generally come in from a wasteful and inefficient administrative process but can just as easily be found in the clinical space and, amazingly enough, in the hands of the patients. In no other business is the vested interest as great as in the healthcare space. Patients and families are more than happy to participate in any effort to reduce variation and potentially adverse outcomes.

Some examples of where Six Sigma might work in healthcare could be

- **Billing Department**. Imagine a billing department that reduced errors in processing patient bills to a 5 sigma process level. While the department might be producing claims at a very efficient and effective rate, it is common knowledge in the industry that many claims are rejected due to errors by personnel at the payer organization. As of Fall 2003, Cigna, Anthem, and many of the Blues are implementing Six Sigma in their organizations. Should a provider and payer agree to implement Six Sigma in tandem, tremendous savings could be achieved solely on the potential to reduce or eliminate claims adjudication in favor of a "trusted" claims chain.

- **Emergency Department**. Imagine an emergency department with a phone-in triage function aimed at "pre-processing" patients for the appropriateness of care. Six Sigma could enable an Emergency Department to send potential ER department patients to more appropriate venues of care or sister facilities for load balancing—a not unheard-of application when most patients could use their cell phones to call on-route.

- **Floor Procedures**. Imagine a system where patients gain control of their stay via meal delivery as a "menu with room service." This psychological "control" leads to faster recovery times, increased patient satisfaction, and potential reduced costs by the food services department through better balancing food preparation throughout the day instead of centered on breakfast, lunch, and dinner.

What would work in one facility wouldn't necessarily work in another, and this is the beauty of the Six Sigma approach. Instead of following the cookie-cutter approach of the healthcare provider down the street, the hospital is able to evaluate its own opportunities and work to improve its unique opportunities. Just as facilities specialize, so too are they empowered by the Six Sigma process to individually identify and improve processes tailored to their individual patient population, payer mix, and staffing situation. Six Sigma truly offers an opportunity for a breakthrough in healthcare.

In the past, we have believed that the healthcare system was too complex with too many players—companies, insurers, medical device makers, pharmaceutical companies, doctors, nurses, hospitals, special interest groups, and others—to actually gain control over a process, never mind a system. These players all have different interests and objectives and, in fact, different motivations for correcting the problem. But if we, the business community, do not step up to the challenge, the government will have to and we believe we can find a better answer. Now, Six Sigma is not the total answer to the problems we are facing in our healthcare system, but it can be a key part. It is time to start making some major changes.

Healthcare organizations may be the type of service organization for the use of Six Sigma. If one considers the very nature of the business, one might notice that in fact healthcare is generally a highly repetitive environment, subject to variation in disease from patient to patient, yes, but generally uniform in the reaction to the variation by patient. While Patient A might require a different dose of a medicine than Patient B in response to an episode, the common factors would be method of ordering and delivering the medication, administering, and documenting the incident. The staff and physicians would be the same—the pharmacy, the crash carts, the floor layouts all generally the same. The only thing that might vary is the patient's reaction to the drug in question at the dose administered. In fact, one could argue that the "practice" of medicine is actually not what we do on the average patient, but what we do in the exception—the day-to-day treatment of our patients is the science of medicine, and science requires a scientific approach to the delivery of medicine. Six Sigma is as close to scientific management than anything that has come before.

Consider the scientific method. One definition we like is "principles and procedures for the systematic pursuit of knowledge involving the recognition and formulation of a problem, the collection of data through observation and experiment, and the formulation and testing of hypotheses."[9] In respect to the methodology of Six Sigma, which we will discuss in greater detail later in the book, Six Sigma allows for:

- Principles and procedures for the systematic pursuit of knowledge; knowledge being about critical to quality characteristics and the understanding and measurement of said characteristics.

- Involving the recognition and formulation of a problem, as formulated in the Six Sigma project charter specifically addressing the problem we will try to solve, the magnitude, and the risks involved.

- The collection of data through observation and experiment, and the formulation and testing of hypotheses, as manifested in the collection of data, development of hypothesis, testing of hypothesis, and development of tests of the hypothesis.

In addition, Six Sigma allows you to utilize the scientific method to actually apply the improvements for immediate benefits to your patients, their families, and the overall well being of the healthcare organization. Accordingly, Six Sigma fits so well with the culture and environment of healthcare that it is one of the most logical and effective extensions of healthcare to come along in the last 50 years.

Medicine, Measurement, and Science

The current healthcare error rate in the U.S. is about 6,210 errors per million opportunities (3.8 sigma) and for some treatment activities runs as high as 1 sigma. Compare this to the manufacturing Six Sigma standard of 3.4 errors per million opportunities for all processes.

According to Altman, at least 150 times since 1996, surgeons in hospitals in this country have operated on the wrong arm, leg, eye, kidney or other body part, or even on the wrong patient.[10] The figure does not include near misses, such as when doctors have started to operate on the wrong part of the patient or even the wrong patient, but stopped before the operation was completed because the error was detected. No one collects such information.

Complex Business

Thirty to forty percent of the cost waste is caused by errors made by specialists.

The U.S. government estimates that IT can save $140 billion per year through improved patient care and the elimination of redundant tests ordered.

In September, 2003, Tawnya Brown underwent surgery at Inova Fairfax Hospital in Falls Church, Virgina. Although the surgery went well, the patient ultimately died. Brown was given two pints of A-negative blood and her blood type was O-positive. To make the condition worse, her doctor called for more blood when he discovered that she was not doing well in recovery. In the following three hours, she received six more pints of the wrong type of blood. (A person her size can hold a volume of about eight pints of blood only.) The day before the surgery, a technician drew a blood sample so that the correct type would be available if needed. The problem was that the technician took the sample from the wrong patient. This should have been discovered by the phlebotomist, but he failed to perform two required identification screens: checking the patient's hospital bracelet and asking the patient to state her name. The financial settlement for this error was about $1.7 million. But not even $1.7 million can make up the loss of a mother to an eight-year old girl.

Brian Bachman, two years of age, died after undergoing a liver transplant at the Fairview University Medical Center in Minnesota. The surgery was uncomplicated, and Brian was doing well initially. However, two days after the surgery, Brian's condition worsened. At 7 a.m., a nurse misread the table on a log of Heparin she was replacing. The new bag contained a much higher concentration of blood thinner than the one she was replacing, and the machine delivering the medication was not reprogrammed. Brian began receiving 10 times the amount ordered by the physician. The staff failed to notice the mistake throughout the day, even though the medication drip was checked every 15 minutes. The error was finally discovered by the evening nurse, but Brian had already experienced internal bleeding and a blood clot in the artery leading to his liver. A blood clot can trigger liver damage, which can cause swelling of the brain and brain death. Doctors determined that the little boy "will most likely remain in a vegetative state." As a result, Brian was taken off life support and died soon thereafter. Mike Sertz, Fairview's Vice President for Risk Management, stated, "It was more a system error than an individual error."

Fraud and Abuse

Healthcare costs run $1.7 trillion a year. Fraud and abuse run between $50 and $75 billion a year. In controlling variation, fraud and abuse can be more easily identified and dealt with.

Six Sigma can be a great tool in fighting healthcare fraud and abuse. For example, billing for services not furnished is arguably the single most common method of deceiving or misrepresenting services delivered. Because Six Sigma utilizes statistical process control as a core tool, variations in standard practice will always be noted. Too many treatments, too many supplies, or too many visits will, by definition, signal the system to investigate the reasons for the variation. This argument can also be made for unbundling or "exploding" charges, and "upcoding."

Another typical healthcare fraud and abuse practice is the misrepresentation of a diagnosis, which can be identified through controls when individual institutions or physicians seem to consistently have sicker patients than the population in general. This argument also works in the case of falsification of certificates of medical necessity, plans of treatment, and medical records.

Only by gaining a true understanding of your healthcare business can you begin to get a real handle on the indicators of fraud and abuse. Six Sigma enables you to spot outliers before they become a big problem for the provider.

Dedication to Perfection and Elimination of Errors

Each year an estimated 1,500 surgical patients have foreign objects (such as sponges) left in them during surgery, leaving many to face crippling health problems. However, there is no mandatory system for reporting errors, leaving the actual number of medical errors in question.

It is often only through malpractice lawsuits that these errors become public knowledge. The article goes on to report that 5 percent of doctors are found responsible for more than 50 percent of successful malpractice suits. One caution: Most malpractice cases don't make it to court. Only one in six victims even file, and about half of those abandon the effort before trial.[11]

Performance

Contrary to popular belief, effective performance metrics in healthcare are virtually non-existent.

Hospitals with an atmosphere and/or culture of distrust have a death rate that is 58 percent higher than average.

Ramon Cruz, 81, had not even been hospitalized when Good Samaritan Hospital Medical Center in Islip, NY, forwarded the incorrect information to government agencies that he had died. Apparently, a hospital worker called up the wrong "Ramon Cruz" in the database. Cruz's monthly Social Security checks were halted, his bank accounts emptied, and Medicare benefits terminated. A spokesman said all Cruz's lost money will be returned, adding that it would take a couple of months.[12]

Customer Focus

According to the Centers for Disease Control, two million patients per year acquire an infection in the U.S. when hospitalized for conditions not related to the infection, and 88,000 die as a direct or indirect result. This adds an additional healthcare cost of $5 billion.[13]

According to the CDC's William Jarvis, MD, and scientific chair of the healthcare-associated infections conference sponsored by CDC, "If you get an infection while you're in the hospital for an operation for heart disease, for example, your hospital stay may be extended by days, and sometimes weeks, before the infection is cured."

In general, the number of extra days a patient has to spend in the hospital varies depending on the type of infection he or she gets: an estimated 1 to 4 days for a urinary tract infection, 7 to 8 days for an infection at the site of a surgery procedure, 7 to 21 days for a bloodstream infection, and 7 to 30 days for pneumonia.

"The costs vary, too," Dr. Jarvis said. "Anywhere from $600 or so for a urinary tract infection to $5,000 or more for pneumonia. Prolonged bloodstream infections can top $50,000."

According to some experts, a patient improves faster at home by 10 to 60 percent than in a healthcare facility.

Complaints about hospital bills are as common as complaints about hospital food. *Consumer Reports* recently surveyed 21,000 readers on satisfaction with hospital stays. Of the 11,000 respondents who had reviewed their itemized hospital bills, 5 percent said they found major errors. Respondents with out-of-pocket expenses of $2,000 or more were twice as likely to have found billing errors.[14]

Consumerism in healthcare is another hot topic. Health Savings Accounts were introduced in 2005 to mixed reviews. Since then, they have been growing in popularity with employers and insurers. While some might be advocating a repeal of the law, the plan, which allows customers to opt into a high deductible health plan while investing their own money in healthcare expenses below the deductible, is proving to be popular.

What this means to the healthcare provider is that customers/patients now have a say in how, where, and with whom they will spend their money. It is doubtful that customers will spend their discretionary money at healthcare organizations that cannot or will not invest in quality and customer-focused care.

Staffing Shortages

There is a critical shortage of nurses. This is caused by several factors, including

- A growing demand as the baby boomers retire.
- The high cost of training a nurse. Because many universities find that tuition stratification is difficult (that is, charging different amounts based on the major), classes and majors that require labs, small classes, and highly skilled instructors are not as profitable as others.
- A nursing instructor with a Masters degree is paid less than half that of a hospital nurse. Given the pay differential, universities are finding it very difficult to recruit nursing professors.
- Finally, nursing can be difficult and sometimes hazardous. In general, the hours are long, the work is dirty, and the pay is less than a comparable position outside the hospital. Accordingly, many nursing professionals leave the field each year for easier work at software companies, pharmaceutical companies, and doctors' offices.

Patricia Ann Hottois, age 53 of Phoenix, died of septic shock after the abdominal pad was left in her surgical wound. She had her surgery on June 8, 2003, at Maricopa Medical Center. About two weeks after the surgery, she was still complaining about the pain when her doctors discovered that the pad was left inside her. She died on July 1, 2003. This medical malpractice case was settled for $320,000.[15] These types of errors should be eliminated by just doing a sponge count. According to a 2003 study in the *New England Journal of Medicine*, this type of surgical error occurs in about 1 out of every 1,000 to 1,500 abdominal operations, a lot more than the six sigma goal of 3.4 per million.

On March 19, 2004, two patients died at Foothill Medical Centre because they got an incorrect solution during dialysis treatment. They were given a potassium chloride solution instead of sodium chloride. The mix-up took place in the hospital's pharmacy. Dr. Bob Johnston, the CHR's Chief Medical Officer, stated "Despite our best efforts, errors do occur." Barry Cavanaugh, Chief Executive of the Pharmacists Association of Alberta, stated, "An adverse event could happen because they are overworked."[16]

Costs to Society

In the U.S., healthcare accounts for 15 percent of the GNP, and it will continue to rise to 18 percent. This compares to 8 percent and 10 percent in developing regions such as Japan, Europe, and Canada.

Two percent of hospital patients experience an adverse drug reaction, resulting in an increased length of stay and $4,700 added needless expenses. This accounts for 2.5 percent of the hospital's budget.[17]

One person in the U.S. dies every eight minutes as a result of nosocomial infection, and 95 percent are preventable.[18]

About 20 percent of U.S. "products and services" extra cost is caused by our legal system.[19]

"Survey: 40 percent of public experienced medical errors," which appeared in the *New England Journal of Medicine*, reports that more than one-third of practicing physicians and 40 percent of the public have experienced a medical error in the care that they or a family member received as patients. One of the findings of the survey is that "physicians disagree with national experts on the effectiveness of many of the proposed solutions to the problem of medical errors."[20]

ENDNOTES

1. Harrington, H James. "Process qualification manufacturing insurance policy." *IBM Technical Report*, September 15, 1980.

2. Coppola, Anthony. Six Sigma Programs. *DoD Reliability Analysis Center START Sheets*, 1990. Volume 6, Number 5.

3. Byrne, John A. "How Jack Welch Runs GE". *BusinessWeek*, June 9, 1998, p. 47.

4. Harrington, H. James. *The Improvement Process*. (McGraw-Hill, 1987).

5. Cutler, A.N. (2001, August 22). http://www.sigma-engineering.co.uk/, Sigma Engineering Partnership.

6. Trusko, Brett E. (2006, November 14). http://www.jointcommission.org/Codman/Avedis_Donabedian.htm, Ernest Emory Codman Award.

7. Taylor, G. Don and English, John. "A Benchmarking Framework for Quality Improvement." *Quality Engineering*, Vol. 6, No. 1, July 1993, pp. 57-69

8. Hammer, M and Champy, J. *Reengineering the Corporation: A Manifesto for Business Revolution* (New York: Harper Business, 1993).

9. tangents.home.att.net/data/rlgdef.htm.

10. Altman, L.K. "The wrong foot, and other tales of surgical error," *The New York Times*, December 11, 2001.

11. Burton, Susan. "The Biggest Mistake of Their Lives," *The New York Times*, March 16, 2003.

12. Associated Press. "Government Declares Man Very Much Alive, Dead." *Associated Press*, February 19, 2002.

13. Centers for Disease Control (United States). Hospital infections cost U.S. billions of dollars annually. *Media Relations.* Monday March 6, 2000. http://www.cdc.gov/od/oc/media/pressrel/r2k0306b.htm.

14. *Consumer Reports*, 2003. "Decoding your hospital bills. You can find and fix costly errors."http://www.consumerreports.org/cro/personal-finance/decoding-hospital-bills-103/overview/index.htm.

15. Leonard, Christina. "Surgery Mistake Is Costly," *The Arizona Republic*. June 25, 2004.

16. Trusko, B and Harrington, H.J., "The Prescription for Health Care Excellence - Take Six Sigma As Needed." *Quality Digest.* http://qualitydigest.com/IQedit/qdarticle_print.lasso?articleid=8889&-session=ACCESS:40A788221b3f61DA5DynTy16AE15. 2006.

17. Institute of Medicine. Preventing Medication Errors: Quality Chasm Series. July 20, 2006.

18. Centers for Disease Control (United States). Hospital infections cost U.S. billions of dollars annually. *Media Relations.* Monday March 6, 2000. http://www.cdc.gov/od/oc/media/pressrel/r2k0306b.htm.

19. Council of Economic Advisors. Who pays for tort liability claims? An economic analysis of the U.S. tort liability system. April 2002.

20. Davis, Robert. Survey: 40 percent of public experienced medical errors. *Asbury Park Press,* December 15, 2002.

METHODOLOGY, TOOLS, AND MEASUREMENTS

THE HEALTHCARE OPPORTUNITY

SECTIONS

Launching the Six Sigma Initiative
Defining Six Sigma Vision and Mission

Successful implementation of Six Sigma must begin with a clear identification of the opportunity for improvement in the healthcare organization. The opportunity could exist in support functions, in interaction with patients, in the operation room or the emergency room, in the supply chain, in regulatory compliance, or in facilities. Application of the Six Sigma methodology must be directly related to improved financial performance. The opportunity analysis leads to specific projects for application of the Six Sigma methodology.

The rapidly rising cost of healthcare and a degrading quality of services have been of concern for businesses and individuals. A checkup for a heart problem can cost as much as $15,000. The cost of healthcare accounts for about 15 percent of the cost of product or services, which used to be about 8 percent several years ago. The continual rise and consequential effort to control the cost of healthcare has led to the evolution of managed healthcare and reduction in availability and quality of healthcare services. For practicing physicians, the cost of insurance for protecting against malpractice has forced them to move from metropolitan to suburban areas. The main players in the healthcare services involved are insurance companies, managed healthcare services providers, pharmacies, hospitals, and doctors. Each one is trying to preserve available healthcare resources contentiously, and is feeding each other. For example, insurance will not allow for filling a prescription for three months at a time, thus forcing individuals to make three co-payments. The healthcare services are still evolving and almost completing a circle by the advent of midwife services, pharmacy-based practitioners, and uncontrolled medical service providers. Consumers must weigh between quality and availability of medical services. For some people, it is better to have insurance of some quality rather than have no insurance. Much of the cost of the increase in healthcare has been attributed to increases in malpractice insurance and associated lawsuits. The increased cost of malpractice implies degradation in the quality of healthcare, unless we assume that people had decided to claim malpractice intentionally.

Another global phenomenon in healthcare is increasing utilization of outsourcing. People from European countries have been visiting hospitals in Thailand and India where the cost of superior healthcare is about 20 to 30 percent less. The advent of the Internet has already launched the remote provision of healthcare services. For example, aspects of radiology are being performed in remote villages or cities in India for U.S. healthcare service providers. Medical transcription and billing are other areas which have been outsourced to providers in India. One can see that healthcare services are being fragmented for cost reasons. This trend in healthcare services implies opportunities for improvement in these areas through various means. The sources of problems are everywhere from registration, checkup, illegible prescriptions, tests, hospitalization, billing, and customer service. Hospital care accounts for about a third of the cost of healthcare. It appears that we have developed excellent and expensive methods to treat bones, heart, and brain diseases. However, we have become worse in treating patients for common variations in health.

Six Sigma was developed when the competition in the electronics industry became intense around 1985. Despite being the industry leader in the telecommunication industry, Motorola recognized that in order to continue to be the market leader, its leadership realized that something different had to be done to survive the challenging times. Interestingly, the healthcare industry is experiencing similar challenges in terms of spiraling increases in cost of services, competitive pressures, government regulations, complexity of operations, lack of traceability, and concerns about quality of service. Pressure to perform better, faster, and cost-effectively is mounting daily in the healthcare industry. The Motorola leadership set out their quality improvement journey with ten times improvement in five years (10x5), which later became ten times in two years (10x2), and that is still true. Like any new technology initiative, awareness and understanding through education is the first step. Motorola University became the vehicle to transform Motorola into a high-performance company. Managers were trained in Change management to create a culture to work under challenging and competing environment. Along with this, a strong management review process was established.

Before officially launching Six Sigma on January 1, 1987, the company practiced principles of Six Sigma, especially setting "stretch" goals. Every employee was required to participate in stretch goals of improving performance and generating savings. Besides the stretch goals, an employee participation management program was established to share savings with employees. Employees earning extra money and a strong performance review program propelled the principles of Six Sigma, which led to the official announcement for its corporatewide implementation in five years. About halfway through 1986, the concept of Six Sigma was ready for implementation, and projects were identified for prototyping the concepts. The first four projects, called *Small Wins for Six Sigma*, were in product development and manufacturing. The Six Sigma measurement methods were applied to establish accountability that drove the improvement. Then the graphics department, corporate law, human resources, and new product development departments followed implementation of Six Sigma.

Several companies, including healthcare facilities, have launched Six Sigma and reported significant savings using Six Sigma. One of the prerequisites for applying Six Sigma is that one does not use the Six Sigma approach unless one can show significant and visible savings. There is no hidden savings even though Six Sigma can eliminate hidden costs. There has been no methodology other than Six Sigma that has been credited with saving billions of dollars.

There have been challenges and failures associated with Six Sigma. Some of the reasons for struggling with Six Sigma are the following:

- Not being able to demonstrate the savings
- Missing the intent of Six Sigma
- Lack of creativity
- Too many or no projects
- Too much Black Belt training
- Too many consultants without hands-on experience
- Too many introductory books and consultants
- Six Sigma as a program of the year
- Minimal leadership commitment
- Too much statistics without statistical thinking

To ease into Six Sigma, the leadership must first understand Six Sigma well. Six Sigma has four components, as follows:

Component	Description
Intent	Lots of improvement very fast
Methodology	Define, Measure, Analyze, Improve, and Control
Key Tools	Various tools corresponding to the various phases
Measurements	Defect Per Unit, Errors Per Patient (Product level); Defects Per Million Opportunities

Having understood that Six Sigma is beyond statistics and numbers, a well-thought out approach must be formulated and implemented. The approach must remedy pitfalls and prevent false launches. The most important aspect of the approach must answer the question of why one should implement Six Sigma. The following steps describe a practical approach to implementing Six Sigma in the healthcare industry:

1. Identify improvement opportunities in the organization for savings, and define the value proposition for Six Sigma.
2. Ensure strategic alignment of the organization for achieving desired business objectives and employee incentives.

3. Develop a business case for Six Sigma, identify leading team members, and develop a plan for successful implementation. Innovation must be an integral intent of the Six Sigma initiative.

4. Establish measurements, evaluate performance, and analyze for causes of problems.

5. Plan and manage change through communication and participation.

6. Sustain improvement through performance review and recognition.

A cornerstone of the Six Sigma methodology has been to aim for a dramatic improvement, an improvement that is visible, meaningful, and profitable. Merely setting an incremental improvement goal is not what Six Sigma is about—it can drive for a 70 percent improvement rather than a 10 percent improvement. Setting an ambitious goal for improvement requires a totally different approach. As a result of dramatic improvement, and the resultant savings, everyone can benefit from their commitment to Six Sigma. Depending upon the size of facility, and complexity of organization, savings per project could range from $50,000–$250,000. The projects could be reducing patient waiting time, reducing donors' blood collection errors, reducing surgical errors, reducing excessive consumption of disposables, or reducing the post-surgery infection rate.

The first five years of Six Sigma at Motorola were very rewarding for the company. Sales grew dramatically; better products with higher margins were introduced that focused on quality, and the company's reputation soared. Such benefits of Six Sigma could not have been realized just by focusing on some projects. Instead, it was an organization-wide, leadership-driven, process-oriented, middle managerial-led, and employee-owned initiative to improve the corporate performance.

To ensure the basic intent of the Six Sigma methodology is effectively implemented, a practical approach to planning should begin with setting aggressive goals for improvement.[1] An implementation plan for Six Sigma focuses on the strategic intent that will move the company forward, understanding the critical requirements in each area and the key indicators of progress. The plan for Six Sigma should include opportunity analysis, development of a vision, establishment of drivers, definition of strategies, planning for superior execution, and a desire for continual improvement.

LAUNCHING THE SIX SIGMA INITIATIVE

The organization must have brainstorming sessions to understand drivers for Six Sigma before launching the Six Sigma initiative. Attending an executive overview of Six Sigma concepts would create an appropriate level of appreciation for the methodology, and generate interests in using Six Sigma for improving performance. Experience teaches us that success or failure of the Six Sigma initiative largely depends upon active involvement of a well-informed leader. Once the leader learns the methodology, opportunities to benefit from the Six Sigma methodology can be identified, and realistic value proposition can be established. Capitalizing on the right opportunity can be a profitably rewarding experience, maximizing return on investment.

Healthcare Scorecard

Launching a Six Sigma initiative starts with a lot of enthusiasm from the "champion" who has found courage and conviction to persuade management to commit to it. With enough resources, interest, excitement, and the help of some consultants, the Six Sigma initiative gets off the ground. After initial training, the promise of Six Sigma starts fading. The interest level wanes, the "champion" moves on, and the Six Sigma crew starts losing its touch. In the Six Sigma journey, it's only a matter of time before the team loses its momentum and ceases to progress. Sustaining a Six Sigma initiative is at least as important as launching it.

One of the main tenets of Six Sigma is "measure what we value." Thus, it is important to establish a methodology to ensure performance of the Six Sigma initiative and a scorecard for monitoring performance of the entire healthcare organization, be it emergency, outpatient, pharmacy, surgery, clinical trials, purchasing, or even the senior leadership functions. The *Six Sigma business scorecard* offers a framework for measuring and managing performance of a healthcare organization. The Six Sigma business scorecard combines the Six Sigma methodology for dramatically improving customer satisfaction with the balanced scorecard approach to achieving financial objectives.[2] The Six Sigma business scorecard is a balanced and complete corporate scorecard that promotes inspiration by the leader, improvement by the managers, and innovation by employees. Most importantly, the Six Sigma business scorecard produces a *Business Performance Index* (BPIn), which is linked to expected profitability, therefore providing a direct indication of financial performance. Some of the benefits of implementing a Six Sigma business scorecard include a quantifiable sigma level; alignment with the organizational structure; clear visibility of cost, revenue, and profitability; and the clear expectation of the leadership and management. Any healthcare related organization can develop a performance index similar to the BPIn.

The seven elements of Six Sigma business scorecard include the following[3]:

1. Leadership and Profitability
2. Management and Improvement
3. Employee Involvement and Innovation
4. Purchasing and Supplier Management
5. Sales and Distribution
6. Operational Execution
7. Service and Growth

These categories provide a launching pad for establishing a set of realistic, easy-to-implement measures that drive improvement using the Six Sigma methodology. Correspondingly, the following is a list of initial set of operational measurements that will provide leading indications of the sustainable performance:

1. Recognition of employees by the chief for superior performance (Rule of 2, either doubling the value, or halving the problems is a good start to define superior performance).

2. Profitability of the organization for continual enhancements of services and returning value to stakeholders for their investment.

3. Rate of improvement in performance of all major functions in an organization.

4. Employee ideas for excellence in idea generation and management.

5. Cost of purchasing as a percent of revenue.

6. Quality of supply chain measured in terms of Sigma.

7. Operational excellence measured in terms of Sigma.

8. Operational responsiveness measured as a deviation from the planned.

9. Customer satisfaction with a maximum score of 90.

10. Sales growth through new services or capabilities.

Because Six Sigma is a data-driven methodology, one must look at more process measurements such as error rate, cycle time, and human capital utilization instead of depending on the financial measurements. Sometimes, financial measurements may be too late to learn about the Six Sigma initiative's progress. Moreover, after the initial success, it's tough to sustain a management system without a compelling measure of success and profitability.

DEFINING SIX SIGMA VISION AND MISSION

Once the leadership understands the intent and methodology of Six Sigma, a corporate story must be written that communicates opportunity, participation of the leadership team, and role of employees. It is important to establish clear roles for physicians, nurses, support staff, administration, and the leadership for the purpose of achieving the desired level of the performance improvement.

A company's Six Sigma vision provides a futuristic outlook of an organization. Superior companies establish their vision irrespective of the Six Sigma initiative. When a company commits to a Six Sigma initiative, supporting homework, such as communication, compensation, recognition, and exciting value proposition, must be completed before launching the initiative. Creating a vision for a Six Sigma initiative requires a complete understanding of the Six Sigma methodology, its intent, and its benefits. Without clearly understanding its benefits, the corporate vision could miss its sense of direction. For example, one company understands Six Sigma as a DMAIC (Define, Measure, Analyze, Improve, and Control), and therefore, a five-step methodology. For another organization, Six Sigma has been understood as a strategy to dramatically improve business. For another company, Six Sigma may mean another type of certification. Management leaders continue to evolve the application of Six Sigma and reap new benefits. Is it a strategy, a methodology, or an enabler? GE sees Six Sigma as its DNA; Motorola sees it as a "culture thing"; and Honeywell sees it as a Standard of Excellence. Six Sigma, which was born as an approach for accelerating improvement, promoting employee teamwork, and achieving total customer satisfaction, has been analyzed to its limits and institutionalized at many corporations. Six Sigma was initially criticized for being unrealistic due to the associated 3.4 defects per million opportunities. Yet today, Six Sigma has become a strategy to improve corporate performance through a culture of continual reengineering and structured self-assessment, a methodology for dramatic improvement, and employee innovation used to produce the best products and services at highest profit. Defining a vision for a healthcare facility could be in terms of handling more patients with highest satisfaction at lowest possible cost, maximum profits, and superior financial returns for investors. This may require understanding patients' needs, stakeholders' expectations, trends in treatment methods and technologies, potential collaboration with other healthcare facilities, continually informing the community of its performance, and participating in community activities. The healthcare facility must envision preventive and reactive care for its customers.

Rush Copley Medical Center, located in Aurora, Illinois, has published its Vision 2010 on its website that incorporates its strategic initiatives, its objectives to transforming Rush Copley into a regional medical center beyond the Aurora community. Its key aspects of vision include the following (see http://rushcopley.com):

- Dominate market share in all institutes.
- Lead market in customer and physician satisfaction with scores in the 95th percentile or higher.
- Achieve and sustain Magnet designation.
- Attain employee satisfaction at the 95th percentile.
- Become a renowned technology leader with full system integration, wireless applications, and eHealth initiatives.
- Become an A+ financially rated hospital—with ready access to capital.

Yale New Haven Hospital (YNHH) had adopted Six Sigma for improving aspects of its operations without clearly stating its vision to utilize Six Sigma. In working together with GE, Six Sigma was practiced at one of its medical centers. However, YNHH'S mission represents its priorities without mentioning Six Sigma (see http://www.ynhh.org):

- **Patient Care**. To provide sensitive, high-quality, cost-effective healthcare services to all patients, regardless of ability to pay.
- **Teaching**. To be the primary teaching hospital for the Yale University School of Medicine and offer training opportunities for nurses and allied healthcare professionals.
- **Research**. To provide the setting for ongoing clinical research that helps bring medical advances from the laboratory to the patient's bedside.
- **Community Service**. To serve the community as a public health advocate and provide support and services which respond to the area's healthcare needs through health education, health promotion, and access to care.

Virtua Health is a non-profit, multi-hospital healthcare system located in Marlton, New Jersey. Its mission is to deliver a world-class patient experience through its programs of excellence in women's health, pediatrics, cancer, cardiology, orthopedics, and geriatrics. In early 2004, the hospital formed a strategic alliance with GE to redefine 21st century patient care. The arrangement will enable Virtua to leverage the resources and strength of GE in order to attain its vision for patient-focused healthcare delivery. Virtua has adopted a Six Sigma approach to problem-solving and performance improvement, which has delivered tangible, measurable results having a positive impact on patient care, employee morale, and the organization's bottom line. As a result of the improvement initiatives over the last few years, Virtua Health reports total annualized savings of more than $5 million in early stages of implementation (see http://www. virtua.org). Virtua's mission, values, and STAR initiatives represent its way to provide outstanding service to patients (as shown in the following section). Interestingly, Virtua has shared its experience using Six Sigma on its website, and shows active involvement of its CEO.

Virtua's Mission

We are dedicated to providing each patient and their family with an outstanding experience, and to ensuring the highest quality healthcare for the community. We are committed to providing our healthcare team with resources, technology and training as well as with opportunities for professional growth.

Values

Integrity: We will be accountable for and take pride in our actions, while maintaining a customer focus. Our values in action:

- We are ethical and trustworthy.
- We maintain the confidentiality of all our customers.
- We are true to ourselves and others.
- We are respectful of others' needs and concerns.
- We maintain a positive attitude towards each other.

Respect: We will treat our customers with high regard while honoring and valuing their requests and decisions. Our values in action:

- We really listen to our customers.
- We show courtesy and respect our customers' privacy.
- We accept customers as they are.
- We value one another.

Caring: We will have understanding, empathy, compassion, and the ability to meet the needs of our customers. Our values in action:

- We have a sincere positive attitude.
- We put others' needs ahead of our own.
- We show genuine sensitivity and concern for our customers.

Commitment: We will be dedicated to acting in accordance with the mission, vision, and values of Virtua Health. Our values in action:

- We exceed the expectations of our customers.
- We follow through to ensure positive outcomes.
- We promote Virtua within the community.
- We go the extra mile.
- We fulfill our responsibilities.

Teamwork: We will work with our customers in a reliable and dedicated fashion toward a common purpose/goal. Our values in action:

- We foster a supportive environment.
- We respect each others' differences.

Excellence: We will be dedicated to providing the best quality care and services to our customers. Our values in action:

- We strive towards continually improving ourselves and the organization.
- We set and achieve high performance standards.

Outstanding Patient Experience

To ensure that patients are at the center of everything we do, Virtua launched the STAR Initiative in 2000. Virtua employees are committed to these five STAR points:

1. Best People
2. Caring Culture
3. Excellent Service
4. Highest Clinical Quality and Safety
5. Resource Stewardship

One can see that vision for a healthcare facility can demonstrate business focus to its core purpose, or excellence in healthcare services to patients and stakeholders. In order to develop a vision for a healthcare organization, one may incorporate the following:

- **Vision:** A patient-focused futuristic statement specifying purpose of the organization, and providing direction to all aspects of the clinical as well as staff activities.
- **Mission:** An operational statement of major activities to achieve a certain performance objective by a specified time.

- **Beliefs:** Perpetually constant core values of the organization representing leadership style, culture, and priorities for making daily decisions in daily activities. Typical beliefs relate to mutual respect for each other, personal integrity, and commitment to serve patients.

- **Goals:** Healthcare business objectives such as happy patients, leadership in the marketplace, superior return on investment, and strategic adoption of specific methods such as Six Sigma.

- **Initiatives:** Key tactics that must be implemented to achieve goals and meet the vision, such as implementing Six Sigma by a specified timeframe, achieving specified rate of improvement in key operations, realizing a specified rate of return, or implementing enterprise-wide systems or tools.

There is no prescribed method of capturing objectives of vision, values, tactics, or even measurements. Leadership of the organization must succinctly document its intent, and communicate to all stakeholders in a consistent and constant manner over a period of time.

Conducting Business Opportunity Analysis

Success of Six Sigma initiative begins with a good understanding of needs for Six Sigma, and evaluation of business performance in terms of its leadership processes, business systems, culture, operational performance, financial results, patient satisfaction, and cost of nonvalue-add activities. In a healthcare organization, identifying opportunities for improving business performance means utilizing tools such as checklists, scorecards, surveys for assessing compliance to regulatory Joint Commission on Accreditation of Healthcare Organizations (JCAHO) requirements, implementation of best practices, levels and trends in internal and external failures. The internal failures could mean unacceptable care of patients, physicians' efficiency in terms of daily number of patients per physician, number of treatments or tests per patient for full recovery, incorrect prescriptions, illegible prescriptions, patient wait time, ratio of staff to doctor, and external failures may include relapses in patients' treatment, excessive patient follow-up visits, malpractices or legal complications, and patient or doctor defection.

While analyzing the performance of the healthcare organization, one must first document the business process flow, identify available attributes or variable data, analyze existing data using statistical tools, and quantify inconsistency in various areas. One can use simple statistics such as mean, standard deviation, or the range, median, and mode. Having completed the basic statistical analysis of the available data, one must look into disconnects in the flow, inconsistencies at processes, and causative relationships. At this stage, one must question every incidence of non-normal observations for assignable causes, and excessive variation for redesigning the process in question. In either case, there will be a group of opportunities that will show promise of significant savings. These opportunities would be the candidate projects for application of the DMAIC methodology.

However, Six Sigma is beyond the application of DMAIC to specific opportunities. The leadership must select certain projects at the first go, and initiate the awareness campaign throughout the organization. The sustained benefit of Six Sigma comes from heightened awareness to recognition of dramatic improvement very fast. During the awareness campaign, physicians and staff members must accept the fact that processes and systems can be improved, and there is a potential waste of 15 to 20 percent, if not more. This will be a major challenge for the healthcare community to accept the existence of opportunities for improvement. For so long, healthcare organizations have come to believe that they are unquestionable because they are providing personal health-related services, including saving lives. The healthcare community does recognize that cost of healthcare has been skyrocketing; however, they are fingerpointing the other members of the community. Hospitals point to patients, patients point to PPOs, and PPOs point to malpractice and doctors.

According to Bob Manam, chief of the staff at Rush Copley Medical Center, increase in cost of healthcare is somewhat related to the sense of entitlements expected by patients. Pharmaceutical companies have not targeted their marketing budget informing consumers directly. As a result, patients demand specific medicines, tests, or treatments from their physicians. If they do not get it, patients change their physician, thus creating a demand for more services and increased cost of healthcare. Thus new technology, medications, scans, or treatments all have contributed to an increase in expenses. Our aggressive approach to prolong life using heart surgery, brain surgery, or ventilating has increased life expectancy. Especially, a larger portion of the population, known as the baby boomers, has reached a stage for higher utilization of healthcare services, thus adversely affecting the cost. Greater awareness of health issues such as breast cancer, diabetes, and obesity has led to more demand for medical services, thus pushing the cost up. Additionally, the freedom to choose a service provider or the physician creates competition, increasing the cost of acquisition of the customer. Moreover, malpractice suits have also increased the cost of healthcare premiums.

With the increase in cost of healthcare, there is a burden on physicians to see more patients to increase revenue. As a result, physicians are spending less time with patients, requiring more follow-up visits. Even though there are established best practices, it is difficult to follow them due to the productivity constraint. Physicians are struggling with their ability to see an adequate number of patients and provide the highest quality service. Measurements are being established for physicians to score themselves, thus the resistance to measure objectively. Another issue that has been dragging down quality of healthcare is established DRGs (Diagnosis Related Groups) This makes the in-hospital care driven by certain costs, rather than the quality of patient care. In other words, the cost per disease has been pre-established. Any variations in the patient care would have to be adjusted within the known DRG.

A national campaign to save 100,000 lives in response to the expected 100,000 deaths per year has highlighted investigation of various processes and root cause of errors. According to Dr. Manam, the errors in prescribing medicine stand at about 1 percent that have serious impact, and errors in prescribing medicine with minimal impact stands about 10 percent. The opportunity to reduce waste includes over utilization of resources, unnecessary medicines, unnecessary tests, and lack of implementation of best practices. At Rush Copley, there are many measurements and goals in place to monitor performance and trigger remedial actions. Patient satisfaction is measured to be at 87 percent against the goal of 92 percent. Dr. Manam says that the leadership has been working on various aspects of business to improve patient satisfaction and reduce cost of services. However, to reduce the cost of healthcare, everyone must participate to minimize utilization and maximize effectiveness.

At Mount Carmel Health Providers, a set of ground rules was established for selecting projects that included targeted defect reduction of 70 percent, annualized savings of $175,000, and estimated completion time of 2 to 4 months per project.[4] Improvement projects at Mount Carmel included physician documentation, accounts receivable, support staff hours, defects in registration documentation, discrepancies in patient type between pre-certification and admission, first-year employee turnover, and processing errors.

At Virtua Health, projects included chemotherapy medication errors, defining "Captain of the Ship" to raise quality and patient satisfaction, reducing bloodstream infections in one surgical intensive care unit (SICU), and improving infertility rates.[5] One of the challenges in introducing Six Sigma within healthcare has been the existence of legacy or manual systems making it difficult to collect data, and the missing management system for systematically reviewing levels and trends in the performance of key processes, be they clinical or staff. Another challenge has been the litigious impact of reporting medical errors. However, to remedy the perceived barrier of litigation, a law has been passed. Accordingly, "The Federal Office of Personnel Management now requires preferred provider organizations (PPOs) and other fee-for-service plans to collect and report quality performance measures".[6] Even though initial areas for reporting performance include breast cancer screening, cholesterol testing, and diabetes care, this is a good start for launching the Six Sigma initiative.

Even though the healthcare industry is at the early stage of adopting Six Sigma-like methods to accelerate its effort for achieving healthcare excellence, opportunities for reaping rewards are abundant. Whether radiology error, medical effort, patient safety, top and bottom line enhancement, supply chain improvement, or the patient wait time, National Healthcare Disparities Report (NHDR) has identified key performance measures for cancer care, diabetes, maternal and child health, respiratory disease, nursing home, home health, access to information, patient perception of care, healthcare utilization, and timeliness. Even establishing right measures could be a Six Sigma project to start dialogue and diagnostics based on facts, rather than just accepting all outcomes as status quo.

Healthcare organizations have been operating as businesses for many years due to the growing cost of healthcare and competition among providers. Each healthcare organization can be viewed as business, staff, and clinical operations. Therefore, one must evaluate all aspects for evaluation health of the healthcare business. The factors to monitor performance would include leadership processes, business management processes, employee related processes, clinical operations, staff processes, and patients' perception of services. Sources of information may include the following:

- Performance data for clinical operations
- Patient feedback throughout the healthcare service utilization
- Marketing process for revenue growth
- Marketing data (such as regional market share and market size)
- Employee ideas or suggestions
- Employee recognition

- Purchasing and suppliers performance
- Supply inventory level and trends
- Financial reports including balance sheets for the last three years
- Business plan or equivalent document
- Comparison to Best Practices analysis
- Monthly, quarterly, or annual reports

In addition to this information, one must review operations and interview a sample of employees for their observations for identifying opportunities for improvement and seeking recommendations for solutions, thus making their organization more profitable and better serving.

Providing Leadership for Six Sigma

Implementing Six Sigma requires a personal understanding of its intent, commitment to a lot of improvement very quickly, passionate interest for results, constant desire to stay engaged, and networking with employees through communication. Because Sigma requires an enormous amount of improvement, it requires total synergy in the organization that can be realized through planning for execution, communicating performance, participating through reviews, and recognizing superior results. The leadership must demonstrate its explicit and unquestionable commitment to Six Sigma by making it an opportunity for growth rather than a fear of loss of jobs for employees. It is imperative that the leadership must focus on growing revenue in order to benefit from the freed up resources due to improvement through Six Sigma. Thus, the leadership must lead the organization for growth and profitability, allowing employees to benefit financially as well as professionally.

Planning and Expecting Dramatic Improvement

Achieving incremental improvement requires a different mindset than realizing dramatic improvement very fast in an organization. Six Sigma thrives on a sense of urgency and challenge of aggressive goals for improvement. One of the key aspects of achieving dramatic improvement is to engage employees intellectually for generating innovative solutions. Six Sigma requires up to 20,000 times improvement from the current level of performance. Only well planned and executed strategies will work. Thus, the leadership must emphasize homework through planning, scoping, providing resources, and expecting results. Typical Six Sigma projects last about 4 to 6 months, require interdepartmental teamwork, common priority, and a positive attitude toward hard and smart work. Six Sigma projects must produce results that have a directly visible impact on the bottom line. The projects must generate savings that can be shared with employees beyond planned level of profits. During the planning, the following issues must be considered:

- Integration of Six Sigma in strategic plan
- Clearly defined responsibilities, and aligned organization
- Fair compensation and recognition system

- Continual inspiration for excellence, and expectation of results
- Demand for breakthrough solution for visible change
- Publicity of success stories
- Dynamic adjustment to the approach to implementing Six Sigma
- Focus on activities and outcomes

Communicating Outcomes and Errors

A direct communication of commitment to Six Sigma from the chief executive is the first critical communication for an organization-wide implementation. If the Six Sigma initiative is evolving from a department or a division, some level of communication is important in communicating the strategy. Many organizations start the Six Sigma initiative with a set of projects. In such cases, a memo communicating with the selected employees may be sufficient. However, still the leadership communication could be helpful just to inform employees of the intent and evolving plan of the potentially organization-wide initiative. In absence of such a communication, employees may resent the lack of information and perceived involvement.

For the organization-wide communication, a much broader approach is taken. Besides, the message from the leader, press releases, publicity brochures, or pamphlets describing Six Sigma in context of the corporation are prepared; trinkets like lapel pins, mugs, shirts, sweaters, or caps are distributed; a video of the personal message from the chief executive is shown; or the announcement in a multi-facility corporation is broadcast through a satellite link. Even a better demonstration of the leadership interest, the chief executive presents the Six Sigma initiative in person to employees through meetings.

The departmental communication follows up the corporate communication because various departments initiate Six Sigma-related activities to support the corporate initiative. If Six Sigma is launched corporate-wide, the departments may start the awareness training first, before selected employees for further project related training. Once the projects have been identified, a periodic communication of the project performance within and outside the department helps maintain the necessary support for projects.

When a corporate level Six Sigma scorecard is established to monitor progress, each department publishes trends and levels of outcomes and errors. These measurements are reported monthly in an Operations Review, like meeting and shared with the other center directors for resolving any competing issues.

When Six Sigma is being institutionalized, it gets down to the process level, where the objective is to achieve Six Sigma level performance (for example, 3.4 errors per million opportunities for its key output or related in-process characteristics). Key measurements are tracked on a trend chart plotted against the continually improving goal line. The monthly process performance is fed into the center or department measurements, and the weekly or daily performance is reviewed within the department. The process level information is communicated to affected employees by displaying trend charts on bulletin boards, and brainstorming in departmental teams for continual improvement.

Participating in Reviewing Performance

Executive participation in the review meetings and expecting extraordinary results from Six Sigma projects is a norm. Six Sigma has been designed to focus on a clearly defined opportunity for economic benefit very fast. Therefore, there must be an expectation for results at the conclusion of an improvement project. Besides, the leadership must also relate improvement to the bottom line, and gain sharing with employees. If the results from the Six Sigma effort are not as expected, an objective analysis and necessary correction in the approach must be made, including providing additional resources. Employees must see the leadership involvement through expectation, performance, and recognition.

Recognizing Excellence at All Levels

With all the objective measurements for quality, response time, and cost, a strong leadership and its inspiration through recognition and incentives play a significant role in successful implementation of Six Sigma. Such subjective measures are difficult to quantify. Successful companies come up with some creative approaches to inspire employees. For example, Motorola used Total Customer Satisfaction (TCS) Team Competition and a CEO Award for extraordinary accomplishment. Publicizing successes breeds success. Recognition of employee excellence inspires more employees to excel. Companies can measure and publicize a number of projects with exceptional improvement or significant savings.

ENDNOTES

1. Gupta Praveen. *The Six Sigma Performance Handbook: A Statistical Guide to Optimized Results*, McGraw Hill, NY, 2004.

2. Kaplan Robert S. & Norton David P. *The Balanced Scorecard: Translating Strategy into Action*, Harvard Business School Press, MA, 1996.

3. Gupta Praveen. *The Six Sigma Business Scorecard: Creating a Comprehensive Corporate Performance Management System*, McGraw Hill, NY, 2003.

4. Schutte, P. "Using Six Sigma Management System to increase primary care office efficiency," *Group Practice Journal*, 51 (7), 2002.

5. Kooy & Pexton. iSixSigma.

6. www.ncqa.org.

Six Sigma Methodology

SECTIONS

Six Sigma Defined
Six Sigma Readiness
Six Sigma Methodology
Six Sigma Measurements
Six Sigma and Other Quality Systems
Making Six Sigma Work

Six Sigma was developed in an environment of extreme competition in new industries, poor economic conditions, and where survival was at stake. Seeds of Six Sigma were sowed in 1981 by the leadership of Motorola when they decided to do some thing different in order to continue to stay in business profitably. Continuing on the success of process improvement efforts in 1986, the leadership team decided to accelerate improvement through employee participation. The rate of improvement was changed from ten times in five years to ten times improvement in two years. Concepts of Six Sigma evolved based on the incremental performance of then improvement techniques such as Statistical Process Control (SPC), Pre-Control, Variability Reduction Methods, and Design of Experiments. It was observed that each function was disjointedly improving its performance without assessing impact on other departments. Besides, the personal computer age was at its beginning and about to explode. Complexity of products and services was increasing, even though the physical size was decreasing. For example, a computer chip could have millions of devices and hundreds of process steps. The more complex an operation or product becomes, there are more opportunities for things to go wrong. On top of the intrinsic variables, competition was intensely growing from domestic as well as international players, which led Motorola to look ahead to the year 2000 in 1985 for strategic reasons. Benchmarking was performed, and best practices were studied in products as well as services. Competitive products in telecommunication and consumer electronics were analyzed, and manufacturing technology was examined to establish the direction.

Bill Smith, the inventor of Six Sigma, recognized that something different had to be done. Different intent, methodology, and measurements had to be devised. Bill created the Six Sigma model that was built on experiences of various corporate initiatives, along with his visionary approach to address the expectations for Motorola products in 2000. This visioning led to the customer expectation of virtual perfection in everything, and thus quantified to be at 3.4 parts per million. The absence of such a model of perfection will lead to wrongly prescribed, or filled prescriptions, erroneous surgeries, and eventually deaths in the healthcare industry, just like defective products or services delivered to customers. The extent of malpractice insurance and risks highlights the level of performance that needs a step up in the level of performance to its customers, and thus reduce risks associated with its practices.

SIX SIGMA DEFINED

Six Sigma initially was developed as an improved methodology of process improvement to meet customer expectations and maintain Motorola's leadership position in the marketplace. The Six Sigma methodology consists of the following six steps:

1. Define your products or services.
2. Know your customers and their critical needs.
3. Identify your critical needs to meet customers' critical needs well.
4. Establish a process of doing your work consistently.
5. Error-proof your process and eliminate waste.
6. Measure and analyze your performance. If not perfect, improve your process.

These six steps are supported by various tools already known in the Total Quality Management (TQM) environment, and strong and demanding leadership throughout and with measurements. Most importantly, employee participation was demanded and success rewarded. During the first five years of Six Sigma implementation, even suppliers were required to participate in the process, and customers were encouraged to benefit from the Motorola experience. The four courses that propagated the Six Sigma philosophy throughout the Motorola supply chain were the following:

- **Understanding Six Sigma**. Basic concepts of Six Sigma, measurement, process mapping, and implementing six steps to Six Sigma.

- **Design for Manufacturability**. Designing products, Motorola being a product company that could be manufactured virtually perfectly.

- **Cycle Time Reduction**. Streamlining operations through removal of nonvalue activities and waste of resources, including of time. The five elements of cycle time of a process are setup time, wait time, move time, queue time, and runtime. The runtime happens to be the only value added time, and is estimated to be about 5 percent.

- **SPC (statistical process control) Overview**. Overview of various statistical concepts and tools, integrated into the four-phase methodology: Visualize, Analyze, Improve, Optimize.

Success of initial implementation of Six Sigma at several companies led experts to package Six Sigma into a robust approach that included the DMAIC methodology, application of methodology through projects, and standardized training programs such as Black Belt or Green Belt, and roles as Champion and Sponsors.

GE, led by its CEO Jack Welch, innovated Six Sigma through rigorous implementation at all levels, and enabled GE to grow profitably for several years. GE leadership credited its success explicitly to Six Sigma, besides other strategic initiatives. After some time, GE executives took the Six Sigma discipline to their new employers and replicated success. This continual success of Six Sigma transformed Six Sigma from a simple process improvement methodology to a business strategy at the highest level, even to the level of corporate values.

One of the distinct and visible aspects of a successful Six Sigma campaign has been the visibility of the chief executive. The leader must be the Six Sigma crusader; the crusade cannot be delegated to the vice president or a subordinate. Certainly, a Six Sigma campaign must not become a quality campaign; otherwise, it would be treated as a program for compliance certification, bureaucracy, or paperwork. Six Sigma must be implemented as a business strategy to improve profits and achieve growth with the help of improved capacity and employee-driven innovation.

Thus, one can define Six Sigma as a futuristic strategy to immediately improve corporate profitability through waste reduction, achieve growth through sustained profits, and create a culture of continually achieving best-in-class performance through process reengineering.

Six Sigma can be thought of as having the following five elements:

1. **Intent**. The intent of Six Sigma is to achieve a lot of improvement very fast (for example, rapid improvement to achieve best-in-class status).

2. **Strategy**. Six Sigma can be applied in a limited sense at project level, or with a strategic intent to implement throughout a corporation.

3. **Methodology**. DMAIC is the methodology to achieve results. The discipline to follow the methodology is bound to produce results. The most important step is the Define phase of DMAIC.

4. **Tools**. Numerous tools have been incorporated in the Six Sigma methodology. The unique tools that have been found to be useful are Kano's model to capture customer critical requirements, SIPOC (Suppliers, Inputs, Process, Outputs, Customers), statistical software for analysis, multi-vary analysis for identifying predominant family of variation or inconsistencies, planned experimentation, and methods to sustain gains.

5.   **Measurements**. The three commonly used measurements are DPU (defects/errors per unit), DPMO (defects per million opportunities), and Sigma level. The *DPU* is a unit or the output level measurement, *DPMO* is the process level measurement, and *Sigma* is a business-level measurement. Sigma provides a common theme for the organization, and requires a lot of improvement to show a positive change.

SIX SIGMA READINESS

One of the reasons for false starts of the Six Sigma initiative is not identifying opportunities for improvement in the bottom line, and blindly committing to the Six Sigma initiative. As a result, the initiative gets launched with fanfare; however, the fun and commitment dwindles over time due to lack of value creation. Thus, for management to commit to a Six Sigma initiative, the questions that must be answered are what can the Six Sigma initiative do for the company, in the short term and in the long term? How much would it cost? Table 5.1 provides some answers in order for a company to realize benefits of Six Sigma methodology during the first year.

TABLE 5.1   Estimated Costs of the Six Sigma Initiative

Number of employees	100	500	1000
Annual sales ($ million)	10	50	100
Cost of Implementing Six Sigma ($ million)	0.5	1.5	3
Cost of poor quality at 20 percent ($ million)	2	10	20
Cost of implementing Six Sigma as a percent of cost of poor quality	25	15	15
Minimum number of projects to be identified for breakeven	3	10	20
Minimum number of projects to be identified for 100 percent return on investment	6-8	15-25	35-50

Gupta, www.CircuitsAssembly.com, 2002

Once the implementation of the Six Sigma initiative becomes an economically viable strategy, management must consider giving it the highest priority. Any competing initiative, conflicting priority, or strategic initiative in progress must be clearly identified. Besides the economic viability, the other success factors must be addressed. A list of critical success factors is as follows:

1.   Leadership needs to have an unwavering commitment to Six Sigma.
2.   Common language is used for setting up common goals..
3.   Aggressive improvement goals will promote employee engagement.
4.   Innovation is the key to achieving dramatic improvement.

5. Process thinking allows decisions to be made based on knowledge and data, instead of just the data.

6. The company needs to maintain continued interest in the Six Sigma initiative.

7. The company needs the right metrics for identifying opportunities for new projects and dramatic results.

8. Rapid improvement must become a way of life.

9. Reward for creating value is essential for continually engaging employees in the Six Sigma initiative.

For the executive leadership to be engaged in the Six Sigma initiative, they must develop a proper understanding of the principles behind Six Sigma. The understanding of intent of the methodology, key tools associated with various phases of DMAIC, and any organizational bottlenecks are critical requirements for launching a successful Six Sigma initiative. The leadership involvement in the Six Sigma must be documented for clear understanding and consistent implementation. They must see the big picture of the Six Sigma initiative which goes through various functions of the organization. The table in Table 5.2 identifies key tools recommended for executives. Having understood the intent of Six Sigma, and key executive tools, the leadership is able to appreciate the effort required to achieve the desired business objectives.

TABLE 5.2   Key Executive Tools

Tool/Concept	Description
Employee Recognition	Process of recognizing exceptional improvement activities and employees
Process Thinking	Understanding business is a collection of processes, and the process must be designed for virtual perfection
Business Scorecard	An organizational performance measurement system balanced for growth and profitability
Operations Review	Role of internal audits, corrective action, and operations management review
Statistical Thinking	Understanding random and assignable variation
Six Sigma Overview	Understanding of Intent, Impact, DMAIC and Requirements
Pareto Principle	A graphical tool to prioritize commitments based on added valued
Process Mapping	Flow charts used to understand information flow, value streams to profitability
Cause and Effect Analysis	Understanding causative relationship between performance and processes
Rate of Improvement	Differences between incremental and dramatic improvement, and commitment to dramatic improvement through innovative thinking

Printed with permission: Gupta, Six Sigma Performance Handbook, 2004

SIX SIGMA METHODOLOGY

The Six Sigma methodology has been known as DMAIC representing the Define, Measure, Analyze, Improve, and Control phases. The methodology is applied to the projects selected from multiple projects based on the *project prioritization index* (PPI), which is calculated as follows:

PPI = (Benefits/cost) × (Probability of success/Time to complete the project in years)

Because the project duration for a Six Sigma project is expected to be four to six months, and the probability of success must give the project a chance to succeed, which can be estimated to be at .7, then the PPI becomes as follows:

$$PPI = (Benefits/Cost) \times (.7/.5)$$
$$= 1.4 \times (Benefits/Cost)$$

To benefit from the project beyond any chance, the recommended PPI is 3 × (Benefits/Cost). If the project is critical to business, lower PPI numbers may be accepted with the management's approval.

Once the project is selected, the team representing various functions is formed to work on it. The team receives the Six Sigma training at the Green Belt level while working on the selected project. During the Define phase, the expected outcomes are as follows:

1. A clear definition of the project and its scope
2. A determination of the customer's critical requirements
3. Benefits of the project completion, or the value proposition
4. A common understanding of the process
5. Identification of various elements of the process
6. Plan to complete the project

In the Measure phase, the process performance and elements are reviewed for establishing a causative relationship. Team members review all the available data, and establish a performance baseline in terms of error rate, or its capability with respect to requirements. In establishing the baseline, a commercially available statistical software program can be used for developing the basic statistics. The basic statistics consists of at least the following information:

- Central Tendency measures such as mean for variable data or median for attribute data
- Variation or inconsistency measures, such as range or standard deviation
- Defective PPM based on distribution, or defect counts

Besides establishing the baseline, one must also analyze trends in the performance related to the critical process elements that would include inputs, process steps, or any other opportunity for making mistakes. In the Define phase, we identified variables relating to the process elements. We recognize that now the problem-solving task is to eliminate trivial variables from further analysis.

In the Analyze phase, team performs the cause and effect analysis using either the Ishikawa diagram or the Fishbone diagram. The objective is to analyze the $Y = f(X_i)$ relationship, and reduce the number of variables such that either team is able to identify necessary actions to improve the process, or prepare for planned experimentation in the Improve phase. The *Multivari analysis* is a unique tool that is simple to use. This tool apportions the process variation in three families of variation and reduces the scope of the problem. The three families of variation are called *Positional*, *Cyclical*, and *Temporal*. The Positional variation relates to the location of errors in the process. The location could be influenced by the process such as same step, certain individual, or certain tool or equipment. The locational variation is repeatable and typically corrected through process or product design. The Cyclical variation is related to a process cycle, which is normally affected by the process set up affecting the cycle. The Temporal variation relates to the trends in the process output which is affected by maintenance or degradation of certain process elements. Thus, the family of variation with maximum inconsistence is selected to work on, and variables associated with the other two families of variation, are temporarily set aside.

Besides the Multivari analysis, other tools in the Analyze phase include *FMEA* (Failure Modes and Effect Analysis) and testing of hypothesis, which are used for anticipating potential problems with a process and statistical evaluation of various process conditions, respectively.

The Improve Phase is used to develop alternate solutions to achieve the desired process outcomes. In an unstructured or non-Six Sigma method of problem-solving, one jumps into the Improve phase directly without properly defining the problem, establishing the baseline, or an appropriate root cause analysis. Once alternate solutions are developed, the best solution is selected based on statistical evaluation, and the process further optimized. The intent of the Improve phase is to develop a breakthrough solution that would lead to significant improvement in the process performance. Again, statistical software is used for evaluation and validation of the proposed solutions.

The Control Phase is used to sustain the improvement using statistical process control techniques such as control charts, or monitoring the process using trend charts. Besides statistical methods, some of the important activities in the Control phase may also include modification in the work procedures, training, communication, and management reviews.

Table 5.3 lists various tools associated with various phases of the DMAIC methodology. Some of these tools are discussed in the next two chapters.

TABLE 5.3 Key Simple Six Sigma Tools

Define	Measure	Analyze	Improve	Control
Kano's Analysis	Terminology	Cause and Effect	Triz Analysis	Process Thinking
Pareto Chart	Normal Distribution (Random vs. Assignable)	Multi-vary Analysis	Comparative Experiments (t-test, and Z-test)	Pre-control Charts

(continued)

TABLE 5.3   Continued

Define	Measure	Analyze	Improve	Control
Process Mapping	Cost of Poor Quality	Failure Modes and Effects Analysis	Components Search	Control Chart Concepts
SIPOC	Measurement System Analysis	Regression Analysis	Full Factorial Experiments	Internal Audits, Corrective Action and Management Review processes
	Performance Measurements (Cp, Cpk, DPU, DPMO)	Testing of Hypothesis	Response Surface Methodology for Optimization	Six Sigma Business Scorecard
		Analysis of Variance	Lean Thinking and Lean Tools	Theory of Constraints

Printed with permission: Gupta, Six Sigma Performance Handbook, 2004

SIX SIGMA MEASUREMENTS

The Six Sigma methodology incorporates a simple but powerful set of measurements, such as DPU, DPMO, Sigma level, Cp, and Cpk. The DPU stands for *defects per unit*, which is a measure of product performance with respect to customer expectations. In healthcare organizations, DPU may be labeled as *errors per unit* (EPU), where the unit could be a patient visit, a surgery, clinical event, or a process cycle. The DPU is a measure of internal performance of the product before delivering it to the customer. Once we know the DPU level, we can question unacceptable levels of DPU and perform root cause analysis. Besides, if the DPU of a complex operation is compared with that of a simple operation, the comparison could be misleading. Thus, the DPMO (Defects Per Million Opportunities) measurement has been created where the DPU is normalized for the complexity of an operation. For example, the complexity of a patient's visit for a normal checkup and the complexity of a surgical operation are quite different, thus a different error rate would be expected. Thus to improve the error rate, one must simplify operations and reduce opportunities for errors. The formula for calculating DPMO is as follows:

$$DPMO = (DPU * 1000,000) / \text{Average number of opportunities in a unit}$$

Once the DPMO is calculated, a sigma level can be determined using Table 5.4, or equivalent methods.

TABLE 5.4 DPMO to Six Sigma Conversion Table

DPMO	Sigma	DPMO	Sigma	DPMO	Sigma	DPMO	Sigma
66807	3.0	6210	4.0	233	5.0	3.4	6.0
54799	3.1	4661	4.1	159	5.1	2.1	6.1
44565	3.2	3467	4.2	108	5.2	1.3	6.2
35930	3.3	2555	4.3	72	5.3	0.8	6.3
28717	3.4	1866	4.4	48	5.4	0.5	6.4
22750	3.5	1350	4.5	32	5.5	0.3	6.5
17864	3.6	968	4.6	21	5.6	0.2	6.6
13903	3.7	687	4.7	13	5.7	0.1	6.7
10724	3.8	483	4.8	9	5.8	0.06	6.8
8198	3.9	337	4.9	5	5.9	0.03	6.9

The Sigma level can be used to compare departmental level performance and accelerate improvement in the Sigma level. As one can see that to change Sigma level from 3 to 4 about ten times, from 4 to 5 about 30 times, and from 5 to 6 about 70 times, improvement is needed. Overall, to improve sigma from 3 to 6, about 20,000 times improvement is needed. We have never heard of such a high requirement for improvement. In the absence of such a measure, we tend to establish incremental goals for improvement and achieve invisible improvement in our operations.

Here's an example: If a surgery for a hernia is being performed, there are several steps, which are listed as follows:

1. **Initial visit**. Visit with the doctor for hernia pain or discomfort, and fill out insurance paperwork.

2. **Follow-up visit**. Schedule the surgery, determine the method of surgery (laser or mesh), sign a liability release, and inform the patient of surgical risks.

3. **Pre-surgery preparation**. Give anesthesia and prepare the patient for surgery.

4. **Surgery**. Prepare for surgery (the operation table, tools, nurses, doctors) and perform the actual surgery (mark, cut, mesh, close).

5. **Post surgery**. Monitor recovery and administer painkillers.

6. **Release**. Provide instructions for home recovery, and make a follow-up call.

7. **Follow-up visit**. Verify surgery outcome, patient's satisfaction, and close paperwork.

8. **Receive payment from patient**. Collect the co-payment from the patient.

9. **File claims**. Submit necessary paperwork to insurance companies or Medicaid for payments.

One could see that a hernia operation includes nine processes, and each operation has opportunities for making mistakes (see Table 5.5).

TABLE 5.5   Hernia Operation Analysis for One Month

Operation Number	Number of Patients Treated	Errors	Estimated Opportunities	DPU	DPMO	Est. Sigma
1	20	3	2	0.15	75000	< 3.0
2	20	0	3	0	0	>> 6.0
3	15	0	2	0	0	> >6.0
4	15	5	20	0.33	16666.67	3.6
5	15	2	2	0.13	66666.67	<3.0
6	15	4	2	0.27	133333.3	<<3.0
7	15	1	3	0.07	22222.22	2.5
8	15	0	1	0	0	>>6.0
9	12	4	10	0.33	33333.33	3.3
Total			45		347,222	~1.89

From the data analysis, one can see that operation number four, which is "surgery," operates at the best Sigma level among all processes, even with the highest number of errors. This may confuse some of us, and lead us to believe that Six Sigma is a counterproductive methodology. We can conclude the following:

- The surgery operation is the most critical operation.

- We must focus on making it at least Six Sigma level, or even higher. This may even impact our malpractice insurance rates because of lower risks.

- We do have some operations that perform almost perfectly, thus focusing our attention on areas that are critical and need improvement. We should learn from people working in those areas how they ensure perfection over a period of time.

- We should not pay too much attention to the absolute value of the measurement, because it may depend upon the measurement methods. Instead, we must strive to improve critical processes very fast to benefit from saving resources in those areas.

Such analysis of the data for various departments will assist us in identifying opportunities for improvement and defining projects to implement Six Sigma methodology.

If one wants to determine overall sigma level for the hernia operation, one adds all DPUs and the opportunities, and determines the DPMO and Sigma level. In this case, the overall Sigma level is 1.89, and DPMO is 347,222. This implies that overall the hernia operation has a long way to go to become virtually perfect, and if 100 surgeries are performed in a month, about 3 would be unacceptable. The risk of malpractice in the three cases may wipe out profits realized from the other 97 surgeries. That's how one must look at the performance of healthcare services, rather than just accepting that there is a risk of 3 percent failure and have patient accept the risk helplessly.

SIX SIGMA AND OTHER QUALITY SYSTEMS

Healthcare organizations, especially hospitals, already have too many regulatory and compliance requirements. There are accreditation programs for various departments, disease-specific certifications, staffing standards, professional licenses, and best practices. However, there is a need for business-like management systems and performance standards. Customers have not been able to drive performance of the providers; instead, providers have been controlling the patients' expectations. Currently, patients are at the mercy of providers instead of driving improvement in the providers' performance. Pharmaceutical manufacturers, insurance companies, and healthcare service providers have been working together to provide more services; however, they are less concerned about the quality of services. As a result, the lack of quality feeds into the fear of malpractice and an increase in insurance premium for physicians.

However, some hospitals have already taken the leadership position of implementing quality management systems, initiating continual improvement programs, and committing to Six Sigma initiatives. Six Sigma works well with both management systems and certification requirements. A license authorizes individuals, certification qualifies specific treatments, and accreditation recognizes facilities. Thus, the management system will integrate various elements of the healthcare organizations, and Six Sigma will accelerate improvement in the quality and cost of the healthcare. Today, the cost of healthcare is more than many businesses' profitability, thus hurting viability of employee benefits and retention of good employees. Therefore, the healthcare providers and support organizations and professionals must commit to improving performance, responsiveness, and cost. Otherwise, more self-insurance, deregulated healthcare services, alternative medicines, global providers, tele-healthcare, and off-shoring of healthcare services will become a common practice, changing the current healthcare system dramatically.

MAKING SIX SIGMA WORK

So, why was Six Sigma developed? Six Sigma was developed to become best in class by achieving virtual perfection in everything. It was simply a methodology that was rigorously implemented and passionately championed. It produced results and savings of billions of dollars. Most successful champions have been the CEOs. Following are basic tenets of Six Sigma:

- Common goal
- Aggressive goal-setting
- Effective learning
- Sharing savings and rewards
- No fear!

There may be a few more, but this list is quite comprehensive. A company becomes successful when one understands Six Sigma correctly, makes Six Sigma a visible goal, continually talks about it, and works hard to achieve it. The aggressive goal-setting is fundamental to Six

Sigma. As we know that Six Sigma is associated with breakthrough improvement, it really means the solution must be different from simply tweaking the process. One can see that Six Sigma is not for the faint of heart. One must have vision, guts, courage, and wisdom to achieve such monumental improvement. However, one must remember that Six Sigma is applied for customer-critical aspects of products or services in order to benefit from it quickly. One must apply Six Sigma in every process, but not to everything in the process.

Effective learning of Six Sigma implies that one should learn the intent first before learning the methodology and tools. It is like getting a car for partying on the go. The intent is statistical thinking for achieving a lot of improvement. Statistical thinking is different from rigorous statistics. Actually, statistical thinking is very simple to understand, but difficult to internalize. Statistical thinking means understanding the nature of variation, cause and effect relationship, and making adjustments accordingly.

One of the subtle aspects of a successful Six Sigma journey is driving out fear. Dr. W. Edwards Deming, the quality guru, has emphasized driving out fear in bringing out the best in people. Employees are encouraged to take risks, learn from mistakes, and accomplish breakthrough results. Six Sigma was used for becoming the market leader (for example, higher sales and the highest profit in the industry through performance improvement). Focusing on sales and cost together will alleviate employee fear of failure and losing jobs. The leadership may want to focus on sales equally aggressively because implementing Six Sigma means more capacity for facilitating growth, creating a positive environment, and driving out fear.

UNDERSTANDING PROBLEMS: DEFINE, MEASURE, AND ANALYZE

SECTIONS

Define Phase
The Measure Phase
The Analyze Phase
Concluding Understanding Problems
Endnote
Sample Healthcare Excellence Project Forms: Understanding the Problem

Six Sigma was initially developed for manufacturing processes. In the manufacturing environment, machines and tools play a more dominant role than people do. However, in healthcare, people and methods play a more important role in delivering services than the equipment, which is still a critical aspect of providing healthcare services. Thus, the DMAIC must be adapted and simplified for the healthcare environment. First, DMAIC can be divided into two parts. The first part can be called *Understanding the Problem* and consists of the Define, Measure, and Analyze phases. The objective of the "Understanding Problems" part is to recognize the significance of a problem, learn about the process, establish a performance baseline, and establish the causative relationship between the problem symptoms and process variables. The second part can be looked at as the *Solving Problem* part consisting of Improve and Control phases. The objective of "Solving Problem" is to develop a breakthrough solution and sustain its benefits.

Healthcare excellence Project Forms have been designed to apply the Six Sigma DMAIC methodology for reducing cost and improving quality in a specific area. Samples of these forms appear at the end of the chapter.

DEFINE PHASE

It has been said that a well-defined problem is half solved. Many times, we jump into solving a problem without even knowing what we are trying to solve. Then, we find out that by solving some mystery problem, we have created new problems. Many solutions we implement we do not verify, and thus end up creating new problems. The list of problems grows rather than shrinks.

Thus, the *Define* phase requires us to spend enough time to gather sufficient information to clarify the opportunity for improvement, learn about the process, and learn about the organizational barriers to solving the problem, and then develop a plan to address it. An important aspect of Six Sigma is to produce breakthrough results fast by scoping out the problem such that the project is completed in no more than six months. A team of three to five qualified individuals is formed to solve a problem. Additional individuals of desired process knowledge may be invited as needed. At the end of the Define phase, the project team has learned significantly about the problem symptoms, process, and organization, and have prepared a project charter to accomplish tasks to successfully solve the problem.

Common Define Tools

Following is a list of some of the tools that are widely used to filter out the high-impact problem that has a direct bearing on the bottom line:

- Listening to customers
  - Kano's Model
  - Affinity Diagram
  - Pareto Analysis
- Gaining Process Knowledge
  - Process Mapping
  - SIPOC Analysis
- Sizing the problem
  - Force Field Analysis
  - Developing Project Charter

Listening to Customers

Our customers can be internal or external. *Internal customers* could be other departments, nurses, physicians, pharmacies, or the staff. We primarily provide services to *external customers* such as patients or institutions. Thus, by listening to customers, by understanding what customers consider critical, we can design healthcare services or products that meet customer requirements. Our objective must become to know the patient and understand the patient's needs, desires, wants, whims, and if possible those things that the customers don't even know they want just yet.

To implement the customer focus culture and remove the departmental barriers, organizations treat each employee as a customer. Every one is a customer for something and a supplier for something. This creates a culture of understanding of satisfying the customer needs within the organization and then extends to the external customers. While customers' needs vary, our inability to respond to customers' needs arises from our rush to get busy and our over-confidence in knowing our customers, without any effort to even listen to them. The external customers may be a group through HMOs or individuals. Ultimately, it is people who are customers of healthcare organizations.

As a physician or an HMO, listening to customers means asking patients questions personally or as a group. As a healthcare organization, the customers' needs may include:

- At the medical facility
  - Easy parking
  - Clear directions
  - Clean facility
  - Prompt attention at reception
  - Pleasant registration staff
  - Assigning the right doctor
  - Medical record availability
  - Shorter waiting time
  - Easy registration
- Treatment
  - Availability of necessary tools and supplies
  - Availability of doctors and support personnel
  - Doctor's success rate for the treatment
  - Availability of backup experts
  - Being treated with respect
  - Communicating with the patient/attendee(s)
  - Collecting correct sample(s)
  - Receiving correct treatment
  - Timely reports
  - Availability of medicines/substitutes/generic
  - Correct medicine

- Completion on schedule
- Legible prescription
- Stay at the medical facility
  - Caregivers
    - Cheering
    - Positive attitude
    - Responsive
    - Caring
  - Room
    - Ambiance
    - Available
    - Clean and well made
    - Entertainment devices
    - Good food
    - Periodic doctor visits
    - Space for visitors
- Post treatment
  - Easy discharge process
  - Easy to understand bills
  - Correct billing
  - Support for transportation
  - Total cycle time
  - Follow-up calls
  - Scheduling follow-up visits

One can see that the list of needs can be quite extensive. Interestingly, people feel that they have no voice in their healthcare services for which they pay. Insurance companies do not listen to them; HMOs do not listen to their needs, and doctors are always rushed and have no time for patients. Physicians are treating the disease, not the patient. In order to provide collaborative caring healthcare services, organizations must establish a process to listen to their customers. The methods could include random brainstorming sessions, surveys, lunch with the staff at the healthcare facility, or focus groups. The easiest method appears to be just take time, demonstrate care, and ask for time with the patients or visitors to learn more about their needs, their satisfaction, and for their ideas how to improve their services.

Kano's Model of Customer Requirements

Noriaki Kano developed a model of the relationship between customer satisfaction and customer requirements. Accordingly, most of the customer requirements are unspoken. What we are told is little, and the customers expect a lot more than what they ask for. Besides, a business organization would love to have its customers patronize its services or products. Kano's model provides an excellent platform to understand customer requirements and expectations, and leads the organization into becoming a best-in-class service provider. According to the Kano's model, customers have three types of requirements:

- **Assumed Requirements (Unspoken)**. When a patient plans to visit a healthcare facility, or deals with a provider, there are certain basic expectations, such as being able to find a parking space, get taken care of, or receive necessary treatment. If the service provider does not have the capability, the patient really becomes frustrated and annoyed. Given a choice, the patient will not visit the same facility again. These unspoken assumed requirements are called *dissatisfiers*. The best the service provider can do is to not upset the customer, because one upset patient shares personal stories with many potential customers in the neighborhood.

- **Marketplace Requirements (Spoken)**. The marketplace requirements are commonly known expectations built through branding or general awareness of the industry. Patients know that these days there are options for treatment for various diseases, whether angioplasty, bypass surgery, medicine treatment, dietary treatment, and so on. On the other hand, it may also appear that providers always chose the best approach to ensure treatment of the disease and prevent medical errors, thus eliminating malpractice claims. Currently, patients do not appear to have choices about treatment or services they receive at healthcare facilities. Instead, they feel helpless going to the facility and surrender to the service provider and pray.

  As competition from global service providers grows, listening to the customer would become important. The quality and cost of healthcare service must become competitive through improvement and competitive strategic planning based on the customer requirements. Many hospitals have started talking on their websites and literature about patients' safety as a major customer requirement. That is an assumed requirement of the customers and an understood requirement from the provider. Evidently, there is a gap between the patient and the provider of healthcare services.

- **Love-to-Have Requirements (Unspoken)**. In the age of customer-and-supplier relationship management, organizations are learning to love their business partners. Any relationship requires knowing what your partner loves to have; similarly, in case of *customer relationship management* (CRM), the project team must learn what it is that customers would love to have. In case of healthcare customers, it is important to know what patients would love to have during their visit. One of the first "love-to" requirements could be the zero wait time, or provision of caring services, such as games for adults, gentle care for extremely sick patients, interesting books to read instead of the generic cheapest magazines, coffee or snacks, or pre-recorded favorite TV shows. While visiting, if the co-payments are easily handled upfront, patients' prescriptions are sent to the pharmacy of their choice for easy pickup, and rides are available to go back home as needed, patients might feel as though their needs were being addressed.

It has been observed that customers love the providers who furnish what they love to have, and customers are willing to pay a premium of 10-20 percent for such additional services. The challenge for providers is to learn customers' "love-to-have requirements" because customers do not easily share them. It requires an extra effort for providers to find out through caring attitude and creative practices. Fulfilling "love-to-have requirements" does not always mean costly freebies. Patients love to have an element of surprise from their service providers.

Figure 6.1 shows Kano's model of customer requirements. The X-axis shows level of effort by the provider, and the Y-axis represents extent of customer satisfaction. The intersection of two axes represents "do not care" on the Y-axis. One can see that by providing the services to meet the assume requirements, the best one can do is to achieve customer's ignorance of performance. As to the spoken requirements, in terms of getting treatment for the specific disease, when needed, and with minimal pain, or additional side effects, the customer satisfaction grows proportionately. In other words, the more we satisfy patients' needs, the more they are satisfied with the services. The final element of the customer requirements, "love to have" is beyond the spoken requirements. The customer satisfaction exponential grows with the provision of "love-to-have" requirements. Customers love such an experience, brag about the service provider, and bring in new customers through word of mouth. The challenge for the providers is to keep up with the customer's "love-to-have requirements" because customers continually ask for more, better, and cheaper. If an organization wants to grow the business, it must habitually meet "love-to-have requirements." Otherwise, its competition will be growing.

Affinity Diagram

The *Affinity Diagram* is an excellent method used to solicit input from various stakeholders, be they patients, staff, nurses, doctors, or directors. Many organizations have methods to collect ideas in a suggestion box and dump them in another box. Those ideas are not exploited to create value. Sometimes, the ideas in the suggestion box are too suggestive, thus ignored. In a brainstorming session, a few outspoken individuals take over the meeting, and the meeting ends up with a bunch of old, limited-in-number ideas.

An Affinity Diagram is a wonderful tool to gather ideas from anybody and everybody in a room. Experience has demonstrated that by using Affinity Diagram methods, a group can generate many ideas very fast. Once the ideas are generated, they are grouped and themes of ideas are developed for identifying action items for creating solutions from the ideas. An Affinity Diagram can also be used to generate new ideas from patterns and combinations of facts and team. Thus, the Affinity Diagram is a tool that organizes ideas based on their affinity and discovers new valuable ideas.

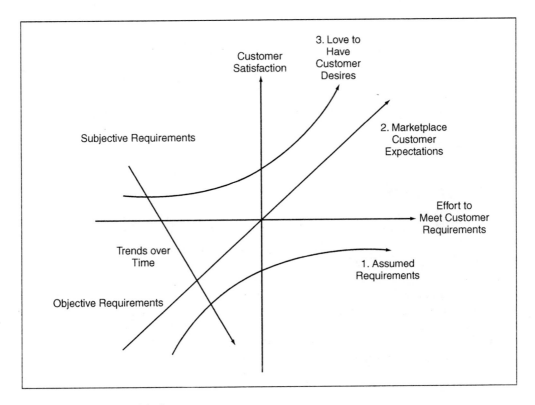

FIGURE 6.1 Kano's model of customer requirements.

An Affinity Diagram is used when there is a

- Shortage of ideas by allowing everyone to participate in generating ideas.
- Large number of ideas by organizing them in groups of related ideas.
- Bottleneck by opening new direction of thinking.
- Disagreement by objectively evaluating ideas.

Constructing an Affinity Diagram involves the following steps:

1. Write a statement clearly defining the problem or goal.
2. Identify the cross-functional team that would work to create the Affinity Diagram.

3. Provide 3" × 5" cards or Post-It notes to each member of the team for writing ideas.

4. Ask team to be silent for five minutes, and write down as many ideas on their 3 × 5 cards as they can. Any incentive to write more ideas can be helpful.

5. Collect the cards and spread them out on a flat surface (such as a desk or wall) so everyone can see them.

6. Have team members arrange the cards into groups of related ideas.

7. Develop a main category or a theme for each group. That main category idea becomes the affinity card. Members move around cards to fit in best-suited group.

8. Once all cards or notes have finally been placed under a proper affinity card, the diagram can be drawn up.

9. The main theme or ideas are then used to build solutions and identify action items.

Gaining Process Knowledge

We require sufficient process knowledge to work on a project successfully. As a fact of matter, one can solve a problem only with process knowledge. However, we tend to substitute with the experience in an area with the process knowledge. To gain process knowledge, one must deliberately attempt to learn details of the process, be able to answer various questions about the process, fix its problems, or guide others to replicate the process. For example, if a physician is an expert in heart surgery, it implies that the physician knows the ins and outs of the heart. He knows how to open it, how to operate on it, and how to properly work with it, and if an anomaly occurs how to handle it. Many times, having the false perception about the process knowledge we tend to resist new ideas or alternate methods. Based on concepts of the process thinking, it is expected that process experts must be able to answer the following aspects of a process[1]:

- **Purpose**. *Purpose* is the most important aspects of a process. Team members must be able to articulate what the basic purpose of a process is. Is the process needed? Does it add any value? Can the project be done without the process?

- **Process description**. The process owner must be able to describe the process from beginning to end. The one responsible for the process should be able to explain key aspects of the process, measurements to monitor it, and its deliverables.

- **Process details**. The process knowledge includes knowing details such as process inputs, critical process steps, process outputs, process parameters, and workmanship standards. There must be a clear understanding of the target and tolerance conditions for the process.

- **Process performance**. An important aspect of the process knowledge consists of knowing process performance at key measurement points throughout the process operation. The process performance includes knowing typical performance levels, trends in the performance, and the amount of improvement. If there are visual standards of excellence, they must be clearly known.

- **Handling of nonconforming material**. In addition to knowing the good product or process output, employees working on the project must also know how the nonconforming material is handled. What kinds of exceptions are made, and what is sent on "as-is?" This represents the "knack" of a process.

- **Statistical performance**. In addition to the qualitative knowledge of the process, a process expert must understand the process variability and the process performance in statistical terms. Jeff Hawkins, the author of *On Intelligence*, defines intelligence as "an ability to predict."[2] Statistical understanding of a process provides the ability to project and predict.

Process Mapping

To understand a process better, *process mapping* is an excellent exercise to identify various activities and their interrelationships. The *SIPOC* (supplier, input, process, output, and customer) is another tool to identify opportunities in the process. These opportunities, if performed incorrectly, may result in an unacceptable performance.

A *process* can be defined as a series of tasks that transform a set of inputs into desired outputs. Our objective should be to establish the shortest and simplest process of doing a task. The more the steps, the more complex the task becomes, and the more opportunities there are for errors. The basic building block of a process is the *4P model*, where the 4Ps stand for *Prepare, Perform, Perfect*, and *Progress*.[3] In the Preparation stage, a process requires material or information, method or approach, tools or equipment, and people with the required skills. A successful outcome of a process depends on a good preparation. The Perform stage focuses on excellent execution of certain tasks. The Perfect stage highlights the target performance rather than acceptable performance. The knowing target is the essential minimum requirement for achieving excellence in anything. The Progress stage focuses on actions to reduce inconsistencies in the process.

A well-defined process must address the following:

- Process has a purpose.
- Process has beginning and end states.
- Process has needs or inputs.
- Process must have a clear target performance.
- Process output does vary due to uncontrolled sources of variation.
- Process must be evaluated based on its mean or typical performance, as well as range between worse and better performance levels.

Constructing a Process Map

A *process map* is a graphical representation using standard symbols of a set of activities arranged in a sequence from start to the end. Process maps provide a picture of how the work is done and are used as training tools to reinforce the process training. Examples of process are Registration Process, Patient Release Process, Post-surgery Care Process, Clinical Trial Process, Patient Visit Process, Patient Feedback Process, Physician Ethics Process, Billing Process, and Handling of Rude Patients Process.

To construct a process map, follow these steps:

1. Select a process to be mapped.
2. State purpose of the process, and define its boundaries.
3. List all the activities that occur in the process
4. Sequence the activities.
5. Construct the flow chart using a standard set of symbols.
6. Connect various process steps to describe the flow of information.
7. Identify areas where review or verification is to be performed.
8. Include redo or repair activities.
9. Highlight critical activities and associated measures of performance.

The process map can be generated at the business level, department level, or the process level. The business level map is at a high level to depict information flow of the major business processes. The business level process map crosses the departmental boundaries and shows the information flow across the departments. The process level map identifies details of a process.

An example of a process of visiting doctor is shown in Figure 6.2. The map displays the flow of information and can act as a visual tool for training, identifying disconnects, and opportunities for improvement to reduce cost and responsiveness.

SIPOC

SIPOC, an abbreviation for *Supplier, Input, Process, Output*, and *Customer*, is used to expand the process map to identify players in the theater of operation. The main benefit of constructing a SIPOC is to identify practically all variables affecting performance of a process. From such understanding, we can prioritize critical customer outputs, process inputs, and the critical process steps in delighting patients, or the customer. A sample of SIPOC for a typical patient visit is shown in Figure 6.3.

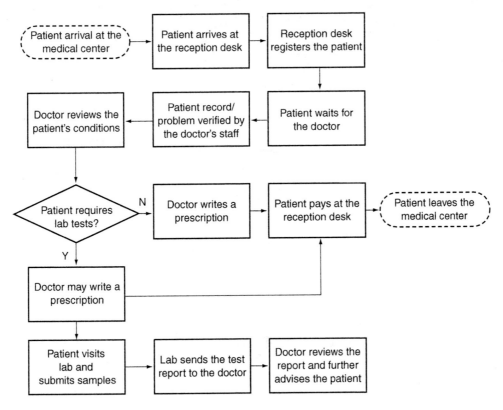

FIGURE 6.2　A sample process map for visiting a doctor.

Constructing a SIPOC

To construct a SIPOC effectively, one can first complete the middle column by writing the process steps from the process map. Then, complete two columns on the right related to the customer. First identify the process outputs, and then identify who the process output is going to. The customer could be external or the internal. The internal customer could be another department, such as radiology providing services to surgical operations, or the next process within an operation. The final steps would include completing the inputs column which can be a little tedious. The best way to complete the inputs column thoroughly is to ensure material or information, method or approach, machine or tools, or the manpower or people and skills have been considered for each process. We suggest that a cross-functional team is used to construct the SIPOC as it represents the cumulative knowledge of a process within the organization.

Suppliers	Inputs	Process	Outputs	Customers

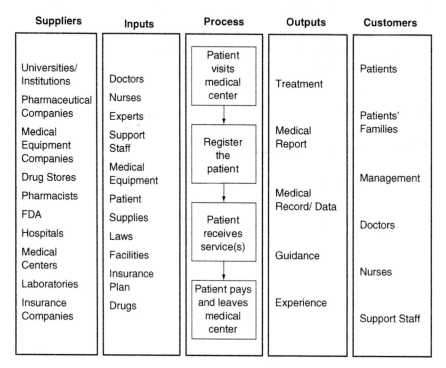

Suppliers	Inputs	Process	Outputs	Customers
Universities/ Institutions	Doctors	Patient visits medical center	Treatment	Patients
Pharmaceutical Companies	Nurses			
	Experts		Medical Report	Patients' Families
Medical Equipment Companies	Support Staff	Register the patient		
Drug Stores	Medical Equipment			Management
Pharmacists	Patient		Medical Record/ Data	
FDA	Supplies	Patient receives service(s)		Doctors
Hospitals	Laws			
Medical Centers	Facilities		Guidance	
Laboratories	Insurance Plan			Nurses
Insurance Companies	Drugs	Patient pays and leaves medical center	Experience	
				Support Staff

FIGURE 6.3   An example of a SIPOC for a general physician visit.

In working on the Six Sigma project, the process map and SIPOC are used to establish a baseline of the process knowledge. This knowledge enables us to identify and prioritize areas for improvement in order to achieve the improvement goal.

Pareto Analysis

Pareto analysis is also known as the 80:20 rule. The Pareto analysis is a powerful tool to develop our ability to make decisions based on importance instead of convenience. In our daily lives at work, we tend to get busy with easy to-do activities, rather than important things to do. As a result at the end of the day or even over a period of time, one does not see any improvement. In case of working on a project, Pareto analysis is used to prioritize process steps, process inputs, and process outputs based on their significance to the organization, instead of some arbitrary criteria. According to the Pareto principle, a few vital opportunities exceed many trivial ones combined for their impact. For example, most of the deaths in a hospital occur due to few diseases, or most of the malpractice premium is affected by the few risky practices, or most of errors are caused by a few individuals.

The Pareto analysis demonstrates that all customers, suppliers, activities, problems, or opportunities are not equally important. Pareto analysis is used to prioritize limited resources to maximize their return on investment. While selecting a project from many opportunities, one can prioritize based on their social or economical impact on the organization. It helps to focus on a few vital opportunities rather than working on many trivial ones.

Pareto analysis includes a graphical representation of a set of data, be it deaths by disease, errors by departments, waste by functions, or complaints by a group of customers. A *Pareto chart* is a bar chart showing attributes of the problem on x-axis and frequency of occurrence on y-axis. The data is arranged in descending order such that the tallest bar is plotted on the left representing the most significant opportunity for improvement. It has been observed that the two or three bars on the left together account for most of the unacceptable performance. Thus, we deploy limited resources to the most significant opportunity.

Some Pareto charts also plot a cumulative line accumulating the contribution of each category, thus highlighting areas for improvement and accounting for about 80 percent of the opportunity. Some examples of opportunity for improvement include the following which can be prioritized using the Pareto analysis:

- Causes of variation in diagnosis
- Causes of variation in the cost of treatment of a particular disease
- Type of diseases requiring medical attention at a particular facility
- Causes of various diseases
- Types of infections
- Reasons for delay in attending a patient
- Reasons for wrong prescription
- Reasons for the patient loyalty
- Cost (lower than the others)
- Comfort (quality of treatment)
- Convenience (location)
- Care (by the doctor)
- Choice (lack of)
- Consistent (good experience)
- Competent (doctors)

The following steps describe the process of constructing a Pareto chart:

1. Draw X and Y axes, where the X axis represents data categories, and the Y axis represents frequency of occurrence. Label axes appropriately.
2. Establish the attributes or categories for analysis of data.
3. Select a time interval for analysis. This interval should be a representative of typical process performance.
4. Calculate the frequency of occurrence or determine the significance of category.

5. Arrange categories in descending order based on the frequency of occurrence.

6. Plot data on the bar chart. Work on the tallest bar for improvement.

One of the challenges in constructing a Pareto chart is too many categories. The typical rule of thumb is to plot seven bars, and the last bar is designated "miscellaneous," which includes all categories beyond the top six categories. An example of the Pareto chart for the late delivery of food to patients is shown in Figure 6.4.

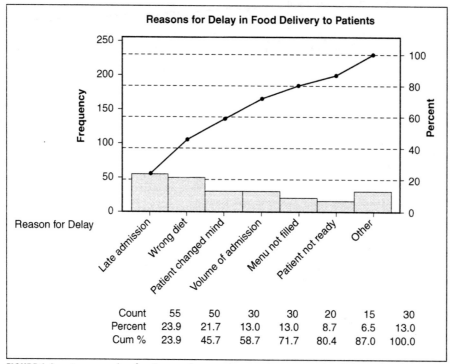

Count	55	50	30	30	20	15	30
Percent	23.9	21.7	13.0	13.0	8.7	6.5	13.0
Cum %	23.9	45.7	58.7	71.7	80.4	87.0	100.0

FIGURE 6.4   An example of a Pareto chart explaining the reasons for delay in food delivery to patients (Minitab® Statistical Software).

Force Field Analysis

While working on Six Sigma projects that require cooperation of other departments or individuals, we experience resistance to cooperating due to conflicting priorities. *Force Field analysis* is a simple method used to identify supportive and resistive resources that could be utilized effectively toward the project goals. The Force Field analysis includes identification of factors or individuals that support (drivers) the project objectives and those that may distract (restrainers) from the project objectives. Our objective is to identify supporting individuals or factors that we can exploit to accelerate change, and identify resistive resources in order to manage them effectively considering the project objectives. For example, in an attempt to reduce waste in the emergency department, one may start monitoring use of supplies. Initially this may cause a little concern because of the monitoring or discomfort in reducing the use of cleaning supplies. By identifying the people's concern upfront, we can address the issue through raising awareness or training, and converting the resistive emergency staff into staff supporting the project objectives.

Force Field analysis is widely used in planning for change management. The Force Field analysis is mostly used at the planning stage to maximize the ration of Drivers to Restrainers. For example, Figure 6.5. shows how Driving and Restraining forces have an impact on reducing the waiting time.

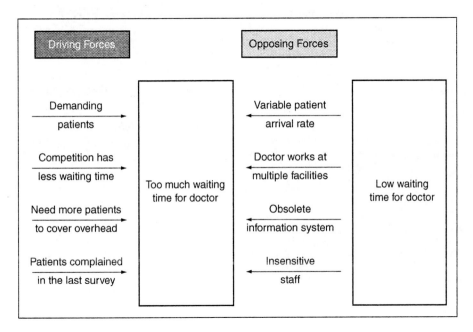

FIGURE 6.5 An example of force field analysis for waiting time.

Project Charter

Once we understand our process, customer, and customer's critical requirements, a *project charter* is created to document planned steps. The *project chart* compiles the problem definition, goals, objectives, and action plans to achieve them. The project charter is a written roadmap that

- Justifies the project efforts with the financial impact.
- Describes the problem and its scope to be addressed by the project in the specified timeframe.

- Declares the goal, objectives, and measures of success.
- Defines the roles of the team members.
- Establishes the timeline, milestones, and key deliverables.
- Identifies required critical resources.

THE MEASURE PHASE

Once the process knowledge has been gained through process maps and SIPOCs, we need to baseline the performance. One of the main tenets of Six Sigma is measure what we value. The purpose of the *Measure phase* is to identify correct measures, establish a baseline, and eliminate trivial variables or issues from further analysis.

We see data everywhere, and sometimes there is too much to handle. However, we are too busy to plan for data analysis and do something with it. The purpose of data collection has been to ensure compliance regulation or industry requirements. Instead, the purpose of the data collection should be to identify areas for improvement and ensure compliance to various requirements. Healthcare facilities have been more focused, with exceptions, on ensuring compliance rather than on improving operations. While applying the Measure phase, the following concepts and tools are important to understand:

- Basic statistics
- Statistical thinking
- Cost of quality
- Measurement system analysis
- Critical parameters
- Critical to Quality (CTQs)

Statistics is of two types: descriptive and inferential. The *descriptive statistics* summarizes the historical data, while the *inferential statistics* is based on analysis of the sample to infer performance of the process. One can consider statistics as a science of natural behavior of a process. Several statistical tools have been developed to analyze two types of data, such as variable and attribute. The *variable data* is a measure of performance on a continuous scale such as temperature, time, quantities of medication, and duration of stay. Examples of variable data include the following:

- Patient waiting time
- Initial
- Treatment
- Discharge

- Duration of a procedure
- Hospital mortality
- Mortality after a defined period from the date of hospital discharge
- Duration of hospital stay
- Days lost from work or normal routine
- Hospital readmission rates
- Complication or "adverse event" rates
- Bed turnaround time

The other type of data is called *attribute data* which has pass or fail, low or high, up or down, good or bad, cured or not cured, and zero or one values. Here the data does not have value, but has attributes. Such data is used by counting the frequency of occurrence.

Obtaining good data requires careful planning about what is required, why is it required, how often data should be collected, and where is the data stored or filed. In a healthcare organization, data is collected in clinical as well as staff areas. Staff areas will have employee, financial, facility, purchasing, supply, or patient's personal data, while the clinical data will include disease specific, clinical trials, or patient's health data.

Basic Statistical Analysis

Basic statistical analysis utilizes descriptive statistical tools such as mean and range, median, or mode. Such data are plotted to examine trends or distribution. Data are summarized by studying their central tendency or their typical values and variation or spread of the data. The *mean value* tells us the expected performance, and variation tells us about the consistency of a treatment or an action.

Mean or average is the most commonly used measure of location for a variable. The *mean* provides a measure of the most likely value of the observed data. The mean for a sample is represented by x-bar (a bar over x), and for population by a Greek letter μ (mu). A *sample* is a part of the population, with a much larger set of data. Examining a sample of a population is an economic way to learn about a process. The mean is calculated by summing all the numbers divided by the number of observations.

Median identifies the middle point in our dataset. Median is used when we count occurrences, and we want to look into percentiles for analysis. The lower quartile marks the 25 percentile point, and upper quartile marks the 75 percentile point. For example, if one looks into internal medicine data for a month, the median would imply how 50 percent of the people responded within a specific amount of time. For an odd number of observations, the middle value obtained by arranging the observations in an ascending order is called the median. For an even number of observations, median is the average of the two middle values. For example, for 49 observations, the 25th data point of sorted data will be the median, and for 50 observations, the average of 25th and 26th points will be the median. Median is a more meaningful measure of central tendency when data has some extreme values.

Mode is the value that occurs with greatest frequency. For example, the value that occurs most frequently in the Call Handling dataset is 5. Patients' calls for flu in the allergy season may represent the mode. Sometimes it happens that two diseases may become most frequently occurring diseases; the data is said to be *bimodal data.*

Range is the simplest measure of variability or spread in the data. It is the difference between the largest and the smallest values in the dataset. It has limited application because of its sensitivity to just two of the observations.

Variance is a more accurate measure of variability as it utilizes all data points. Variance is calculated by determining the difference between a data point from its mean value, squaring, and summing it. The formula for variance is described as follows:

$$\text{Variance} = \text{Sum}\{(x_i - \text{x-bar})^2\}/N$$

where N is the number of data points, and subscript "i" represents the sequence of data point between 1 to N.

Standard deviation is the square root of variance. While calculating sample standard deviation, we divide by (n-1) instead of N. Several statistical software programs such as Minitab, Statgraphics, or Microsoft Excel worksheets are available for statistical computations and analysis.

Statistical Thinking

Normal distribution is a bell-shaped distribution of data values where the majority of the items are in the center and some are on the tail ends, as shown in Figure 6.6. The normal distribution is used to determine probability of occurrence of an event based on the knowledge of past performance. The area under the curve helps us define what proportion of values will fall within a certain range. For example, the probability of data points that fall within a range of one standard deviation around the mean is 68.26, or about two-thirds; within two standard deviations around the mean is 95.44, or 95 percent, and within three standard deviations around the mean is 99.73, meaning practically everything.

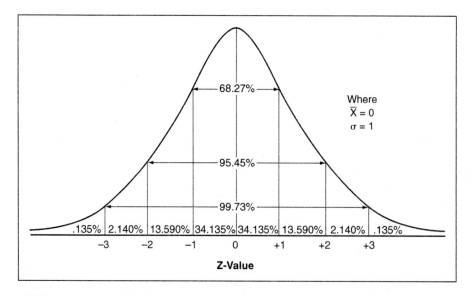

FIGURE 6.6   A normal distribution curve.

The reason we use normal distribution to estimate probability of occurrence is that most of the events in nature follow this distribution, which can be understood by its mean value and standard deviation. A normal distribution helps you make decisions about a treatment based on the sample data.

Random Versus Assignable Variation

Normal distribution has most of the points around its mean and a few on its tail ends. The data within the center of the distribution or within two standard deviations represent the *common variation*, while data outside the two standard deviations represent *special variation*. Walter Shewhart, a quality professional in the 1920s, called these variations *random* and *assignable variations*, respectively. More precisely, data that do not follow the normal distribution represents nonrandom variation, thus considered assignable variation. The statistical thinking means a clear understanding of the difference between the random and the assignable variation:

- Random variation occurs due to uncontrolled variables that exist in the environment around us. For example, variation among patients' response to a treatment can be considered random variation. Random variation is hard to understand and control.

- The assignable variation occurs due to a specific cause. For example, a patient's response that is significantly different from that of the group response to the same treatment can be considered assignable variation. Assignable variation is easier to understand and change.

At a personal level, when we commute to work, we expect a certain time with some give and take due to random variation. However, when an accident occurs, the commute time changes significantly due to an assignable cause; thus this is considered assignable variation.

Understanding the random and assignable variations allows us to make decisions to utilize our resources most effectively. Random variation represents the process capability, while the assignable variation is a deviation in performance from that capability. To improve capability of a treatment takes a lot of resources and fundamental research, while to change the performance of a treatment, some adjustments are needed.

Cost of Quality (COQ)

Dr. W. Edwards Deming, the famous quality guru, has said that variation is evil. Many business problems are caused by inconsistencies. Many organizational inefficiencies or malpractices are caused by inconsistency in our practices. The inconsistency could result from an illegible handwriting on prescriptions, excessive waiting time, poor training, insufficient documentation, and so on. Of course, some of the inconsistencies could be prevented with a good design of process or the product.

The main purpose of Six Sigma is to reduce the cost of quality (COQ). It is estimated that 3 Sigma level can be associated with COQ of about 15–25 percent of sales, and 6 Sigma level with less than 1 percent of sales. The COQ is beyond the cost of errors; instead it includes cost of handling problems, checking or verifying the performance, reworking the service, lost opportunity, or the lost customer. The COQ has three main components: *Failure*, *Appraisal*, and *Prevention*.

The Cost of Failure has two components, internal and external failures. Examples of the cost of quality may include the following:

- Failure costs
- External Failures
  - Cost of malpractice insurance
  - Legal costs of fighting malpractice cases
  - Handling patient complaints
  - Lost patients
  - Lost doctors
  - Revisits
- Internal Failures
  - Lost patient information
  - Long wait for patient
  - Rework
  - Nonstandard working methods
  - Material or equipment waste/scrap
  - Billing errors
  - Other avoidable process losses, such as scheduled admission process
  - Calling a doctor because an order is not clear
  - Retaking an X-ray because the film quality was poor
  - Inefficiencies
- Preventive
- Planning
- Capability studies
- Patient surveys and evaluation
- Training
  - Doctors
  - Patients
  - Staff
- Resource planning
- Procedures
- Appraisal

- Excessive sign-offs or approvals
- 100 percent inspection of diagnostic code capturing when errors rarely occur
- Compliance to various regulatory and industry requirements
- Audits

One of the differences in reviewing cost of poor quality between healthcare and the conventional manufacturing industry is that direct cost of appraisal is not obvious, such as compliance to JCAHO requirements, or various reviews and approvals. However, some of these items are built-in service processes and are difficult to see as separate cost items. Besides, waste of time, reduced inefficiencies of staff and physicians, and overuse of supplies could also lead to increased COQ. Such inefficiencies can lead to fingerpointing among employees. The high frequency of mishaps may result is a negative work atmosphere.

Measurement System Analysis

An inaccurate blood pressure measuring system may show excessively high readings; the patient may be sent to an emergency care center, resulting in excessive anxiety and an enormous waste of expensive resources. I remember one of my friends went in for a quick examination at his workplace. His cholesterol level was detected to be at 300 plus level. He was shocked at such a high number. Even though the test was redone, he was recommended for further tests. Later he found out that the high cholesterol level was due to a bad test device. Another example is buying a blood pressure measuring device from a local pharmacy. It is difficult to get a consistent measure of one's blood pressure, and even more difficult to correlate with another devices at the physician's office or at the pharmacy. Even though the device may be acceptable to use, the measurement system is still questionable. Besides the measuring device, the measurement system includes variability because of the person taking the measurement and the patient who is being measured.

If more than one nurse measures a patient's blood pressure, it is quite possible two measurements may not be the same or equally reliable. The objective is to be as close as possible to the actual blood pressure. One can see that the blood pressure can be inconsistent because of the patient's condition, the measuring device, and the measuring method. The *measurement system analysis* (MSA) is a method of apportioning sources of inconsistencies in the measurement system. The MSA is important to conduct for devices that are used for measuring critical and sensitive measurements. MSA is also known as *Gage Repeatability and Reproducibility* (R&R), which involves taking a number of cases, patients, or test individuals, and measuring them by two or three individuals, gathering the data, and analyzing by using a statistical analysis software. The repeatability indicates how consistent is the measuring device and reproducibility indicates how consistent is the measuring person.

Figure 6.7 shows the difference between repeatability and reproducibility. Together, MSA determines the R&R factor. For good measurement systems, the R&R should be less than 10 percent, and acceptable measuring devices used for noncritical measures of R&R may be as high as 30 percent. In general, the rule of thumb is that the device must have a resolution fine enough to measure the variation in the measurement itself.

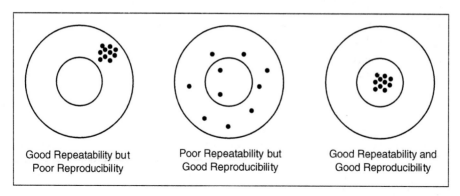

Good Repeatability but Poor Reproducibility	Poor Repeatability but Good Reproducibility	Good Repeatability and Good Reproducibility

FIGURE 6.7   Repeatability and reproducibility.

Process Performance Measures

Besides defect per unit (DPU), or defect per million opportunities (DPMO), two other measurements must be learned to understand how the intent and actual performances must be aligned. Imagine you have a one-car garage with a door width exactly equal to the width of your car. How would you feel about parking in the garage, especially Friday night? Having a garage width exactly equal to the width of the car is considered as a borderline case of your car's parking capability. We understand that it is difficult to drive exactly the same way and very precisely all the time. The inconsistency in our ability to drive like on railway tracks can be thought of as variability, which is measured in terms of standard deviation or the range.

Six times the standard deviation is considered as the *process capability*. One can understand that process capability is defined by the range of your performance, not the target or average of your performance. How frequently a process can achieve its target performance determines a process' capability. Based on the process capability, two indices, Cp and Cpk, are defined.

The Cp, the *process capability index*, is as the ratio of expected to actual performance, tolerance to the process capability, or defined as

$$Cp = \frac{\text{Upper Specification Limit} - \text{Lower Specification Limit}}{6 * \text{Process Standard Deviation}}$$

The difference between upper and lower specification limits is called the *tolerance*, and it represents the garage door width from the left to the right of the garage. The proces 109s standard deviation is a calculated measure of inconsistency of the process. According to the Six Sigma methodology, in order to achieve 3.4 errors per million opportunities, one should have Cp of 2 or better. In other words, having a garage door twice the width of the car can make the driving process to be at 6 Sigma level.

A complementary measure, Cpk, the process capability index adjusted for shift in the process mean, provides a snapshot of the process performance. While Cp deals with the variance,

Cpk deals with the distance from target, or specification limits. Cp represents inherent process capability, and Cpk represents the actual process performance. It implies that for a given Cpk, one can expect a certain error rate.

The Cpk can have two values depending upon the shift in the process. The CPU is determined when the process center is closer to upper specification, and the CPL is determined when the process is closer to lower specification. The smaller of the two values is treated as the Cpk.

CPU = (Upper specification limit – Process mean) / 3 * Standard deviations, OR

CPL = (Process mean - Lower specification limit) / 3 * Standard deviations

$$Cpk = Min(CPU \text{ or } CPL)$$

Thus, Cp can be remembered as a planned capability of the process; yes, having a one-car garage, I can park the car. However, how often I park the car in the garage well will determine its Cpk value.

The following guidelines can be used to evaluate Cp and Cpk values:

Cp > 1.33 (Capable)

Cp = 1.00 – 1.33 (Capable with tight control)

Cp < 1.00 (Incapable)

Cpk > 1.5 means that the process is achieving virtual perfection, and thus requires less control.

Cpk > 1.0 means 6s spread is inside of specification limits, thus lower failure rate.

Cpk < 1.0 means some part of the distribution is outside of the specification limits.

Figure 6.8 shows the concept of Cp, and Figure 6.9 shows the concept of Cpk.

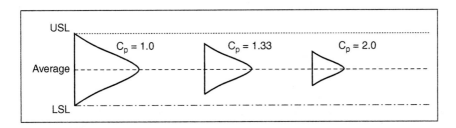

FIGURE 6.8 Process capability index.

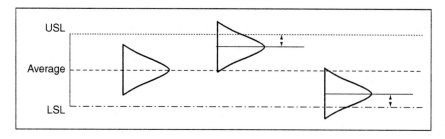

FIGURE 6.9   Process capability index adjusted for the shift in the mean.

THE ANALYZE PHASE

The *Analyze phase* begins the convergence of possibilities toward the root cause of the problem. At the end of the Analyze phase, we identify a list of critical variables. The Analyze phase focuses on the key variables so that problems can be fixed. In the Analyze phase, we investigate the family of variation to pinpoint the type of variation; then we conduct the root cause analysis, and reduce the number of variables to a manageable number. The *root cause analysis* is conducted to the level such that an action item can be identified that would alleviate inconsistency in the process output. In this phase, some hypothesis testing of "what-if" scenarios is also possible. Then, the regression analysis is conducted to ensure at least some statistical relationship between the parameter variables versus the output process performance. The likelihood of solving the problem increases as the problem is addressed through various phases of DMAIC. Finally, the *failure modes and effect analysis* (FMEA) is used to anticipate potential failure modes and address them.

Key Analyze Tools

Multi-vary analysis is a tool that apportions variation into its components and reduces the scope of the problem to a manageable level.

Cause-and-effect analysis is also known as *fishbone* or *Ishikawa diagram*. This tool is excellent to explore potential causes that could impact the problem. The team for further convergence or potential solution then prioritizes the causes.

Regression analysis is used to build process models, or to quantify or prioritize relationship between various causes and effects.

Failure modes and effects analysis, FMEA, is a great tool to anticipate potential problems so some of the problems could be prevented from occurrence in the proposed solution.

Multi-Vary Analysis

A typical process problem can be caused by many potential causes. In solving a problem, we try to reduce the number of potential causes by removing trivial ones. However, sometimes it is difficult to reduce the number of potential causes to a smaller number directly. In such circumstances the multi-vary analysis is used to reduce the scope of the problem. The multi-vary analysis reaffirms the approach that most of the problems are due to excessive variation. Thus, by categorizing the process variation, one can focus on the most significant sources of variation. Accordingly, a process output manifests three types of variation, namely, Positional, Cyclical, and Temporal. The multi-vary analysis is a graphical representation of three families of variation, identifying the most significant family of variation to work on, and reducing the scope of problem to one third of the problem.

The *Positional variation*, also known as *within variation*, represents the family of variation that occurs within a system at certain locations. The system could be a process or product. Thus, the position variation could be the occurrence of unacceptable variation within a process at certain specific steps, within a department at certain activity, or within a treatment at certain stage the results are unacceptable. The position variation occurs frequently, is considered repeatable, and thus relates to the *design* of the process. As a product, one can say that the certain medicine from a certain supplier is less effective than another manufacturer's response to a treatment is more unique at some parts of the body than others. Thus, the treatment shows some location-specific effect.

For example, if one bakes cookies on a tray or the cookie sheet, and places the trays on a conveyor belt into the commercial oven, two cookies at one corner turn out to be uncooked on all trays. One can right away focus on that aspect of the baking process that includes oven, conveyor, trays, or heating element. Isolating the location-related pattern helps us in diagnosing the problem and identifying a solution to the problem.

The *Cyclical variation*, known as *between variation*, represents changes from one process cycle to the next process cycle. It means that at one time a treatment works; the other time it does not work. Or, one tray of cookies looks great; the next one has inedible cookies. Detecting such patterns of problems leads us to look into potential causes that relate to the process setup, rather than its design. If the cyclical variation is large, then one looks into the inconsistency in the setup of the process cycle, which could be due to wrong material, wrong quantity, wrong time, or an unqualified person

The *Temporal variation*, known as *trends*, is defined as the shift in the process output observed over time. Normally, such variation has been observed in decay of a process element over time. For example, in X-ray machines, the intensity of the X-ray source decreases over time, equipment using a laser source diminishes over time with usage, or in the case of cookies, normal decay in the heating element or change in the viscosity of the cookie dough by the seventh or eighth tray.

To conduct a multi-vary analysis, we define the three families of variation, design data collection forms, collect data, and analyze the largest family of variation by calculating range (difference between maximum and minimum) of consistency. The amount of data to be collected should be sufficient to represent most of the variation in the process. Once the largest family of variation is known, the root cause analysis is done to identify causes of the excessive variation, which could be due to design, setup, or maintenance-related activities.

Cause and Effect Analysis

Cause and effect analysis was developed by Kaoru Ishikawa to identify the source of the problem seen at the process output or in the field. The chart representing the cause and effect analysis is called the *Ishikawa diagram* or the *fishbone diagram*. It a systematic approach to perform backward analysis by tracing an effect to its cause(s). The fishbone diagram contains a box (fish mouth) to represent the cause, and major branches represent bones. The four major branches include Material, Machine, Method, and Manpower. However, due to diversity in the workforce and advances in technology, we have relabeled these branches as Material/Information, Machine/Tools, Method/Approaches, and Mind Power/People Skills. The chart is formed in the team environment where expertise representing various branches and problems is available. One of the challenges in conducting root cause analysis using the Ishikawa diagram is that people tend to point to the person responsible for the undesired effect, and take necessary corrective action, which includes training and counseling. After some time, either the person is let go or feels bad; however, the problem recurs. In a performance-driven healthcare organization, when an error occurs, the question must be asked, "What happened?" rather than "Who did it?"

Accidents do occur in healthcare organizations causing dissatisfied, irritated, or helpless patients. Such errors can occur in any area whether at registration, examining the patient, or testing patients. Malpractice or dissatisfaction can be attributed to excessive inconsistency from expected practices at a typical process, or the condition of the patient.

Conditions of excessive deviation must be investigated. The extent of this investigation into root causes varies due to the frequency of the deviation and the severity of its effect. However, many times the extent of the investigation is not sufficient and proportionate to significance of the deviation, and the analysis remains shallow. As a result, problems recur, and soon we have many fires to fight.

The fishbone diagram provides a framework to understand the causative relationships between output and input variables more effectively. When constructing the Ishikawa diagram, one can either populate all four major branches in random fashion, or one at a time. In either case, it is imperative that no idea is left ignored. All ideas are documented first, and then evaluated for significance. A typical branch should have multiple potential causes. To identify the key potential causes, the team selects at least one key cause on each branch. This directly reduces the number of variables from a large number to a smaller number, between four to six variables. Once the key causes have been identified, each cause is drilled down by asking about five "why's" or until clear actions are identified. Due to a lack of depth in the analysis, one cannot identify the appropriate action to remedy the problem. The following thread investigating the causes of long waiting time demonstrates the depth of analysis:

> We have too many patients catching cold in the waiting room. >> Why do the patients catch cold in the waiting room? >> They wait too long. >> Why do they wait too long? >> Doctor spends too much time with patients and takes an interest in patients' care? >> Why? Doctor does not have a standard process >> Why not? >>Because… >> Why not? >> Because doctors know what they are supposed to do?>> Really? >> Yes>> Why haven't we documented the doctors' process then?>> Well, nobody has asked for the procedures.>> Can we document the procedures now? Yes, let's interview doctors, and document a standard procedure for patients' examination to reduce a long waiting time in the reception area. (It should help in reducing the patient to patient variation, and help in scheduling appointments.)

Constructing the Ishikawa Diagram

The following steps may help streamline team meetings and expedite getting to the root cause:

1. Form a cross-functional team with members representing facility, doctors, staff, administration, pharmacy, compliance, and supplies.

2. Construct a cause-and-effect diagram and list potential causes on each branch.

3. Jot down as many causes as possible. Do not exclude any at this time.

4. Prioritize causes on each branch, select at least one important cause for further analysis, and ignore trivial causes.

5. For each important cause, conduct a detailed analysis by asking "Why" at least five times, as many times as needed to identify an action to reduce the undesired effect or eliminate it.

6. After the "Why" analysis, develop an action plan.

7. Follow up until the action item is implemented and the results are verified.

8. If the resultant outcome is unsatisfactory, further analysis or experimentation will be required using tools identified in the Improve phase.

Figure 6.10 shows an example of a cause and effect diagram for poor X-ray quality.

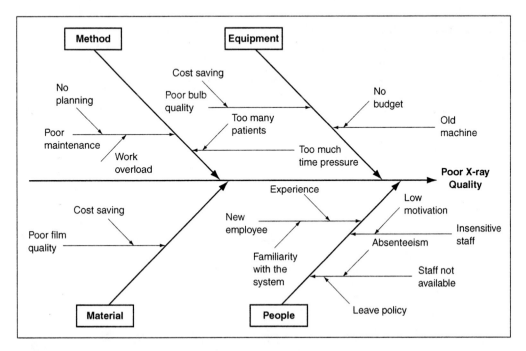

FIGURE 6.10   An example of a cause and effect diagram for poor X-ray quality.

Regression Analysis

The cause and effect analysis identifies potential causes that may relate to the expected or unexpected outcome. The regression analysis helps us in quantifying the strength of the relationship between the dependent (outcome) and independent (input) variables. For example, patients waiting too long in the reception area may be because of unscheduled arrivals, emergencies, or the doctor's process of examining patients. In order to determine which one may be more significant than others, we correlate three potential causes of the delay to the waiting time.

Similarly, there may be other incidences where correlation can be estimated for evaluating the extent of causation:

- Billing error rate versus number of bills issued
- Mortality rates versus number of procedures
- Mortality rates versus number of patients treated
- Hospital re-admission rates versus number of patients treated
- Relapses versus type of disease
- Medication dose versus the patient's weight or health
- Infant mortality rate versus demographics

In a Six Sigma project, regression analysis is used to prioritize independent variables or establish causative relationship between output and inputs. Once the relationship or a model has been established based on historical data, one could predict the dependent variable for a given independent variable. Regression analysis can be seen as analysis of scatter plots by adding best-fit lines and quantifying the relationship between the dependent and independent variables. The regression analysis includes the *regression equation*, *residual variance*, and *R-square*. Regression equation defines the best-fit line. The *best-fit line* is the line that quantifies the relationship between two variables. Figure 6.11 shows an example of the scatter plot for the relationship between the length of hospital stay and the patient satisfaction score using Minitab.

When analyzing a scatter plot, there can be a negative, positive, or no correlation between two variables. If the output increases with the increase in the input, the correlation is called positive. If the output decreases with the increase in input, the correlation is negative, and when the output does not change with the change in input, then there is no correlation. The correlation is represented by a letter "R." However, we examine square of R, represented as "r^2," that is a measure of certainty in the relationship between two variables. If r^2 is more than 64 percent, we have established a correlation that accounts for almost a majority of variation in the relationship. This corresponds to the correlation coefficient of R = .8. The value of R ranges between -1 to 1, where 1 represents 100 percent correlation.

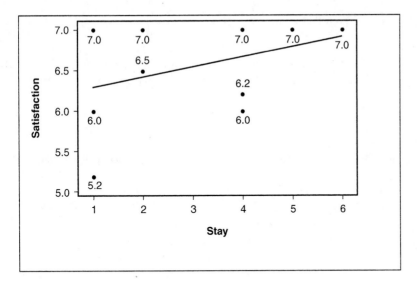

FIGURE 6.11 An example of a relationship between satisfaction score and the length of hospital stay (Minitab® Statistical Software).

Performing Regression Analysis

Following are the steps for performing a regression analysis:

1. Select the key potential causes for regression analysis with the expected response.

2. Draw two axes, label Y-axis for the output (response) variable, and X-axis for input (predictor) variable. Plot the points on the chart.

3. Draw an approximate best-fit line, and interpret the relationship in physical terms. You may observe the relationship to be positive, negative, or no relationship.

4. Calculate the correlation of coefficient using Microsoft Excel or statistical software. If the r^2 is greater than 60 percent, one can investigate for improving the relationship in order to predict response.

5. If r^2 is less than 50 percent, one can use the regression analysis to prioritize potential causes for further analysis.

For performing regression analysis of multiple variables, statistical software is used, which one can learn through help files, tutorials, or some classroom training. At the end of the regression analysis, one may establish a strong relationship between two variables, or prioritize a group of variables for further analysis such as design of experiments (DOE) in the Improve phase.

Failure Modes and Effect Analysis (FMEA)

FMEA was first used in the aerospace industry in the mid 1960s to detect problems with an aircraft before it ever left the ground. FMEA is mandatory in aerospace, automotive, food, and pharmaceutical industries. The U.S. Food and Drug Administration requires FMEA to launch new medical devices or drugs.

FMEA is a tool used to identify the potential failures for maximizing patients' safety and to reduce the chances of critical errors for reducing malpractice claims and achieving patient satisfaction. The failures could be the breakdown of a process, or its impact on the patient or the customer. As the name implies, while performing FMEA in a team environment, we identify various potential modes of failure, evaluate its effects, severity, frequency of occurrence, our ability to detect and control, and estimate associated risk. If the risk is high, preventive actions are initiated to reduce to risk to an acceptable levels. For example, from a manufacturer's perspective while designing an X-ray machine, any potential failure mode that may expose a patient to the X-rays must be identified and addressed because that may lead to injury to the patient. Similarly, in a healthcare facility, one must do the FMEA in the emergency department; any potential for failure may lead to significant adverse effects to the condition of the customer. Even during the patient's visit for a normal checkup, one must identify potential modes which may cause spread of infectious diseases as simple as a cold. While working on a Six Sigma project, FMEA can be used while identifying the potential causes, or evaluating a proposed solution for anticipating failures.

FMEA is more effective when it is proactively applied while designing a treatment, developing a new healthcare facility, or installing a new equipment with significant potential risks. After identifying the potential failure modes, the severity of the failure mode is evaluated for cosmetic, non-functional, or safety impact. If the impact is severe enough affecting patient safety adversely, it must be remedied before using the treatment or equipment. Then, the causes relating to the failure modes are identified, and the frequency of occurrence are identified from rare to all the time. If the causes of failure modes occur, our ability to detect and control is evaluated to minimize impact on the customer. Table 6.1 summarizes the grading criteria.

TABLE 6.1 Ranks of Severity, Occurrence, and Detection[4]

Number	Severity to Organization	Occurrence of the Severity	Detection of Occurrence
10	Damage without warning	Very high (1 in 2)	Absolute Uncertainty
9	Damage with warning	Very high (1 in 3)	Very remote
8	Very high risk	Very high (1 in 8)	Remote
7	High risk	High (1 in 20)	Very low
6	Moderate risk	High (1 in 80)	Low
5	Low risk	Moderate (1 in 400)	Moderate
4	Very low risk	Moderate (1 in 2,000)	Moderately high
3	Minor risk	Low (1 in 15,000)	High
2	Very minor risk	Low (1 in 150,000)	Very high
1	No risk at all	Remote (1 in 1,500,000)	Almost certain

Steps to Perform FMEA

To perform FMEA, follow these steps:

1. Identify the project and understand its functional elements.
2. Form a cross-functional team.
3. Review ranking criteria for severity, occurrence, and detection as shown in Table 6.1.
4. Review SIPOC, and list potential failure modes relating all elements of SIPOC.
5. Identify potential causes relating to the failure modes and ability to detect or control occurrence of the potential causes.
6. Evaluate severity failure modes, occurrence of causes, and detection of controls on a scale of 1–10.
7. Calculate Risk Priority Number (RPN) by multiplying Severity, Occurrence, and Detection as follows:

$$RPN = Severity \times Occurrence \times Detection$$

8. Any severity rating more than 7 and occurrence 1 in 80 or more must be investigated for reduction. Then, address any RPN higher than a predetermined value of significance economic for the organization.
9. While addressing certain RPN, the team must look into implementing failure-free methodologies—for example, error-proofing the methods.
10. After implementing remedial actions, re-estimate RPN.

For example, a physical therapy clinic is interested in performing FMEA. A patient makes an appointment to meet a physical therapist. Table 6.2 shows a list of various failure modes or errors that could occur during the therapy process. Once failure modes are identified, severity and detection grading are assessed on a scale of 1 to 10.

TABLE 6.2   Example of FMEA for Physical Therapy Treatment at a Clinic

Process: Patient receiving physical therapy

Date: _____

Process #: _____

Failure Mode	Severity	Occurrence	Detection	RPN =
	(S)	(O)	(D)	SxOxD
Patient missing appointment	2	3	8	36
Patient providing confusing information about the symptom	5	2	8	80
Improper treatment given to a patient	10	2	6	120
Patient fails to understand physical therapy benefits	6	2	7	84

It appears that improper treatment given to a patient has the highest RPN and is therefore a likely candidate for process improvement.

CONCLUDING UNDERSTANDING PROBLEMS

By applying the first three phases of DMAIC methodology, one can get a better grasp of the process needing attention, establish a performance baseline, and conduct root cause analysis to identify likely causes of the problem. If the causes are too many, screening experiments can be conducted for shortening the list of potential causes; otherwise, you can conduct a concluding design of experiments to quantify the impact of causes on the response and optimize the solution before applying elements of the Control phase. The Healthcare-Excellence Project Forms present a simple way to apply commonly used Six Sigma tools.

ENDNOTES

1   Gupta, Praveen (2005), *From PDCA to PPPP*, Quality Digest, http://accelper.com/pdfs/From%20PDCA%20to%20PPPP.pdf.

2   Hawkins, Jeff and Blakeslee, Sandra (2004), *On Intelligence*, Times Books.

3   Gupta, Praveen (2006).

4   www.fmea_infocenter.com.

SAMPLE HEALTHCARE EXCELLENCE PROJECT FORMS: UNDERSTANDING THE PROBLEM

PROJECT FORM: Understanding Problem

Define

Project Title:	Project Leader:
Team Members:	Project Start Date:

Project Analysis (*based upon experience and expertise*)
Cost (C)_____   Time (T)_____   Net Annual Savings (S)_____   PPI _____

Opportunity/Problem Description:.

Customer(s):

Customer Requirements:	Measures	
	External	Internal
Assumed and Unspoken:		
Spoken and Measurable:		
Love to, but Unspoken:		

Healthcare Excellence_Project Form
Understanding Problem

1

Understanding Problem

Define

Team Members and their Roles

Member	Role

Opportunity/Problem Attributes in the order of significance:

Other observations:

Force Field Analysis:

Drivers:	Distracters:

Understanding Problem

Define

Process Flow Chart
Standard Symbols (additional symbols may also be used)

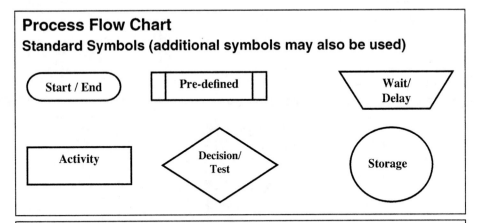

Constructing a Flow Chart
(1. List process activities, 2. Sequence the process activities, and
3. Construct a process map using the above symbols):

Understanding Problem
Define

SIPOC				
Supplier (5)	**Input (4)**	**Process (1)**	**Output (2)**	**Customer (3)**

Resources required for the project, and its source

Project Goal: *(e.g. Reduce the average patient waiting time from 30 minutes to 3 minutes)*

Project Timeline:

Phase	Major Activities	Target Completion	Actual Completion

Healthcare Excellence_Project Form
Understanding Problem

4

Understanding Problem

Measure

Cost of Quality (*Summarize the quality costs as identified under different categories.*)

Internal Failures Items	External Failures Items	Appraisal Items	Prevention Items	Summary	Cost
				Internal	
				External	
				Appraisal	
				Prevention	
				Total	

Performance Measures (Use columns as appropriate)
Summarize and calculate the current performance.

Performance Measure	# of Observations	# of Errors	DPU	# of Opportunities	DPMO	Sigma Level	Process Capability Index (Cp)*

*Process Capability = Sigma level/3

Healthcare Excellence_Project Form
Understanding Problem

5

Understanding Problem
Analyze

Multi-Vary Analysis: *(Identify the key characteristic whose variation is to be measured and fill-in the information below)*

Positional (Within) Variation (Design related)

Definition:

Minimum Value: _____   Maximum Value: _____

Positional Variation (Maximum - Minimum)

_____

Cyclical (Between) Variation (Batch to batch or set up related)

Definition:

Minimum Value: _____   Maximum Value: _____

Cyclical Variation (Maximum - Minimum)

_____

Temporal (Over time) Variation (Over time, or maintenance related)

Definition:

Minimum Value: _____   Maximum Value: _____

Temporal Variation (Maximum - Minimum)

_____

Understanding Problem
Analyze

Cause and Effect Analysis

Identify the key problems from the measure phase and analyze the problem. Using this analysis identify four measures and plot the expected relationship in the visual regression analysis.

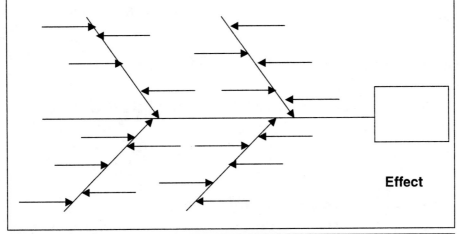

Effect

Visual Regression Analysis

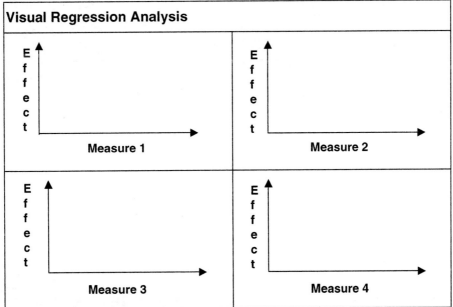

Measure 1

Measure 2

Measure 3

Measure 4

Healthcare Excellence_Project Form   7
Understanding Problem

Understanding Problem

$$Y = f(X)$$

The desired process output (Y) is a function of key variables (Xi).

Thus, your process output (_____) is a
function of the critical variables

1._____

2._____

3._____

4._____

5._____

6._____

SOLVING PROBLEMS: IMPROVE AND CONTROL

SECTIONS

Improve Phase
Control Phase
Endnotes
Sample Healthcare Excellence Project Forms: Solving the Problem

A good problem definition is considered to be the halfway point through solving the problem. During the first three phases of DMAIC, we gained knowledge about the process activities, process performance, process problems, and potential causative relationship between the problems and its sources. In Chapter 6, "Understanding Problems," we ended up with a clear definition of the problems and a reduced number of critical variables that form the likely recipe of the solution.

In this chapter, we work with the remaining key variables and develop a recipe for improvement. In order to reduce the number of variables further, and develop an optimized recipe, one can use one's knowledge, or experiment to determine effects of multiple variables. For evaluating effects of experimental settings, various combinations, or alternate solutions, one must understand statistical testing methods. Having developed a solution to the process problem, sustaining the gain becomes a challenge. Many times, we have the idea or changes required in the process; however, keeping up with the desired changes becomes a challenge. We must create a system to consistently practice the new methods of treating patients, doing surgery, or practicing medicine. The Improve phase and Control phase have been designed to develop a desired solution and sustain the improvement as long as needed.

The Solving Problem portion requires tools for creativity, evaluation, verification, implementation, monitoring, change management, and communication. Thus, the following tools can be implemented to solve a problem and realize benefits over time:

- Improve phase
  - Systems thinking
  - Testing of hypothesis
  - Comparative experiments
  - Design of experiments
- Control phase
  - Control charts
  - Documentation
  - Change management
  - Communication
  - Reward and recognition

IMPROVE PHASE

The improve phase has been designed to identify actions remedying the root cause of the waste or inefficiency of a process, or in a department. People tend to jump to the action or improve phase without taking time to understand the problem and the process. However, the Six Sigma methodology promotes a systemic approach to problem solving, avoiding our tendency to jump to conclusions and take a rash action to be reversed later.

Systems Thinking

Six Sigma is perceived by many as a data-driven expensive methodology that can only be learned or used after six months of intensive training at the cost of more than $10,000 per person. People think Six Sigma implies a lot of statistics and that just by applying those rigorous statistical techniques, one can fix all problems. If that were true, most problems could have been solved using some statistical software. Actually, I had seen this at a company where a statistical consultant ran a design of experiment, and based upon his statistical analysis, he concluded that a certain process was infeasible. I have found that learning everything about the process factually helps in formulating a right solution quickly. As someone has said, "Let the product and the process do the talking." We must *listen* to our product and processes and make decisions based on facts and intuition, rather than either facts or intuition. While applying systems thinking to problem-solving, it has been said that one should solve the problem at least *one level above* the visible symptoms of a problem. For example, if an error is made in improperly identifying patients during a routine examination, then similar mistakes could be made in surgery too. Thus, first we must investigate where else one may have a similar problem, gather facts, and understand the nature and scope of the problem.

One cannot apply the Six Sigma methodology to an organization that has a leadership crisis, or does not have a clear vision or purpose for the organization. Thus, achieving excellence will require more than Six Sigma in specific areas; instead, one must look at the entire organization in order to make substantial improvement. Synergy created at this level has a chance to produce dramatic results.

In applying systems thinking, one must first clearly understand the expected outcome. Then, the details can be worked out to get there. We must clearly visualize the results; in other words, if an organization is implementing Six Sigma, leadership must be clearly able to see what the organization would look like at the end of the Six Sigma journey. Would it be a one-time measure of success, or would it be a continual improvement at an aggressive rate? We should be able to anticipate specific needs for achieving the future state. Thus, we can commit to solving the problem at *system or the process level*, instead of at the symptom level. That's where the root cause analysis becomes more effective.

Testing of Hypothesis

Testing of hypothesis is an inferential statistical technique that is used to make a statement about an activity or process, based on its sample output. A *hypothesis* is a statement about a potential change event (normally an improvement, new treatment, or drug based on an experiment). Validating the statement is called "testing of hypothesis." The technique involves setting up two hypotheses: one about the expected change, and the other about the remaining possibilities. The statement about the expected experimental outcome is called the *alternate hypothesis*, and the other one about remaining possibilities of no interest is called the *null hypothesis*. For example, when evaluating a new cancer medicine or chemotherapy dose during clinical trials, one can set up a hypothesis or make a statement that the new treatment will require a shorter time than the time for current treatment. This will be an alternate hypothesis. If the new treatment causes no improvement, or takes longer time, then the treatment is no good; thus it is null. In other words, we are not interested in the null outcome. The hypotheses can be written as

Null Hypothesis: H_0 = New Treatment Time is no different from Current Treatment Time.

Alternate Hypothesis: H_a = New Treatment Time is less than Current Treatment Time.

A combination of null and alternative hypotheses includes all possibilities and does not overlap with each other. The outcome of any hypothesis testing leads to concluding as follows:

- "Rejecting the null hypothesis," or "Not rejecting the alternate hypothesis"
- "Not rejecting the null hypothesis," or "Rejecting the alternate hypothesis"

This conclusion is made based upon the statistical significance of evidence. The *statistical significance* implies that the shift between two process means or average values are so far apart that it is unlikely to happen by chance. Thus, it can be concluded that the new treatment is due to *planned* changes. Figure 7.1 shows three cases of improvement.

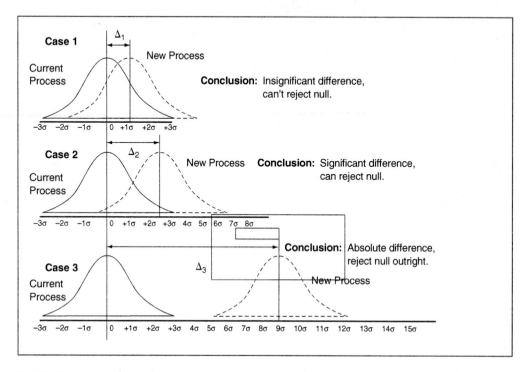

FIGURE 7.1   Testing of hypothesis

In case 1, Δ (delta) represents the difference between the current process and new process. The difference is about one standard deviation. One can see that there is a significant overlap between the current and new processes. It implies that the expected outcome could be the same even with the new process; in other words, there is a good chance that the new process may not produce improved results. Thus, we conclude that there is no difference, and we do not reject the null hypothesis. In case 2, the difference between the current process and new process is a little more than two standard deviation points. This implies that the probability of overlap does not exceed more than 5 percent. In other words, with almost 95 percent confidence, one can say that the new process is better than the current process. In case 3, the difference exceeds more than nine standard deviations, thus there is no likelihood of any overlap. One can say that the new process is absolutely different than the current process. In such case, one does not even need to do statistical validation. So, one can see that case 1 implies rejecting the alternate hypothesis; case 2 rejects the null hypothesis, and case 3 rejects the null without even a test. Of course, in order to create evidence of testing for regulatory requirements, one may still conduct testing of the hypothesis.

When testing the hypothesis, mistakes can be made. Sometimes, we may conclude that the new treatment is better than the current process when in reality there is no difference; then a Type I mistake is made. The risk associated with Type I error is called *alpha* (α) *risk*. This is the risk associated with rejecting the null hypothesis. When we conclude that there is no improvement, in reality there is some improvement; in other words, we missed the improvement, and we commit Type II error. The risk associated with Type II error is called *beta* (β) *risk*. Typical risk values associated with Type I and II errors are 5 percent and 10 percent, respectively. For patient safety related tests, the α-risk could be set at 1 percent or much less. For typical fever-type tests, one can set the α-risk similar to industrial risks at 5 percent. For healthcare professionals who used statistical software programs to run hypothesis tests, the value of p represents the α-risk.

Conducting Testing of Hypothesis

To validate a claim or a new treatment, follow these steps:

1. Make a statement about the expected effect of the new treatment or trial (H_a).
2. With remaining options, make a statement of no change (H_0).
3. Stating the alternate hypothesis could imply type of test. If less is better (<), more is better (>) or dissimilar or different is better ($\uparrow$), we establish the type of test. Based on the sign of inequality, the test is set to be left tail, right tail, or two-tail test.

$$H_0: \mu \leq 5 \qquad H_a: \mu > 5 => \text{Right Tail Test}$$

$$H_0: \mu \geq 5 \qquad H_a: \mu < 5 => \text{Left Tail Test}$$

$$H_0: \mu = 5 \qquad H_a: \mu \uparrow 5 => \text{Two Tail Test}$$

4. Establish the risk associated with the test which is 5 percent or less. In case of having a sign of equality, the risk is divided on both sides, thus have 2.5 percent risk on each side.
5. Collect data from trials or experiments.
6. Compute test statistics to evaluate the outcome.
7. Evaluate significance by comparing the test statistic with theoretical value.
8. Draw a conclusion about rejecting the null or the alternate hypotheses.

Calculating Test Statistic

To determine whether the new treatment is better than the current treatment, one is looking for the average performance, and the consistency of the treatment. Therefore, tests are designed for various situations. Table 7.1 summarizes types of test, their applicability, and evaluation criteria.

TABLE 7.1   Parametric Tests

Type	Test Statistic	DF	Application
Z	$(\bar{X} - \mu)/ (\varphi_x/\sqrt{n})$	NA	Single sample mean. Population standard deviation is known. Sample size > 30.
t- test	$t = (\bar{X} - \mu)/ (S/\sqrt{n})$	$n - 1$	Single sample mean. Population standard deviation is unknown. Sample size 30.
2 Mean Equal Variance t- test	$t = (\bar{X}_1 - \bar{X}_2)/ (S_p/\sqrt{1/n_1 + 1/n_2})$	$n_1 + n_2 - 2$	2 sample means. Variances are unknown, but considered equal. S_p must be calculated.
2 Mean Unequal Variance t- test	$t = (\bar{X}_1 - \bar{X}_2)/ (\sqrt{S_1^2/n_1 + S_2^2/n_2})$	$n_1 + n_2 - 2$	2 sample means. Variances are unknown, but considered unequal.
Paired t test	$t = d/ (S_d/\sqrt{n})$	$n - 1$	2 sample means. Data is taken in pairs. A different d is calculated for each pair.
$\chi 2$ where φ^2 is known	$\chi 2 = (n - 1)S^2/\sigma^2$	$(n - 1)$	Tests sample variance against known variance.
$\chi 2$	$\chi 2 = \sigma (O - E)^2/E$	$(r - 1)(c - 1)$	Compares observed and expected frequencies of test outcomes.
F	$F = S_1^2 /S_2^2$ S_1^2 – Larger Variance S_2^2 – Smaller Variance	$n_1 - 1$ $n_2 - 1$ 	 Tests if two sample variances are equal.

       Table 7.2 shows that there are parametric tests for variable data and nonparametric tests for attribute data. The details of each test becomes a statistician's job; however, the available statistical software, such as Minitab, SPSS, JMP, Statgraphics SAS, and many more, are available to quickly analyze the data and draw conclusions. However, in using the software, conceptual understanding of the testing of a hypothesis is important.

TABLE 7.2   Nonparametric Tests

Test Name	Data Type	Test	Application
Kruskal-Wallis Test	Measurement or Count	$\chi 2$	Data is ranked or converted to ranks for a 1-way ANOVA.
Contingency Coefficient	Count Data	$\chi 2$	A measure of association between two classifications.
Mann-Whitney U Test	Ranked Data	Tables	Determines if two independent groups are from the same population. An alternative if t-test assumptions cannot be met.
Wilcoxon-Mann Whitney Rank Sum Test	Ranked Data	Tables	Same as above. Slightly simpler to use. An alternative if Z and t- test assumptions are not met.

Test Name	Data Type	Test	Application
Mood's Median Test	Sample Medians	$\chi 2$	Determines equality of sample medians by scoring sample medians relative to population median.
Kendall Coefficient of Concordance	Ranked Data	$\chi 2$	Determines degree of association among classifications based on ranked scores.
Spearman Rank Correlation Coefficient	Ranked Data	$r_s = 1 - 6\sigma d^2/(N^3 - N)$	A measure of association (r_s) that requires both variables be measured in at least an ordinal scale.
Kendall Rank Correlation Coefficient	Ranked Data	$\chi 2 = 12s/(KN(N+1))$	Same as Spearman except calculates, r, which also permits determining partial correlation coefficient.

Statistical tests evaluate difference in process means or ratio of inconsistencies (variance) of two treatments. Accordingly, the test statistic for mean and inconsistency are computed as follows:

Test statistic for means = (estimator − equal value in null hypothesis)/
Standard deviation of estimator

(New Process Mean − Current Process Mean)/Standard error of estimate of means

Test statistic for variance = Larger Variance/Smaller Variance

Once we calculate the test statistic, we determine what the expected or theoretical test statistic is. To answer this question, we look up the table, select a test, and determine theoretical test statistic, which is described either in terms of a probability, a coefficient, or a measure of standard deviation. Then we compare the test statistic and theoretical value. If the test statistic exceeds the theoretical value, we conclude that the change is significant, or the new treatment is significantly better; thus, we reject the null hypothesis. At this point, a business decision can be made about whether to conduct more trials and accept the findings for developing new treatments.

Figure 7.2 shows regions of significance.

The region in between two standard deviations represents about 95 percent and is called *common region*. The region on the tail end that represents the probabilities associated with the α-risk is called *critical region* or the *region of significance*. When we test a hypothesis or run an experiment, we evaluate whether the new process mean falls in the region of significance. Normally, when we evaluate a difference, we simply determine based on the extent of difference, and based on our feeling we draw a conclusion about whether or not the difference is enough. In case of determining statistical significance, we always evaluate difference with respect to the variation in the process. Thus, if the difference between means of current and the new treatment exceeds two standard deviations, it is considered significant. This significance is more accurately calculated using the statistical tests from Table 7.1 and Table 7.2.

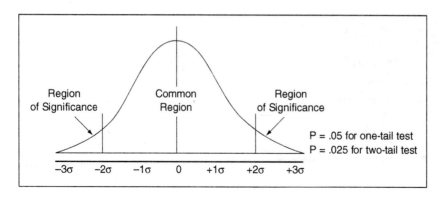

FIGURE 7.2 Regions of significance

Figure 7.2 depicts probability regions for testing of hypothesis. The common region accounts for probability associated with variation by random or uncontrolled causes, and the region of significance is a complement of the common region—for example, the area under the tail ends beyond two standard deviations. In the healthcare industry, nonclinical or routine operations have associated risk similar to industrial applications; thus, the critical area can be designated beyond two standard deviations as shown in Figure 7.3. However, when the applications are critical or with severe effects of a treatment, the region of significance can start beyond three standard deviations, as shown in Figure 7.4. In other words, one must see an improvement using the new treatment by at least two standard deviations for a routine process, and an improvement of three standard deviations for a critical process. For extremely life-threatening applications, one must consider actual probabilities using statistical software along with some help from an expert.

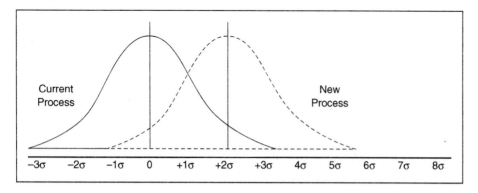

FIGURE 7.3 Testing of Means

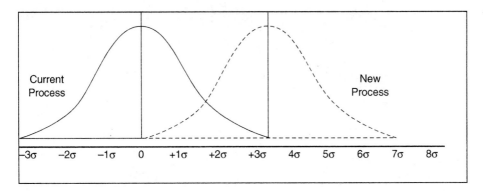

FIGURE 7.4 Testing of Means

Similar to validating improvement in means, sometimes processes or treatments are improved through optimization to improve their consistency and confidence in the treatments. In such cases, the objective is not to improve the mean performance as much as it is to reduce the standard deviation. For evaluating improvement in variances, there are tests such as *F-test* or $\chi 2$ *test*. The method testing for improved consistency is similar to the hypothesis testing, except a different test is used. Figure 7.5 shows two processes where the current process has larger variance than the new process. One can see that the new process is more predictable as its width is tighter than the current process. Similarly, Figure 7.6 shows where the new process ends up having larger variance.

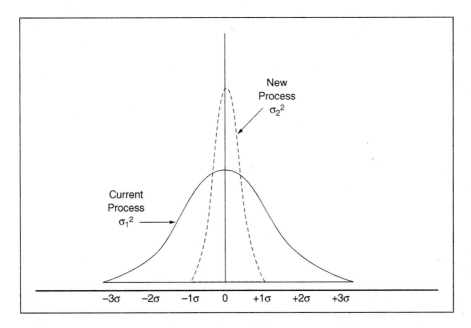

FIGURE 7.5 Testing of Variance

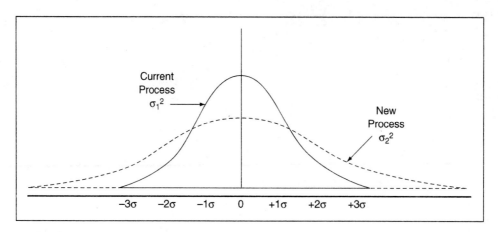

FIGURE 7.6 Testing of Variance

F-Test

The standard procedure to compare the variances is the F-test. To perform an F-test, we make the following hypothesis:

Null Hypothesis:	H_0:	$\sigma^2_m = \sigma^2_p$
Alternate Hypothesis:	H_a:	$\sigma^2_m \neq \sigma^2_p$

where

- σ^2_m is variance of the samples obtained from the modified process conditions, and
- σ^2_p is variance of the samples obtained from the present process conditions.

The test statistic that is used to compare the variances is called *F-test statistic* and is defined as follows:

$$\text{F-test Statistic} = \frac{S_1^2}{S_2^2}$$

where

- S_1^2 is the larger variance and
- S_2^2 is the smaller variance

Calculated F-test statistic is compared with the $F_{critical}$ value from the F-Table or through software. The recommended approach is to use statistical software to evaluate two variances.

Evaluating Multiple Treatments Using ANOVA

Similar to the testing of hypothesis, Analysis of Variance or ANOVA test, developed by Sir Ronald Fisher in 1920s, allows evaluation of multiple treatments. Again, the process of using ANOVA for evaluating multiple treatments is similar to the testing of the hypothesis. Here the objective of evaluation is whether the treatments are different or not different. In ANOVA, we are testing whether the difference among means of multiple treatments is more than the variation within the treatment itself. In the case of two treatments, we evaluate difference with respect to the standard deviation. In the case of ANOVA, we evaluate variance among means with respect to the variance within the treatment using F-test. Thus, we analyze variance to evaluate difference among multiple means.

Hypotheses for ANOVA can be written as follows:

$H_0: \mu_1 = \mu_2 = \mu_3 = \ldots = \mu_k$

$H_a: \mu_1 \neq \mu_2 \neq \mu_3 \neq \ldots \neq \mu_k$ (at least one of the μ's is different)

ANOVA can be used for testing multiple drugs for a same disease, multiple brands for the same medicine, or multiple suppliers of various items.

In performing the ANOVA, we calculate sum of squares (or variance). Total sum of squares (TSS) can be partitioned into two components: sum of squares between treatments (SSB), and sum of squares within treatments (SSW)[1]:

TSS = SSB + SSW

The ANOVA test depends on the following three parameters:

- Size of the difference between group means
  - Sample size in each group. Generally speaking, larger samples will tend to give more reliable data.
  - The variance of the dependent variable.

Conditions for Applicability of ANOVA methods include the following:

- We must ensure that observations in each group are randomly taken.
- The population variances are equal.
- The treatments must be independent of each other.
- The observations within each treatment must be independent of each other.
- The population within each treatment must be (approximately) normally distributed with roughly equal standard deviations.

When conducting ANOVA analysis, you should follow these steps:

1. Use appropriate software for performing the calculation.
2. Enter data appropriately and select the appropriate data set.
3. Perform calculation for the F-value.
4. Compare the F-value with critical F-value.

The F-ratio is calculated as follows:

$$F_{test} = \text{(Observed variation of the group averages)} / \text{(within the group variation)}$$

Thus, the calculated F-value is compared with the theoretical value of F in order for variances to be significantly different. There are F-tables published in statistical books, or available on the Internet. However, it is recommended that we use statistical software for performing ANOVA for saving practitioners a lot of time. When the calculated F-value exceeds the theoretical value, the difference among the means is considered significant, and the null hypothesis is rejected. Otherwise, variance among treatment means is considered statistically insignificant, and we conclude that all means are roughly equal, and thus reject the alternate hypothesis.

Comparative Experiments: Present Versus Modified

Once we understand how to evaluate a hypothesis and draw conclusions based on the statistical evidence, we can use it for evaluating the outcome of a clinical trial, testing of new drugs, or a new treatment. To conduct a comparative experiment, you should run a two-sample experiment. The one sample is a control group representing the present process, and the other sample is an experimental group representing the modified process. We collect new data for the control group as well as the experimental group. The sample size depends upon several factors such as cost, availability, and feasibility. Depending upon the sample size, one can choose to conduct t-tests for smaller samples (less than 30), or a Z-test for larger samples (equal or greater than 30).

The comparative t-test statistic is calculated as follows:

$$t = \frac{\overline{X}m - \overline{X}p}{S_{pl}\sqrt{(1/n_m + 1/n_p)}}$$

where

- $\overline{X}m$ is the mean of the modified process;
- $\overline{X}p$ is the mean of the present process;
- S_{pl} is the pooled standard deviation calculated as

$$S_{pl} = \sqrt{S_{pl}^2} \text{ and}$$

$$S_{pl}^2 = \frac{(n_m - 1) S_m^2 + n_p - 1) S_p^2}{n_m + n_p - 2}$$

where

- S_m is the standard deviation of the samples from the modified process, and
- S_p is the standard deviation of the samples from the present process.

Nonparametric Output

There may be a situation in which we have very few samples to run a trial and the nature of distribution is unknown. Under these circumstances, we assume that the population of the two sets (present and modified conditions) of samples shall have the similar probability distribution.

In such experiments, we rank their output and evaluate for overlapping among the data using Tukey's No Overlap End Count technique. The two possible outcomes are either no overlap or some overlapping. When there is no overlap, then the modified process is better than the present process significantly. However, when there is an overlap, decision of significance is made based on specified number of no overlapping end counts as shown in Table 7.3. The established alpha risk (.05, 0.01 to 0.001) is chosen based on the seriousness of the implications of the incorrect decision.

TABLE 7.3 No Overlap End Counts

Alpha Risk	End Count >=
0.05	6
0.01	9
0.001	12

Let us say that one hospital decides to conduct a monthly review of its performance with the doctors and staff and decides to evaluate its effect on the reduction of re-admission rate. We record observations for six months with and without monthly reviews. The data has been tabulated in Table 7.4. Now this data is sorted in the order from most desirable to least desirable condition. Figure 7.7 shows the sorted data with the associated process condition (no monthly reviews and monthly reviews). We find a total nonoverlapping end count of 7 (4 in most desirable and 3 in least desirable region), which exceeds that specified in the Table 7.3. Hence, we conclude with 95 percent confidence that the monthly review of performance has made an improvement.

TABLE 7.4   Mean Re-admission Rates for Six Months

Re-admission rate with no monthly reviews 'P'	Re-admission rate with monthly reviews 'M'
30	28
31	26
29	25
27	22
32	24
28	29

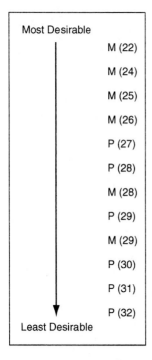

FIGURE 7.7   Ranking of re-admission

Full Factorials Experiments

Moving beyond the Analyze phase into the Improve phase implies further reduction of variables, or evaluation of alternate solutions. To evaluate the effect of alternate solutions and the effects of its variables can be a complicated process that requires planned experimentation, called *Design of Experiments* (DOE). DOE is a statistical method introduced by R. A. Fisher in England in the 1920s to study the effect of multiple variables simultaneously. In his early applications, Fisher wanted to find out how much rain, water, fertilizer, sunshine, and so on are needed to produce the best crop. Similarly, we may find out the certain dose of certain medicine at a specific frequency for an "x" number of days, and so on. Pharmaceutical companies, when developing new medicines, conduct such experiments for best results in drug manufacturing, as well as in the clinical trials.

In the absence of such a technique, we would be conducting experiments by changing one "thing" at a time, which would take forever to complete an evaluation of the new treatment. The DOE methods allow us to accelerate evaluation of a treatment or drug with many components concurrently. There are several methods to conduct the design of experiments such as full factorials, fractional factorials, Taguchi methods, or special-purpose DOE methods. Fractional and Taguchi methods, which are subsets of full factorials, are used when the list of components is very long, and we want to screen out some at the beginning. Once the number of components of a treatment is reduced to two to three components, the full factorial method can be implemented. *Full factorial* implies all combinations of the specified components of a treatment, or variables are tried in order to draw a conclusion. If we have reduced the number of variables down to a smaller number, and the cost of experimentation is not very high, this is an excellent way to quickly come up with the final recipe with a lot of confidence. With the fractional factorial experiments, we sacrifice some confidence for economy.

To run a full factorial experiment, the number of trials is determined by the $\text{Level}^{\text{Variables}}$, where the level is the number of values of the variables one wants to try. Normally, number of levels is kept at two for containing the number of trials. The two levels represent "present" and "modified" values of variables.

To conduct a full factorial experiment, follow these steps:

1. **Define the experiment objective**. The objective is to determine the length of stay in the hospital based upon the patient's age to improve patient satisfaction. Thus, the patient satisfaction is our response variable, and length of stay and age are our two independent variables.

2. **Identify the key variables and their levels**. The two variables are Stay and Age, which could be run at two levels. Stay will be tried at 3 and 5 days, and Age will be 50 years for patients between 30–50 years of age, and 70 years for patients between 50–70 years of age.

3. **Design the experiment**. To determine various combinations, a matrix is draw as shown in Figure 7.8. This shows four combinations ($\text{Level}^{\text{Variables}} = 2^2$). To determine the sample size for $\alpha = 5$ percent, $\beta = 10$ percent, use (n is = $(8\varphi/\Delta)^2$) relationship, where φ is the standard deviation of the process and Δ is the required change to declare the new process better than the current one. Let the improvement be specified at $\Delta = 2\varphi$; thus, the sample size for evaluation will be equal to 16. Because we are able to combine two cells per treatment, the sample size per cell could be 16/2 = 8. In most cases, the samples sizes are much larger in the healthcare industry.

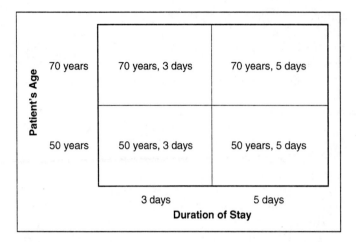

FIGURE 7.8 Experiment Design (Minitab® Statistical Software)

While running these various trials, we randomize the order of trials. In other words, we pick any combination randomly and gather data. Then, another combination, we gather data, and so on. By randomizing we are minimizing effect of other unplanned variables such as a nurse's personality, staff's behavior, food quality, room condition, and so on. For example, Table 7.5 represents our experiment.

TABLE 7.5 Randomized Order of Trials

Trial #	Age	Stay	Patient Satisfaction	Sequence of Experiment
1	50	3	90	3
2	50	5	50	1
3	70	3	60	2
4	70	5	90	4

4. **Data Analysis—Interactions**. The experiment data is analyzed for determining the effects of Stay and Age variables. Effects for each variable are calculated as follows:

Main Effect of Age = Average (Trial 3, Trial 4) – Average (Trial 1, Trial 2)

Main Effect of Stay = Average (Trial 2, Trial 4) – Average (Trial 1, Trial 3)

Interaction Effects= Average (Trial 1, Trial 4) – Average (Trial 2, Trial 3)

Figures 7.9 and 7.10 display main and interaction effects of Age and Stay, respectively. One can see that according to this experiment, the Age and Stay have little positive and negative correlation with patient satisfaction, respectively. However, they have a strong interaction with each other. Note that older patients are more satisfied with the longer duration, but younger patients feel otherwise. Based on this analysis, one may establish two separate policies for two age groups in order to maximize patient satisfaction, instead of having one Stay policy for all age groups. The actions for implementation of the improvement arising out of the experiment can be captured in the Improvement Action Plan as illustrated in the sample forms at the end of this chapter.

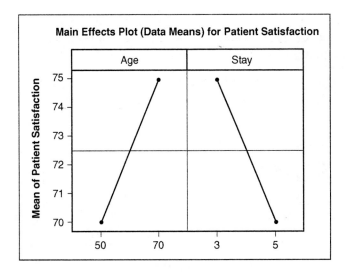

FIGURE 7.9 Main effects of Age and Stay (Minitab® Statistical Software)

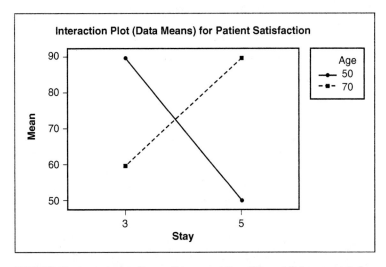

FIGURE 7.10 Interaction effects of Age and Stay (Minitab® Statistical Software)

A benefit of using statistical software is reducing the time to analyze the experiment and spending more time to develop a solution.

CONTROL PHASE

One of the main challenges in implementing Six Sigma is to realize benefits by maintaining the improved process. Many times, we find a solution; however, we have difficulty implementing the change. The impulse to keep moving on to the next project without seeing successful implementation and controls in operations must be checked. Closing a project using the Control phase helps achieve return on investment in the project and provides an opportunity to celebrate. Control Chart is the commonly used statistical tool in the Control phase, besides ensuring the document changes, communication, recognition, and reward.

Control Charts

Walter Shewhart of AT&T developed control charts in 1929 while studying variation in manufacturing. Shewhart identified variation as the enemy of quality. He recognized the two types of variation such as random and assignable, or natural and nonnatural. In order to maintain the natural behavior of the process, he identified the potential situation of disruptions based on patterns in the process and developed charts to display such occurrences. Thus, the *control chart* is a tool that identifies situation when a process loses its statistical control or its natural behavior.

The control chart compares variation in a process with properly established control limits, based on the inherent variation in the process. If the variation is excessive or unexpected based upon the laws of probability, it raises a flag for investigation and necessitates remedial actions. The remedial actions may include shutting down the process, or quarantining, sorting, or inspecting the input or output, such as supplies. The intent of remedial actions is to restore natural or statistical behavior of the process or an activity. Every process does not require control charts. Control charts must be used when it makes economic sense to use them.

Normal Distribution and Control Charts

A control chart compares the current performance with the probability of the outcome based on normal distribution. In other words, it is expected that about two-thirds of the time, the output must fall within one standard deviation around the target performance; approximately 95 percent of the output should fall within two standard deviations around the target, and almost 100 percent should fall within three standard deviations around the target performance. In other words, the intent of control chart is to preserve the bell-shaped distribution of the process output.

To use control charts, data is collected from samples at a predetermined frequency, plotted on a chart, and evaluated for statistical behavior. To make evaluation of the sample data, a set of rules has been developed. By applying the rules, one determines whether the statistical behavior of a process continues or is disrupted. If a process is not in statistical control, it is called out of control condition, and an investigation is initiated to understand sources of assignable variation.

Types of Control Charts

Depending upon the type of data, attribute or variable, control charts are classified into two categories: *attribute control charts* and *variable control charts*. Table 7.6 and Table 7.7 show commonly used control charts.

TABLE 7.6   Attribute Control Charts

Type of Chart	Description
u chart	Defects (errors) per unit in a subgroup
np chart	Number of defective units in a sample for go and no-go data
p chart	Percent or proportion defective in a subgroup
c chart	Number of defects in a subgroup

TABLE 7.7   Variable Control Charts

Type of Chart	Description
X bar-R chart	Plot of mean and range of smaller subgroup size (less than 5)
X bar-s chart	Plot of the mean and standard deviation of subgroup size (more than 5)
X-R chart	Plot of mean and range of individual measurements

All control charts are based on the same principle of statistical variation. Thus, they all have control limits using similar formula. It is recommended that statistical software be used for constructing control charts and highlighting out-of-control conditions automatically without remembering the rules.

Implementing a control chart requires consideration of sample size, sampling frequency, typical value, standard deviation, ownership, and response to out-of-control conditions. The weakest link in successful implementation of control charts is responding to the out-of-control conditions appropriately. The response may include shutting down the process, which operations personnel normally do not like. Another challenge is to determine where and when to implement control charts. One should select preferably the input process conditions to ensure good output performance. Control charts can be applied to processes that are critical, must be maintained at acceptable performance, and are more prone to variation, thus likely to break down. Besides, the processes that have been well understood for causation and are stabilized are good candidates to leave alone with the help of control charts.

Constructing Control Charts

When constructing a control chart, remember the following:

- Select a process parameter at its input, in-process, or output.
- Select a suitable control chart.

- Develop the check sheet to collect data.
- Collect samples and record the data.
- Enter data in the computer using statistical software; it will do the necessary computations.
- Display mean and range charts, and evaluate for out-of-control conditions.
- Review and determine necessary actions to adjust the process.

Interpreting Control Charts

Interpreting control charts correctly is necessary for adjusting the process effectively. There are eight rules for interpreting control charts after plotting a data point, ensuring normality of the process. The rules for out of control conditions are listed here:

- Any point is beyond control limits.
- Two out of three points in a row beyond two sigma.
- Four out of five points in a row beyond one sigma.
- Fifteen points in a row within one sigma.
- Eight points in a row on both sides of the centerline within two sigma.
- Nine points in a row on one side of centerline.
- Six points in a row increasing or decreasing.
- Fourteen points in a row alternating up and down.

One can see that these rules are designed to ensure randomness of the data and thus a bell-shaped distribution. The out-of-control incidence must be investigated to determine the cause, so that appropriate action can be taken. If a point is beyond the three sigma control limits, it could be due to data entry error, measurement system error, or sudden change in the process performance. The control charts rule is looking into sources of nonrandomness that may include recognizing trends, shifts, patterns, and distribution. Thus, if there is a shift, a process needs to be adjusted; if there is a trend, some component wear-out may be the cause; if there is a pattern, the operator may be the cause or some breakdown in the system; and if the distribution is disrupted, some unintentional change might have occurred normally in the inputs to the process.

Control charts have been the most misused tool in the industry due to a lack of willingness to adjust the process for ensuring continuing performance. For sake of short-term production, the long-term productivity is sacrificed. Such short-sightedness can be avoided through proper understanding of the concepts and correct interpretation of the rules.

Figure 7.11 shows an example control chart for a patient's body temperature.

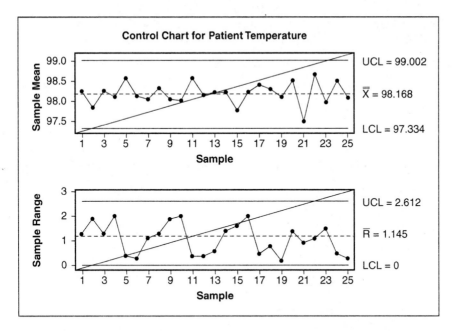

FIGURE 7.11 An example of a control chart for a patient's body temperature (Minitab® Statistical Software)

Documentation

In order to maintain statistical control of the new and improved process, one must ensure consistency in practice. The consistency is achieved through effective documentation, which identifies purpose, needs, critical check points, target conditions, and handling of nonconformities. Documentation of practices allows us to minimize opportunities for errors through reviews, and instills a sense of structure for compliance and consistency. A well-documented process highlights the "right" things to do for effectiveness and requires us to do our activities efficiently.

In order to document our practices effectively for driving virtual perfection in healthcare, we must understand the 4P model of process management.[2] The basic premise of ISO 9001-like management systems has been to promote process thinking. The combination of Six Sigma and the management systems need to pay attention to quality inputs and preparation, to consistency of critical activities, performance targets, and ability to detect inconsistencies for continual improvement. Figure 7.12 shows the 4P model that enhances the commonly known PDCA (Plan, Do, Check, Act) model of process management:

- *Prepare* represents ensuring good input to activities according to Ishikawa's 4M's (material, machines, methods and manpower or people).

- *Perform* implies the process is well understood, and its activities are well defined for error-free and streamlined execution.

- *Perfect*, normally the misunderstood with acceptability, relates to the target performance to be achieved. If an activity is not on target, it must be changed.

- *Progress* allows us to strive toward the ideal performance by reducing inconsistency in the execution.

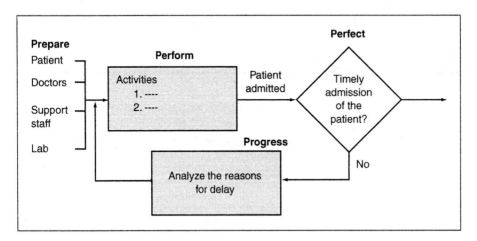

FIGURE 7.12   An example of process thinking for ER

Table 7.8 shows examples of critical parameters to control the process.

TABLE 7.8   Examples of Critical Process Parameters for Control of ER Processes

Sl. Number	Input	In-Process	Output
1	Inappropriate use of ER	Change of shift	Bed dirty
2	Transportation	X-ray down	Delayed discharges
3	Too busy	Change in patient condition	Patient refuses assigned bed
4	Nonavailability of doctor	Registered nurse not available	No patient service

Training

Continual emphasis on learning better practices and training for improvement tends to provide the best return on investment. When a new drug or treatment is to be introduced in the marketplace, we must plan to learn its impact through proper training and education. Training could be achieved through self-learning, in the classroom, or using computer media. Training topics may involve caring for patients, caring for customers, improving listening skills and interpersonal skills, improvement tools and techniques, or even new research in the healthcare field.

A good training program can benefit an organization in many ways, for example:

- Better understanding of the commitment to excellence, not just the throughput
- Better knowledge of the process and expected performance
- Continual cost reduction through simplification and consistency
- Knowledge to handle unusual situations
- How to get help when needed
- Reduced resistance to changes

Leadership training is equally important as much as the training of staff or physicians. Leadership is a learned trait, and leadership skills can be improved through continuing training. Leadership training can be in communicating with employees and stakeholders, in new technology and treatments, new business models or thoughts, reengineering, Six Sigma, teamwork, time management, goal setting, performance review, recognition, and leading through personal commitment. Of course, some training in golf would not hurt, because an improvement in the game improves the personal satisfaction.

Communication

The need for open communication between leadership and employees cannot be overstated. Employees need to receive direction from their leader, for a pat on the back, and just for interaction. Too many organizations exist where the leadership avoids talking to their employees. Open communication policy through closed doors does not work. We must be really interested in listening to employees for their ideas. Employees normally deliver what is asked of them. If they have not delivered the expected outcome, it is likely that communication broke down between the leadership and employees. The employees need to hear the expectations of the leadership, and the leadership needs to build credibility with the employees by working toward common goals. Lack of communication is usually an indication of other problems, quality issues being just one of them.

Employee participation can be increased through formal and informal communication for achieving virtual perfection using Six Sigma. Establishing clear objectives and rewards for achieving excellence can lead to extraordinary performance. Working communication builds trust and demonstrates leadership's respect for and their dependence on employees, which is very rewarding to employees and hence to the organization.

Business Review

The most significant part of sustaining the Six Sigma initiative is conducting periodic business reviews of activities, results, and celebration. If there are not enough celebrations for success going on, most likely business objectives are being missed. The Six Sigma initiative can be reviewed for progress and its impact on the performance along with the operations and financial reviews. The review must follow a standard process ensuring consistency of expectations, participation, and adequacy of the review process. Results of the review must be shared with all employees at the earliest possible time. In absence of active participation of the executives, most likely Six Sigma will be de-prioritized in the interest of fighting fires in the short term. The review leads to challenging the status quo, recognizes successes, and generates action items to drive progress.

Having implemented Six Sigma successfully, the executive management must become the best spokesperson for publicizing successes. It is critical that leadership makes the successes visible inside as well as outside the company. Participation in internal and external forums of sharing success would breed more success. Therefore, companies can use newsletters, websites, conferences, articles, or forums for publicizing their successes, and learning from peers' experience.

ENDNOTES

1. Gupta, Praveen (2004), *The Six Sigma Performance Handbook: A Statistical Guide to Optimized Results*, McGraw Hill, NY.

2. Gupta, Praveen (2005), *From PDCA to PPPP*, Quality Digest, http://accelper.com/pdfs/From%20PDCA%20to%20PPPP.pdf.

SAMPLE HEALTHCARE EXCELLENCE PROJECT FORMS: SOLVING THE PROBLEM

PROJECT FORM: Solving the Problem
Improve

Project Title:	Project Leader:
Team Members:	Project Start Date:

Project Analysis (*based upon experience and expertise*)
Cost (C)_____   Time (T)_____   Net Annual Savings (S)_____   PPI ____

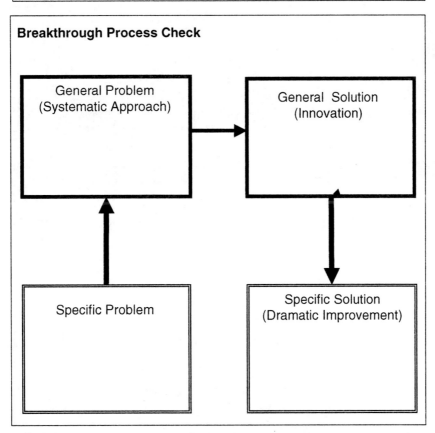

Breakthrough Process Check

General Problem (Systematic Approach)

General Solution (Innovation)

Specific Problem

Specific Solution (Dramatic Improvement)

Solving the Problem
Improve

Design of Experiment - Full Factorial:

Factors	Level 1 (Current)	Level 2 (New)
F1.		
F2.		

Expected Response:

R e s p o n s e | Factor 1

R e s p o n s e | Factor 2

Experiment Design:

Level 2 | $F1_2, F2_1$ | $F1_2, F2_2$

Factor 1

Level 1 | $F1_1, F2_1$ | $F1_1, F2_2$

Level 1   Level 2
Factor 2

Solving the Problem

Improve

Experiment Results and Analysis:

S.N.	Factor 1	Factor 2	Response	Observations
1	$F1_1$	$F2_1$		
2	$F1_2$	$F2_1$		
3	$F1_1$	$F2_2$		
4	$F1_2$	$F2_2$		

Response Plots- Main Effects

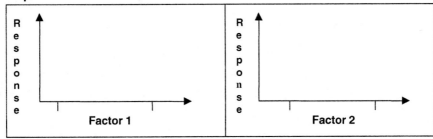

Response — Factor 1

Response — Factor 2

Response Plots – Interaction

Response — Factor 1

Experimental Observations:

- .
- .
- .
- .

Percent Improvement Realized:

New DPU _____

New DPMO _____

New Sigma Level _____

Solving the Problem

Improve

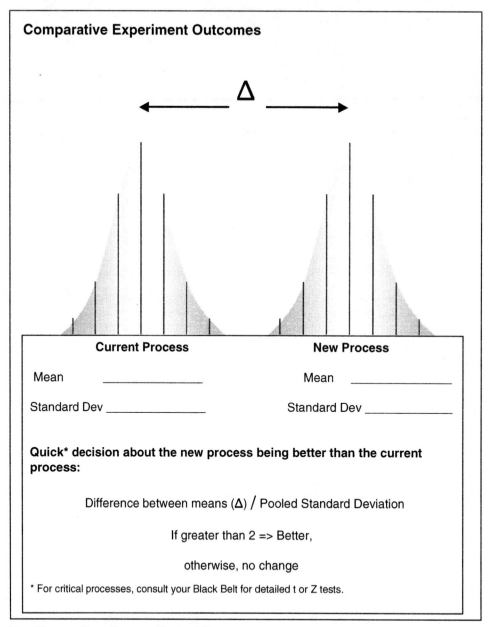

Comparative Experiment Outcomes

Δ

Current Process	New Process
Mean _____	Mean _____
Standard Dev _____	Standard Dev _____

Quick* decision about the new process being better than the current process:

Difference between means (Δ) / Pooled Standard Deviation

If greater than 2 => Better,

otherwise, no change

* For critical processes, consult your Black Belt for detailed t or Z tests.

Solving the Problem

Improve

Anticipatory Analysis for Identifying Potential Problems of New Process

Process	Potential Failure Mode	Potential Effects of Failure Mode	S e v.	Potential Causes of Failure Mode	O c c.	Current Process Controls	D e t.	R P N

A.I.#	Improvement Action Item	Responsibility	Committed Date of Completion
1			
2			
3			
4			
5			

<u>Solving the Problem</u>

Control

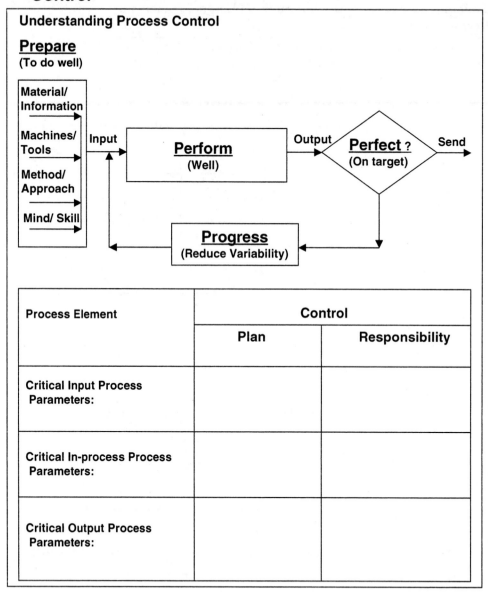

Understanding Process Control

<u>Prepare</u>
(To do well)

Process Element	Control	
	Plan	**Responsibility**
Critical Input Process Parameters:		
Critical In-process Process Parameters:		
Critical Output Process Parameters:		

<u>Solving the Problem</u>

Control

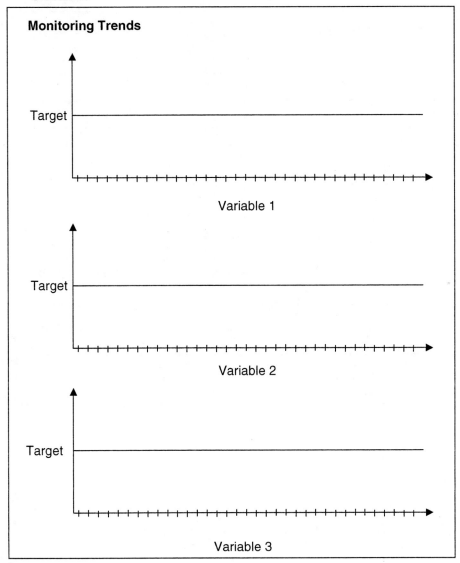

Monitoring Trends

Target — Variable 1

Target — Variable 2

Target — Variable 3

Solving the Problem

Control

Commitment to Six Sigma Initiative

Commitment	Results Achieved	Comments

Corrective Actions for Six Sigma Initiative

Concern with Six Sigma	Root Cause	Corrective Action

Management Review Actions

PART III

BENEFITING FROM SIX SIGMA

CASE STUDY INTRODUCTION AND PROFILES

SECTION

Commonwealth Health Corporation, Bowling Green, KY
Virtua Health, Marlton, NJ
Valley Baptist Health System, Harlingen, TX
North Shore-Long Island Jewish (LIJ) Health System, NY
Thibodaux Regional Medical Center, Thibodaux, LA
NewYork-Presbyterian Hospital, New York, NY
Decatur Memorial Hospital, Decatur, IL
The Nebraska Medical Center, Omaha, NE

During the mid-1990s, the healthcare industry began searching for better process improvement models. Past re-engineering efforts and quality programs had failed to sufficiently address systemic inefficiencies or deliver sustainable results. Short-term cost-cutting measures may have presented a better financial picture temporarily, but the gains tended to unravel over time. Without a viable tool to expose and deal with actual root causes, one of the primary targets for slashing the budget became labor. Unfortunately, simply trimming the workforce wasn't the answer and did not produce the desired long-term effect. By the 1990s, programs like Total Quality Management (TQM) had begun to run their course—at least within the United States—and other approaches had evolved.

"Remember quality circles?" says one hospital Black Belt. "There was a reason we went in circles—we were always coming back to the same issues because they were never fully resolved. Six Sigma has allowed us to really zero in on the right things and make sure solutions stick."

Six Sigma offers distinct advantages over traditional quality initiatives:

- Focuses on customer requirements, instead of vague quality goals
- Targets defects and process variation instead of averages
- Provides a highly structured, data-driven framework for problem-solving
- Includes a robust Control phase and tools to maintain results

In a 1998 article "Is Health Care Ready for Six Sigma?" (The Milbank Quarterly, Vol. 76, No. 4, 1998), Dr. Mark Chassin noted serious challenges facing the industry and discussed the possibility of using Six Sigma to drive fundamental changes within the system. In the end, he noted that "…enough examples of improvement exist to conclude that we can do much better. We can learn a good deal from industries that are working toward the Six Sigma goal. Let's try it in health care and see how close we can get."

Since that article was first published, an impressive track record has steadily developed within the industry. Thousands of projects tackling a host of clinical and operational issues have been completed within healthcare—from small rural facilities to large multi-hospital systems.

Although not every issue requires the rigor of Six Sigma, it is applicable to healthcare because it is adaptable to a wide range of situations and settings—from lengthy wait times to process delays to prescription errors. There are countless opportunities for improvement across the continuum of care. Translating and scoping these opportunities into executable projects with measurable results can have a significant impact on the cost and quality of patient care. When used as part of a broader framework for change, Six Sigma can also have a positive effect on organizational culture. One key to its success—where other change initiatives may have fallen short—may be a higher level of rigor, detail, and follow-through.

Healthcare providers currently considering an improvement initiative that includes Six Sigma methodologies should have a distinct advantage over their predecessors. They will likely have a stronger foundation on which to build, thanks in large part to efforts by early adopters. Reviewing the experiences and lessons learned by healthcare's "Six Sigma pioneers" can offer guidance for the next generation of practitioners.

Many "early adopter" healthcare organizations are now self-sufficient with their own internal training programs and a strategically aligned project funnel. They have demonstrated that with the right planning, guidance, resources, and perseverance, a Six Sigma journey can be truly transformative. This is not to imply, however, that success will materialize overnight, or that the road ahead will be entirely smooth. As Kathy Gallo, Ph.D., RN, North Shore-LIJ Health System, said, "Six Sigma is not for the faint of heart." Challenges are to be expected. Those organizations that invest sufficient time and energy into front-end planning seem to encounter the least resistance as the program is rolled out. The importance of understanding the voice of the customer and gaining early "buy-in" from key stakeholder groups should not be overlooked.

Table 8.1 is not a complete listing of all hospitals and health systems using Six Sigma, but it does provide some idea of both the reach and the staying power of this methodology in healthcare provider organizations.

TABLE 8.1 Healthcare Organizations Using Six Sigma Strategies

Healthcare Provider	Location or Headquarters	Year Six Sigma Program Began
Commonwealth Health Corporation	Bowling Green, KY	1998
Froedtert Hospital	Milwaukee, WI	1999
Women and Infants Hospital	Providence, RI	2000
Mount Carmel Health System	Cleveland, OH	2000
Virtua Health	Marlton, NJ	2000
Charleston Area Medical Center	Charleston, WV	2000
University of Texas MD Anderson Cancer Center	Houston, TX	2000
University of Virginia Health System	Charlottesville, VA	2000
Good Samaritan Hospital	Los Angeles, CA	2001
Thibodaux Regional Medical Center	Thibodaux, LA	2001
Yale-New Haven Hospital	New Haven, CT	2001
Decatur Memorial Hospital	Decatur, IL	2001
Pullman Memorial Hospital	Pullman, WA	2001
North Shore-Long Island Jewish Health System	Lake Success, NY	2001
Good Samaritan Hospital	Dayton, OH	2001
Providence Health System	Alaska, California, Washington, Oregon	2002
Valley Baptist Health System	Harlingen, TX	2002
Nebraska Medical Center	Omaha, NE	2002
Heritage Valley Health System	Beaver, PA	2002
Mount Sinai Medical Center	New York, NY	2002
Queens Medical Center	Honolulu, HI	2002
North Memorial Hospital	Robbinsdale, MN	2002
NewYork-Presbyterian Hospital	New York, NY	2003
Sharp HealthCare	San Diego, CA	2003
University of Pittsburg Medical Center	Pittsburg, PA	2003
SSM Healthcare	St. Louis, MO	2003
Northwestern Memorial Hospital	Chicago, IL	2003
Parkland Health and Hospital System	Dallas, TX	2003
Trinity Health	Novi, MI	2003
Florida Hospital	Orlando, FL	2004
Memorial Hermann Health System	Houston, TX	2004
Rush North Shore Medical Center	Skokie, IL	2004
Sisters of Mercy Health System	St. Louis, MO	2004
St. John Health	Detroit, MI	2004
Bay Medical Center	Panama City, FL	2004
North Carolina Baptist Hospital	Winston-Salem, NC	2004
Tucson Medical Center	Tucson, AZ	2005
East Jefferson General Hospital	Metairie, LA	2005

(continued)

TABLE 8.1 Continued

Healthcare Provider	Location or Headquarters	Year Six Sigma Program Began
Doctor's Hospital of Augusta	Augusta, GA	2005
Deaconess Health System	Evansville, IN	2005
Waukesha Memorial Hospital	Waukesha, WI	2005
Memorial Hospital	South Bend, IN	2006

Within each organization, Six Sigma has been adapted to fit the existing culture, objectives, and readiness for change. It has been applied to address many common challenges in healthcare, including medical errors, technology workflow, market growth, resource utilization, length of stay, and patient flow or capacity issues. A wide variety of hospitals and health systems have used this methodology, often in combination with other tools, to help create a better patient experience, increase efficiency, and improve the operating margin.

In some cases, Six Sigma was initially employed to focus on a specific department or process, and in other cases it has been implemented on an enterprise-wide basis to create self-sufficiency and a common structure for problem-solving. Several profiles are offered in the following sections as examples of various deployment strategies in the healthcare provider sector.

COMMONWEALTH HEALTH CORPORATION, BOWLING GREEN, KY

Generally recognized as the first healthcare provider to implement Six Sigma on a system-wide basis, Commonwealth Health Corporation (CHC) is a 490-bed non-profit organization located in Bowling Green, Kentucky, with more than 2,500 employees.

In late 1997, John Desmarais, president and chief executive officer of CHC, attended a conference and heard Jack Welch speak about Six Sigma and culture change at General Electric. Inspired by the encounter and the results attributed to this rigorous approach, Desmarais soon began working with GE to adapt Six Sigma and related change management methods to his own healthcare organization.

Taking a phased approach to training and implementation, the CHC Six Sigma team focused its initial efforts on four organizational priorities: customer satisfaction, quality of care/service, timeliness/speed/convenience, and cost. Their approach consisted of four phases:

- **Phase One: Radiology**. In May 1998, the first wave of training began with 13 participants focused on issues in radiology. Projects from this phase led to shorter wait times for patients, faster turnaround times for radiology reports, a 25 percent increase in throughput, and a 21.5 percent decrease in cost per radiology procedure.
- **Phase Two: Management Training**. During the second phase, 74 managers participated in ten days of change management training, and cross-functional teams tackled

issues with patient registration, employee empowerment, communication flow, customer service, human resources, and the medication process. The teams acquired skills while addressing major organizational priorities.

- **Phase Three: Billing**. Training for the second Green Belt class began in November 1998, and consisted of 15 participants focusing on specific processes within the billing department. The CEO and senior management team received Green Belt training during this phase and shadowed the projects. This team identified key indicators for the billing process vision, created a process map, and defined the "critical to quality" elements. They analyzed variances and identified potential quality improvement targets. Results from this team's efforts included reduced billing cycle time, more efficient charging procedures, and less returned mail.

- **Phase Four: Training the Trainer**. Two employees were chosen to become Black Belts and eventually Six Sigma instructors and mentors. Eight other employees were trained as change agents. Gaining and transferring skills helped the team to become self-sufficient and pursue other improvement opportunities.

By the end of 2001, more than 2,000 employees had attended at least one full day of Six Sigma awareness training, during which they were introduced to basic concepts of the methodology. Initial projects generated annual savings of $276,188 in billing, decreased annual radiology expenses by $595,296, and reduced errors in the MR ordering process by 90 percent. Within 18 months, CHC had achieved higher efficiency, an improved patient experience, an elimination of more than $800,000 in costs, and perhaps most importantly, a reenergized culture.

Despite challenges and resource fluctuations along the way, the program at CHC has remained on track and evolved over time. As a pioneer in this effort, CHC shared some keys to success with Six Sigma:

- Provide ongoing support from senior management.
- Make sure this is not viewed as just a financial re-engineering effort, but as an evidence-based approach to operational and clinical improvement.
- Persistence is another key: Define your objectives and stick with them.
- Articulate the vision clearly and spell out the CTQs (Critical To Quality elements) to the organization. If you don't have four or five elements you're focused on, the results can become diluted.

"Six Sigma has become the capstone to the pyramid of quality we've built over the years," Desmarais noted in 2000. "It brings everything to a whole new level. The competitive edge the organization has gained through this process is incredible."

The team at CHC develops its own materials, conducts training sessions, and mentors Brown Belts through various levels of operational and clinical projects across the organization. Despite some unavoidable challenges along the way, CHC has seen many positive results.

Pockets of early resistance faded as the "belts" established a track record. The use of change management tools helped by involving those closest to the process and making critical decisions more quickly based on reliable data. To keep the momentum going, they held Green Belt fairs and featured Six Sigma news in the organization's monthly newsletter. Display boards in the hospital are used for posting project summaries and results. CHC's board of directors has remained involved and supportive. Six Sigma projects are highlighted at board meetings.

"Unlike Six Sigma, previous initiatives were not well-defined and provided no data-driven roadmap to follow," says Jean Cherry, executive vice president at CHC. "Having access to solid data and proven processes behind the mission has helped to increase the level of confidence throughout the organization."

CHC is continuing its performance improvement program and will be incorporating other tools such as Lean to eliminate waste or non-value added steps. Projects still flow into one of three dashboards measuring cost, customer satisfaction and timeliness, speed, and convenience.

The Six Sigma program remains active at CHC, but it is more integrated with other quality initiatives now, rather than treating it as a distinct function when the program was first launched. The teams report through the vice president of quality management, and CHC now has three Master Black Belts focused on a variety of clinical and financial projects. There are more than 120 trained Green Belts, along with "Brown Belts" who work on projects on a part-time basis.

CHC is still using the change management tools, and Black Belts continue to mentor and monitor projects. Six Sigma has been used within a Premier/CMS demonstration project focused on five clinical conditions. Coronary Artery Bypass Graft (CABG) compliance is now at 100 percent, and teams are working on improving the care of patients with pneumonia and heart failure, hip and knee replacement, and acute myocardial infarction (AMI). Additional projects have been completed in radiology, adjusting workflow to accommodate a new Picture Archive and Communication Systems (PACS) implementation, and introducing an electronic signature for radiologists.

CHC was one of more than 3,000 healthcare providers who became involved in a 2005 campaign led by the Institute for Healthcare Improvement to save 100,000 patient lives by avoiding unnecessary errors. Projects to support this campaign included reducing central line infections and hospital-acquired pneumonia, and implementing a rapid response team. To align with JCAHO recommendations, they have encouraged managers to use statistical tools such as control charts. One of the most noticeable and lasting benefits, however, has been a change in organizational culture. According to Jean Cherry, managers now make decisions based on a much deeper analysis of their operation.

VIRTUA HEALTH, MARLTON, NJ

Located in southern New Jersey, Virtua Health was formed in 1998 by the merger of two health systems, and now includes four hospitals, outpatient centers, long-term care facilities, home health, ambulatory care, and a fitness center. The system has roughly 8,000 employees and 2,000 physicians. Six years after launching a large-scale improvement initiative that included Six Sigma and change management, the system is now recognized as a high-performing organization and a model for others to follow.

In 2000, however, this healthcare provider was considered somewhat average by most benchmarks. Being average wasn't satisfactory to Richard Miller, president and CEO at Virtua Health, who felt the organization needed a new strategy to drive breakthrough improvements, create a culture of excellence, and support its "STAR" initiative (see Figure 8.1).

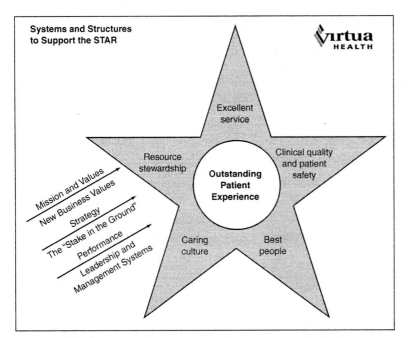

FIGURE 8.1 Systems and structures to support the STAR, Virtua Health

Miller initially had become interested in Six Sigma based on case studies from other industries, and ultimately decided to bring the methodology into his own health system. At Virtua, Six Sigma became part of a broad educational and process improvement initiative enabling staff to become self-sufficient in leading change initiatives. Since the program was launched, every Virtua manager has been trained to at least the Yellow Belt level in Six Sigma, and there are also 56 Green Belts, 20 Black Belts, 5 Master Black Belts, and numerous change agents.

"Change in healthcare is hard no matter what area you are focusing on," says Carol Mullin, RN, Master Black Belt in the Six Sigma program at Virtua. "It is especially difficult with respect to patient safety issues and projects, because you're talking about a huge cultural shift for everyone involved. You can't begin to come up with workable solutions until people first admit there's a problem. The cultural changes in healthcare are often more important than the technical solutions, because they require you to look at how people get their work done and how they were educated to do certain things."

With measurable results in key areas such as the surgical suite, emergency department, and cardiovascular services, this health system in New Jersey has shown it has what it takes to transform its culture, keep the momentum going, and make change stick.

Virtua continues to receive national recognition and awards for its efforts. In addition to improving patient services and transforming the culture, Six Sigma initiatives added roughly $15 million in new revenue to Virtua's bottom line within just five years. This figure does not include projected savings or financial benefit from numerous Work-Out sessions, which also contribute to a healthier operating margin.

"There used to be a mindset in healthcare that raising quality meant raising the costs," says Miller. "But we've learned that in many cases, higher quality also means lower costs."

Miller believes it's important for the CEO to play a very active and visible role in the initiative. "I attend every Six Sigma report-out on a monthly basis," he says, "and I'm involved in our best people review. We also brought in a new learning and leadership approach, and this has fundamentally changed our organization. It has really put accountability in the system, and that was key."

A few of the results so far include projects that

- Reduced the incidence of surgical site infections by improving the administration of antibiotics within one hour of incision from 90 percent to 97 percent

- Improved the accuracy of the home health coding process by the clinical staff, which led to overall agency HHRG (Home Health Resource Group) case weight mix increase to 1.33 for Virtua West Jersey Hospital and 1.36 for Virtua Memorial Hospital, resulting in an increase of $615,000 in Medicare revenues within just six months

- Increased insurance reimbursement for surgically implanted devices such as artificial joints, which saved the hospital more than $2 million

Multiple projects have been able to reach Six Sigma levels of excellence, and the team continues to seek further opportunities to improve. Rich Miller has remained steadfast in his commitment to the program and in continuing to explore new avenues for creating the optimal patient care experience. His visible support, along with recognition for results, has helped to maintain the momentum and enthusiasm among staff. Transparency and accountability—two elements crucial to transforming healthcare—are clearly apparent at Virtua. Employees feel empowered to seek workable solutions instead of becoming complacent or assigning blame. Dr. Mark Van Kooy, Master Black Belt and chief medical information officer at Virtua, puts it this way: "We're more forward-looking now than backward-looking. Everyone understands the concept of accountability; there is no excuse-making or finger-pointing anymore."

According to Van Kooy, Six Sigma is viewed at Virtua as a business tool rather than a quality tool. "Quality, however, is one of our most important businesses. Clinically, we have used Six Sigma to address issues such as the safety and efficacy of acute anticoagulation, administration of CMS cardiac medications for AMI and congestive heart failure (CHF), CHF length of stay, rehab services response time, and restraint usage documentation. Many more of our projects have been in core business functions such as billing and collection. This has had a very favorable impact on our bottom line and allows us to reinvest in critical areas of the organization that directly impact patient care."

Virtua has also adopted new operating mechanisms and Lean techniques to augment their Six Sigma program, and they have created a highly integrated performance improvement structure. Leveraging innovative management methods, Rich Miller and the team have succeeded in creating a high-performing organization at Virtua.

VALLEY BAPTIST HEALTH SYSTEM, HARLINGEN, TX

Valley Baptist Health System, based in Harlingen, Texas is a not-for-profit community health network that includes a 611-bed regional academic referral hospital. Through the leadership of Jim Springfield, president and CEO, it began to implement Six Sigma in May 2002. Since that time, they have improved numerous processes related to the emergency department, outpatient services, surgical services, diagnosis-related grouping (DRG) assignment accuracy, pain management, JCAHO Core measures for AMI, CHF, and pneumonia, and admissions and discharge. They calculate a return on investment of more than $25 million from 2002 to 2006.

As of 2006, 72 Six Sigma initiatives and more than 340 Work-Outs have been completed across Valley Baptist. The projects have had a direct "line of sight" to the strategic objectives of the business and have resulted in decreased cycle times, process standardization, increased customer satisfaction, and financial benefits. A number of initiatives achieved Six Sigma performance levels including AMI , heart failure management, and the patient ID process.

In January 2007, Valley Baptist Medical Center-Harlingen was ranked number one in the United States in the treatment of heart failure, according to a pay-for-performance project conducted by the federal government (http://www.genengnews.com/news/bnitem.aspx?name=11837169&taxid=35).

In addition to the top ranking for heart failure treatment, Valley Baptist placed in the top 10 percent in the nation in treating heart attack (acute myocardial infarction) patients. The U.S. Centers for Medicare & Medicaid Services (CMS) and Premier, Inc. conduct the demonstration program to reward quality and performance among the nation's hospitals.

Valley Baptist attributed the improved patient care for heart failure and heat attack patients to Six Sigma.

Beyond specific financial returns and better quality metrics, Springfield views Six Sigma as 'a means to an end,' with the end being cultural change and the notion of constantly raising the bar to create a better environment for patients.

In 2004, Springfield received the American College of Healthcare Executives' Robert S. Hudgens Memorial Award for Young Healthcare Executive of the Year, in part for his innovative leadership and commitment to creating a better healthcare delivery system through Six Sigma and change management. He has noted that Six Sigma shares similar tenets and statistical tools with other quality improvement efforts, but at a higher level of implementation. He also recognized the importance of addressing the "people" side for change along with statistical process control.

"It doesn't matter how good a solution may be," he says. "If it's not culturally accepted, the results will be diminished."

The Six Sigma team at Valley Baptist strives to ensure that efforts produce both quantitative and qualitative results, taking on projects that are highly visible and touch a lot of people within the organization. As a result of the changes Springfield and his staff have implemented, Valley Baptist has seen significant improvement in many areas throughout the system, including operating room turnaround time, order entry, pharmacy turnaround, discharge process, emergency room turnaround time, and laboratory results reporting. Launching this initiative required a significant up-front investment in terms of training, resources, patience, and dedication, but the benefits have been even more significant. Springfield has noted that financially, they have probably seen a 15-fold return on their investment.

"Healthcare is generally ineffective, and we focus on the wrong things," says Springfield. "So we asked how can we afford *not* to invest in this? We initially spent a lot of money—but we got a huge return, both qualitatively and quantitatively. I would counsel other organizations not to take a shallow view. If they don't want to make the investment, they may be saying they don't believe they can get these results. You're investing in better quality and the capability of your people."

One early project targeted staff scheduling and led to an overall reduction in the higher hourly cost of overtime and agency use, achieving Six Sigma performance from a baseline of zero. This project translated to $460,000 in savings for one unit; Springfield offered a conservative estimate at the time that if it were spread across the system to all units, the project could potentially save more than $5 million. This also provided a classic example as to how Six Sigma can be used to either corroborate or dispel original theories. Management had initially assumed they were over budget on labor costs due to sick leave, FMLA, vacation, and people not showing up, causing the need for the additional overtime and agency hours. Statistical analysis disproved those assumptions, pointing to factors such as nursing dissatisfaction with frequent rotation between different units and issues with the staffing matrix, which attempted to set parameters based on volume.

Internal training efforts have continued, and as of May 2006, the program included 297 Change Agents, 5 Master Black Belts, 4 Black Belts, 61 Green Belts and 34 Yellow Belts. Springfield has emphasized that their program is really about cultural acceptance and changing both processes and behaviors. "We always respect people, and that's important," he said. "And we recognize effort. But we reward performance."

All the improvement initiatives at Valley Baptist Health System are tied to a rigorous performance measurement system and structured operating mechanisms that enable project linkage to their top goals and objectives. Managers track results using control charts and trend reports with data from human resources, time and attendance, and payroll systems. This provides real-time information on productivity, tracking worked hours versus patient days to show alignment with targets on an ongoing basis.

NORTH SHORE-LONG ISLAND JEWISH (LIJ) HEALTH SYSTEM, NY

The North Shore-LIJ Health System is headquartered in Great Neck, New York, and includes 15 hospitals, 4 long-term care facilities, 3 trauma centers, dozens of ambulatory care centers, and 5 home health agencies throughout Long Island, Queens, and Staten Island. It is the third-largest nonprofit, secular healthcare system in the U.S., with about 37,500 employees and more than 6,000 beds.

In January 2002, North Shore-LIJ launched its Center for Learning and Innovation (CLI) in conjunction with General Electric and the Harvard School of Public Health. The CLI features several programs:

- Learning initiatives for new and existing employees and managers
- An "Innovative Solutions" division that focuses on organizational development, leadership practices, workforce development, and performance management
- An Operational Performance Solutions group that uses Six Sigma and Lean methodologies to improve efficiencies and enhance quality within its hospitals and facilities
- Nursing and physician leadership institutes for clinical managers
- Critical Care and Emergency Department Nurse Fellowship programs
- A technical education arm that provides certification programs in the allied health professions
- Patient Safety Institute, which features a simulation lab with three computerized mannequins that allow medical students, surgical residents, nurses, and other healthcare professionals to practice their clinical skills without risk to real patients.

Since CLI opened in 2002, North Shore-LIJ has achieved positive results throughout the organization. In addition to improving the environment for both patients and employees, it has achieved more than $5 million in cumulative cost savings from Lean and Six Sigma efforts, and is able to explore a variety of growth opportunities (see Table 8.2).

TABLE 8.2 Examples of Six Sigma/Lean Projects at North Shore-LIJ

Project	Effect
Turnaround of routine lab work from draw to result	Decreased TAT (turnaround time) from when a specimen is drawn on the floor to received in the lab from 61 minutes to 16 minutes. Decreased TAT from draw to result from 105 minutes to 60 minutes.
Customer satisfaction with discharge instructions	Increased customer satisfaction with discharge information from 66% to 86.8%. Created printed packet to supplement handwritten instructions. Piloted 48-hour call back to patients.
Customer satisfaction with ambulatory care appointment scheduling	Increased customer satisfaction scores for scheduling ambulatory care appointments on a scale of 1–5 from 2.57 to 3.96. Improved call back response time by 50%.
Chart completion within 30 days	Decreased the number of medical records not complete within 30 days from 62% to 48%.
Material operations reconciliation process	Decreased the number of daily manual orders from an average of 78/day to 54/day. Increased the accuracy of the replenishment report by 30%.
CT throughput	Increased CT outpatient scheduling by 17 additional appointment slots per week. Financial impact: additional $217,000 per year.

"We're a much better place because we made a solid commitment to improving our workplace," says Michael Dowling, president and CEO of North Shore-LIJ.

Developing the Six Sigma program and building a full curriculum through the CLI represents a clear commitment to ongoing education and continuous improvement. It also indicates a substantial investment in the development of their people.

"While we recognize the importance of demonstrating quality and financial improvement, the impact on the team is perhaps even more important," says Alan Cooper, Ph.D., MBA, vice president of learning and innovation. "We have certainly seen some great results from projects that contributed to our bottom line, but it's the professional and leadership development that has really made a difference in our organization."

Nancy Riebling, MS, MT (ASCP), is a Master Black Belt and director of operational performance solutions at North Shore-LIJ. She has been instrumental in driving numerous improvement projects for the health system. "By leveraging a common set of tools and techniques, we have continued to achieve solid results in a variety of areas across the organization."

Kathleen Gallo, Ph.D., RN, said hospital executives had decided to use Six Sigma as a management vehicle because they wanted to improve productivity and efficiency. North Shore-LIJ became self-sufficient within three years. The executive leadership team remains actively involved in the program, and educational initiatives through CLI have continued to expand to include the use of Lean and other key management strategies.

THIBODAUX REGIONAL MEDICAL CENTER, THIBODAUX, LA

Located in southeastern Louisiana, Thibodaux Regional Medical Center (TRMC) is a case in point to prove that organizational size is not the determining factor for successfully implementing a Six Sigma or Lean program within a patient care environment. A growing, acute-care medical center with 187 beds, TRMC provides a wide range of outpatient and inpatient services to the surrounding region.

In addition to weathering the usual financial storms and resource issues that affect other hospitals, TRMC had to weather storms of a different kind in 2005 when Hurricanes Katrina and Rita barreled into the Gulf Coast. Along with caring for hundreds of hospitalized patients, the physicians and staff worked around the clock for weeks on end to treat the thousands who came through Thibodaux Regional's emergency department and the shelter located at nearby Nicholls State University.

Greg Stock, president and CEO at TRMC, said he was extremely proud of his team's performance during this chaotic time, and believes their ability to function well as a team came in part from the strong foundation they had built over the years with Six Sigma and change management techniques.

"Nobody could fully prepare for the sheer size of the storm and the aftermath," says Stock, "but we found that all the hard work we'd put into improving processes and strengthening leaders really paid off. Disasters deserve our immediate attention and critical thinking. Although we can't predict or control them, we can prepare our own organizations so that we're in a constant state of readiness. This has a lot to do with the processes you have in place, teamwork, and the vibrancy and flexibility of the culture."

The hospital uses Press Ganey to measure both employee and patient satisfaction, and their scores have been very high in both areas. Using Six Sigma and other tools, they have consistently ranked in the top 1 percent in the nation for patient satisfaction within the past six years, and their employee satisfaction survey went from the 53rd percentile in 2000 to the 97th percentile in 2005.

"Pursuing and achieving excellence with regard to patient satisfaction and quality requires a high-performance culture," says Stock. "Staff members must be enabled through disciplined performance improvement methodologies that drive best performance."

Internal training and projects continue to focus on the issues that are most important to achieving excellence in patient care. To support system-wide quality initiatives and complement their Six Sigma program, TRMC also adopted Lean methods and DIGs, or "Do It Groups," which are guided by trained facilitators and are designed to quickly resolve problems and take advantage of opportunities within a 30-day period. Keeping everyone informed about the improvement initiatives is accomplished through departmental meetings, town hall meetings, project report-outs, and presentations at leadership sessions.

"Communication is essential to the success of any performance improvement effort," says Darcy Prejeant, RN, Master Black Belt at TRMC. "The more staff you have involved in generating solutions, the greater buy-in you will have in maintaining improvement efforts. It is essential to have the masses thinking performance improvement in their daily roles, in order to create a culture of excellence."

NEWYORK-PRESBYTERIAN HOSPITAL, NEW YORK, NY

NewYork-Presbyterian Hospital (NYP) is the flagship of the NewYork-Presbyterian Healthcare System, the largest nonsectarian, nonprofit healthcare system in the U.S. The hospital is a 2,335-bed academic medical center affiliated with two of the nation's leading medical colleges: the Columbia University College of Physicians and Surgeons, and the Joan and Sanford I. Weill Medical College of Cornell University. At the 2006 Global Six Sigma Awards, NYP received the Best Achievement of Six Sigma in Healthcare Award and also were recognized with the Platinum Award for Outstanding Organizational Achievement for their embrace of the Six Sigma culture.

NYP developed a vision to provide the highest quality service in the healthcare industry using a collaborative, interdisciplinary approach to performance improvement. In 2003, senior leadership took a major step toward transforming this vision into reality. After carefully considering the need to anticipate and respond to shifting trends in the industry, they decided to embrace the Six Sigma philosophy for performance excellence. Chief Quality Officer for the system, Mary R. Cooper, M.D., J.D., became the champion for the implementation and helped to guide the program. Some of the criteria for selecting projects included clinical excellence, regulatory and safety, physician satisfaction, staff satisfaction, patient satisfaction, ease of implementation, financial benefits, time to complete, and sustainability.

Several objectives factored into the organization's implementation of Six Sigma:

- Achieve knowledge transfer
- Foster transformative cultural change
- Build accountability
- Instill management discipline
- Ensure no one is left behind
- Reach all levels, all disciplines

The curriculum was designed to include DMAIC, Change Acceleration Process (CAP), Work-Out, Lean and Design for Six Sigma, and training was conducted for 17 days over a six-month timeframe. The training was based on completion of actual projects, and each team was composed of a Black Belt working with three or four Green Belts. Project teams eventually expanded to include other key stakeholders. Abbreviated training was delivered to senior administration, medical staff, management staff, and line employees. The curriculum has been repeated five times over subsequent waves of training.

Completed projects include the following:

Cath/EP Room Turnaround Time

Patient Wait Times in Radiology

CT OR Room Turnaround Time

Hip Fracture LOS

Housekeeping Turnaround Time

Noninvasive Cancellation Reduction

PACU Criteria Met to PACU Exit

Billing Compliance for Screening Mammograms

ED Throughput

Craniotomy LOS

Radiology Report Turnaround Time

Transport Response Time for Patient Care Units

Outpatient Lab Charge Capture

Hem/Onc Infusion Center Cycle Time

Outpatient Transplant Room Utilization

Medical Records to Ambulatory Care

Attending of Record Accuracy

Antibiotic Utilization

Discharge Instruction Process

Psych ED LOS

C-Section LOS Reduction

Accuracy and Timeliness of Pharmacy Charge Posting

Medication Delivery Turnaround Time

Radiology Turnaround Time in ED

Timeliness of Cancer Registry TNM Staging

Ambulatory Surgery Turnaround Time

Antibiotic Delivery in Cardiothoracic ORs

Scheduled Induction Wait Time in Labor and Delivery

Blood Delivery Turnaround Time

Pyxis Overrides

Smoking Cessation Counseling

Nursing Communication Patient Satisfaction

Ambulatory Surgery Wait Time

ICU Throughput

Intradisciplinary Plan of Communication

Isolation Room Throughput

Use of Abbreviations in Medical Records

Information Transfer for Antenatal to Labor and Delivery

Improve AOB Process in Radiology

Inpatient Tray Accuracy

Call Bell Response Time

Pediatrics LOS Reduction

By the end of 2004, the program's first full year, the hospital had realized a savings of $47 million through 130 completed projects that were linked to the hospital's strategic objectives. The hospital takes pride in the fact that many Black Belts have now been promoted back into the organization. In 2006, the hospital received 105 applicants for 10 open Black Belt positions—the majority of which were internal—demonstrating the momentum that had been established and allowing the organization to be selective in choosing candidates. Two were promoted to vice president level from the Black Belt position; four became Master Black Belts. All Black Belts from the first wave of training and half of the Black Belts from the second wave have been promoted back into the organization.

"I believe this is a testament to the leadership development aspect of Six Sigma," says Mary Cooper, M.D., J.D. "Participants in the program are very attractive to those who are hiring, and having the Black Belts dispersed out into the organization has been very helpful. There are now more than 200 Green Belts trained, and all the Black Belts are still committed and highly motivated."

In 2005, NYP also adapted GE's management and leadership systems, and created a year-round operating calendar with clear deadlines, hand-offs, and accountability. Projects have effectively addressed a wide range of safety, quality, operational, and technical issues. As of August 2006, the health system reported $68 million in financial benefits from improvement initiatives within two years. Since 2003, NYP has succeeded in building a solid framework that includes Six Sigma, Lean, CAP, Work-Out, and new management models.

DECATUR MEMORIAL HOSPITAL, DECATUR, IL

Decatur Memorial Hospital is a 300-bed community-based hospital in Illinois with approximately 2,500 full time employees. In 2001, the hospital launched a Six Sigma program to train staff and pursue projects that align with the organization's strategic objectives.

As part of this alignment, the team is encouraged to focus on "noble goals," or efforts that support a noble purpose, such as raising patient satisfaction or preventing hospital-acquired infections. Results are monitored through the hospital's scorecard. Employees receive education in Lean, Six Sigma, change management, and "Imagine 21" to create a better focus on goals and performance.

Physicians at Decatur often play the role of "consultant" at various stages and offer advice or input to specific processes. Using tools such as the Stakeholder or GRPI Analysis helps to determine whether a clinician needs to be involved and at what level—in other words, whether they will participate periodically, receive information on a "need-to-know" basis, or serve as the chief decision maker.

Since their deployment began, more than 50 Green Belts have been trained at Decatur, and every formal project has an internal Black Belt assigned to provide mentoring. A monthly review process helps to keep their efforts on track and includes executives, Six Sigma leaders, and others in the organization. "These reviews have become an important communication tool within the hospital," says Don Miller, Master Black Belt at Decatur.

Decatur has also developed Yellow Belts who are trained in basic Six Sigma concepts and Lean techniques, and who focus on improving their individual work units. The combined methodologies are integrated into the fabric of the organization, and results are measured in terms of higher satisfaction, increased efficiency, and better service quality. While initially receiving outside help to get its programs started, the hospital is now able to manage its own internal training and projects.

THE NEBRASKA MEDICAL CENTER, OMAHA, NE

The Nebraska Medical Center is a 690-bed hospital in Omaha that includes regionally and nationally recognized programs in cancer treatment and transplantation, neurology, and cardiovascular services. The hospital was formed by the merger of Clarkson Hospital and UNMC's University Hospital in 1997. Although it had dealt with the complexities of joining two distinct cultures and maintained a performance improvement department, some frustrations had begun to arise due to lack of strategic focus in this area and recommendations not always being implemented.

As CEO at The Nebraska Medical Center, Glenn Fosdick always placed a strong emphasis on sustainable quality. Under his leadership, the hospital began a Six Sigma program in 2002, with specific goals to help the organization achieve measurable, sustained results that significantly improve its key processes, and advance its focus and commitment to continuous quality improvement.

"We have had quality initiatives for a long time in our organization," Fosdick says. "Bringing the Six Sigma tools in allowed us to have a common approach to issues and has given us great strategic advantages. For a successful project, you need to improve outcomes, increase efficiency, or make somebody's job easier. If all you've done is make someone's job easier, it's well worth the effort."

As of August 2006, the status of the Six Sigma improvement program includes

- 44 DMAIC-Lean projects initiated
- 1 Manager, Six Sigma (Master Black Belt Trained)
- 2 Master Black Belts
- 5 Black Belts dedicated full-time to quality improvement projects
- 6 Trained Green Belts actively applying DMAIC and Lean Tools/Methods

The return on investment for The Nebraska Medical Center has been significant and exceeded the expectations of the hospital's leadership team (see Table 8.3). "In addition to better quality results, the structure we've put in place is working well for us financially," says Fosdick. "We haven't laid anyone off for budget-related reasons for four consecutive years."

TABLE 8.3 Financial Impact, Nebraska Medical Center (as of 11/05)

Hard $ To Date	Soft $ To Date	Unused Capacity $
$1,921,397	$3,664,485	$2,083,724

The organization continues to seek and adopt a variety of management best practices, and in 2006, The Nebraska Medical Center was recognized for service excellence under the J.D. Power and Associates' Distinguished Hospital Program, acknowledging a strong commitment to provide an outstanding patient experience.

The approach draws interest from employees, who are identified and asked as high-potential future leaders to be part of the Six Sigma program. Jason Lebsack, Six Sigma Manager at The Nebraska Medical Center, noted that while the program requires a lot of work and dedication, they owe it to their patients to come as close to perfection as they can.

Keys to their continued success include creating a "quality umbrella" and integrating methods, having dedicated resources, building acceptance, and focusing on sustainability. Moving forward, the hospital's plans include further integration of Lean and DMAIC tools, increased communication, and providing advanced change agent training in such topics as Lean Thinking, Project Management, and FMEA.

CLINICAL CASE STUDIES

SECTIONS

Six Sigma and related methodologies have proven valuable in removing barriers and bringing greater consistency to the healthcare environment. Although many healthcare executives will readily admit they have been able to achieve some measure of cost savings or revenue enhancement through the use of Six Sigma, they often cite other reasons for pursuing this strategy. In some cases, the organization is seeking to equip their workforce with new skills and a stronger set of problem-solving tools. One of the most prevalent reasons for Six Sigma adoption in healthcare, however, is to provide a rigorous, evidence-based structure for improving services and supporting the goal of delivering safe, high-quality clinical care. From medication administration to the prevention of hospital-acquired infections, healthcare providers are finding numerous opportunities to apply methods such as Six Sigma and Lean.

Partly because of its origination in the manufacturing environment, there is a broader track record of operationally focused projects such as supply chain management, billing cycle time, variability in product quality, and so on. The uniquely human aspects of healthcare have required a special adaptation of Six Sigma and ongoing collaboration with clinicians so that the benefits are not lost in translation. Because of the scientific nature of Six Sigma, physicians in particular tend to respond favorably after they have seen how the process actually works and the impact it can make on their ability to care for patients.

The following case studies demonstrate the versatility and widespread relevance of this approach within the clinical environment.

CARDIAC MEDICATION ADMINISTRATION AT VIRTUA HEALTH

To support a "Cardiac Program of Excellence" launched in 2002, Virtua Health began a Six Sigma project that would focus on key aspects of the initiative. During the Define phase, the team developed the following project description: "Increase quality of patient care by use/ non-use and appropriate documentation of aspirin, beta-blockers, and ACE inhibitors in congestive heart failure (CHF) or acute myocardial infarction (AMI) patients to achieve or exceed Virtua benchmark goals."

The project would include Virtua's four acute care facilities, within all medical disciplines, to meet guidelines set by the Joint Commission on Accreditation of Healthcare Organizations (JCAHO). The team anticipated the project would yield better outcomes for patients with AMI/CHF diagnoses by adhering to evidence-based practice, compliance with regulatory standards, and enhanced quality of care.

During the Measure phase, data analysis indicated variation between reports from the quality review analysts (QRAs) and Virtua's review. Gage R&R was used to examine the existing process, reconcile the differences, and develop an accurate measurement system that would meet CMS standards (Centers for Medicare and Medicaid Services, http://www.cms.hhs.gov/).

Inconsistencies with data measurement were addressed during a working session with the QRAs and case management directors to examine process flow and establish standard operating procedures (SOPs) for chart review. The team also developed a plan to communicate the new SOPs to the nursing and medical staffs.

The levels of defects per million opportunities (DPMO) were identified for each indicator for AMI and CHF. With a goal of zero defects, the team found significant room for improvement since baseline data indicated a 4 percent defect rate for AMI patients and a 10.2 percent defect rate for CHF patients (see Figure 9.1).

The team initially focused on administering a beta-blocker within 24 hours of admission and prescription of an ACE inhibitor when discharging AMI patients. They instituted 100 percent chart review and involved nursing staff, case management, quality teams, and physician's staff in education and review.

During the Measure phase, a Gage R&R revealed variation on assessment between the QRA review of charts. A Work-Out was held with the QRAs and case management directors to develop SOPs in reviewing CHF and AMI patients for core indicators.

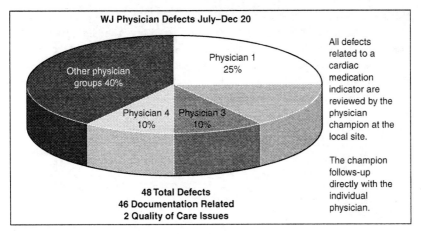

FIGURE 9.1 West Jersey physician defects

Analyze and Improve

As the project entered the Analyze phase, the team held bi-weekly meetings and focused on data analysis to ensure the data collection process had improved. They created detailed process maps and identified drivers of variation.

Based on data from the chart review, they found that 46 out of 48 defects involving physicians were due to documentation issues. The team held another Work-Out, piloted best practices, and coordinated medical leadership with nursing and case management to standardize practice and eliminate some variables. They also developed a root cause analysis (see Table 9.1).

TABLE 9.1 Root Cause Analysis

Factor	Root Cause	Proposed Solutions
MICU run sheets not available on charts.	Medics unable to complete; shortened documentation not part of permanent chart.	Sponsor to work with Ambulatory Quality Director to have MICU run sheets completed and submitted concurrent with care.
Inconsistent availability of patient census with diagnosis for nursing and case management.	IS integration with Canopy system; initial information input by ICD-9 code, not description	Word order placed with information services with actual cases to research and advise on proper input process.
Physician compliance in completion of discharge instructions.	Inconsistent follow-through.	Directive from medical staff leadership to complete discharge instructions; two week trial period in April, 2003 by HIM to tag all charts without discharge instructions.
Consistent practice of multi-disciplinary care of the patient across Virtua.	Need for champion at each campus to lead initiatives of the Cardiac Programs of Excellence.	Appointment of nurse leader within each facility to coordinate activities of Cardiac Programs of Excellence at local level.

The team established standard processes for regular physician-to-physician correspondence, and created a flow chart and monthly reports for tracking purposes. Another key step was the use of Failure Mode and Effects Analysis (FMEA) prior to closing the project and the development of a standardized data collection form. As shown in Table 9.2, Virtua has consistently achieved overall improvement in CMS cardiac standards as a result of the project and implemented changes.

TABLE 9.2 Virtua Health Performance of CMS Cardiac Medications Standards

Measure	Benchmark	1st Qtr 2002	4th Qtr 2002	4th Qtr 2004	1st Qtr 2005
Use of ASA with Acute MI patients within 24 hours of arrival to hospital (%)	95*	87	95.8	97.8	98.3
Use of beta blockers within 24 hours of arrival to hospital (%) in AMI	95*	83	97.1	100	99
Use of aspirin at discharge (%) in AMI	95*	83	90	98.5	92
Use of beta blocker at discharge (%) in AMI	95*	85	100	100	98
Appropriate use/non-use of ACEIat discharge (patients with LVEF, 40% (%) in AMI	95*	72	100	95	54**
Appropriate use/non-use of ACEIat discharge (patients with LVEF, 40% (%) in CHF	95*	48	90.5	85**	90

*2005 Virtua/NJ PRO Goals
**Change in Regulatory Practice

Six Sigma helped identify root causes for process failure in appropriately administering and documenting cardiac medication. Solutions included physician and staff education, stocking aspirin on each hospital floor and shortening the form paramedics must complete. The project surpassed benchmarks, and the results have been maintained (see Table 9.3).

TABLE 9.3 Realized Results of Implemented Solutions

Improvement	Y Benefit	Quality Benefit
MICU run sheets on patient charts within 24 hours of admission.	Increased compliance for aspirin given within 24 hours.	Compliance with PRO indicators for aspirin given within 24 hours of admission; Department of Health regulations for transfer of patient care.
Physician completion of written discharge instructions specific to medications for cardiac patients.	Compliance and proper documentation of care for discharge medication indicators.	Quality of care documented.

Improvement	Y Benefit	Quality Benefit
Standard operating procedures by nursing and case management in chart review, 'sticky' reminders for physicians, and availability of discharge instructions.	Increased compliance in care and documentation for all indicators.	Coordination of care for the cardiac patient by the multi-disciplinary team.
Consistent education of nursing per cardiac medication indicators.	Increased compliance for medications given within timeframes.	Increased knowledge base of the nursing staff of the cardiac medications for AMI and CHF patients.
Accurate daily census with diagnosis available through proprietary information systems.	Increased compliance in care and documentation for all indicators.	Timeliness of care improved.
Appointment of a process owner at each hospital to coordinate care with directives from Cardiac Programs of Excellence.	Sustained improvement in all indicators.	Sustained results maintained and reported to CMS and public appropriate recognition and reporting of quality of care.

REDUCING SURGICAL SITE INFECTIONS AT CHARLESTON AREA MEDICAL CENTER

The Centers for Disease Control estimates that 500,000 surgical site infections occur each year in the U.S., out of approximately 30 million surgical procedures performed. A single infection may require an additional hospital stay of seven days, an extra $3,000 in charges, and a 60 percent greater chance of being placed in an intensive care unit. The patient is also five times more likely to be readmitted to the hospital, with twice the incidence of mortality. In 2002, a Surgical Infection Prevention Project (SIPP) led to the issuance of new guidelines by the Centers for Medicare and Medicaid Services and the Centers for Disease Control and Prevention, seeking to reduce surgical site infection (SSI) rates by improving the selection and timing of prophylactic antibiotic administration.

As part of an ongoing improvement program, Charleston Area Medical Center (CAMC) in West Virginia brought together a multidisciplinary Six Sigma team to address SSIs, including two surgeons, an anesthesiologist, an epidemiologist, safety personnel, the chief of CRNAs, a Six Sigma Black Belt, and a Six Sigma Green Belt.

The team scoped the project to include the immediate pre-operative phase and up to 30 days post discharge for colon and vascular surgery patient populations only. Because the focus was on prophylaxis, patients already on antibiotics for any reason prior to surgery would not be considered in scope.

The following indicators for antibiotic administration would be measured:

- Recommended antibiotic appropriate for specific surgery.
- Dose administered at the right time (0–60 minutes prior to incision, with the exception of vancomycin which is in the 0–120 range). (Antibiotic must be completely infused prior to tourniquet inflation.)

- Administration of right dose based on weight. Medication and antibiotics are not "one size fits all."
- Appropriate intraoperative re-dose if the surgery is longer than 240 minutes.
- Discontinuing the prophylactic antibiotic within 24 hours of surgery to reduce the risk for development of antibiotic-resistant organisms.

Define and Measure

The project began with data collection and building a business case for action. With initial process measurements at 0 sigma and 660,828 DPMO, there was obviously room for improvement. The team looked at the percentage of surgical patients acquiring an infection during their hospital stay, and considered factors such as mortality and morbidity rates and length of stay. Baseline data indicated that many patients arrived in the pre-operative holding area of the OR without a written antibiotic order, and that antibiotics may be administered too early or too late. Consistently assuring weight-based dosage was also an issue. Finally, patients undergoing procedures longer than 240 minutes (360 minutes for vancomycin administration) did not routinely receive an appropriate re-dose of antibiotic.

Figure 9.2 illustrates the ideal process designed to ensure that the antibiotics are administered correctly and at the right time.

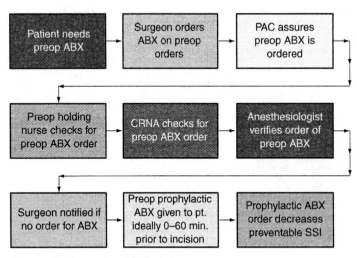

Source: Charleston Area Medical Center

FIGURE 9.2 Ideal prophylactic antibiotic process

Tools such as FMEA and fishbone diagrams were used during the Analyze and Improve phases to identify critical factors impacting infection rates. The data pointed to variability among surgeons and anesthesiologists, and processes were examined to find and share best practices.

Even with an early order for antibiotics from the surgeon, OR delays could prevent timely administration. A stakeholder analysis helped to support the statistical findings and create a shared need. Gaining acceptance from the staff, the team began to introduce new procedures and solutions, including a database for indicator monitoring reporting, revision of the pre-operative order set, development of a physician report card, and education of physician office staff, CRNAs, anesthesiologists, surgeons, residents, and OR staff.

Additional changes included having RN staff and anesthetists prompt the physician for an antibiotic order if the patient arrives in the pre-operative holding area without one or with one that is not recommended. They began posting appropriate antibiotics and doses for colon and vascular surgeries beside each patient and nurse's station, in the medication preparation area, and in key locations within the surgical area. Error-proofing techniques were used to revise the pre-operative physician order form to include recommended antibiotics with proper doses and re-dose times.

A "Who-What-When" (WWW) plan was created to track more than 200 tasks, and the team gave staff a new post-op order set to quickly check the right boxes instead of writing every-thing out. Posters, signs, and a puzzle displaying indicators were developed, while visual reminders in the OR prompted the staff regarding timely re-dose of the antibiotic.

Ongoing education is helping to maintain results, and as new residents enter the hospital they learn the processes that have been established to reduce infection rates. Following the close of the project, the rate at which surgical patients receive the right dose of antibiotic at the right time improved 91 percent from 0 sigma to 2.86, and progress is continuing. In addition to improving patient safety, the business case demonstrated annual savings in excess of $1 million. When CMS began monitoring the SSI indicators, CAMC was already one year and nine months into the project, and was able to demonstrate measurable improvement.

Several measures were put in place to control results:

- Prophylactic antibiotics added to the pre-induction and pre-incision time-out.

- Pre-operative and intra-operative indicators to be monitored by the Surgical Quality Improvement Council, with individual results sent to surgeons, anesthesiologists, and CRNAs.

- A Six Sigma team completed a project for the discontinuation of post-operative antibiotics in 24 hours.

- A Six Sigma team completed a project for the glucose control for cardiac patients and is working on one for all surgical patients.

- A Six Sigma team completed a project for inadvertent hypothermia prevention.

- A Six Sigma team is currently addressing VTE prophylaxis.

- A project binder documenting the entire project was prepared for the administrators and physician champion.

- The results and project process were shared with the Peripheral Vascular Services Collaborative Practice and Surgical Quality Improvement Council.

CAMC continues to monitor these completed projects, and they are still in control with consistent results of 98-100% compliance.

According to Deborah Young, RN at CAMC, this project translated to benefits for the patient, but it also helped to raise staff satisfaction and save valuable resources and time that can be spent in other care areas. By avoiding the longer length of stay, the hospital can improve capacity and access to care for other patients. "Multiple Six Sigma projects have positioned Charleston Area Medical Center as a leader in the nation regarding the CMS indicators. We won a Premier Award for Quality for our Hip and Knee Surgery in July 2006 and were number one in the country for open heart surgery. The awards are wonderful recognition, but the greatest reward is that we know we are providing the highest quality of care for our patients."

NOTE

An article on this project was first published in the July/September 2004 issue of *Patient Safety and Quality Healthcare*, written by Carolyn Pexton and Deborah Young (http://www.psqh.com/julsep04/pextonyoung.html).

REDUCING CVC-RELATED BLOODSTREAM INFECTIONS AT FLORIDA HOSPITAL

In addition to surgical site infections, another issue hospitals are confronting involves infections acquired through central venous catheters (CVC). The catheters provide critically ill patients with necessary fluids, medication, nutrition, and monitoring. The use of CVCs, however, presents a risk of bloodstream infection (BSI), with associated treatment costs ranging from $34,508 to $56,000.

At Florida Hospital, a 1,800 bed healthcare system with seven campuses in central Florida, a Six Sigma project led by Lois Yingling, RN, MSN, CPHQ, helped to target this critical issue. The hospital closely monitors BSI rates, and the internal benchmark is the aggregate top quartile for critical care set by the National Nosocomial Infections Surveillance (NNIS) System.

The overall BSI rate is calculated by dividing the number of central line associated BSIs by patient days multiplied by 1,000. Patient days are used for overall BSI calculation, as device days are not tracked for all units. Internal benchmarks are adjusted downward on an annual basis, per control charts and trends.

For this project, baseline metrics were the overall BSI rate and BSI cases secondary to CVCs in 2003. During the year, efforts to reduce BSI included a policy banning artificial nails for direct care providers, conversion to 2 percent chlorhexadine skin prep on supply carts, and BSI staff education. As a result, the overall BSI rate decreased by more than 40 percent in 2004.

Applying Six Sigma was seen as furthering the effort to prevent bloodstream infections. It was also viewed as a learning opportunity for the cross-functional project team led by a Black Belt and mentored by a Master Black Belt, with participation from an infectious disease physician, infection control practitioners, a nurse manager, nursing educators, front-line nursing staff, an intravenous access nurse, a laboratory technician, and a nurse from materials management.

Define and Measure

The scope for the project included inpatients older than 17 year of age with a positive blood culture within 48 hours of admission or re-admission within two weeks with a confirmed CVC-related BSI based on the CDC definition. Considered out of scope would be patients with BSI secondary to tunneled lines, port line, dialysis lines, peripherally inserted central catheter (PICC) lines, or peripheral lines. Historical data indicated 43 percent of BSI infections were in scope.

The team set a target for 2005 to achieve a 20 percent reduction from the baseline average of 6.33 CVC-related BSI cases per month, or 16 or less annually. Baseline measurement of variable cost and average length of stay was determined by comparing diagnosis-related groups (DRGs) for patients with confirmed central line-related BSI with a patient population of identical DRGs without a bloodstream infection. Based on this metric, variable cost was $16,699 more for patients with BSI, and length of stay was 20.6 days longer than the non-BSI population.

Analyze Phase

Statistical analysis found normal distribution of data for the overall BSI baseline rate with a p value of 0.308. The process was in control with no special cause variation and a sigma of 0. A SIPOC chart was developed to illustrate process flow, while a fishbone diagram helped to pinpoint the most important drivers or critical Xs, which included hand hygiene, maximal barrier precautions, skin prep, and an antimicrobial catheter. Figure 9.3 shows the SIPOC process.

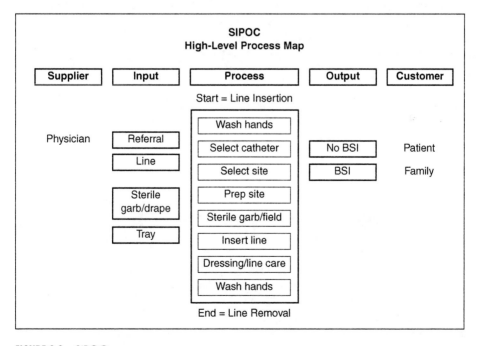

FIGURE 9.3 SIPOC process

Successfully implementing such a large-scale change effort requires a focus on gaining acceptance from others in the organization. The team used a stakeholder analysis to verify support from administration, the hospital's infection control committee, infectious disease specialists, critical care intensivists, advanced registered nurse practitioners, and clinical nurse specialists.

Results from a Gage R&R assessment demonstrated 100 percent accuracy for repeatability and 90 percent accuracy for reproducibility for infection control surveillance by infection control practitioners. The audit accuracy is now incorporated for new employees and annually for all employees.

Measuring and Maintaining Results

To further improve processes and reduce the risk of BSIs, the team introduced a hand hygiene campaign, and completed a conversion to custom trays for CVC lines in November 2005. An employee poster contest increased acceptance and awareness. New SOPs for tray distribution were put in place and distributed to each campus, and additional error-proofing was accomplished by placing sterile barriers in all custom trays.

By June 2005, the team had achieved its goal to reduce the number of CVC-related BSI cases by 20 percent or 16 deaths annually, translating to the prevention of 2 deaths based on a baseline 13 percent mortality rate. Savings have been estimated at $318,029 for the first two quarters, using a per diem room cost. Internal analysis demonstrated an average of $16,699 additional variable costs per case, equating to a savings of $271,984. The Sigma score went from 0 to 1.8, and the overall BSI rate is well below the initial target and continues to improve. Monthly infection rates continue to be measured. Estimated savings are calculated monthly and year-to-date by the finance department, and reported to process owners.

NOTE

This project was the subject of a poster at the Institute for Healthcare Improvement's (IHI) National Forum in December 2005, and an article by Lois Yingling was published in the May/June 2006 issue of Patient Safety and Quality Healthcare (www.psqh.com). http://www.psqh.com/mayjun06/sixsigma.html

PREVENTING INFECTIONS AT DECATUR MEMORIAL HOSPITAL

Eliminating hospital-acquired infections is one of the top goals for the Six Sigma team at Decatur Memorial Hospital in Illinois, and the team has completed several projects focused on this critical quality issue. One such project targeted three key operational areas: intensive care, intermediate care, and the cardiovascular unit.

The project was successfully completed, and the hospital has been able to sustain improvements over time. Another successful project focused on the reduction of surgical site infections, specifically looking at all total joint replacements for hips or knees. Again, by analyzing the data and following the DMAIC (Define, Measure, Analyze, Improve, Control) process, they were able to make and maintain changes that have measurably improved patient care.

The hospital also launched a project to look at the administration of antibiotics. The CDC (Centers for Disease Control) recommends that for certain cases, antibiotics should be delivered prophylactically to the patient in order to reduce or eliminate the risk of infection. The focus is on the length of time between complete delivery of the antibiotic and the surgery or "cut time" on the patient. The CDC recommends this should be less than an hour, and early analysis by the Six Sigma team found that although averages were close, there were variability issues in consistently meeting the recommended guidelines.

Figure 9.4 illustrates the before-and-after results for a separate project that focused on improving the timeliness of antibiotic administration to pneumonia patients.

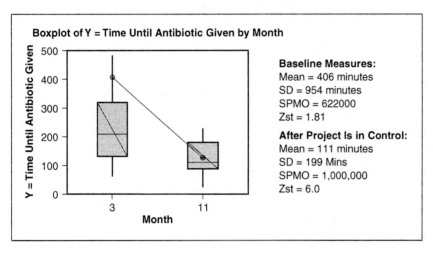

FIGURE 9.4 Antibiotic administration

REDUCING THE INCIDENCE OF POST-OPERATIVE INFECTIONS IN BOWEL CASES AT COMMONWEALTH HEALTH CORPORATION

In August 2001, Commonwealth Health Corporation (CHC) began a Six Sigma project to assess the number of post-operative infections that occur in surgical bowel cases, seeking to identify key variables and ultimately reduce the rate of infections. CHC had noticed a higher than expected number of post-op infections in bowel cases, which negatively impacts patient days, cost, and morbidity.

The team set a goal to reduce the number of post-operative infections and related wound problems. The beginning Z score was 1.90, and a defect was defined as any post-operative infection or wound integrity problem occurring within 30 days of surgery. The Brown Belt who headed this project was an infection control practitioner. The hospital epidemiologist was the sponsor, and the project team also included an operating room (OR) scheduler, OR nurse, PACU nurse, outpatient nurse, and surgery clinical manager.

Statistical data analysis using Chi Square revealed three significant variables in such cases: use of Betadine on the post-operative wound, oxygen concentration administered post-operatively, and Hibiclens bath pre-operatively.

Based on the need to address the issues, specific recommendations were presented to general surgeons and anesthesiology:

- Hibiclens shower within 48 hours pre-op
- Dry sterile dressing or only Bactroban or Bacitracin ointment
- More than 40 percent oxygen in the OR
- More than 40 percent oxygen during the immediate two-hour post-operative period

The surgeons were essentially receptive to the recommendations, and anesthesiology was very willing to implement the suggested oxygen delivery.

With new procedures in place, the project team noted a statistically significant reduction in the number of post-op infections. By December 2002, the Z score had risen to 2.70, and the project had documented a 64 percent process improvement. The team also developed a control chart for monthly updating as part of ongoing infection control efforts.

Because bowel cases are part of ongoing infection control surveillance, the hospital will be alerted to any significant deviations over time. A control chart monitors this process and determines whether the improvements are maintained (see Figure 9.5). Immediate action will be taken if the process shows signs of going out of control.

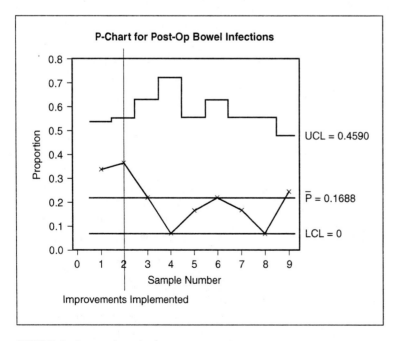

FIGURE 9.5 Post-op bowel infections

The cost analysis for this project involved research by the finance department into cost, charges, reimbursement, and insurance group for this set of patients. The spreadsheet analysis was broken out by patients who had developed an infection and those who did not. By calculating average cost, average charges, average reimbursement, and average profit for each set of patients, the financial impact per defect was set at $263.87 (20 defects for 6 months). Annualized project savings approved by the finance department are estimated at $6,755. Because all the infections identified during the study period were superficial, the financial impact was not significant. However, through time more serious and costly infections will be prevented. The increase in patient satisfaction is difficult to quantify, but there is significant benefit associated with satisfied customers.

The project continues to be monitored by the process owner. Any warning signs are reported to the infection control team for appropriate action as indicated. The process continues to improve at CHC, and in 2005 the bowel surgery infection rate was at its lowest point in five years.

REDUCING NOSOCOMIAL PRESSURE ULCERS AT THIBODAUX REGIONAL MEDICAL CENTER

Since 2001, Thibodaux Regional Medical Center (TRMC) in Louisiana has applied Six Sigma and change management methods to a range of clinical and operational issues. One project that clearly aligned with the hospital's strategic plan was an initiative to reduce nosocomial or hospital-acquired pressure ulcers, because this is one of the key performance metrics indicating quality of care. Although the pressure ulcer rate at TRMC was much better than the industry average, the Continuous Quality Improvement (CQI) data detected an increase between the last quarter of 2003 and the second quarter of 2004.

In October 2004, a Six Sigma project to address this issue was approved by the hospital's senior executives. A team began to clarify the problem statement. Their vision was to be the "Skin Savers" by resolving issues leading to the development of nosocomial pressure ulcers. The project team included a Black Belt, enterostomal nurse, medical surgical RN, ICU RN, rehab RN, and RN educator.

Through the scoping process, the team determined that inpatients with a length of stay longer than 72 hours would be included, while pediatric patients would be excluded from the scope. The project Y was defined as the nosocomial rate of Stage 2, 3, and 4 pressure ulcers calculated per 1,000 patient days. Targets were established to eliminate nosocomial Stage 3 and Stage 4 pressure ulcers and reduce Stage 2 pressure ulcers from 4.0 to <1.6 skin breaks/1,000 patient days by the end of the second quarter of 2005.

The team developed a Threat/Opportunity Matrix to help validate the need for change (see Table 9.4). They encountered some initial resistance from staff, but were able to build acceptance as the project began to unfold.

TABLE 9.4   Threat/Opportunity Matrix

	Threat	Opportunity
Short Term	Increase length of stay Increase costs Increase medical complications to patient	Improve quality of care Decrease medical complications to patient
Long Term	Decrease patient satisfaction Increase morbidity rate Decrease physician satisfaction Increase number of lawsuits Decrease reimbursement Loss of accreditation	Improve preventative care measures Improve hospital status/image Increase profitability Improve customer satisfaction

During the Measure phase, the team detailed the current process, including inputs and outputs. Using cause and effect tools, process steps having the greatest impact on the customer were identified as opportunities for improvement. The team also reviewed historical data and determined that overall process capability was acceptable, but that the sub-processes had a great deal of room for improvement. Improving these sub-processes would positively impact the overall process and further improve quality of care.

Measurement system analysis on the interpretation of the Braden Scale was performed to verify that results obtained by staff RNs were consistent with the results obtained by the enterostomal therapy registered nurse (ETRN), because this is the tool used to identify patients at risk of developing a pressure ulcer. This analysis indicated that the current process of individual interpretation was unreliable and would need to be standardized and re-evaluated during the course of the project.

A cause and effect matrix was constructed to rate the outputs of the process based on customer priorities and to rate the effect of the inputs on each output (see Figure 9.6). The matrix identified areas in the process which have the most effect on the overall outcome, and consequently the areas which need to be focused on for improvement (see Table 9.5).

The team identified several critical Xs affecting the process:

- **Frequency of Braden Scale**. *Braden Scale* is an assessment tool used to identify patients at risk of developing pressure ulcers. Policy dictates how frequently this assessment is performed.

- **Heel protectors in use**. *Heel protectors* are one of the basic preventative treatment measures taken to prevent pressure ulcers.

- **Incontinence protocol followed**. Protocol must be followed to prevent against constant moisture on the patient's skin that can lead to a pressure ulcer.

- **Proper bed**. Special beds to relieve pressure on various parts of the body are used for high-risk patients as a preventative measure.

- **Q2H turning**. Rotating the patient's body position every two hours is done to prevent development of pressure ulcers.

Customer Priority — Process Inputs (importance weights shown in the header row):

#	Process Step	Process Input	1. Patient Demographics (1)	2. Admit Patient Risk Factor (8)	3. Admit Assessment Findings (4)	4. Preventative measures (10)	5. Documents Order (2)	6. Prevents skin breaks / stops progression (10)	7. ET RN notified (2)	8. Coordination of skin care (8)	9. Prevention / treatment verified by ET RN (9)	10. Daily skin condition (5)	11. Detailed skin assessment findings (3)	12. Repeat Patient Risk Factor (8)	13. Decreased Nosocomial Pressure (7)	Total
1	Patient Admitted	HIS Admit Module	10	0	0	0	0	0	0	0	0	0	0	0	0	10
2	Admit Assess-Braden Scale	HIS Admit Assessment	0	10	10	7	0	8	9	2	2	0	0	0	5	357
3		Braden Scale (Admit)	0	10	10	5	0	7	9	6	3	0	0	0	7	382
4		Professional Judgement	0	10	10	0	5	8	10	0	0	0	0	0	7	279
5	Initiate Prevention Protocol	Braden Scale result	0	10	0	9	0	8	10	8	0	0	0	0	5	369
6		Staff Compliance	0	8	0	10	0	10	0	0	0	8	0	8	10	438
7		Prevention Protocol	0	0	0	10	0	10	0	0	7	0	0	8	8	383
8	Treatment Protocol on Chart	Manual Placement on Chart	0	0	0	0	10	5	0	0	0	0	0	0	4	98
9	Initiate Treatment Protocol	Staff Compliance	0	0	0	9	8	10	0	0	0	8	0	0	10	316
10		Treatment Protocol	0	0	0	4	0	10	0	7	3	7	0	0	7	307
11	ET RN Notified via Clinical Alert	HIS Documentation	0	0	0	0	0	0	10	0	0	0	0	0	10	90
12	ET RN Physical Assessment	HIS Documentation	0	0	0	0	0	0	0	9	9	0	0	8	9	280
13		ET RN Professional Judgement	0	0	0	0	0	0	0	10	10	0	0	8	9	297
14	ET RN Verifies Prevention/Treatment Protocol	Chart Verification	0	0	0	0	8	7	0	6	10	0	0	0	5	259
16	Daily Dept. Skin Assessment	HIS Daily Skin Assess	0	0	0	8	0	10	10	0	8	10	7	8	10	477
17		CNA Reports Skin Condition	0	0	0	0	0	10	9	9	0	8	0	0	6	272
18	Wound Assessment	Daily Skin Assess. Findings	0	0	0	6	0	10	10	9	0	10	10	6	10	450
19		HIS Wound Assess	0	0	0	0	0	0	0	8	4	0	5	0	5	150
20	Repeat Braden Scale (7days)	Braden Scale (Repeat)	0	0	0	10	0	10	10	5	0	0	0	10	8	396
21		Professional Judgement	0	0	0	0	0	8	9	0	0	0	0	10	6	220
22		Skin Policy Defined Frequency	0	0	0	0	0	7	9	0	0	5	0	10	6	235
23	Patient Discharged	Consistency of Care	0	0	0	9	3	10	0	0	6	9	0	5	10	405

FIGURE 9.6   Cause and effect matrix

TABLE 9.5 Data Analysis

Process	Defects	Opportunities	% Defective	Z Score
Overall Process	64	16,311	0.39	2.66
Braden Scale Frequency	10	76	13.16	1.12
Proper Bed	24	76	31.58	0.48
Q2H Turning	49	76	64.47	-0.37

Data analysis revealed that the bed type was not a critical factor in our process, but the use of heel protectors, incontinence protocol compliance, and Q2H turning *were* critical to the process of preventing nosocomial pressure ulcers. The impact of the Braden Scale frequency of performance was not identified until further analysis was performed (see Figure 9.7).

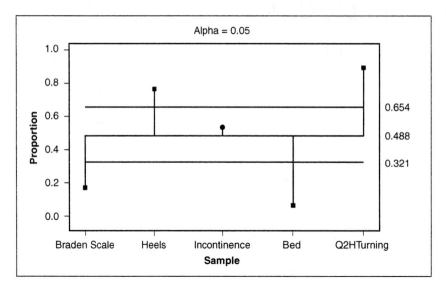

FIGURE 9.7 One-way analysis of means for sub-process defects

Evaluating data specific to at-risk patients, the team separated populations who developed nosocomial pressure ulcers from those who did not have skin breakdowns. The Braden Scale result at the time of inpatient admission from each population was analyzed to see the affect on development of a nosocomial pressure ulcer. One unexpected finding was that the admit Braden Scale result was higher for patients who develop nosocomial pressure ulcers than for those who do not develop them, showing that patients at risk are not being identified in a timely manner, thus delaying the initiation of necessary preventative measures.

The team then looked at defects for Braden Scale frequency of performance for each population of patients using Chi Square. They found the frequency of Braden Scale performance did have an effect on the development of nosocomial pressure ulcers. This was confirmed with Binary Logistic Regression (see Table 9.6).

TABLE 9.6 Binary Logistic Regression

Process	Coefficient	Odds	Probability	Odds Ratio
No Defects	−0.5222	0.59	0.37	N/A
Braden Scale Defects	2.54322	7.55	0.88	12.72
Bed Defects	1.56220	2.83	0.74	4.77
Q2 Turn Defects	−2.16870	0.07	0.07	0.11

The most significant "X" is the Braden Scale frequency of performance. This analysis confirmed the need to increase the frequency of Braden Scale performance to identify at-risk patients.

During the Improve phase, recommended changes were identified for each cause of failure on the FMEA with a RPN score of greater than 200. Some of them include the following:

- Increase frequency of Braden Scale performance to every five days
- Braden Scale assessment in hospital information system (HIS) to include descriptions for each response
- Global competency test on interpretation of Braden Scale to be repeated annually
- Add "prompts" in HIS to initiate prevention/treatment protocols
- ET Accountability Tracking Tool issued for non-compliance with prevention and treatment protocols as needed

The Braden Scale R&R was repeated after improvements were made on the interpretation of results. The data revealed an exact match between RNs and the ETRN 40 percent of the time and RNs were within the acceptable limits (+/−2) 80 percent of the time. Standard deviation was 1.9, placing the results within the specification limits. The data indicated that the RNs tend to interpret results slightly lower than the ET RN, which is a better side to err on because lower Braden Scale results identify patients at risk of developing pressure ulcers.

Another round of data collection began during the Control phase to demonstrate the impact of the improvements that had been implemented. A formal control plan was developed to ensure that improvements would be sustained over time, and the project was turned over to the process owner with follow-up issues documented in the Project Transition Action Plan.

The team implemented multiple improvements, including compilation of a document concerning "Expectations for Skin Assessment" with input from nursing and staff. They also gave a global competency test on interpretation of Braden Scale which will be repeated annually. The Braden Scale frequency was increased to five days, and they corrected the HIS calculation to trigger clinical alerts for repeat Braden Scale. Prompts were added for initiating Braden Scale, and monthly chart audits were developed for documentation of Q2H turning. A turning schedule was posted in patient rooms to identify need and document results of Q2 turning of patient. Additional solutions included the following

- ET RN attends RN orientation to discuss skin issues
- Revise treatment protocol to be more detailed

- Re-organize wound care products on units
- Unit educators to address skin issues during annual competency testing
- CNA and RN report at shift change to identify patients with skin issues
- Task list for CNAs
- ET Accountability Tracking Tool issued for non-compliance with prevention and treatment protocols as needed

Results and Recognition

Since this was a quality-focused project, the benefits are measured in cost avoidance and an overall improved quality of care. A 60 percent reduction in the overall nosocomial pressure ulcer rate resulted in an annual cost avoidance of approximately $300,000.

To make sure their initiatives are producing a positive impact on the patient care environment, the hospital continuously measures patient and employee satisfaction through Press Ganey. Inpatient satisfaction is consistently ranked in the 99th percentile and employee satisfaction in the 97th percentile. TRMC has also received recognition in the industry for their achievements, including the Louisiana Performance Excellence Award for Quality Leadership (Baldrige criteria: http://www.quality.nist.gov/) Studer Firestarter Award, and Press Ganey Excellence Award.

"This project is a perfect example of the need to verify underlying causes using valid data, rather than trusting your instincts alone," says Sheri Eschete, Black Belt and leader of the pressure ulcer project at TRMC. "Six Sigma provided us with the tools to get to the real problem so that we could make the right improvements. There had been a perception that not turning the patients often enough was the issue, but the data revealed that it was really the frequency of the Braden Scale. Leveraging the data helped us to convince others and implement appropriate changes."

The nosocomial pressure ulcer rate is monitored monthly as one of the patient-focused outcome indicators of quality care. The results are maintained on the performance improvement dashboard (see Figures 9.8 and 9.9).

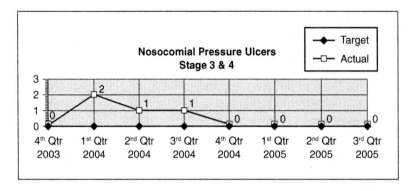

FIGURE 9.8 *Stage 3 and 4 nosocomial ulcers*

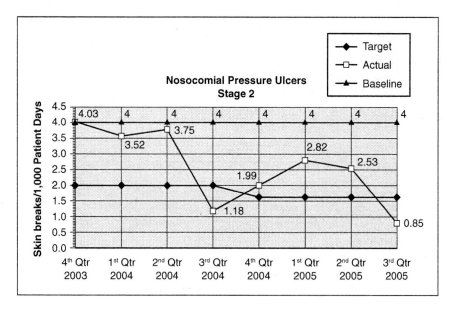

FIGURE 9.9 Stage 2 nosocomial ulcer

GLUCOSE CONTROL IN THE ADULT ICU AT VALLEY BAPTIST HEALTH SYSTEM

Ensuring effective glucose control for patients within an intensive care unit (ICU) has been shown to decrease morbidity and mortality rates. Studies supporting the role of glycemic control have used continuous infusion of insulin and glucose. With this protocol, glucose should be monitored frequently after initiation of the protocol (every 30 to 60 minutes) and on a regular basis (every 4 hours) once the blood glucose concentration has stabilized. At Valley Baptist Health System in Texas, a Six Sigma project completed in 2006 focused on controlling blood glucose levels in all critically ill patients, regardless of diagnosis, within 85mg/dl and 125mg/dl.

At the outset, data indicated the adult ICUs lacked a standardized process to manage glucose levels, with 31 percent of patients admitted to ICUs from June to August 2005 not receiving a glucose level measurement (see Figure 9.10). Of those measured, 70 percent were outside the recommended parameters of evidence-based medicine (85mg/dl to 125mg/dl).

The hospital felt that the potential benefits of this initiative would include improving patient care and outcomes, decreasing ICU length of stay, increasing ICU bed availability, reducing ICU cost, and increasing ICU revenue. To obtain Voice of the Customer (VOC), the team relied upon a combination of sources, including evidence-based medicine indicating appropriate guidelines, 32 surveys completed by physicians, and 41 surveys completed by the nurses.

The team determined that the Y for this project would be glucose levels of all adult patients admitted to MICU and NICU, glucose levels at the time of admission, glucose levels after 24 hours of admission if initial glucose is greater than 175mg/dl or after 24 hours if glucose level becomes clinically elevated at more than 175mg/dl.

METRICS	BASELINE
Dates	6/1/05– 11/14/05
Sample Size	2,644
Mean	148 mg/dl
Standard Deviation	58.53 mg/dl
DPMO	307,634
Yield	69%
Z Score	2

FIGURE 9.10   ICU glucose levels

Project specifications included the following:

- Target: 85mg/dl to 125mg/dl
- USL: 175mg/dl
- LSL: 80mg/dl
- Defect: Any glucose reading more than 175mg/dl or less than 80mg/dl

Based on the data analysis, the team decided to pursue several changes, including limiting the protocol selection to one, providing physician education, obtaining key stakeholder support, conducting one-on-one education for nurses, and obtaining additional glucometers and docking stations for NICU and MICU. They also relied upon evidence-based medicine research to develop and standardize glucose management protocol that would include

- Admission glucose and potassium levels
- 1,800-calorie ADA diet
- Endocrinologist consult
- Standardized glucose targets

Going forward, here are some of the roles and responsibilities that have been assigned to ensure project results will be maintained:

Evaluate CareVue documentation every 12 hours	Shift coordinator
Review electronic data system glucose report daily	Owner
Review physician compliance log daily	ICU medical director

| Ongoing nurse competency assessments | Individual ICU nurses |
| Set individual compliance/competency goals | Nurse manager |

From Baseline to Pilot, the process showed a statistically significant improvement (see Figure 9.11). Using Mood's Median, the team determined that the factors that were significant in terms of driving process variation were glucose IV, diet, and protocol.

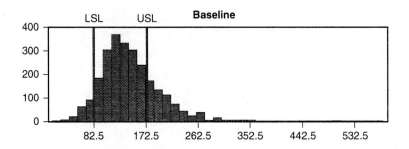

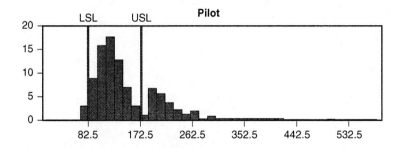

METRICS	BASELINE	PILOT
Dates	06/01/05–11/15/05	2/13/06–2/17/06
Sample Size	2,644	70
Mean	148 mg/dl	119 mg/dl
Standard Deviation	58.43 mg/dl	22.18 mg/dl
DPMO	326,558	14,286
Yield	69%	98.6%
Z Score	2	3.69
P-Value	Hypothesis Testing	0.00

FIGURE 9.11 ICU glucose baseline to pilot

A variety of control mechanisms were put in place and accountability assigned to ensure that the results of the project could be maintained over time. These included regular physician meetings, posting flyers in ICU for physicians and nursing staff, adding Glucometers and docking stations, creating a data order set and report for protocol implementation, reviewing reports on a daily basis to ensure compliance, and reviewing glucose levels every 12 hours.

Figures 9.12 and 9.13 illustrate the project measurements and percent improvement as of the Control phase.

METRICS	BASELINE	PILOT	CONTROL	Percent improvement from baseline to control
Mean	148 mg/dl	119 mg/dl	119 mg/dl	20%
Standard Deviation	58.43 mg/dl	22.18 mg/dl	25.94 mg/dl	56%
DPMO	307,634	14,286	30,973	
Yield	69%	98.6%	96.9%	40%
Z Score	2	3.69	3.37	69%

FIGURE 9.12   ICU glucose baseline to pilot controlled

Diagnosis	BASELINE All in scope diagnosis	PILOT & Control All in scope diagnosis	Improvement from baseline to control
Number of patients	92	42	
ALOS	8 days	6 days	2 day decrease
Mortality	49 / 92 = 53%	17 / 42 = 40.5%	24% decrease

FIGURE 9.13   ICU glucose baseline to control results

Chapter 10

Operational Case Studies

SECTIONS

It is sometimes difficult to categorize improvement efforts as either truly clinical or operational because the goals and processes often overlap to some degree. Clinical efforts, such as medication error reduction, may be linked more directly to patient care at the bedside. However, many of the projects within healthcare target opportunities in areas such as

- Reducing report turnaround time
- Improving accuracy in billing and collections
- Increasing radiology throughput

- Streamlining patient registration processes
- Optimizing information technology implementation
- Reducing patient wait time in ED
- Improving OR scheduling and room utilization
- Expanding volume and bed capacity

Addressing such issues successfully contributes to the overall capacity of the organization to function efficiently and with optimal resource utilization. Efforts to reduce paperwork and streamline nursing workflow, for example, can translate to additional time spent caring for patients. Money that is saved by eliminating redundant or unnecessary steps in one area can be used to expand services, hire additional staff, or introduce new life-saving technologies in another area.

Process improvement projects that reduce errors and inefficiency help to create a better environment in which to give and receive care. The case studies in this chapter illustrate this point and highlight the benefits of operational Six Sigma projects when appropriately selected and driven by the voice of the customer.

Timeliness of Self-Pay Collections on Commercial Accounts at Commonwealth Health Corporation

One Six Sigma initiative that provided Kentucky's Commonwealth Health Corporation (CHC) with some early financial results targeted the timeliness of self-pay collections on commercial accounts. As employers increasingly pass healthcare costs to employees through higher deductibles and co-pays, this issue is one that many hospitals will eventually need to address.

Six Sigma Master Black Belt Pam Jones and her team began an effort to study the process for patients presenting with commercial insurance in an attempt to collect co-pays, deductibles, and co-insurance at point of service. In scoping the project, the focus was on reducing the length of time required to collect on commercial accounts and increasing the collection percentage on patient balances.

The team presented a strong business case for this initiative. The initial Z-score was 1.8, and the preliminary cost of a defect was $1,504,099. In addition to the financial aspect, this issue also represented a customer satisfaction issue and a significant amount of re-work.

They decided to implement the pilot in the emergency department (ED) because data analysis had demonstrated that this area held the greatest opportunity for improvement, as shown in the Pareto chart for location in Figure 10.1. ED patient flow processes were modified to ensure all patients were routed through a formal "checkout" after being treated and discharged by clinicians. Financial counselor positions were established and comprehensive training was provided prior to implementation.

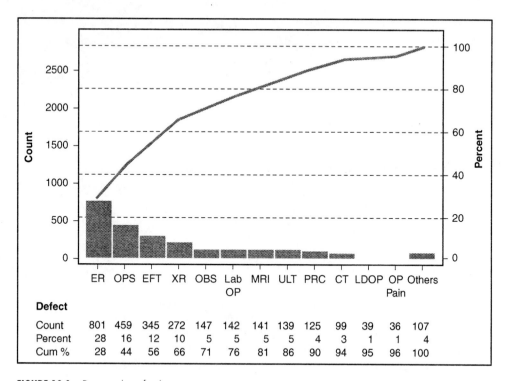

Defect	ER	OPS	EFT	XR	OBS	Lab OP	MRI	ULT	PRC	CT	LDOP	OP Pain	Others
Count	801	459	345	272	147	142	141	139	125	99	39	36	107
Percent	28	16	12	10	5	5	5	5	4	3	1	1	4
Cum %	28	44	56	66	71	76	81	86	90	94	95	96	100

FIGURE 10.1 Pareto chart for location

The following information was provided by Commonwealth Health Corporation as background on the implementation plan for this project:

IMPLEMENTATION OF A POINT OF SERVICE COLLECTION INITIATIVE–EMERGENCY DEPARTMENT

The emergency department will be the starting point of the collections initiative as it is a self-contained environment with a well-defined process flow and co-pays are usually fixed, eliminating the need to estimate patient financial responsibility.

HARDWIRING ED CHECKOUT:

- Examine and modify ED patient flow processes to ensure that all eligible patients are routed through a formal "checkout" after being treated and discharged by clinicians.
- Establish a financial counselor position for the ED to work the hours of 11:00 am-7:00 pm Sunday through Thursday (days and hours may vary

later in the pilot period according to needs and feedback from appropriate personnel). The pilot period will run for three to six months based on data analysis.

- All eligible patients will be asked to pay their ED co-pay if insured or an estimated balance if self-pay. A minimum of $20.00 will be requested from all eligible patients if they can't pay in full.
- Comprehensive education and dialogue will take place prior to rolling out new processes to secure buy-in and compliance from staff. Careful scripting will enhance customer interactions.
- Continuous tracking and regular analysis of results will assist in identifying problems, setting goals, and targeting intervention to ensure successful implementation.

TIMELINE FOR IMPLEMENTATION:

Week 1—*Assessment and Planning* (week of January 10th)

Recommended Implementation Team:

- Establish preliminary goals: Vice President, Business Office Services
- Evaluate physical location: Clinical Manager, Emergency Department
- Identify financial staff: Director, Patient Registration
- Develop Job Description: Registration Supervisor
- Meetings with Clinical and Clerical Staff: ED Registration Clerk
- Identify any potential additional needs: ED Nurse

Cashier, Patient Registration

Week 2—*Education and Training* (week of January 17th)

Customer Service Representative, CFM:
- Evaluate and modify process flows

Management Engineer:
- Complete education plan and staff training
- Develop standardized cash collection procedures and forms
- Develop necessary tools, including sample scripting, payer matrix, patient education leaflet, monthly trend analysis.

Week 3—*Roll-Out* (one week after new personnel is on board)

- Continue staff training
- Roll-out new protocols
- Monitor performance against established goals

Improving and Controlling the Process

Using Chi Square, the team re-evaluated the process and found a statistical difference between the before and after measurements (see Table 10.1).

TABLE 10.1 Chi-Square Test: Remeasure Pass, Remeasure Fail

Expected counts are printed below observed counts

	Remeasure Fail	Remeasure Pass	Total	
1	37	3304	3341	(Before Pilot)
	122.69	3218.31		
2	209	3149	3358	(After Pilot)
	123.31	3234.69		
Total	246	6453	6699	
Chi-Sq =	59.846 +	2.281 +		
	59.543 +	2.270 +	123.941	
DF = 1, P-Value = 0.000*				

*P-Value of 0 indicates a statistical difference between the before and after process.

By the Control phase of this project, the Six Sigma team at CHC had achieved a 92 percent process improvement with final cost savings of $1,388,401 (see Figure 10.2).

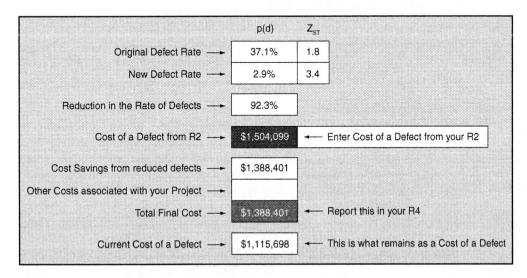

FIGURE 10.2 Final cost savings and cost of a defect

Extending the benefits of this initiative, the project findings and solutions have since been replicated in other areas of the health system. The final results underscored the success of the initiative. Using the Six Sigma DMAIC process, the team was able to reduce the probability of a defect occurring from 37 percent to 2.9 percent, and improve the overall process by 92 percent, as shown in Figure 10.2.

REDUCING AMBULANCE DIVERSIONS AT PROVIDENCE ALASKA MEDICAL CENTER

Many hospitals across the U.S. have had to confront the issue of emergency department overcrowding. In some cases, hospitals are forced to divert ambulances to other facilities due to lack of space or inpatient capacity. Several years ago, Providence Alaska Medical Center (PAMC) began to notice an increase in its ambulance diversion rate, which had risen from 3 percent to 5 percent in 2000 and then to 16 percent in 2001. The divert rate peaked at 21 percent in 2002—the hospital put policy and process changes in place and developed a web-based inpatient capacity tool.

Although the diversion rate fell to 12 percent in 2003 and to 8 percent in the first three months of 2004, the numbers again began to rise. In the second quarter of 2004, the diversion rate tripled to 24 percent and peaked in the month of July with the ED being on diversion 51 percent of the time.

In June 2004, a new ED project was launched using Six Sigma and change management methods. The project targeted reducing diversions as a result of critical care at capacity to zero, and reducing diversions as a result of ED at capacity to 3.4 percent.

The team began by trying to correlate multiple sources of information, using tools such as Work-Out to reach consensus on a common data set that would be made accessible to all stakeholders. Prior to this project, different departments had maintained multiple data sets on the same diversion episodes. Definitions and time stamps were not standardized, and access to the various databases was restricted.

The team quantified the financial impact by estimating that the average cost for one hour of diversion was $3,400. A review of the data during the Analyze phase of the project indicated that the solution must focus on the adult critical care (ACC) unit (see Figure 10.3).

The project team established clear definitions for each type of diversion and simplified the data-entry process, saving all raw entries in an electronic record designed to reduce errors. They created new standard operating procedures and defined roles and responsibilities to minimize variation in the way data would be gathered and interpreted.

With greater rigor in the data collection process, the team began to develop solutions for the primary causes of diversion. According to Dr. David Ingraham, Black Belt at PAMC, one of the most enlightening aspects of the project came from using the process to disprove an assumption that critical care diversions were due to not having an available bed. When "No Bed Available" was indicated, however, it was often because there was no *staffed* bed, indicating staffing issues rather than a lack of physical beds.

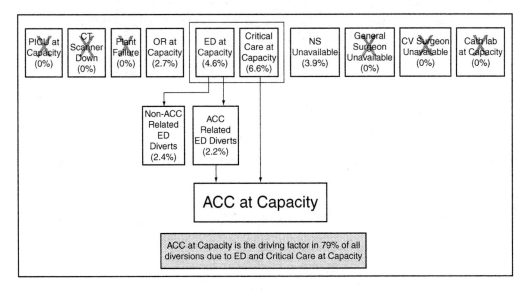

FIGURE 10.3 Linkage between diversion and access

Through statistical analysis, the team was able to develop viable solutions:

- New SOPs were created for the collection of diversion data
- An electronic data collection tool was developed
- SOPs were developed for the translation of raw data to a summary sheet
- Diversion summary data was published on an accessible hospital intranet site
- Goals and targets for diversion were established
- Staff was educated on the importance of length of stay as a contributor to staffing needs in the adult critical care unit
- A high census policy was developed to correct resource issues before a diversion becomes necessary
- An interventional cardiac recovery unit was developed to reduce burden on the critical care unit
- Alternatives were established for placement of critical care patients with prolonged lengths of stay
- Critical care house conveniences were identified at times of high census
- The team recommended proper use of float pool staffing for unexpected vacancies rather than supporting core staffing

After changes were implemented, the diversion rates dropped and ED access improved, as illustrated in Figures 10.4 and 10.5.

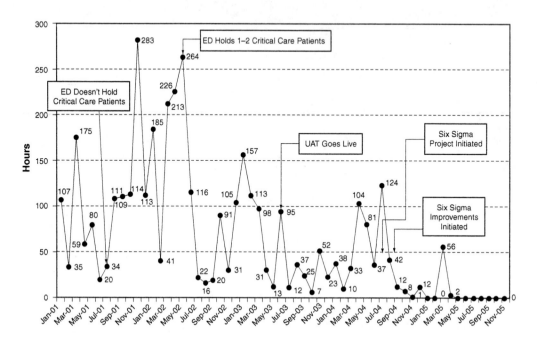

FIGURE 10.4   Critical care diverts 2001–2005

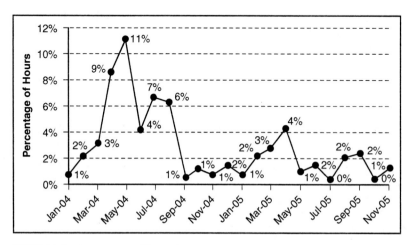

FIGURE 10.5   Percentage of hours ED at capacity 2004–2005

The original timeline to achieve the target rates was 1.5 years, or by the end of 2005. The project was completed well ahead of schedule in January 2005. Key project benefits included:

- Net revenue increase of $1.04 million on annualized basis
- Better patient access through decreased diversions due to "critical care at capacity" by an average of 26 hours per month
- Provided substantial opportunities for organizational learning, collaboration, and growth

The project to reduce emergency department ambulance diversions was part of a larger improvement initiative at Providence Alaska Medical Center and across the Providence Health System. The organization has trained its own Master Black Belts, Black Belts, and Green Belts and is now incorporating Lean into its performance improvement toolset.

Note: This project was originally shared through an article by John Kalb and David Ingraham, MD, published in the iSixSigma healthcare newsletter (http://healthcare.isixsigma.com/library/content/c061011a.asp).

BETTER PATIENT CHARGE CAPTURE AT YALE-NEW HAVEN HOSPITAL

Hospitals lose millions of dollars each year due to patient care items that are used but somehow never charged or reimbursed. A Six Sigma team at Yale-New Haven Hospital (YNHH) in Connecticut decided to look at the opportunities related to patient charge capture and began the scoping process for a project.

Previous attempts to address this issue had not met with great success due to the large number of items that might be included in a review. To ensure the project would be both manageable and measurable, the team decided to focus on the top 12 supplies based on quantity and expense, and also limit the scope of the project to 7 pilot units.

As they began the data collection and analysis process, they found that only 35.7 percent of medical/surgical supplies were being captured on inpatient nursing units. Based on this finding, they calculated an opportunity to increase gross charges by an estimated $4.5 million for just the top 12 supplies.

Another observation the team made was that there wasn't a standard method of processing patient charge items within the inpatient units. Beyond the "Big Y" of patient charge capture, there were several sub-cycles to focus on. They created a process map that revealed numerous intertwined steps—making it difficult to see how any items could be properly charged. The process was divided into three sub-cycles with three sponsors (see Figure 10.6).

One of the sub-cycles the team decided to target was improving the documentation of the five required data elements on the charge cards. They believed this could help to reduce cycle time, beginning with use of product to charging of product, defects such as cards that can't be billed, and re-work associated with manual data capture.

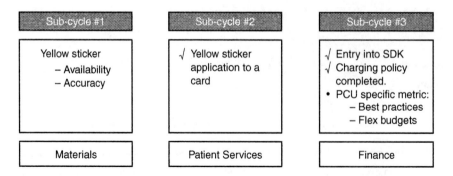

FIGURE 10.6 Three sub-processes and sponsors (sub-cycle 1: items without stickers)

Technology was another area to consider. Although a variety of technology solutions are available for inventory management and billing, they are often costly and do not guarantee a return on investment. Furthermore, as many healthcare organizations have discovered the hard way, implementing a new technology on top of a broken process can lead to disappointing results. Simply automating a broken process isn't the answer.

To address some of the issues and determine the factors and solutions within its immediate control, the team held a Work-Out with nurses, patient care associates, and business associates. Frequently, the staff would point to missing yellow stickers on products. This was considered out-of-scope for the first Work-Out. The patient care unit staff was informed that another team would explore reasons for missing yellow stickers.

The primary factor within the immediate control of the unit staff was incomplete information on the charge card to which the yellow stickers were affixed. Cards were not accessible to clinicians, or one of the five essential data elements was missing from the charge card. Many business associates complained that the product names on the yellow stickers did not match the computer name. After the Work-Out, a new process was implemented in which the five data elements would automatically be printed on labels, replacing the handwritten process. This prevented missing and illegible data elements on the charge card. It was also determined that the current process of business associates entering cards into the computer would be replaced with a centralized data-entry process that could be more easily monitored. Ensuring appropriate staff training on the new procedures and written reference materials was another key change the team put into place.

Figure 10.7 illustrates an effort to streamline and simplify sticker application to a patient charge card. One area of concern involved making sure all products had yellow stickers for capturing charges, because an audit revealed that 10 percent of the items were arriving from vendors without them. Auto-substitution and back-ordered items were the two factors most often behind the missing stickers. Also, the outer package sometimes had yellow charge stickers affixed, but the product inside did not. The team held a second Work-Out to simplify some of the process steps, making sure stickers were on the products when they were delivered to the units.

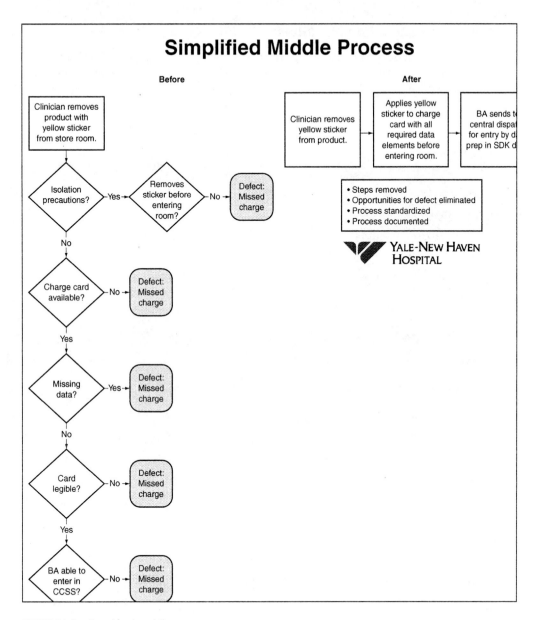

FIGURE 10.7 Simplified middle process

Developing and Piloting Solutions

As a result of the second Work-Out for the first sub-cycle, three solution areas surfaced: improving the pick process, developing an accurate list of patient charge items, and improving communication systems.

There were a number of suggestions to improve the pick process, and several changes were implemented:

- Training and awareness programs for pickers both at YNHH and the supplier
- Develop solid QA procedure to ensure patient charge items were labeled at supplier and YNHH
- Develop procedure to flag auto-substitutions
- Achieve visual control by flagging on shelf what is to be a patient-charged item at YNHH and the supplier
- Instruct all YNHH pickers on how to print out own labels
- Supplier to scan all YNHH orders for charge items
- Education and QA orders to ensure labels are attached in the proper spot
- Supplier and YNHH representative to meet regularly to provide feedback and discuss problems

To address the accurate list of items, the following solutions were proposed:

- Finance and Materials to agree on what is chargeable
- Supplier and YNHH materials department will complete an accurate list of patient charge items
- A new process for reconciling different lists between YNHH and supplier using automation
- New patient charge policy and standard operating procedure
- Users educated with "getting-to-know you" patient charge items
- Any patient charge item will be reviewed with "unit of measure," which is each item versus carton/pack to validate that patients are charged for each as appropriate

With respect to the communication systems, solutions included the following:

- Communicate with supplier when product was not labeled; standardize this communication daily and then weekly
- All parties work off accurate list of patient charge items
- Materials should always check for yellow stickers to ensure consistent training

- Floor staff (RNs, PCAs, BAs) should be aware of which items are patient charge items, and ensure stickers on bins

- Identify a clear point of contact in Finance

- Develop regular update process to verify all systems have same patient charge items flagged, minimize manual verification, investigate common data field for each system, and send summary to supplier for verification

- Identify in product catalog which items are chargeable

- Communicate to floor staff new chargeable items added to formulary

New Systems and Fewer Defects

As a result of the project, the team was able to eliminate some of the unnecessary steps and opportunities for defects involved with the patient charge capture process. The charge card was redesigned so that the required data elements would automatically print out to a label. To minimize confusion, the team had the cards placed in the same highly visible places within every care unit. They also developed a unit report to reconcile differences between items purchased and what is being charged to patients. One unit may borrow supplies from another unit, which can throw off the tracking system. For instance, an ICU may purchase multiple kits that don't necessarily make sense for the entire floor to stock, so people tend to borrow the items when needed. As the hospital was looking for technology to automate the charge capture process, it was important to ensure that vendors had a mechanism for charging borrowed supplies.

The project team succeeded in implementing key changes and achieving statistically significant results. Within the seven pilot units, they moved from 35.7 percent capture of patient charges to 87.5 percent captured. For the 12 products on the 7 pilot units, the hospital was able to capture $197,000 more in gross charges than it would have at the January charge capture rates. On an annualized basis, this is estimated to be $600,000 for 7 pilot units and 12 items, or for all 34 inpatient units, the annualized gross revenue is estimated at $3 million. Assuming net revenue at 10 percent of gross, net revenue on $3 million is $300,000.

By capturing the right information by patients in the database, the hospital is able to increase accuracy as to what is spent on each DRG (diagnosis-related group) and better reflect the actual cost of caring for patients.

ENSURING ACCURACY IN MANAGED CARE OPERATING ROOM CARVE-OUTS AT VIRTUA HEALTH

One of the early Six Sigma initiatives at Virtua Health targeted revenue generation by improving the process to identify, charge, and bill carve-out items for managed care and Medicare. Leveraging opportunities uncovered through these initial efforts led to scoping a project in 2005 to focus on managed care operating room (OR) carve-outs at Virtua's Marlton and Memorial campuses.

Within managed care contracts, "carve-out" arrangements have become common practice for particular conditions or types of services. Payers and health plans use carve-outs to separate specific items from the overall plan's risk pool. Potential revenue can be gained from managed care carve-outs if the costs can be tracked and charged accurately.

"For a variety of reasons, we had been struggling for some time to accurately capture costs for implantable devices," says Adrienne Elberfeld, Master Black Belt on the project. "When we originally looked at the data in 2001, we found we weren't capturing charges to the tune of about $7 million. We had made improvements through our first project, but learned some lessons as well. We actually built a process that was dependent on one person generating reports, and without that person the process fell apart. Many things were happening at once that impacted our ability to control the project results—including changes in process owners and leadership, and the introduction of new OR systems. We decided a follow-up effort would be required."

Despite all the work they had done initially, something had slipped. By carefully scoping a new project, they were able to take a fresh look at the issue and uncover opportunities to review internal processes to make sure paperwork got through and charges were appropriately captured.

The goal for this project would be to increase revenue by ensuring all managed care OR carve-outs are correctly billed and documented to meet compliance standards. The "Y" to be measured was identified as the number of managed care OR carve-outs that were accurately billed, and the sub-Y defect would be any managed care OR carve-out not posted within five days of the procedure or discharge. Both factors would be measured through the "Managed Care OR Carve-Out Report," and data sources would include 100 manual chart reviews from each hospital. To analyze measurement system accuracy, a gage R&R was completed and found 96 percent agreement among the sources of information.

Education frequently is a key component in Six Sigma projects to make sure that employees understand and embrace any process changes or workflow adjustments that are introduced through the initiative. At Virtua, focused educational sessions were conducted in November 2005 to help OR staff understand the importance of proper implant documentation. Monitoring the frequency, descriptions, and volumes of "like" items would help to determine the need for an action plan to help control costs by reducing the amount of supplies being ordered unnecessarily.

During the Improve Phase, a review of the Employer Sponsored Insurance (ESI) category/revenue codes from the 100 chart reviews revealed opportunities for improvement. The probability of a defect was measured at both campuses: 30.9% at the Marlton campus and 19.3% at the Memorial campus. The root cause analysis shown in Table 10.2 illustrates the team's effort to identify the underlying drivers for the defects and propose solutions. The revenue code defects are shown in Figure 10.8.

TABLE 10.2 Root Cause Analysis

Factor	Root Cause	Proposed Solutions
Managed Care carve-outs billed accurately	Incorrect ESI category/ revenue codes	• Update of the 16,000 items in the CDM • Monthly review by the Surgical Services Practice Council of the new OR supplies upload to confirm correct revenue codes • New requisition form with space to add product category and check box "Is supply an implantable device?"

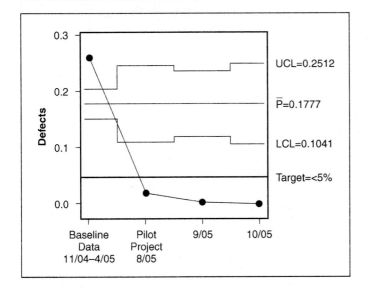

FIGURE 10.8 Revenue code defects

At the outset of the project, the Z score was measured at 2.14, with a 26 percent probability of a defect. After the project entered the Control phase, the Z score was measured at 3.60 with a 1.8 percent probability of a defect. Initial measurements indicated the accuracy of managed care OR carve-outs at Marlton was 69.1 percent and at Memorial it was 80.7 percent. In August, results from the pilot project demonstrated a 98.2 percent accuracy. The team noted one change in September and 0 changes in October. Statistical analysis indicated that September results were 99.7 percent accurate, while results for the month of October were 100 percent accurate. The Chi-Square analysis in Figure 10.9 shows the significance of the pilot project results.

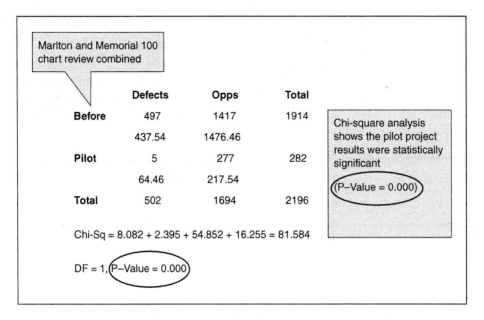

FIGURE 10.9   Chi-square analysis MHBC and Marlton—Combined versus pilot project

The projected financial benefit from this initiative was estimated at $196,000, with $115,000 from the CDM review (1/05-7/05) and $82,000 (8/05-6/06) if the changes were not made to the CDM and the activity remained unchanged. The surgical services council now reviews all information on a monthly basis. They also were able to benefit from a multidisciplinary approach. By educating clinicians and finance staff, and making everyone aware of the issue, they instituted a workable review process to make sure charges are consistently captured in the system. The financial benefits are demonstrated in Figure 10.10.

Data results confirmed that the improvements had achieved the goal defined in the DMAIC team charter. The team selected ongoing measures to monitor performance of the process and ensure continued effectiveness of the solution, and determined that key charts or graphs would be used within a "process dashboard." With changes implemented, the team created a plan to sustain the process. This would include having the hospital's Surgical Services Practice Council conduct a monthly review of the new OR supplies uploaded the previous month to confirm accuracy of the revenue codes. The plan also called for product coordinators to use the new requisition form that had been developed.

To facilitate better communication and staff education, part of the Control plan involved establishing clear roles, policies, and standard operating procedures. The team carefully documented the revised process, and then identified a process owner to assume responsibility for maintaining results and managing operations going forward. They also developed charts detailing requirements, measures, and responses to problems in the process, and updated the project binder documenting the work that had been done and the key findings.

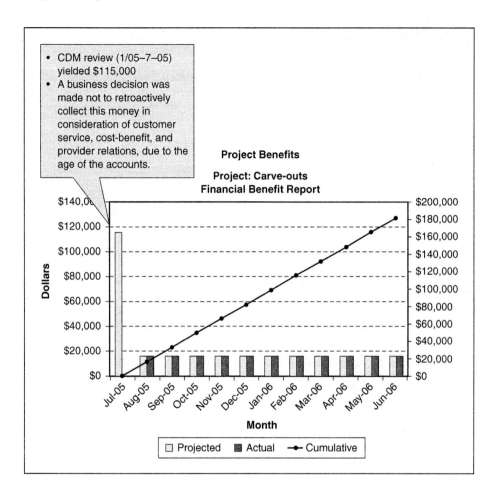

FIGURE 10.10 Project financial benefits

Other issues or opportunities that couldn't be addressed adequately during the course of the project were shared with senior management. The team took time to recognize and celebrate their achievements, which is a key aspect that helps build enthusiasm for improvement initiatives. The carve-outs project had measurably improved service quality, decreased expense, and created a more accurate process for revenue collection.

Carve-Out Project Team

> **Sponsors**: J. Dower/B. Segin
> **Process Owners**: D. McKenna/M. Paglione/P. Schultz/L. Walker

> **Ad-Hoc Team Members**:

K. McRory	M. Schultz
C. Sambucci	N. Rivera
S. Fiorini	K. Pape
D. Flagg	C. Bosco
C. Childress	R. Altmark
A. Annuzzi	J. Kurz
B. Cain	M. Paglione
L. Ackley	

> **Finance Approvers**: R. Rueblinger/W. Christie
> **Green Belts**: H. McNally/A. Kitz
> **Black Belt**: K. Goodman
> **Master Black Belt**: A. Elberfeld

ADDRESSING BED MANAGEMENT AT THE NEBRASKA MEDICAL CENTER

In many hospitals, a certain number of inpatient beds are unavailable each day due to staffing-related issues. This restricts access to care and can result in lower patient, staff, and physician satisfaction; reduced physician referrals; quality issues; and lost revenue or market share. At The Nebraska Medical Center, an effort to deal with bed restrictions became one of three individual projects derived from a larger scoping effort initially described as "bed availability."

In December 2002, the hospital began its first round of training and initial wave of Six Sigma projects. Following discussions with senior leadership, three Black Belts were asked to focus on the general topic of bed availability. The hospital considered this to be an important issue given the impact on patients who might have to wait for a long time in the ED or who may be referred to other facilities for admission. By targeting issues related to staffing utilization and bed restrictions, the hospital hoped to identify ways that nursing staff could be better deployed to increase the capacity to care for more patients.

As the project began, team members included managers from a rehab unit, the patient placement unit, a medical surgical floor, an intensive care unit, a telemetry floor, a nursing director, and a nursing resource coordinator. This level of participation illustrates how broad the initiative was even after initial scoping. The team began by analyzing the daily reports that indicate whether or not a bed is available. By following the Six Sigma process, their goal was to find solutions that would help them to reduce the number of unavailable beds and thereby improve their ability to admit and care for patients. As they entered the measure phase of the project, 75 to 80 percent of beds in the hospital were still in scope.

"In addition to helping the hospital resolve a key issue impacting access to care, this project served as a great learning opportunity for the team," says Jason Lebsack, Manager of Six Sigma at The Nebraska Medical Center, who in 2003 served as the Black Belt on this project. "It wasn't simply a matter of identifying a problem with bed availability and deciding to launch a project to fix it, given the complexity and amount of scoping required. We all learned to be more focused in our efforts and to set clear, measurable parameters."

As it turns out, bed availability was not a single project in itself, but rather a focal point from which separate projects could be scoped and executed. They were starting from scratch, given that data was either hard to come by or at least widely dispersed throughout the organization.

To set reasonable boundaries, the team made some decisions on the areas that would be in scope and out of scope for this particular project:

- In scope
  - Medical/Surgical, Telemetry, intensive care units
  - All unit staffing practices
  - Use of nurse/patient ratio
  - Use of current acuity rating approach
  - Sick call, holiday, vacation approach
- Out of Scope
  - Burn, LSCU (Liver Special Care Unit), OB, pediatrics, PICU, NICU, LTCC (Lied Transplant Cooperative Care) and TRU units (Transitional Rehabilitation Unit)
  - Redefining medical necessity
  - Nursing shortage
  - Non-staffing bed restrictions
  - Process for determining patient acuity
  - Student nurses

Obtaining the "voice of the customer" (VOC) helped to ensure alignment with the organization's strategic plan and validate connections with two key objectives, which are two of The Nebraska Medical Center's five Priorities for Excellence:

- **Most attractive employer**. Internally, there were concerns that issues surrounding lack of bed availability could make it difficult to recruit and retain staff, and to adequately manage the patient load taking safety and acuity into account. Referring physicians had become dissatisfied with the capacity issues.

- **Highest quality of customer service and care.** Feedback from patient surveys indicated concern over waiting too long for a bed, or being turned away to other hospitals
  for care. Being able to address bed restrictions would positively affect the hospital's
  ability to provide high-quality patient care in a timely manner.

At the outset of the project, there were some hard feelings between staff on the various
floors making requests for beds and others who were taking the calls. "Decentralized patient
assignment requires a lot of cooperation and teamwork," says Lebsack. "Interactions over the
phone were sometimes tense because they were based on a sense of urgency."

The goal or "Y" for the project would be that at 3PM each day, each unit should have at
least as many available beds as budgeted beds. By measuring current performance they found
they were starting with a 29 percent defect rate.

Simply arriving at the basic formula of available beds divided by budgeted beds required a
tremendous amount of effort and discussion. There had previously been no set target for nurse
managers as to the number of beds they needed to have open. Figure 10.11 shows the available
beds in the areas that were within scope, and points to the variability between different floors.

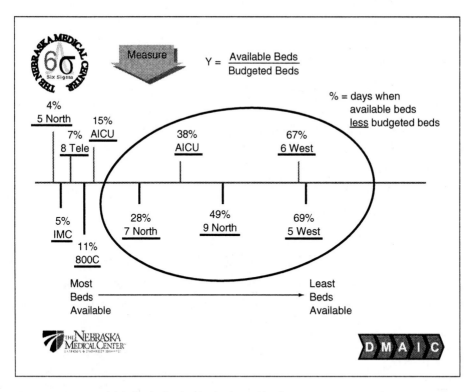

FIGURE 10.11 Available beds divided by budgeted beds

Analyzing this information was another key aspect of the scoping process. Of the 10 units evaluated, data revealed that at least 5 did not present availability issues. They narrowed their focus to staffing issues within the five units that had the highest percentage of unavailable beds.

Further scoping led to a concentration on 6 West with a 67 percent rate of defects. They decided to exclude 5 West from the study at the time, even though the rate was slightly higher, because their issues with vacancy rates would be addressed by recent new hires.

The team then began to prioritize the underlying factors, narrowing down to people-related (see Figure 10.12) and "other" (see Figure 10.13). This didn't necessarily reveal a trend, other than the obvious with regard to staffing rates, as indicated in Figures 10.12 and 10.13.

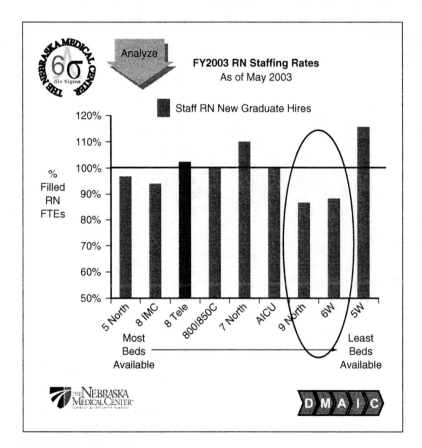

FIGURE 10.12 RN staffing rates

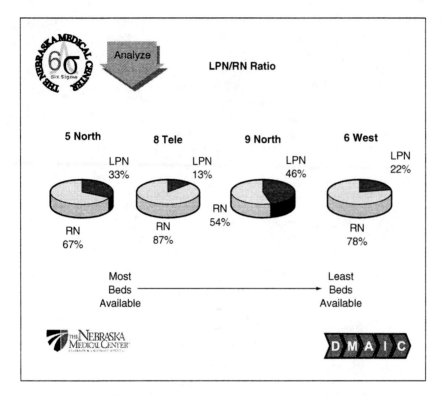

FIGURE 10.13 LPN/RN ratio

It was initially assumed that the more established units would be able to take more patients, but in fact the opposite relationship was identified. As shown in Figures 10.14 and 10.15, they analyzed data on daily admissions and discharges, staffing ratios, and critical elements such as specific time periods to see if they could statistically confirm the most important factors.

During the critical elements analysis phase of this project, the application of Lean Thinking provided critical insights into factors contributing to beds unavailable due to staffing-related issues on 6 West. A detailed analysis of the RN and LPN shift structure on 6 West revealed a number of opportunities for improvement.

At the time of the project, nursing schedules on 6 West included various combinations of 4-, 8-, and 12-hour shifts. Having so many different shifts built in numerous handoffs of patient care throughout the day (non-value-added time from the patient's perspective) and created an almost daily nursing gap in the number of nurses working to provide care in the late afternoon.

In fact, 6 West chronically had vacancies in the 3 PM-to-11 AM shift and frequently had to scramble to find additional nurses to work during this time. This scramble placed a significant amount of stress on Lead RNs each day.

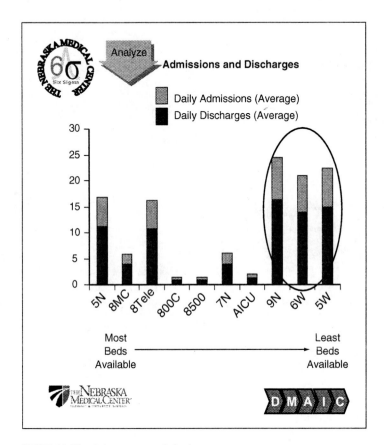

FIGURE 10.14   Admissions and discharges

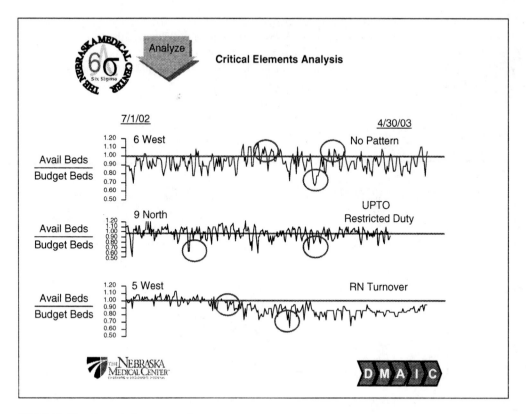

FIGURE 10.15 Critical elements analysis

Developing Solutions

In all, the project team identified three major improvement strategies for 6 West as well as four main improvements to improve the overall utilization of nursing staff:

- 6 West Improvements
  - Improved floor aesthetics and computer upgrades (installed in hallways close to patients)
  - Creation of an Admission and Discharge RN role
  - Simplified RN shift structure
- Overall Improvements
  - Nursing staff floatation
  - Bed Status report simplification

- Lead and Charge RN/Patient Placement Unit RN job shadowing program ("Trading Places")
- Lead and Charge RN response timeliness to Patient Placement Unit pages

During the course of the project, the team identified other possible changes that could be addressed later, and placed them on the project "parking lot." The issue of nurse staff flotation eventually became one of several Work-Out sessions. Through another separate Work-Out, the team developed revisions to the bed report to increase usability, streamline content, and provide clearer definitions.

Sometimes necessity really is the mother of invention. When one of the nurses had to be on restrictive duty for medical reasons, the team decided to pilot the idea of a specialist role for admissions and discharge. The nurse would handle some of the duties in this critical area to reduce the workload for other staff, and would also back up an LPN in this role. Although this idea originated because a nurse happened to be on restrictive duty, it turned out to be such a positive change that they figured out a way to make it work long-term. According to Lebsack, several different nurses now fill this role, and they are very pleased with the arrangement.

One innovative solution coming from this project was the creation of a shadowing program where the lead staff was asked to spend a few hours at the bed desk and learn about what they do, while others went to the floors. Because of its power to create a more collegial atmosphere, this framework for trading places has since been integrated into the hospital's orientation process. It allows staff to meet face to face and gain some appreciation for the complexity of other jobs, and has helped strengthen relationships between the two groups.

In looking at the unit aesthetics and layout, the team brought in some useful Lean concepts, particularly around the 5S method to Sort, Set in Order, Shine, Standardize, and Sustain. They helped to clean and organize the nurses' lounge, fix monitors, install two additional computers, and revamp traffic patterns to reduce some of the back and forth travel to the nurse's station. The changes enabled caregivers to stay closer to the patients.

The team also re-instituted a 10/10 bed assignment process with the expectation that floors would return a page within 10 minutes, then be paged again, and then if there was no answer in 10 minutes the manager would be paged. This system was devised through a Work-Out to monitor response time from page to floor to bed desk, and it continues to be monitored on a quarterly basis. The team had found that about 50- to 60 percent of the time calls weren't being returned in a timely basis, but this has is now consistently under 25 percent and has been tracked for more than two years since the project was completed. One of the keys to making the monitoring of this Work-Out possible was the Patient Placement Unit's transition from a paper monitoring system to a computerized database.

Project Results and Sustainability

Two years after the changes were implemented on 6 West, the hospital has continued to see positive results, while also working through remaining challenges. The admission/discharge nurse is still in place, and this change has been well received by the staff. The 12-hour only shift structure has been maintained, and 6 West has been fully staffed for more than a year, although two LPNs did leave the unit at least partially due to the 12-hour shifts. All beds, other than those with isolation restrictions, are usually available for patients. All ten private beds on the floor were converted to pediatric beds in January 2005. The lack of private rooms presented challenges with patient bed assignment, especially given isolation patients treated on the floor. Improvements in bed availability are demonstrated in Figure 10.16.

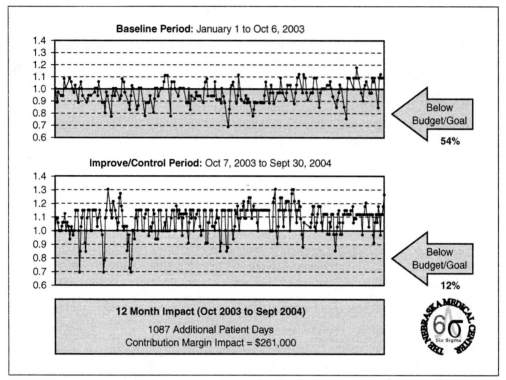

FIGURE 10.16 6 West available beds (Monday-Sunday 3 PM)

Gaining VOC is important at each phase of the initiative. For this project, positive impact on the staff was evident through comments such as the following:

- "We don't have downtime from direct patient care at 3 PM anymore."
- "Most of staff is content with 12-hour shifts and would not go back to an 8-hour shift structure."
- "Nurses love it that they only have to work every third weekend."
- "Admission/Discharge RN role still working well. Exploring the need to expand hours and further specify duties."
- "6 West is fully staffed. In fact, currently there are three RN students interested in working on 6 West but there are no open positions."

THE CORPORATE ADVANCE DIRECTIVE AT VALLEY BAPTIST HEALTH SYSTEM

One of the many successful Six Sigma projects at Valley Baptist Health System in Harlingen, Texas, targeted the existence of an advance directive. The hospital sought to institute a single, consistent and effective process to ensure that 100 percent of the adult patients at Valley Baptist Medical Center-Headquarters (VBMC-H) have an advance directive in their medical record.

For the purpose of this initiative, the groups considered in scope would be all VBMC-H adult inpatients, 18 years of age or older, and ED and direct admit patients. Surgery and outpatients would not be included in the scope of the project.

The team believed that one of the primary benefits of the project would be compliance with the JCAHO standard to address the wishes of the patient regarding end-of-life decisions. In addition, the hospital sought to enhance patient education and improve patient and caregiver satisfaction. The project aligned with the overall strategic plan in terms of integration, simplicity, and relentless service and Six Sigma quality. The team looked for input from a variety of stakeholder groups including patients and families, physicians, nurses, case managers, social workers, pastoral services, admissions, medical records, risk management, and JCAHO.

The first Y to be measured would be VBMC-H adult inpatients with an advance directive or its refusal in the medical record. The second Y would be time elapsed from the advance directive order placed until advance directive documentation is added to the medical record (see Figure 10.17).

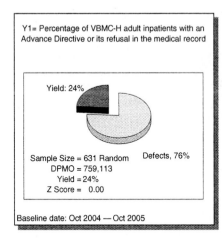

Y1= Percentage of VBMC-H adult inpatients with an Advance Directive or its refusal in the medical record

Yield: 24%

Sample Size = 631 Random
DPMO = 759,113
Yield = 24%
Z Score = 0.00

Defects, 76%

Baseline date: Oct 2004 — Oct 2005

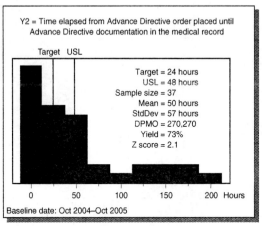

Y2 = Time elapsed from Advance Directive order placed until Advance Directive documentation in the medical record

Target   USL

Target = 24 hours
USL = 48 hours
Sample size = 37
Mean = 50 hours
StdDev = 57 hours
DPMO = 270,270
Yield = 73%
Z score = 2.1

0   50   100   150   200 Hours

Baseline date: Oct 2004–Oct 2005

FIGURE 10.17 Baseline metrics/process capability

Y2	Target = 24 hours
	USL = 48 hours
	Defect > 48 hours

Statistical analysis revealed that the critical Xs causing most of the variation were the nurse unit and the patient language (see Figure 10.18).

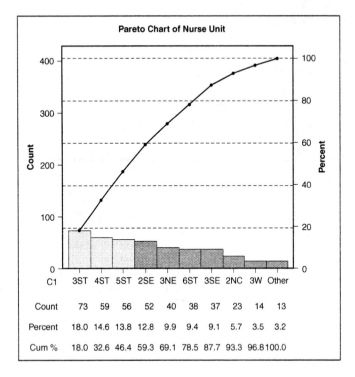

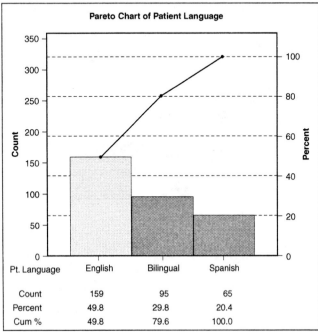

FIGURE 10.18   Pareto charts

The Valley Baptist Health System team implemented several improvements during the course of the project, including streamlining processes and removing rework, improving accessibility and clarity by introducing online forms, improving process control and accountability by introducing an order-based system, and simplifying interpretation by creating a combined English/Spanish form.

CATH LAB UTILIZATION OF IMPLANTABLE DEVICES AT MEMORIAL HERMANN HEART & VASCULAR INSTITUTE-SOUTHWEST HOSPITAL

The Memorial Hermann Heart & Vascular Institute on the campus of Memorial Hermann Southwest Hospital in Houston is one of Houston's largest heart programs, and the only freestanding heart facility in Houston. The Southwest Heart & Vascular Institute is one of three in the 16-hospital Memorial Hermann system. As part of a large training and improvement initiative, a Six Sigma team began a project to address the rising cost of implantable devices in the Cath Lab. The effort aligned with one of the organization's key strategies to achieve and maintain operational excellence.

The team included a Black Belt, two Green Belts, a Project Sponsor, Executive Champion, and Physician Champion. They began to focus on defibrillator and pacemaker utilization as the two primary cost drivers in the Cath Lab, collecting data on the type of implant used, the implant description, physician, manufacturer, and implant cost.

Data was collected during a three-month period. Implant utilization and cost by physician, implant cost by manufacturer, and implant type (biventricular versus dual-chamber versus single-chamber) were used to benchmark against other facilities in the system. This provided useful background for the team and revealed that the average implant cost per case for both defibrillators and pacemakers exceeded the organization's benchmark, which was set as the upper specification limit to determine process capability.

With clinician support, the team shared its findings with the cardiologists on the hospital's Cath Lab Review Committee, which was responsible for overseeing program development. The data analysis and discussions with cardiologists led to the following conclusions:

- Significant variation in implant utilization existed among cardiologists
- Manufacturer presence during procedures heavily impacted implant selection
- Cardiologists were unaware of the cost of the device used in the case
- No specific control or attention was paid to implant pricing and utilization by the cardiologists

The cardiologists realized the need to manage the increasing implant costs and assumed responsibility for implementing a physician-owned accountability system and structure. Two sub-committees were designated: Defibrillator/Pacemaker and Stent Utilization. Both meet monthly and report back to the parent committee.

Changes identified to help positively impact implant cost per case included educating cardiologists on implant cost through use of a physician pocket card listing all devices by manufacturer in order of price. Similar devices (biventricular, dual-chamber, and single-chamber) were also grouped together. Using this tool, conversations began to change between manufacturer and physician.

As the cardiologists became more involved in implant selection, the manufacturers were required to bring in more than just "high-end" devices. With strong physician influence and leadership, manufacturers began to explore avenues to help the hospital appropriately manage implant cost.

The project began in May 2005, and results were monitored for a 12-month period starting in July 2005. The hospital saw a $1,006,913 hard dollar cost savings for fiscal year 2006. The average defibrillator implant cost per case decreased by $4,420, leading to a 54 percent reduction in defects. This surpassed the project goal of 50 percent defect reduction compared to the organization's benchmark. In addition, average pacemaker implant cost per case decreased by $1,146, leading to a 44 percent reduction in defects (see Figure 10.19).

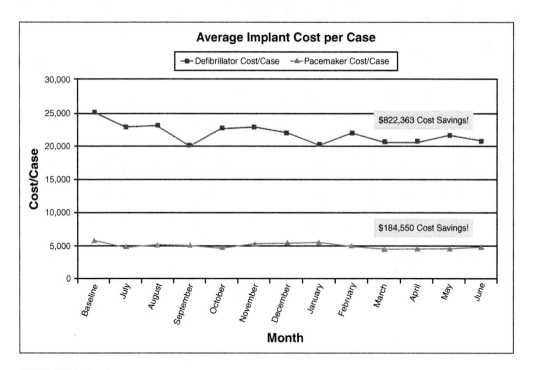

FIGURE 10.19 Implant average cost per case

According to the team, the success of this project was due in large part to physician support and having a motivated group of cardiologists involved in the process. In addition, having participation and support from the Project Sponsor and Executive Champion was key in working with physicians to remove barriers. The team's persistence was also a factor, along with the development of a solid control plan to sustain project results.

OPTIMIZING RESPIRATORY CARE SERVICES AT VALLEY BAPTIST HEALTH SYSTEM

In Fall 2005, the area of respiratory care services at Valley Baptist Health System became a target for a Six Sigma improvement initiative when a retrospective chart review uncovered a number of treatment and documentation errors. Feedback from staff confirmed that this was an important issue affecting patient care, and would require a focused effort to validate root causes and put sustainable solutions in place.

A Six Sigma team was assembled with the specific goal to improve the timeliness of respiratory treatments and eliminate incomplete and inaccurate documentation. The objective clearly aligned with the organization's strategic plan in terms of ensuring excellence in service, quality, integration, and simplicity.

In scoping the project, the team determined it would include all inpatient therapeutic respiratory treatments on 2T, 3T, Pediatrics, Telemetry, MICU and SICU, but the ED and NICU patients would be considered out of scope. To gather VOC and understand how respiratory services could be improved, the team surveyed physicians, nursing staff and case managers.

The project involved the following details:

- Y1: Timeliness of subsequent treatment (measured in minutes)

- Y1 defect: Treatment administered less than 30 minutes before or after scheduled treatment time

- LSL: 30 minutes before treatment due (target: scheduled treatment time)

- USL: 30 minutes after treatment due

- Y2: Accurate and complete documentation of initial and subsequent treatments (measured as "yes" or "no")

- Y2 defect: Documentation that is not accurate and complete

- Y2 target: 100 percent

Looking at the baseline metrics and process capability for both focus areas revealed significant opportunity for improvement (see Figure 10.20). At the outset of the project, the "Y" dealing with timeliness of subsequent treatment had a Z score of 2.21, and the "Y" that focused on accurate documentation had a Z score of 0.

Y1 Baseline Metrics	
METRICS	**BASELINE**
Dates	11/5/05–11/15/05
Sample Size	125
Mean	47.9 Min.
Standard Deviation	122.2 Min.
DPMO	240,000
Yield	76%
Z Score	2.21

Y2 Baseline Metrics	
METRICS	**BASELINE**
Dates	11/5/05–11/15/05
Sample Size	199
DPMO	914,573
Yield	8.5%
Z Score	0.0

FIGURE 10.20   Baseline metrics

When the team analyzed the data to determine statistical significance, it found that for subsequent treatments, the RT (respiratory therapist) was a key factor. With respect to the second "Y", the team did not find any significant statistical difference, accounting for variation, because the incomplete documentation was common to every unit, respiratory therapist, and shift.

During the Improve phase, several new standard operating procedures (SOPs) were developed and implemented for equipment techs, handling codes, load leveling and staff assignment criteria, unit-based RTs, charging for treatments, and order retrieval from IDX. The team also created RT notes to replace the orange stickers and charge sheets that had been previously used.

The documentation process was streamlined from five down to just two documents, including the multidisciplinary care plan, which is now completed once every 24 hours. All other documentation is done with every treatment on one single form. Other changes that were put in place as a result of the project included the development of supply par levels and the replacement of existing pagers with alpha numeric pagers to eliminate the RTs having to call back to the units.

Two pilots were conducted to test the viability and impact of the solutions that had been introduced. While documentation had significantly improved in the first pilot, treatment times had actually increased. The staff was informed of this situation, and increased surveillance of the process was implemented before the second pilot began. Stricter adherence to the new SOPs was required, and the second pilot was successful for both timely treatments and improved documentation.

As a result of the pilot, several process changes were integrated into daily operations, including unit-based RTs, streamlined documentation by reducing the number of forms the RTs were using, and the development of supply par levels (see Figure 10.21).

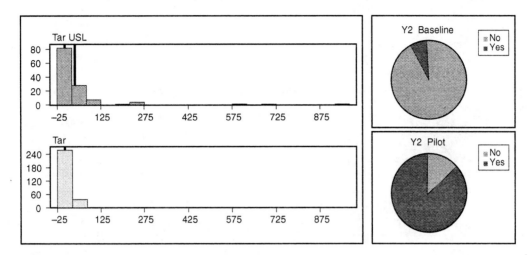

FIGURE 10.21 Performance metrics: baseline versus pilot

The RT project proved to be both successful and sustainable, given the fact the initiative is already house-wide, and showed improvement from pilot to control, even though the Pyxis medication system was a new component of the process added after the pilot.

Maintaining results long-term will require adherence to the control plan and staff accountability. The control plan has specific alerts and processes to deal with defects when performance drops below certain levels. SOP accountability will be strictly monitored and enforced, and the control plan and control charts will be monitored by the process owner on an ongoing basis.

Reaching Six Sigma levels of excellence will be accomplished by ensuring that every step of the process adheres to the SOPs, with the clear understanding of the staff's role and accountability. Staff will be accountable for adhering to the new SOPs, knowing there will be consequences for poor performance and rewards for excellent performance. To ensure results are maintained, the process must be constantly monitored and immediate actions taken when defects occur (see Figures 10.22 and 10.23).

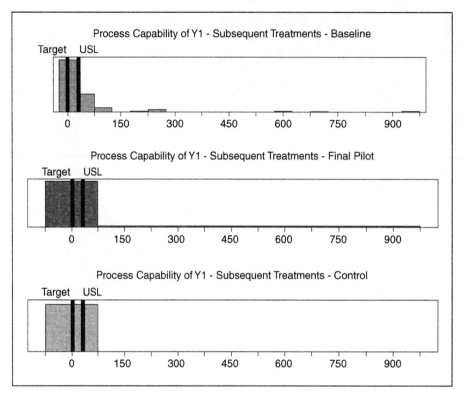

FIGURE 10.22 Process capability before and after

Performance Summary–Y1 Subsequent Treatments				
METRICS	**BASELINE**	**PILOT**	**CONTROL**	**Percent improvement from baseline to control**
Mean	47.9 min	15.1 min	14.6 min	69.5%
Standard Deviation	122.2 min	14.4 min	9.6 min	92.1%
DPMO	240,000	88,737	26,490	
Yield	76%	91.1%	97.4%	28.2%
Z Score	2.21	2.85	3.44	55.7%

Performance Summary–Y2 Documentation				
METRICS	**BASELINE**	**PILOT**	**CONTROL**	**Percent improvement from baseline to control**
DPMO	914,573	144,538	960,96	
Yield	8.5%	85.8%	90.4%	963.5%
Z Score	0.00	2.57	2.80	

FIGURE 10.23 Performance summary Y1 and Y2

PART IV

ROLLING OUT AND SUSTAINING SIX SIGMA

CHAPTER 11

IMPLEMENTING A SIX SIGMA CULTURE

SECTIONS

Implementation Process
Phase I—Mobilizing
Phase II—Planning
Phase III—Piloting
Phase IV—Implementing the Six Sigma System
Summary
Endnotes

"First, have a definite, clear practical ideal: a goal, an objective. Second, have the necessary means to achieve your ends: wisdom, money, materials, and methods. Third, adjust all your means to that end."

—Aristotle

Six Sigma is not green, black, or any color belt. It is not DMAIC (Define, Measure, Analyze, Improve, and Control), DMADV (Define, Measure, Analyze, Design, and Verify), or DFSS (Design for Six Sigma). It is not saving money. It is not the silver bullet that corrects all problems. Organizations that think it is are in for a big surprise and limited success.

What then is Six Sigma? It is a new way of thinking, behaving, and managing. It is a firm belief that we all can be nearly perfect and do nearly perfect work all the time, and that we all have the inert potential to be creative. We need to think of applying this kind of thinking to each of the healthcare stages (see Figure 11.1).

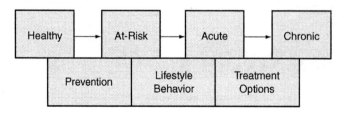

FIGURE 11.1 The healthcare stages

We are always surprised at the number of organizations that look at Six Sigma initiatives as groups of Green and Black Belts running around solving problems. This has a negative, not a positive, impact upon the organization. They relieve management of accountability for change. In the past, management used the technical talents that were assigned to them. Process optimization was done by design, manufacturing, and quality engineers. Organizations that just use Six Sigma to solve problems have limited success. The organizations, which were the most successful in using Six Sigma as just a problem-solving tool, were the ones that had the most problems to solve. But organizations that used Six Sigma to change their culture were the ones that reaped the big harvest. The difference between these two types of approaches is that the first type of organization measures its success on dollars saved, while the second type of organization measures its success on improving customer satisfaction.

> "In healthcare, a million dollar savings is unimportant compared to saving one life that could have been lost."
>
> —H. James Harrington

In healthcare, there are many opportunities to reduce the number of errors that occur every day and to save lots of money, but most of all there is a unique opportunity to save lives. A typical hospital has millions of opportunities to be successful or fail every day. Healthcare professionals cannot rely on a few groups of Black and Green Belts who are looking for million dollar savings' project opportunities. At the Six Sigma level, an organization could have more than 1,200 (based upon 1 million opportunities per day) needless deaths per year in just a single hospital. We are lucky that not all of the errors that occur result in death. For example, a nurse could drop a bedpan; it would cause a mess, but not a death. The checks and balances already placed in the system catch some of the other errors. In healthcare, we need to be much better than 3.4 defects per million critical opportunities. We need to be closer to 3.4 per *billion* critical opportunities. This means that everyone within the healthcare organization needs to be actively involved in the Six Sigma process.

The healthcare professional is faced with a major problem because the specification limits on their product (the patients) they are working with is very broad. A manufacturing operation has many close tolerances on all parts that provide consistency in the process. They all go together in the same way. In healthcare, each patient is different. They have different allergies, different blood types, different medical histories, and so on. It is like having a one-of-a-kind manufacturing production line. This means that the healthcare professional has to be more creative and more adaptive than most other types of professionals. All of these things make up the complexity and increased risk that the healthcare professional faces each day.

In spite of all of this, or maybe because of all of this, there are many opportunities to apply Six Sigma concepts in the healthcare arena. For example, at North Carolina Baptist Hospital, a Six Sigma team attacked the problem of getting patients from the emergency department into the Cardiac Catheterization Laboratory for treatment in the shortest possible time. As a result of this, they were able to reduce the cycle time by more than 41 minutes.[1] It is this type of result that converts skeptics into believers.

Bank of America had the right idea. Its Six Sigma program focused on customer satisfaction and resulted in a 25 percent improvement and saved more than $2 billion. They focused on improving customer satisfaction and credit risks assessment reduction plus fraud prevention.[2]

> "In the medical field (alone), bioscience will shift the health paradigm to such a degree that (within two decades) we'll look back on the medical practices of today the way we now look back on those in medieval Europe."
>
> —The Long Boom: Schwartz, Leyden and Hyatt

IMPLEMENTATION PROCESS

> "For 40 years, I have been lecturing and writing on Process Improvement, and each time management thinks it is a new idea. They must be deaf, blind and forgetful."
>
> —H. James Harrington

It is not easy to make the required transformation in a healthcare unit. Everyone is already doing their best to do a great job already. Everyone is overworked. Everyone has their own job to do. They all are trying to satisfy the patient, the doctors, the government, the insurance companies, the patient's families, and yes, each other. Prices keep going up. The medical technology is changing so fast that it is almost impossible to keep up with it, and everyone is looking for a way to earn some easy money by suing the healthcare provider (HCP). With all this going on, who has the time or the desire to take on an additional project? The real answer is that you just cannot afford to fail to continuously improve. The trick is, "How can you convince the Executive Team, key doctors, and enough of the staff that the Six Sigma activities are worth investing their valuable time and effort in so that the Six Sigma project can get started and keep expanding?"

Based upon our experience, the following five-phase approach is one of the most effective methods that we have run across to bring about the required transformation:

- Phase I —Mobilizing
- Phase II —Planning

- Phase III —Piloting
- Phase IV —Implementing the Six Sigma System
- Phase V —Internalizing the Six Sigma Culture

"When I climb Mount Rainier, I face less risk of death than I'll face on the operating table."

—Donald M. Berwick, CEO of the Institute for Healthcare Improvement,
Harvard Medical School

PHASE I—MOBILIZING

"A useful motto during the start-up phase is 'Think big—Start small.'"

—Ernst & Young

The mobilization phase is subdivided into seven activities:

- Activity 1—Finding and Developing a Six Sigma Advocate
- Activity 2—Analyzing Six Sigma Fit with the Strategic Plan
- Activity 3—Defining Six Sigma Improvement Opportunities
- Activity 4—Building a Six Sigma Business Case
- Activity 5—Approving and Organizing for Phase III Pilot
- Activity 6—Setting Preliminary Objectives for the Pilot
- Activity 7—Selecting an External Consultant

Activity 1—Finding and Developing a Six Sigma Advocate

"Someone has to lead. Why not you?"

—H. James Harrington

All Six Sigma projects start with a single individual or a very small group of people who want to get more information about Six Sigma and how it can be used to improve the healthcare provider's performance. We will call this individual —the *Six Sigma Advocate* (this person may be you). This individual is often a forward-thinking individual who has read articles or talked to friends who have experienced implementing Six Sigma initiatives in healthcare or other industries. Often the Advocate is a new hire who has come from another healthcare provider that is doing Six Sigma, and he/she has already had some experience with the results that a Six Sigma initiative has on the organization that he/she left. Based upon these early contacts related to Six Sigma, the individual will continue to expand his/her knowledge of Six Sigma until reaching a point where he/she feels comfortable enough to contact executive management, requesting permission to conduct a concept study to determine whether Six Sigma is right for the organization. Once the Executive Team approves the concept study, the individual (or group) will start to collect more articles, read more books, and even attend conferences to become knowledgeable about what Six Sigma is and what it can do for the organization. Often the individual will contact consultants to get their advice about what they would do to start a Six Sigma program within the organization.

If the Advocate is convinced that a Six Sigma initiative may be in line with the organization's culture, the Advocate is ready to move on to Activity 2.

Activity 2—Analyzing Six Sigma Fit with the Strategic Plan

"If the glove doesn't fit, it is time to quit."

—H. James Harrington

If the initial study phase convinces the Advocate that the organization could benefit from the Six Sigma initiative, the Advocate will need to prepare a business case that will be used to convince the Executive Team that the investment in time and effort will provide adequate return on investment and improve the organization's competitive advantage. This business plan has to answer two questions that are on everyone's mind:

- Why should we do something different?
- Would the Six Sigma initiative be the best answer to the problems we are facing?

We find that during this activity, it is best to have a small group developing the business case. This team should be made up of members from the strategic planning group, finance, practicing physicians, administration, sales, and quality.

The business case should be directed at ensuring that the goals set forward in the strategic plan are met or exceeded. By doing this, the Six Sigma initiative is directly connected to the organization's day-to-day operations. We cannot overemphasize the importance of developing a good business case, as it will determine whether the organization will go forward with the Six Sigma initiative. It must provide the Executive Team with a compelling reason to go forward with the initiative. The business case must provide logically researched answers to these two questions.

The strategic plan is the baseline and targets all rolled up into one. It should define the future of managed care evolution and its impact upon the HCP. It should answer and incorporate plans to questions such as

- Is our leadership capable of handling dramatic change?
- Has the time come when we need to compete on costs?

- Do we have the ability to shift from treatment to health maintenance?
- Do our rewards and recognition systems motivate staff (support, administration, nurses, and physicians) to invent new creative approaches to medical care?
- Do we have the ability to serve the needs of the population we service, and do we understand how our service population and services' needs will change over the next five to ten years?
- Do the board, management, clinicians, suppliers, alliance partners, and medical community realize and want change to take place, and if so, what type of change does each stakeholder want?
- Do we understand the difference between customer's needs (must have), expectations (things they should get), and niceties (things that set the HCP apart from other healthcare providers)?
- How big a change do we need in order to compete in the market today and in the future?

One of the key parts of the strategic plan is a set of vision statements that defines the changes that are required in the HCP. The primary vision statement is the one for the total HCP that defines where the organization is heading. Back in the 1930s, doctors used to come to people's homes when they were ill. Today, the sick person drags himself/herself to the HCP. Even with the expansion of outpatient care, we still rely on the patient to come to the HCP location for diagnostics and treatment. The future is leading to in-home care where the patient will not have to come to the HCP location. Electronic monitoring devices will become more and more prevalent, allowing the physician to monitor and treat the patient using IT technology as a communication system. This virtual treatment will replace the need for many of the long stays in the hospital.

Kurt Miller, partner with Arthur Andersen Consulting, depicts the traditional healthcare system as laid out in Figure 11.2.[3]

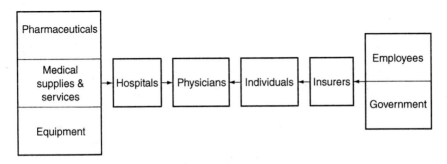

FIGURE 11.2 Traditional healthcare system

You will note that in the historical, traditional healthcare system, the groups and individuals involved were connected in a logically sequential flow of activities. Each one had individual and segregated roles and positions in delivering the healthcare cycle.

As Kurt Miller points out, "Managed care has brought together the supplier, selectors, and payers or physicians, hospitals, and insurers. Most importantly, it has aligned hospital and physician incentives to reduce inpatient utilization, and therefore, cost."

We predict that in the future the individual will become an active participant in the healthcare delivery process and incentive structure.

Based upon considerations like these, you can see why the overall vision statement has to really address what direction the organization is going to take.

Vision statements can define how the key business drivers need to change over the next five- to ten-year period. *Business drivers* are the controllable factors within the HCP that impact the performance of the HCP. Business drivers are the major parts within the organization that management has the power to change—things that impact the organization's performance by adding or subtracting resources, changing standards, redesigning processes, or modifying behavioral patterns. There are usually 8 to 12 business drivers in a HCP. One business driver that is common to all HCPs is leadership and support. Another one is the organization's processes. For each of these business drivers, a vision statement needs to be developed that defines how this business driver needs to change over the next five years. For example, the following is a typical vision statement for operating procedures:

"Major processes are documented, understood, followed, easy-to-use, prevents errors, and are designed to be adaptable to our stakeholders' changing needs. Staff members use them because they believe that they are more effective and efficient than the other options. Technology is effectively used to handle routine, repetitive, time-consuming activities and to remove bureaucracy from the processes."

Other types of vision statements focus on things such as

- **Technologies**. How will the technologies' information need to change to keep up with the needs of the HCP industry and to remain competitive in the future?

- **Structure and facilities**. The future configuration and facilities will need to be much different to accommodate the home care approach.

- **Markets and customers**. Today, we have a hard time even defining who is the customer. Is it the patient, employee, employee's family, health plan member, insurer, physician, or all of these? What are their future needs? How will we need to service this changing market, and what markets do we need to service? In the future, we will need to establish strategic alliances and partnerships with key customers, suppliers, and other HCPs. There will be a change in the HCP's scope and variety of products and services to bring them in line with their specific target markets and patient population.

- **People**. Our people will have even more need for technical knowledge that can be obtained and assimilated much faster than it is today. Teams will give way to teamwork. The future HCP must send a daily flow of communications concerning "What is going on in the HCP?" "How is the HCP changing?" "What is changing that impacts each specific individual?" and "What is the new knowledge related to the individual's profession?"

The business-driver vision statements are very important because they provide the HCP suppliers, employees, and management with a clear vision of how the organization will be changing and its impact upon how they will be required to perform and be treated. The gap between the present performance and the business-driver vision statement will drive the performance improvement activities over the coming years and will have a major impact on the application of Six Sigma concepts.

Why is improvement for HCPs so important? The National Committee for Quality Assurance (NCQA) in its 2005 "The State of Healthcare Quality" report, produced by the *U.S. News and World Report* magazine, reported that over the past six years, quality improvements in healthcare has resulted in the prevention of 67,000 deaths. These improvements were applied to 64.5 million people. If the payment in a wrongful death suit is only $1 million, that amounts to a savings of $67 billion to the HCP industry.

"Any kind of health plan might potentially be an excellent plan. But realistically, only the ones that measure quality are going to achieve excellence."

—Margaret E. O'Kane, NCQA President[4]

As healthcare providers, we can't just focus on servicing the sick. We also have to help the well stay well and live longer. The estimated deaths attributed to failure to deliver recommended care in 2004 were by category:[5]

- Controlling high blood pressure: 12,000 to 32,000 deaths
- Smoking cessation: 8,300 to 13,200 deaths
- Diabetes care—HbA1c control: 5,300 to 11,700 deaths
- Colorectal cancer screening: 4,100 to 6,200 deaths
- Cholesterol management: 3,400 to 7,200 deaths
- Prenatal care: 1,000 to 1,750 deaths

The strategic plan should also include a set of Performance Indicators measurements called *KPIs* (Key Performance Indicators). There are different performance indicators for each of the many levels and departments within the organization. The HCP should have a high level set of measurements that are in keeping with the balanced scorecard concept. Typically, these high-level KPIs are things such as

- Customer satisfaction level
- Percent of customers who document complaints
- Bed occupancy percentage
- Percent utilization of high-cost special equipment
- Staff satisfaction level
- Turnover rates
- Operating cost ratio to dollars collected
- Percent increased in collections per year
- Percent of insured inpatient stays billed
- Percent of insured outpatient visits billed
- Average age of insured claims outstanding

The HCP should have a set of lower-level measurements called CPIs (Critical Performance Indicators) that back up and support the higher-level measurements. They may or may not be included in the strategic plan, but there should be a relationship of the CPIs in the individual units and departments to the high-level KPIs. Often these CPIs are efficiency and/or effectiveness measurements of the processes within the departments. For example:

- Average wait time to be admitted
- Average time to process specific lab work
- Percent lost records
- Average response time to a bed call
- Average time in critical recovery by operation type
- Percent billing errors
- Percent of patients who receive recommended healthcare

"In a study conducted by Rand Health and Pfizer Inc. in 2005, evaluating 182 measurements of health for 22 common medical conditions covering more than 300 patients, they found that only 55 percent of the patients received the recommended care."[6] This study revealed that the current practice of examining administrative records alone does not provide an accurate picture of how the recommended procedures are being implemented. When just the administrative information was used, it indicated that 83 percent of the patients received the recommended care. This is more than a 50 percent higher rate than the actual quality of the treatment.

Having a good set of measurements that relate to the HCP's vision statements is a good starting point. But, to understand what needs to happen, there should be a set of improvement objectives year by year for each KPI and CPI. These improvement objectives provide good insight into the areas that are in need of and have the priorities for major improvement.

The Strategic plan should have both strategic initiatives and tactical initiatives included in it. Examples of strategic initiatives include the following:

- Financial stability plans
- Formation of Knowledge networks
- Continuous care model

Examples of tactical initiatives include the following:

- IT expansion
- Training plans
- New equipment plans
- New Service Plans

Activity 3—Defining Six Sigma Improvement Opportunities

"The big opportunities that lead to renewal and the strategic decisions that capture them seem more like the whimsical flight of a butterfly than the path of a carefully aimed arrow."

—Robert H. Waterman, Jr.

The Six Sigma team needs to also review the customer satisfaction data to define hot spots that provide opportunities for increased customer satisfaction. It is also recommended that meetings with some small focus groups of employees and customers are conducted to define the important improvement opportunities as viewed from their standpoint and to provide them with a quick overview of Six Sigma.

Another good information source is the projects that are being implemented or that are approved for implementation. Many of these projects are IT projects that will result in major changes in the organization's processes. Frequently these proposed projects are excellent candidates for the Six Sigma initiative.

Six Sigma has built into in it some effective approaches to redesign the HCP processes. Making a list of the HCP business processes and then evaluating them to define how well they are performing is another way to identify Six Sigma improvement opportunities. The following lists provide examples of typical HCP core processes and sub-processes that could be Six Sigma improvement opportunities.

Typical HCP core processes:

Market information capture	Customer engagement
Market selection	Inventory management and logistics
Inpatient services	Direct business
Outpatient services	Plan business
Customer fulfillment	Develop processes
Customer relationships	Manage process operation
Customer feedback	Provide personnel support
Marketing	Market products and services
Solution integration	Provide consultancy services
Financial analysis	Plan the network
Accounting	Provide support services
Human resources	Management information resources
IT infrastructure	Manage finance

Typical HCP sub-processes:

Perform diagnostic testing	Perform surgical procedures
Perform pharmacological procedures	Perform therapeutic procedures
Perform psychological social service care	Render clinical support
Render patient transport	Provide charging, billing, and collection services
Render quality and cost control	Assess and protect against financial and not-clinical risk
Provide communication	
Coordinate processes and interfaces	Provide accounting and financial services
Promote referring physician and PCP relations	Scheduling patients and resources
Continuing care referrals	Discharge, bill, and transfer patients
Housekeeping process	Transporting and movement of patients
Distributing materials and medicine	Purchasing materials and medicine
Education and training	Staffing process
Billing and collection process with insurance organizations	Admitting and registering patients

In the Riddle Memorial Hospital's 2006 Process Improvement Initiative Business Plan, it defined the following processes as core processes:

- Emergency room
- Inpatient encounter
- Pharmacy
- Imaging
- Physician practices
- Advanced life support
- Operating room
- Out-patient encounter
- Registration and scheduling
- Housekeeping
- Cerner information system

In addition, it defined the following processes as support processes:

- Labor relations
- Technology
- Facilities management
- Supply chain management
- Project management
- Billing
- Credit and collections
- Legal

The Patient Journey

"The truth of the matter is that when it comes to quality, the customer has all the votes."

—John Guaspari

One of the best ways to identify improvement opportunities is to define the patient journey throughout the care cycle. Figure 11.3 shows a typical journey.

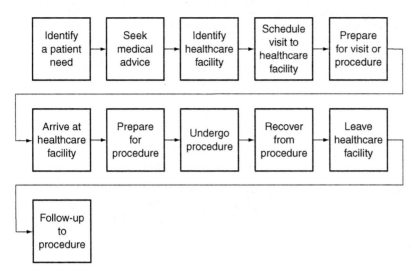

FIGURE 11.3 The patient's journey through the care cycle

In order to understand how the physicians' and staff's daily behaviors and practices in the
HCP setting follow the patient journey, the following approaches may be used:

- **Walking in the Patient's Shoes**. In this approach, team members actually go through
  the patient treatment process. Often these individuals are not identified to the hospital
  staff as "test patients," so they get no special treatment. In the consumer business,
  these individuals are called *mystery shoppers*. This allows them to experience anxi-
  eties, expectations, discomfort, and emotions that a real patient would experience.

- **Document tracking**. Using the patient's chart, analyze each step the chart takes. This
  helps to understand how the chart-handlers feel about how the patient is being taken
  care of.

- **Shadowing Staff**. Team members accompany the doctors, nurses, and staff, observing
  their work and the bottlenecks they face in their daily routines.

- **Patient and Family Interviews**. This approach provides data about their expectations,
  feelings, and disappointment as they progress through the patient journey.

- **Process Walk-Through**. Using the major processes as a starting point, a team follows
  the process flow, reviewing each step in the process. This helps define problems in the
  hand-off between each department.

- **Workflow Analysis**. By looking at the movement of patients and staff, you are able to
  identify wasted effort and increased cycle time. This can include workflow mapping
  by area or in some cases, just observing what is going on in a specific location within
  the HCP (for example, emergency care admittance).

Typically, the patient's journey has six improvement opportunities:

1. Entering the HCP
2. Being informed
3. Finding the way
4. Waiting for service
5. Using the care facilities
6. Paying the bills

Based on this body of knowledge and information, the team should be able to identify a number of opportunities to apply the Six Sigma methodology to. We suggest that the team review these opportunities based on a set of guidelines that the team develops. Figure 11.4 is a two-dimensional analysis based on

- Impact on the HCP
- Likelihood of success

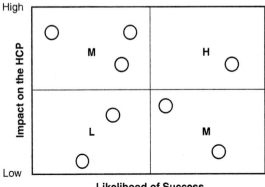

FIGURE 11.4 Selecting the right project

In most cases, these two-dimensional approaches are inadequate to make these important divisions, as many factors need to be considered. The following are typical factors that HCP may use to help select the opportunities that will make up the pilot phase:

- Does it support the strategic plan?
- Is it a patient safety issue?
- Will it improve patient central care?
- Will it decrease death rates or just save money?

- Will it improve the work environment?
- Is there a high payback if the problem is solved?
- How hard is the problem to solve?
- Is it a problem that the Six Sigma methodology can address?
- Will it provide a competitive advantage?

Informed Approach to Selecting Opportunities

"Make a habit of discussing a problem on the basis of the data and respecting the facts shown by them."

—Dr. Kaoru Ishikawa

World-class organizations continuously strive to provide superior products and services to their customers. As a result, they ensure that all improvement efforts focus on improving external customer satisfaction. Because a Six Sigma effort is a major undertaking for all organizations, which directly impacts the service-related customer interface, it should be linked to customer satisfaction.

Traditional approaches to define improvement opportunities can be thought of as "internally focused" and "defensive mechanisms" that try to correct and prevent problems from recurring. A more appropriate approach is "customer-focused" and "offensive mechanisms" so that business processes are truly world-class. The informed approach we are going to describe in this section is an objective method for prioritizing business processes, based on the importance of the process (as determined by external customer expectations), and the degree to which the process can be improved (as determined by its current quality).

This approach embodies the following principles:

- Linking improvement efforts to customer expectations
- Focusing on prevention, as well as correction, activities
- Emphasizing the areas with the greatest potential for improvement
- Working on a manageable number of projects
- Using facts, not perceptions, for selection of projects
- Ensuring constancy of purpose

The informed approach differs from the other approaches because it is based largely on actual data collection from customers and internal operations, instead of opinion. It is therefore more time-consuming. The Executive Improvement Team should undertake this effort by

- **Understanding External Customer Requirements**. External customers have several requirements related to the facilities and the services (both healthcare- and administration-related) that are provided by the HCP. The service-related requirements are satisfied by the organization's business processes; therefore, it is essential to understand these requirements. This can be done by actually talking to customers and documenting their requirements, or by using information that already exists in various parts of the organization (comment cards, customer service data, and so on). It is important to understand not only the requirements but also the importance of each of those requirements, because the aim of the organization should be to focus on the key requirements.

- **Evaluating the Importance of Business Processes**. External customer requirements are met by the organization through the execution of one or several business processes. This needs to be understood by management, and is best achieved by identifying the processes that directly and indirectly impact the external customer. Once the business processes that impact the external customer have been identified, the importance of these processes can be evaluated. Those processes that have major impact on important external customer requirements will be rated the highest, and will be considered primary candidates for the Six Sigma project.

- **Evaluating the Improvement Opportunities**. No process is so perfect that it cannot be improved. Continuous improvement is the basic principle of quality and business everywhere; the degree of improvement possible depends on the current state of the process. There are several key indicators of effectiveness, efficiency, and adaptability, such as cycle time, rework, backlog, cost, and so on. The Executive Team should select a handful of meaningful indicators and then rate every process based on the information it can gather about the process. Processes with greater opportunities for improvement should be rated the highest, because they are primary candidates for DFSS (Design For Six Sigma).

- **Selecting the Critical Processes**. After gathering the data on the processes, the Executive Team is now ready to select the critical processes for improvement. It should be obvious that the critical processes are those that are high in importance as well as high in improvement opportunities, and these are the ones that should be attacked first. Correspondingly, processes that are not very important from a customer viewpoint and appear to be functioning quite well should not be selected for initial improvement efforts. Figure 11.5 shows a matrix that can be constructed based on the data gathered. It is a helpful tool that provides a clear overview of all processes and helps make the final selection.

The same approach can be applied to improving the internal workings of the organization, by replacing the external customer with the business unit. This is not as self-serving as it might seem. As you improve the internal workings of the organization, you reduce cost and provide a better quality of work life for the employees. As internal costs go down, the cost to your external customer can be reduced. As the quality of work life improves, the organization's output improves.

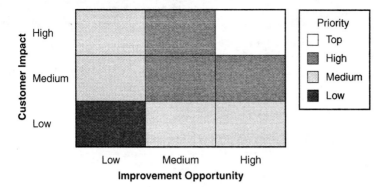

FIGURE 11.5 Matrix for setting process priorities

Remember that every process, every activity, and every job within an organization exists for only one reason: to provide our customers and/or consumers with products and services that represent value to them. The rippling effect of improving any activity should have a positive impact on the external customer.

Weighted Selection Approach

"It is not the employer who pays the wages. Employers only handle the money. It is the customer who pays the wages."

—Henry Ford, Sr.

In this opportunity-selection approach, each opportunity is evaluated on a number of parameters. For example:

- How changeable is it? = 2 points
- Will it reduce cost? = 2 points
- Decreased death rates = 5 points
- Improve patient care = 4 points
- Improve staff morale = 3 points
- Reduce wait time = 1 point

Each of these parameters is weighted by a point score from 1 to 5. A rating of 1 indicates that it is a low priority and a 5 that it is a very high priority.

In Table 11.1, typical improvement opportunities are listed with the six parameters defined in the previous example.

TABLE 11.1 Typical Improvement Opportunities

Opportunities	A=2	B=2	C=5	D=4	E=3	F=1	Total
1. Reduce billing errors	2x2	1x2	1x5	1=4	2x3	1=1	
	4	2	5	4	6	1	22
2. Present bell response time	4x2	1x2	2x5	4x5	2x3	5x1	
	8	2	10	20	6	5	51
3. Improved coronary artery bypass graft process	3x2	4x2	5x5	4x4	2x3	1x1	
	6	8	25	16	6	1	62
4. Medication Administration Records (MARs) error rates	1x2	4x2	5x5	5x4	4x3	2x1	
	2	8	25	20	12	2	69

- Reducing inpatient wait time
- Reducing billing errors
- Reducing pharmacy errors
- Reducing response time to bed calls
- Improving information sharing
- Reducing record errors
- Offering better customer parking
- Increasing inventory turns
- Reducing tobacco cessation
- Improving risk management
- Reducing medication administration
- Recording Medication Administration Records (MAR) errors
- Reducing critical-care recovery time
- Standardizing procedures for different treatments
- Reducing outpatient processing cycle

The six evaluation parameters are listed A through F in the top of Table 11.1 along with the related weighting factor. Each of the improvement opportunities are evaluated on a scale of 1 to 5 for each evaluation parameter. A rating of 5 indicates that the opportunity will be easy to take advantage of or that it will have a big impact on the HCP. This rating is then multiplied by the weighted factor for the parameters being evaluated to define a score for the opportunity/evaluation parameter combination. For example, in Table 11.1, Reduce Billing errors was evaluated at the 2 level (difficult to change) and column A (how changeable is it) has a weighting factor of 2. The total score for the "Reduce Billing Errors / How Changeable Is It" combination is 4 (2x2=4).

By summing up the individual scores for each parameter for an opportunity, the total weight for that opportunity can be calculated.

Based upon the analysis in Table 11.1, MAR errors are the most important improvement opportunity. Prescription errors are estimated to kill up to 25,000 people a year.[7] You might think that physicians care more about their money than the health of their patients. When they write a check, they write out the dollar amount and then double-check it by writing out the amount in numbers. The same physicians scribble in almost illegible instructions on prescription forms. Errors are very common—for example, the interpretation of the prescription was 10mg and it should have been 1.0mg.

Selection Process

As you finalize your selection of the business processes that will have Six Sigma applied to them, remember the 4 Rs:

- **Resources**. There is a limited amount of resources available, and the present processes must continue to operate while we are improving them. Often, this means that a new process will be operating in parallel with the old process while the new process is being verified. Don't overextend yourself.

- **Returns**. Look closely at the potential payback to the business. Will the process reduce costs? Will it make you more competitive? Will it give you a marketing advantage?

- **Risks**. Normally, the greater the change required, the greater the risk of failure. Major changes always are accompanied by resistance to change. Breakthrough activities have the biggest payback, but they also have the biggest chance of failure.

- **Rewards**. What are the rewards for the employees and Six Sigma Team (SST) members working to improve the process? How much will their quality of work life be improved? Will the assignment be challenging and provide them with growth opportunities?

Based on the results of this analysis, the Executive Team will typically select 10 to 25 critical processes to which the Six Sigma approach will be applied. The number will vary based on the size and complexity of the organization.

Using one of these three approaches, the Executive Team can decide which opportunities will be part of the pilot phase and which can be scheduled for later analysis. Consideration should be given to balancing the workload within the organization and ensuring that all functions are participating. This approach concentrates attention on critical issues, sets priorities for resources, and ensures that the effort is manageable. While it is a relatively simple and useful way to select business opportunities, this approach has a number of drawbacks, including

- "Pet projects" commonly are identified.
- Management perspectives may not be supported by hard facts.
- Top management may sway the decision.

Medication Administration Records (MAR) Errors

Although MAR errors are a big healthcare problem, it is not one that should be tackled by the SST. Six Sigma projects should last less than three months in most cases.

> "We believe we can change how healthcare uses I.T. and it starts with the federal government."
>
> —President George W. Bush speech at Vanderbilt
> University Medical Center, May 2004

The U.S. Department of Health and Human Services awarded more than $8 million in contracts in 2005 to 15 projects designed to help clinicians, facilities, and patients implement evidence-based patient safety practices.[8]

Dr. David Brailer, the former National Health IT coordinator, defines his goal as improving the nation's quality of healthcare and reducing cost through the use of technologies such as electronic health records and electronic prescription-ordering systems. It is estimated that these types of IT systems will save the U.S. $140 billion per year by improving patient care and eliminating redundant tests.[9]

Brailer worked with the Santa Barbara County Health Data Exchange to design and install the first peer-to-peer electronic healthcare information data exchange in the U.S. It allowed hundreds of physicians, hospitals, and labs to have timely access to patients' medical formation.

As you can see, correcting MAR errors is a big problem and a major project with a lot of IT involvement. It is not a SST-type project that can be put to bed in three months. That does not mean that the Six Sigma approach cannot help to solve this problem. In fact, you should at least have one Six Sigma Black Belt on the MAR transformation team to help them analyze the problems and the potential solution.

Activity 4—Building a Six Sigma Business Case

> "If we look at Quality as it has been implemented in the past, we won't be successful in reducing patient errors."
>
> —Monica Berry, President, American Society for Healthcare Risk[10]

With the help of the selected guidelines, the team should select a small quantity (two to five projects) to build a business case around. The business case should include both tangible and intangible impacts. It also should include the estimated cost to investigate, analyze, and define the solution to the selected opportunities. In most cases, the projects should last less than three months. If the business case looks good (and it usually does look good), the team should schedule a meeting with the Executive Team to provide them with a quick overview of the Six Sigma methodology and present the business case to them.

Often it helps if you use some examples to back up your business case. Typical Six Sigma savings as reported in "Six Sigma and Its Impact on American Business," a presentation by Dr. Ronald Snee (Sigma Breakthrough Technologies, Incorporated, October 17, 2000,), are as follows:

- Increase dryer throughput — $100,000
- Reduce freight cost (shipping) — $700,000
- Reduce warranty manufacturing — $150,000
- Reduce cost of waste disposal environmental — $320,000
- Reduce time to issue bills by 50 percent ($2.6 million)
- Implemented forecasting model sales — $500,000
- Reduce obsolete inventory and production planning — $1.7 million
- Increase warehouse input by 100 percent — $250,000
- Reduce travel cost — $1.3 million

Activity 5—Approving and Organizing for Phase III – Pilot

"You must have your senior leadership team committed to doing this (Six Sigma). Expect that the first year will be the most difficult, but it will be easier from there."

—Louise Goeser, Vice President of Quality, Ford Motor Co.

The desired outcome from this meeting is an improved budget to train three to five teams of Green Belts and cover their efforts to solve the selected projects. These Green Belts will make up three to five Six Sigma Improvement Teams. It should also include the cost of bringing in a consultant Black or Master Black Belt to provide the training and to work with the Green Belts to take full advantage of the pilot improvement opportunities. Sometimes the HCPs prefer to select an internal person to train as a Black Belt to lead the pilot projects. On the surface, this may look like a less-expensive way to go. In reality, it is usually more expensive as it slows down the projects and decreases their impact.

The Executive Team should also, at this point in time, select an individual to become the Six Sigma Champion. The *Six Sigma Champion* is typically an upper-level manager who leads the implementation of the Six Sigma program. Often, as a result of this meeting, a Six Sigma Executive Improvement Team is formed. Sometimes this is a very small team made up of three to four members. In other cases, it becomes a very big team. The following is an example of the people who could make up the team:

- Chief Executive Officer
- Chief Medical Officer
- Chief Financial Officer
- Chief Operating Officer
- Vice President, Management Care
- Vice President, Hospital Administration and Nursing

- Director, Quality Improvement
- Director, Quality Management
- Director, Care Management
- Vice President, Sales and Marketing
- Chairman, Primary Care
- Chairman, Medical Specialties
- Chairman, Surgical Specialties
- HCP Health Plan Director
- Associate Director, Care Management
- Associate Director, Information Systems
- Outside consultant

For each of the selected opportunities, an *Executive Sponsor* should be assigned. This individual will watch over the Six Sigma activities to be sure they are on schedule and help if SST runs into any organizational bottlenecks that it cannot address.

Activity 6—Setting Preliminary Objectives for the Pilot

"We must stop comparing ourselves against yesterday and start measuring ourselves against tomorrow."

—Colby Chandler, past Chairman and CEO, Eastman Kodak Company

Once the Executive Team has selected the pilot opportunities to which Six Sigma will be applied, it should develop a set of preliminary objectives that will be used to provide vision and direction to the Six Sigma Teams (SST). These preliminary objectives will ensure that an initial common understanding exists between the SST and the Executive Team. Depending on the amount of knowledge and the data that the Executive Team has about the selected processes, these objectives will be more or less quantified. In some cases, the objectives may only set the direction for the SST (for example, reduced cycle time). In other cases, improvement objectives may be provided (for example, reduced cycle time by 20 percent). The preliminary objectives should address effectiveness, efficiency, adaptability, and cycle time. In all cases, the objectives should be focused on meeting or exceeding customer expectations and can drive incremental or breakthrough improvement, depending on the degree of improvement desired.

It is very important not to blindly accept the preliminary objectives as the goals for the SST. Normally, these objectives are set without detailed data or understanding of the present opportunity. Letting the SST set its own goals provides needed ownership. These goals often are more aggressive than the Executive Team-set objectives.

Activity 7—Selecting an External Consultant

The last activity in Phase 2 Planning is selecting an External Consultant to help with the training and implementation of your Six Sigma initiative. This is one of the most important activities in your Six Sigma initiative.

> "All of the most successful implementations have used experienced external consultants who have saved these companies months and even years in their implementation process."
>
> —Michael Brassard and Diane Ritter

This is no place to try to save money. The consultant cost will be 2 percent of the total cost and less than .1 percent of the savings. It has always been my dream to find an organization that would let me put in a Six Sigma program for free and just give me 10 percent of the savings. Time after time, it has been proven that you get the best return on investment when you select the very best consultant without basing your selection on consulting cost. Your risk of failure goes up exponentially when you try to cut cost by using less experienced consultants or when you decide you can do it yourself by just sending a few people to Black Belt classes. It is just like taking a doctor right out of school with no internship and putting them in charge of the Heart Surgery Protocol Flow Committee. Time after time, when we have talked with organizations that complain that Six Sigma or TQM did not work for them, we find that they tried to do it without the proper experienced help and with little or no budget set aside for the initiative. You cannot expect an individual who you send to a Six Sigma Black Belt class to have the depth of understanding to attack all of the complex problems that your organization is facing without years of experience in using these complex approaches. The problems you are facing today are very complex or you would have already solved them. Even a trained Black Belt is an apprentice until he/she has five or six different projects under his or her belt.

Six Sigma consultants can be divided into three major categories, each of which has their own advantages and disadvantages:

- Instructors
- Implementers
- Process Experts

Instructors

Instructors are those individuals who usually come out of universities and have a great deal of experience in adult learning. They can take a book, a curriculum, or another person's material and do an excellent job of presenting it in an interesting and informative way. They typically have read a lot and, as a result, have some excellent examples that back up the materials they are presenting. They do an excellent job of presenting materials for management, and Green Belt and Black Belt certification. Their disadvantage is they have had little or no experience in implementing Six Sigma programs and are only familiar with the Black Belt body of knowledge. It is difficult for them to relate theory to practices.

Implementers

These consultants are experts in installing Six Sigma initiatives throughout an entire organization. They know what steps need to be taken to bring management on board. They know how to sell Six Sigma programs across the entire organization. They do an excellent job of developing business cases. They work very well with the Executive Team and finance. They are big-picture consultants that need to understand the corporate strategy. They usually are less effective at working with and motivating the first-line managers and employees. They do not like to get their hands dirty. They are very good in the conference room but not as good in the classroom.

Process Experts

These are the people who want to understand the details. They spend most of their time in the processes not at their desks. They can be found in the operating room, morgue, test laboratories, and admissions. They are excellent net workers. They know the processes and problems firsthand. Their weakness is they are not as good at teaching as the other two types of consultants but get to the heart of the problem much faster and are usually much better change agents.

Making the Selection

How do you know which type you need? Table 11.2 indicates the strength of these three types of consultants and should help you make your selection. You may want more than one consultant. Select an organization that has all the skills that you need, but stay with one consulting firm so they get to know your culture.

TABLE 11.2 How Different Types of Consultants Perform

	Teach Classes	**Design and Installation**	**Problem-Solving**
Instructor	Excellent	Fair	Good
Implementer	Good	Excellent	Fair
Process Expert	Fair	Good	Excellent

Of course, you would like consultants that do all three activities outstandingly, but this is really not the case. When you do find these consultants, they are more generous and do an acceptable job in all three areas, but do not excel in any one of the areas. As a customer of the consultants, define what activity is most important to you and target to get a consultant who excels in that activity. In most HCP Six Sigma initiatives, you will want to find a consulting firm that will provide three different consultants who excel in each of the three areas.

The following are other things to consider when using and selecting a Six Sigma consultant:

- Have they managed a business?
- Have they had experience working with SSTs solving problems?
- Do they have experience in dealing with and mentoring senior executives?
- Do they understand the IT enablers?
- Is their expertise limited to Six Sigma?
- Do they have good chemistry with the senior executives?
- How will they get the total HCP personnel involved?
- What kind of result have they had in improving customer satisfaction?

NOTE

Most consultants want to talk about dollars saved. The true value of Six Sigma is improving customer satisfaction.

- Are they Certified Quality Engineers?
- Are they Certified Project Managers?
- What software do they used to track assignments?
- What software do they used to track project status?
- How have they been recognized by their professional societies? (Example: The American Society for Quality in the United States, The European Organization For Quality in Europe, The Asian Pacific Quality Organization in Asia.)
- What books have they written? Are they creators or followers? What approaches do they have to training Green Belts and Black Belts?
- How many Master Black Belts do they have in their organization?
- Who will be working on the floor helping solve problems on all three shifts? (Be sure that you meet these individuals and like them.)
- What kind of results have they had in the HCP industry? Who on their team was on the SST that solved the problem and what was that consultant's role?

Our advice is to select the consultant who can help work with you on the floor to the advantage of your opportunities, not the one who has the flashiest presentation.

PHASE II—PLANNING

"The healthcare system is not built around quality. It also doesn't really care about costs."

—Michael Porter, Professor, Harvard Business School

Once the pilots are approved by the Executive Team, the Six Sigma initiatives start in earnest. The external consultants and the Six Sigma Sponsor will be the primary drivers of this phase. It is made up of the following seven activities.

- Activity 1: Define the Scope of Each Opportunity
- Activity 2: Define the Six Sigma Team (SST) Members
- Activity 3: Train the SST Members
- Activity 4: Organize the SSTs
- Activity 5: Define Measurements
- Activity 6: Prepare a Project Plan
- Activity 7: Prepare the Organizational Change Management Plan

"It is better to prepare and prevent rather than to repair and repent."

—H. James Harrington

Activity 1—Define the Scope of Each Opportunity

What is the difference between 3 Sigma and 6 Sigma in HCP? Let's look at one example. Let's assume that the HCP treats 2 million patients per year, and 50 percent of them undergo medical tests. What would be the impact on the HCP services?[11]

- 2 Sigma = 106 prescription errors per day
- 3 Sigma = 11 wrong medical tests per day
- 4 Sigma = 2 misplaced personal items per day
- 5 Sigma = 1 wrong test per month
- 6 Sigma = 1 customer complaint in 2.3 years

It is very important to bring the external consultant into the organization and provide him/her with an excellent understanding of the organization's objectives and culture. At a minimum, consultants should have an excellent understanding of the following documents:

- Vision statement
- Mission statement
- Values
- Strategic focus
- Critical success factors
- Five- to ten-year business objectives
- Performance goals
- Improvement strategies and active projects

The consultants also should understand the product and services that the organization provides, the types of customers that it services, and the culture within the HCP organization. The consultants would need to know how you define customer needs and how you measure customer satisfaction. This type of indoctrination pays off big as the consultant helps you get full value from the Six Sigma initiative.

Armed with this type of understanding and knowledge, the consultant would be able to aid the Six Sigma Sponsor or the Sponsor's delegated representative to define the scope of the opportunities that make up the pilot phase. The scope of each opportunity needs to be defined so that the people who make up the SST will have the right background and interest. The scope of the opportunity can vary all the way from a single task in an activity that is part of a bigger process, made up of hundreds of activities, to other opportunities that will include the total process that flows through many departments and functions within the HCP.

Another consideration is determining what needs to be accomplished. Basically, there are two options:

- Reduced variation
- Relocate the medium or center point

In the first case, we reduce the deviation around a center-preferred operating point. For example, if an injection was defined as 1.0mg + or −0.1mg of fluid and through experiments, you were able to calculate that the 3 Sigma limit was + or −0.1mg, the objective for the SST would be to reduce the 6 Sigma level to + or −0.05mg. As Figure 11.6 indicates, during Phase A the major effort is directed at bringing the process under control. During Phase B, the processes stabilize so we can start to focus on reducing variation at that activity. In Phase C, we reached the Six Sigma point where the variation at a 3 Sigma level is equal to or less than half of the specified limits. This approach is often used to improve manufacturing operations that have specific tolerances which combine to produce a deliverable end-product.

In the second case, the SST will be assigned to set a new center point (see Figure 11.7.) It is typically used when the objective is to reduce cost, cycle time, or processing time. This type of opportunity is usually directly related to a complex process that goes across many units (see Figure 11.8).

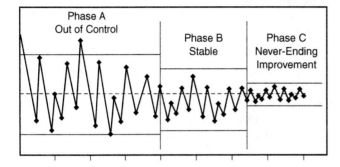

FIGURE 11.6 Reducing variation

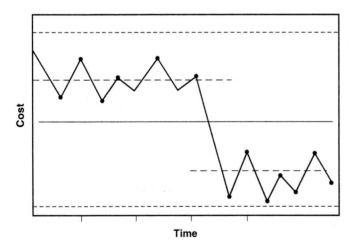

FIGURE 11.7 Setting a new center point

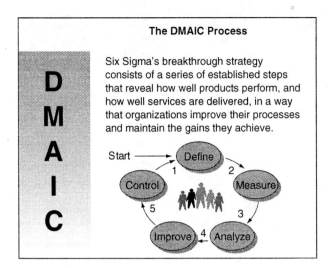

FIGURE 11.7 The DMAIC process

The *DMAIC* (Define, Measure, Analyze, Improve, and Control) is used to reduce variation on simple process improvement projects. The *DMADV* (Define, Measure, Analyze, Design, and Verify) is used to define new products and processes and to improve present products and processes (see Figure 11.9).

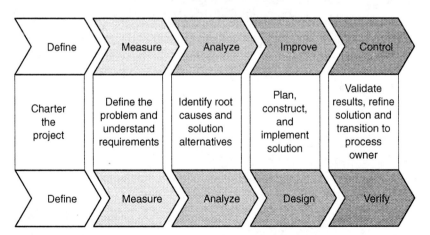

DMAIC - (Process Improvement)

FIGURE 11.9 Two Six Sigma improvement concepts

Note that in both cases the first three activities are the same (Define, Measure, and Analyze). It is only in the last two activities that there is a change, but don't be misled. The activities that go on during Define, Measure, and Analyze are very different in the two improvement cycles. The DMAIC cycle is used to reduce variation and to improve simple processes. It is usually applied when

- Customers' needs can be mapped by refining the existing process
- The project is part of an ongoing continuous improvement program
- A single activity or task within the process needs to be changed
- A single customer performance requirement needs to be changed
- Competitors' performance is relatively stable
- Customers purchasing behavior is stable
- Technology is stable

The DMADV cycle is a more rigorous cycle and can be applied to major processes. It is based upon the process redesign and benchmarking methodologies previously developed. It is used when

- No processes exist in the present time
- Existing processes need to undergo a major improvement greater than 20 percent
- The project is of strategic importance
- Multiple activities need to be changed
- Multiple customer requirements need to be addressed
- Customer behavior patterns are changing
- Competitors' performance is improving rapidly
- Supporting technology is changing

Activity 2—Define the SST Members

"Few incentives are more powerful than membership in a small group engaged in a common task, sharing the risks of defeat and the potential rewards of victory."

—Robert Reich

The consultant and the Six Sigma Sponsor need to define the make up of the individual SST based upon the types of changes that will need to be made. For example, if the opportunity is limited to one natural work team's environment, the SST will need to be made up of these people who are involved in the activity being studied. You may also need technical people who support the equipment the natural work team is using and someone from IT who is familiar with the supporting software. Often, the problem is not the fault of the natural work team; it might be because the supplier is not providing the correct inputs to allow the natural work team to do error-free work. It is sometimes good practice to have the customer for the output on the SST, particularly when that customer is an internal customer.

For complex, cross-functional processes, the consultant should prepare a block diagram of the process that identifies who is performing each key operation. This is a very important step in the cycle because it forces the consultant to mentally walk through the total process. It is strongly recommended that the consultant do some research before he or she starts to construct the block diagram. He/she should read the prevailing procedure and talk to the people in the process. The consultant must have a good view of the total process before putting pencil to paper.

Figure 11.10 is a typical block diagram that was used by a consultant and the Six Sigma sponsor to define the team members. Once the block diagram is prepared, the consultant should meet with the manager of each department on the block diagram to discuss the project with them and explain what the project's mission will be. They should also define who the proper person is within that department to represent the department as part of the SST.

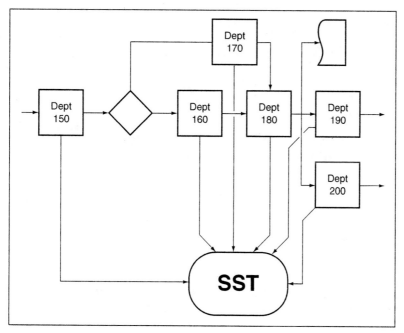

FIGURE 11.10 Block diagram of selecting the process team

SST Members

An SST is a group in which members are working together as a collective, cooperative, and cohesive force. Great care should be taken in selecting the members of each SST because individuals will be working together for an extensive period of time.

The SST members will be charged with the responsibility for creating a solution that takes advantage of the assigned opportunity. They primarily represent his or her department on the team and will be trained to become Six Sigma Green Belts.

Major responsibilities include the following:

- Participate in all SST activities (Example: training in Six Sigma techniques, attend meetings, conduct walk-through, participate in problem-solving, collect and analyze data)
- Conduct SST activities in his or her department as required by the Black Belt (Consultant) (Example: Obtain local documentation, develop a flow chart of the department's process activities, measure efficiency, and help implement department changes)
- Obtain appropriate resources (Example: Time for the activities to be performed within his or her department)
- Implement changes in the process as they apply to his or her department (Example: Supervise production of new documentation, organize training, and perform follow-up work)
- Chairs a sub-process team as appropriate
- Support Change (Example: Provide information, encouragement, and feedback, and listens to complaints)
- Train and evaluate other department members as appropriate
- Solve process-related problems
- Provide his or her department with a better understanding of how it fits in to the total process and Six Sigma program
- Collect and analyze data

SST Membership Time Requirement

The SST members should expect to devote roughly four hours per week to the project. However, depending on the application selected, the time requirement could be as much time as 50 percent of the work week during the first two months. For example, the Executive Team might decide that a critical process (billing, accounts payable, outpatients' treatment) requires immediate attention. This could mean a full-time assignment for about four weeks for all team members. The full-time approach is frequently used to prepare a business process for computerization or to have a significant immediate impact on the organization's near-term performance. Although the Executive Team should be ready to make the appropriate investment, launching an SST generally does not require this level of commitment. It is important that the SST members are relieved of some other normal work in order to participate on the SST. It is not fair or practical to expect them to continue all of their present assignments that are already keeping them busy 125 percent of their time and add to it an additional assignment as a Green Belt.

Activity 3—Train the SST Members

"World-class companies realize that firms have access to the same equipment, technology, financing, and people. The 'half-life' of any academic degree is extremely short; therefore, the real difference among companies is the degree to which employees are developed."

—Ernst & Young

The implementation model we are suggesting makes use of a consultant as the Six Sigma Master Black Belt that will manage the three to five opportunities (pilot project). The team members will be trained as Green Belts and function as Green Belts. At the end of the pilot, the best performing Green Belts will be recommended for Black Belt training.

Green Belt training is typically 40 classroom hours. Subjects to be covered are

- Introduction
- Enterprise-Wide Deployment
  - Why companies initiate Six Sigma
  - The necessity to revise cultural thinking
  - Six Sigma roles and responsibilities
  - Six Sigma deployment models
  - Cost of quality
  - Business examples
  - Beginning the case study
- Focusing on the Customer
  - Customer analysis
  - Customer CTQs (Critical-to-Quality requirements)
  - Changes in customer needs over time
  - Customer requirements versus customer needs
  - Customer alignment matrix
  - Continuing case study and applying new knowledge
- Business Process Improvement
  - What is a business process improvement?
  - Looking at the organization as a system
  - Process flow
  - Reengineering versus process improvement
  - Process matrix

- Process levels
- Moments of truth
- Detailed process mapping
- SIPOC analysis
- Business examples
- Continuing the case study and applying new knowledge
- Define
  - Target (board)
  - Benchmarking
  - Area activity analysis
  - SIPOC
  - Process definition and mapping (high level)
  - Continuing the case study and applying new knowledge
- Measure
  - Detailed process map ("as-is")
  - Identification of process Xs and Ys
  - What to measure
  - Why, where, and when to measure
  - How to collect data
  - Five-step data collection plan
  - Continuing the case study and applying new knowledge
- Analyze
  - Visually interpret data
  - Value-stream analysis
  - Vital few analysis
  - "Should-be" process map
  - Opportunity analysis
  - Continuing the case study and applying new knowledge
- Improve
  - Solution analysis
  - Charter revision
  - Final revision of "as-is" map
  - Cost-benefit analysis finalized

- Completion of project plan components
- Scheduling models
- Change management strategy
- Project planning strategy
- Risk analysis
- FMEA (plus other risk analysis models)
- Continuing the case study and applying new knowledge
- Control
  - Maintaining the gain
  - Measurement plan
  - Control tools
  - Standards
  - Procedures
  - Accountability
  - Continuing the case study and applying new knowledge
- Introduction to Lean Thinking
  - What is "lean thinking?"
  - "Lean" topics for the Black Belt
  - How is lean thinking applied to DMAIC?

This training can be presented in a number of ways. The most conventional way is to have the consultant conduct a five-day class for each of the teams. We believe that this approach is not the correct one for HCPs. Taking a group away from the day-to-day activities puts a big strain on the organization. Our experience is that it's next to impossible to get a physician to take five days off in a row, let alone the 20 days that are recommended for a Black Belt.

One of the big advantages of having a consultant leading the pilot programs is that this person can give Just-In-Time training to the SST members. We suggest that the team meets two times a week for two to three hours for 12 weeks in order to complete its assignment project. At each of these meetings, the consultant will present the SST members with the tools needed to continue their assigned project. This way, they will learn the required Green Belt tools while they are working with real-time improvement opportunities that they will get credit for solving. Not only will the organization benefit from the new skills these teams acquire, but also it will benefit from the money saved as a result of taking advantage of the improvement opportunities. In most cases, the money that is saved by the SSTs will more than pay for the consulting cost, the SST members' time away from their normal jobs, and the cost of making the change. At the end of the 12-week period, the consultant will provide the SST members with an instructional class that will fill in any of the Six Sigma tool requirements that they have not had an opportunity to use in solving their specific opportunity. There should also be a Green Belt competency test given to them at this point in time to be sure they understand the Green Belt tools.

Activity 4—Organize the SSTs

"You can't make bread with just flour. The same is true of teams. It is the mixture of skills that makes the breakthroughs."

—H. James Harrington

The SST has been formed for a specific purpose. The Sponsor has initiated this team because there is a process or problem to address or a new innovation is soon to be launched. The SST members have been chosen as a part of this team because they have specific knowledge, expertise, or experience that is considered invaluable to the success of the team's task. Do not make the mistake, however, of assuming that this assignment is already translated into the goals that are necessary for a successful team outcome. The goals are set when the group can wholeheartedly agree on them. Figure 11.11 is a typical project charter worksheet.

6 Sigma Project Charter Worksheet		
Project Title WHAT		
Project Leader WHO	Team Members WHO	
Business Case WHY		
Problem/Opportunity Statement WHY and WHERE	Goal Statement - HOW MUCH	
Project Scope: Constraints, Assumptions WHAT	Stakeholders - WHO	
Preliminary Plan - WHEN	Target Date	Actual Date
Start Date		
DEFINE		
MEASURE		
ANALYZE		
IMPROVE		
CONTROL		
Completion Data		

FIGURE 11.11 Typical project charter worksheet

The Charter

The *charter* is a written project plan that identifies what will be done, how it will be done, why, and when. It should be no more than two pages. It is generally written by the Sponsor (sometimes with the Black Belt) as a starting point, and should be modified by the team as needed.

The team should carefully review its charter and make necessary modifications to ensure that the charter accurately reflects the objectives and the scope of this team. The team will also need to change the charter to reflect any change in direction that the team deems necessary.

Once the team finalizes the charter, team goals should be developed along with operating ground rules. (See Figure 11.12 for a typical Facilitator's team charter.)

FACILITATOR
TEAM CHARTER

Objective:
To support the ABC HCP and its cross-functional teams by:
- Providing recommendations for facilitation and the teaming process at ABC HCP
- Supporting teams and team leaders at ABC HCP

Scope:
Facilitators will support teams sponsored by ABC. This includes Resource Management, Patient Acquisition, Health Maintenance, and Health Restoration.

Deliverables:
1. Improve the Facilitator Selection Process flowchart and communication map.
2. Standardize meeting minutes and communication.
3. Provide Facilitators and effective facilitation to ABC teams.
4. Offer guidelines for Sponsors and Team Leaders on available team training.
5. Develop a facilitation feedback process.

Benefits:
- Better resourcing for the sponsors and team leaders
- More cohesive teams with higher levels of synergy
- Trained Team Leaders and Team Members

Methodology:
The five-step DMAIC will be the methodology to examine the Facilitator selection process and the communication process between Facilitators, Sponsors, and Team Leaders.

Team Roster:
Sponsor: John A., Human Resources Department
Team Leader: Sally K.
Facilitator: Ken L.
Team Members: Bob L., Mike L., Joe B., Jesse H., and Karen L.

FIGURE 11.12 Facilitator team charter

Goals

Although your charter has a stated objective, the team will need to decide whether that objective should be divided into goals. Discussing and agreeing on specific goals will help the team get on the "same page" regarding the implications of the charter objective and how the team plans on achieving it. The team should never assume that everyone on the team understands the charter in the same way until they have discussed and agreed on its meaning.

Common goals provide team members with the following:

- Purpose. Goals are designed to help the team accomplish its charter.
- Clarity. Goals help the team transition from abstract ideas to concrete tasks.
- Direction. Goals help the team identify next steps to take.

SMART goal characteristics are as follows:

- **S**pecific. Goals should be specific
- **M**easurable. Goals must be measurable
- **A**ttainable. Goals are attainable
- **R**elevant. Goals are relevant to the charter
- **T**ime-bound. Goals are time bound

Ground Rules

The *ground rules* are a set of standards of behavior and attitudes that the team agrees to abide by. They should be established in the beginning stages of the team's formation and should include expectations regarding

- Punctuality
- Respect for team members
- Member responsibilities/commitments
- Meeting etiquette
- Juggling team tasks with normal work tasks

The entire team is responsible for seeing to it that the ground rules are established and followed.

The following is a set of typical ground rules:

- **Attendance**
  - Arrive on time, and stay until the end.
  - Start on time and finish on time, unless otherwise agreed.
  - Make every effort to attend. Provide advance notice to the meeting chairperson if you cannot attend, and arrange for a representative to attend in your place.
  - No unannounced interruptions.
- **Objectives and Agenda**
  - Publish an agenda and stick to it unless otherwise agreed.
  - Clearly state the objective for the meeting and stay focused.
  - Use the group's time wisely; deal with the most important issues, or share information of general interest.
- **Communication**
  - Use active listening; recognize that every idea or concern may be valuable.
  - Do not dominate the conversation.
  - Be concise.
  - Use sensitivity; question, do not challenge.
  - Participation is essential. Express your honest viewpoint or concern.
  - No hidden agendas.
  - Focus *constructive* criticism at exposing or removing obstacles.

- **Respect and Courtesy**. Avoid behaviors that discourage involvement:
  - Interrupting
  - Side conversations
  - "Killer" phrases, body language, or gestures.
  - Not paying attention.
  - Respect and understand others' position and feelings.
- **Teamwork**
  - Explore and disagree within the meeting. Present a single approach outside.
  - Strive for consensus. Use appropriate decision-making tools if necessary. Resolve irreconcilable differences outside the meeting.
  - Have some fun: Set up $1 fines for improper behavior, or go out to dinner together each month or quarter.
- **Support and Follow-up**
  - Review meeting effectiveness periodically.
  - Address problems openly.
  - Assign a facilitator to monitor team processes and behaviors.
  - Assign a scribe to record and issue minutes.
  - Assign a timekeeper to keep the meeting on schedule.
  - Make clear action assignments and carry them out.
  - Use visual media (flipcharts, overheads) to share ideas.

Team Development

HCP executives who are familiar with Six Sigma will understand the benefits of having ordering physicians, medication supplies' dispensing, pharmacists, delivering nurses, and support staff work as a team to reduce medication errors. Together they can define how prescription errors occur (for example, a pharmacist read it incorrectly), when it occurred (physician wrote it incorrectly) and/or why it occurred (technician inputted it incorrectly).

It is well understood that a team does not begin functioning at full efficiency from its very inception. Basically, the team is like a husband and a wife who have to learn how to live together, to respect the other's good points, and to forgive their weaknesses.

Stages of Team Development

There are four key stages (see Figure 11.13) in the development of a team. Each stage is important to the successful lifecycle of your team.

The stages of team development are

- Forming
- Storming
- Norming
- Performing

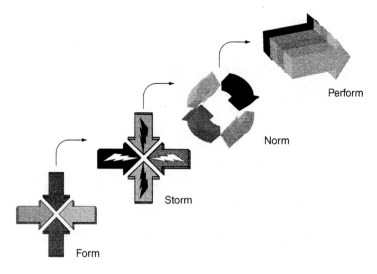

FIGURE 11.13 Four key stages of team development

The *Forming Stage* is marked by uncertainty and tentativeness:

- Accepted behaviors are not yet clear.
- Member feelings may reflect excitement and anticipation.
- Statements about what the team should do are ambiguous.
- Members usually try hard not to offend each other.

The *Storming Stage* is signaled when members are no longer tentative and ambiguous and are willing to express their differences of opinion:

- Resistance to different approaches may develop.
- Members express strong opinions.
- Members who agree may try to band together.
- Sharp attitude changes may accompany disagreement.
- As conflict is expressed, some members may attempt to withdraw.
- If handled improperly, tension and disunity can undermine the success of the team.

During the *Norming Stage*, the team begins to "rally" around their ability to accomplish the team objective:

- Members learn how to communicate with each other.
- Members develop trust and respect.
- Dissent and social conflict die out.
- Members have learned how to give and receive feedback.
- Responsibilities are evenly distributed.
- Decisions are made.

At the *Performing Stage*, both the team dynamics and the team's product become tangible to the members (see Figure 11.14).

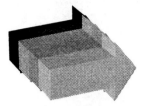

- Members experience a high level of interaction.
- Members experience positive synergy and increased performance.
- Members are comfortable with each other.
- Members reach consensus and are confident of their solutions.

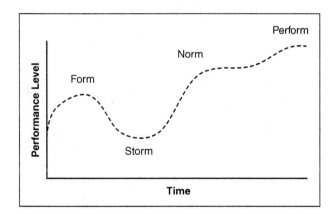

FIGURE 11.14 Life cycle of a team

There can be many circumstances that trigger a return to a previous stage, such as a new Sponsor, a change of scope, or a change of deliverable (see Figure 11.15). If a new member joins the group, the team will return to the Forming Stage until everyone is familiar with the new team member. If a Sponsor adds a specification to the charter late in the project, the team may return to the Storming Stage.

Types of Teams

"The greater the loyalty of the members of a group toward the group, the greater is the motivation among the members to achieve the goals of the group and the greater the probability that the group will achieve its goals."

—Renis Likert

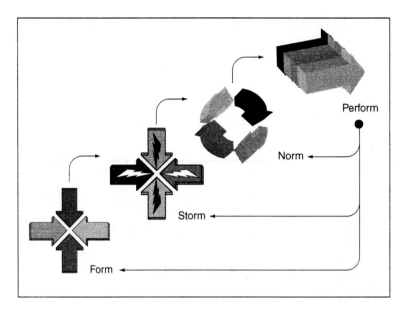

FIGURE 11.15 Looping back to previous stages

In the sports world, there are many types of teams. Most of us were first introduced to the team concept in school while playing on or watching sports. In sports, you have three outcomes: The team can win, lose, or tie. When the team ties, no one wins or loses. In business, we need an outcome where everyone wins.

Football is an example of a group of people working *in a team*. The decisions are made by the quarterback or the coach. Everyone has his/her own role to play, and each person plays that role independently. The plays are pre-planned, and everyone has his/her own work assignment. This is very much like the way the laboratories perform in HCP organizations. Working in a team has its own set of characteristics:

- Activities are pre-planned and go on in parallel.
- Management makes all the decisions, as decisions are centralized.
- Personal focus is hierarchical.
- The major disadvantages are the lack of flexibility and the long cycle time to make a decision.

Another type of team has its members work *as a team*. Basketball is a good example of this type of team. The activities of a basketball player have to be integrated with the other team members. Decisions must be made fast and on the spot; everyone is involved and contributing all the time. Anyone can score. The players are continually making the decisions. The coach develops their skills and builds their morale, but success depends on the decisions that individual players make during the game. The nurse and the physician working in the operating room work in much the same way that a basketball team works together. Working as a team has its own set of characteristics:

- Activities are not pre-planned. The team's activities are interdependent and integrated.
- The players make most of the decisions spontaneously.
- Players have on-the-spot flexibility.
- The weakness to working as a team is that it takes time to build the required level of trust.

When playing baseball, the players work *on a team*. They all are working toward the same goal. They all have different jobs and their own set of measurements. Most of the decisions are made by the manager. In this case, the team is a lot like a project management team in HCP organization. Each team member is doing his/her job of batting, pitching, or catching, but the result of the activity is not based upon help from other team players. The characteristic of working on a team are

- Activities take place in sequence, usually independent of input from the previous activity.
- Each player is an independent expert.
- Although the team is measured on the final score, each team member is also measured individually.
- Decisions are a combination of decentralized ("Shall I swing at this pitch?") and centralized ("When will the pitcher be removed from the game?").
- The weakness in working on a team is the lack of opportunity for the players to help each other. An example is that no one on the team can help the person who is up to bat.

The Different Ways SST Are Influenced

"If management is split about teams, implementing them won't work, plain and simple."

—Deborah Harrington-Mackin

In a Six Sigma project, a number of types of people influence the SST. They can be classified as

- Managers
- Team Leaders
- Facilitators
- Advisers

The *Manager* is the one who makes the final decision. The organization's employees are charged with the responsibilities but do not have the authority to deviate from the manager's direction. This leads to bureaucracy throughout the organization (see Figure 11.15).

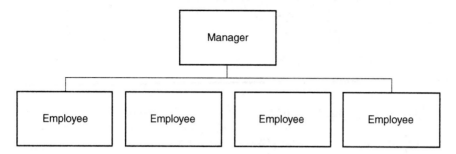

FIGURE 11.16 Manager influence on SST

The *Team Leader* is an individual who is part of the team and shares decision-making with the team. The leader takes an active role in keeping the team on track and growing the abilities of the team. He/she is a Green or Black Belt (see Figure 11.17).

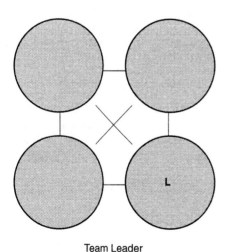

Team Leader

FIGURE 11.17 Team Leader influence on SST

The *Facilitator* for a team does not get involved with the team's decisions, but he/she is involved with the team decision-making process. The Facilitator focuses on the team process, not on the problem the team is solving (see Figure 11.18).

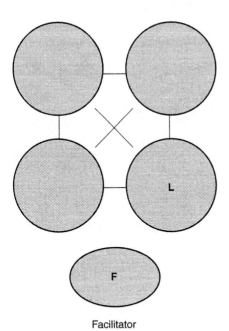

Facilitator

FIGURE 11.18 Facilitator influence on SST

The Adviser is not a member of the team, but he/she is invited to help the team when its members feel that they have reached a point where they need someone with specific technical skills. For example, a Master Black Belt could be asked to help design a very complex experiment, or someone from IT could be asked to recommend a software package or to evaluate a number of software packages before they are purchased (see Figure 11.19).

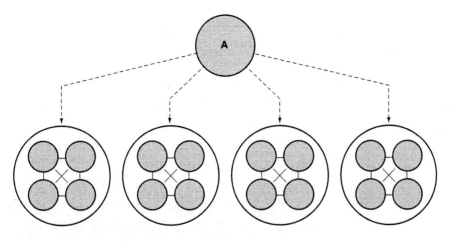

FIGURE 11.19 Advisor influence on SST

Activity 5—Define the Measurements

"A good measurement system listens to many voices."

—H. James Harrington

When you talk about measurements, you have to consider five different voices:

- The Voice of the Customer
- The Voice of Management
- The Voice of the Supplier
- The Voice of the Employee
- The Voice of the Process

Each of these voices tells you different things, and usually they have different requirements. You need to listen carefully to all five voices.

"In Japanese, the same word—okyakusama—means both 'customer' and 'honorable guest.' Disney World has always thought of its customers as its 'guests,' and many companies address their customers as being part of their 'family.' Customers in today's marketplace are looking for the special treatment that typically honors guests—and they are receiving it."

—Peter Capezio and Debra Morehouse

The *Voice of the Customer* is a very key part of the Six Sigma process, as Six Sigma is specifically designed to meet customer expectations. Typically, the Voice of the Customer has three different ingredients:

- It defines what they *must have*. These are the basic ingredients; without them, the customer will be very dissatisfied.
- It defines the things that they *expect to have*, although these are not things that they *need* to have. They will compromise these to get a lower price.
- It defines things they *would like to have*. These are the nice things—the frosting on the cake. If they get these, they're delighted with you. These are the ones that really lead to long-term customer relationships—customers for life. These customers feel that they have been given the greatest value by interfacing with your organization.

"The Voice of the Customer guides world-class leaders' every action and decision."

—Y.S. Chang, George Labovitz, and Victor Rosansky

The Voice of Management is also a very important input. Management has an obligation to keep the company profitable, to be able to meet payroll, and to pay the investors a reasonable return on their investment. Management focuses heavily on efficiency and cost control.

The Voice of Supplier is another important input. We are all very dependent on the suppliers, and if the supplier cannot meet our requirements, there is little chance that we will succeed. Imposing unrealistic requirements on your supplier can lead to failure throughout the organization.

> "If your employees are your most valuable asset, your suppliers run a very close second."
>
> —H. James Harrington

The Voice of the Employee is a key element. Our employees are a major asset, and we must take care of them. We must ensure that they are properly trained and motivated. We have to understand that change is difficult for them, and we need to control the amount of stress that change is subjecting them to. Our employees are an investment, not a cost.

The Voice of the Process involves the process itself. It speaks loud and clear about its capabilities. Too often, we ignore the Voice of the Process or don't listen to it. It is absolutely essential that we certify each piece of equipment and each step in the process to understand its capabilities, and when it goes into the unreliable and erratic state, we correct the situation. The least complicated condition for the SST is when the assignment is to reduce variation related to a specific dimension on a print. In this case, the customer requirements are specified and the tolerance limits are documented. All the SST needs to do is to reduce the variation down to the point that the calculated Six Sigma limit and the print limits are the same. Unfortunately, that is often a lot easier to say than to do. We have seen SSTs working for weeks trying to refine a specific sequence of activities to reduce variability when the equipment's capability exceeded the specification tolerance. Don't accept that the print tolerance is correct. Often, the print tolerance is set arbitrarily, and it is much easier and more effective to change the print specification than to buy new equipment. Often, a combination of refining the task and adjusting the print limits is the correct answer.

When it comes to process type improvements, there are three main measurements:

- **Effectiveness**. The extreme to which an output of a process or sub-process meets the needs and expectations of its customer. A synonym for effectiveness is *quality*. Effectiveness is having the right output at the right place at the right time at the right price. Effectiveness impacts the customer. Typical effectiveness measurements are appearance, timeliness, accuracy, performance, reliability, usability, serviceability, durability, cost, responsiveness, adaptability, and dependability.

- **Efficiency**. Relates to the extent that resources' usage is minimized and waste is eliminated. Productivity is a measurement of efficiency. Typical effectiveness measurements are

  - Processing time

  - Resources extended per unit of output

- Value-added cost per unit of output
- Percent of value-added time
- Poor-quality cost
- Wait time per unit
- **Adaptability**. The flexibility of a process to handle future changing customer expectations and today's individual special customer request. It is managing the process to meet today's special needs and future requirements.

Adaptability is an area largely ignored, but it is crucial for gaining a competitive edge in the marketplace. Customers always remember when you don't handle their special needs. Basic quality involves satisfying customer requirements; however, for many customers today, good enough is not enough anymore. HCPs must exceed customer needs and expectations, now and in the future, by

- Empowering people to take special action
- Moving from meeting basic requirements to exceeding expectations
- Adjusting and adapting to ever-changing customer expectations
- Continuously improving the processes to keep ahead of the competition
- Providing a non-standardized activity to meet a special customer need

Typical measurements of adaptability would be

- The average time it takes to get a special customer request process compared to standard procedures
- The percentage of special requests that are turned down
- The percentage of time the special requests are escalated (for example, in the HCP industry the more people a customer has to talk to in order to get a need satisfied, the less chance that person will be satisfied)

Adaptability requirements should be established at the beginning of a process improvement cycle so that the improvement activities can consider these parameters and data systems can be established to measure adaptability.

Activity 6—Prepare a Project Plan

"Plans are nothing; planning is everything."

—Dwight Eisenhower

Project management is one of the most important Six Sigma tools that the SST has available. It is very important that each project uses this tool effectively to manage the assigned project. The Project Management Methodology has been well defined by the Project Management Institute in a methodology they call *PMBOK* (Project Management Body of Knowledge). The project management knowledge areas are

- Integration Management
- Scope Management
- Planning and Estimating Management
- Documentation and Configuration Management
- Time Management
- Financial and Cost Management
- Quality Management
- Human Resource Management
- Communication Management
- Risk Management
- Procurement Management

Everyone who manages a project should have a detailed understanding of each of these knowledge areas. It also advisable that all members of the project team have a working knowledge of them. We feel that every Master Black Belt should also be a Certified Project Manager if he/she is going to work well in leading the Six Sigma activities.

The project plan is used to pull together the key project information into a single place. It should include things such as

- Project mission
- Project budget
- Project objectives and goals
- Risk analysis
- Assumptions
- Schedules (work breakdown structures)
- Training plans
- Project charter
- Team Members' names and committed times
- Any special directions/limitations

One of the most important parts of the project plan is the work breakdown structure. It defines what will be done by whom and when. Figure 11.20 is a sample work breakdown structure. We feel that the Microsoft Project software package is an effective tool to generate work breakdown structures for the SST. It does an excellent job of organizing a single project and defining the critical path through the project. However, it has major drawbacks when it comes to managing a portfolio of projects like the Master Black Belt needs to do.

NOTE

For more information on how to manage projects, we suggest reading *Project Management Excellence* by Dr. H. James Harrington and Dr. Thomas McNellis (Paton Press, 2006). Appendix A in that book provides a list of the PMBOK 75 tools and techniques along with a self-evaluation quiz to determine how good your project management skills are.

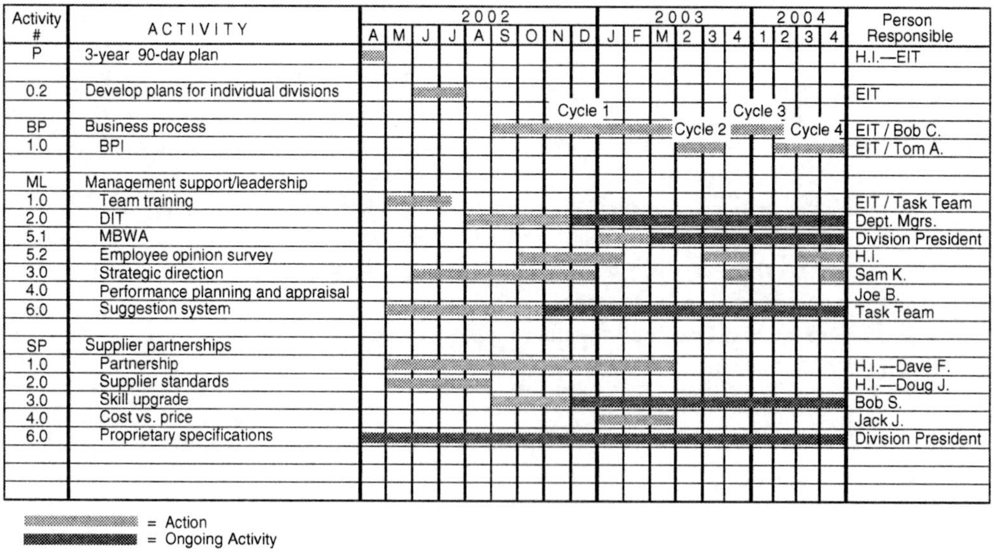

Activity #	ACTIVITY	2002									2003						2004				Person Responsible
		A	M	J	J	A	S	O	N	D	J	F	M	2	3	4	1	2	3	4	
P	3-year 90-day plan	▨																			H.I.—EIT
0.2	Develop plans for individual divisions			▨	▨																EIT
									Cycle 1				Cycle 3								
BP	Business process						▨	▨	▨		Cycle 2 ▨			Cycle 4							EIT / Bob C.
1.0	BPI												▓				▓				EIT / Tom A.
ML	Management support/leadership																				
1.0	Team training	▨	▨																		EIT / Task Team
2.0	DIT						▓	▓	▓		▓	▓	▓	▓	▓						Dept. Mgrs.
5.1	MBWA										▓			▓	▓						Division President
5.2	Employee opinion survey							▨	▨						▨						H.I.
3.0	Strategic direction						▓	▓	▓						▓						Sam K.
4.0	Performance planning and appraisal		▨	▨																	Joe B.
6.0	Suggestion system	▨	▨					▓	▓		▓	▓	▓	▓	▓						Task Team
SP	Supplier partnerships																				
1.0	Partnership				▓	▓				▓	▓										H.I.—Dave F.
2.0	Supplier standards		▨	▨																	H.I.—Doug J.
3.0	Skill upgrade					▓	▓			▓	▓			▓	▓						Bob S.
4.0	Cost vs. price										▨	▨			▨						Jack J.
6.0	Proprietary specifications	▓	▓																		Division President

▨ = Action
▓ = Ongoing Activity

FIGURE 11.20 Combined three-year improvement plan

"Defining an objective is like telling a railroad ticket clerk your destination before you buy a ticket. If you have not decided on a destination, you cannot buy a ticket."

—Katsuyoshi Ishihara

Activity 7—Prepare an Organizational Change Management Plan

The biggest single reason that Six Sigma and TQM programs have failed is that they have focused on the technology, knowledge, and processes and have forgotten the "people side" of the equation, and people is what change management is all about. (see Figure 11.21).

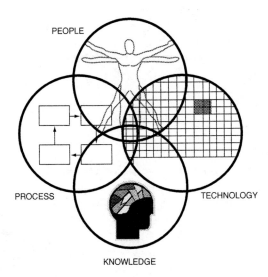

FIGURE 11.21 Change management

Almost all the major Six Sigma process changes have a major impact upon the people working in the process that is being improved. Sometimes it affects just one person; other times it affects everyone within the process. Many of the Six Sigma programs have eliminated many jobs, because the re-work assignments and no-value-added jobs are removed and business-value-added activities are removed from the process. In Six Sigma, we treat organizational change management as a process (see Figure 11.22).

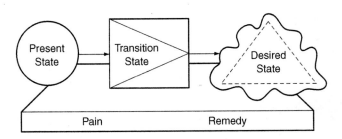

FIGURE 11.22 The change management process

The Change Management Process starts with the individual in the *current state*. This is a state where he/she feels very comfortable. The person is in control, has his/her own specific job, and knows more about it than anyone else. As we apply change to the process, the individual goes into a *transition state*. At this point, the person has lost control of his/her job and doesn't know if he/she will be able to function in the new environment. The person is worried, and often resistance groups are formed. Eventually, the individual moves into the *future state* with the promise that this new state is a better condition than he/she had in the current state. Unfortunately, it's very difficult to get the individual to move from one state to another. If he/she feels that there is less pain in the current state than the pain he/she perceives will be subjected to during the transitional period and in to the future state, it is next to impossible to get anyone to change (see Figure 11. 23).

You would think that the individual understands the pain he/she is having in the current state better than anyone can, and it's usually true they do. But, there is another part of current-state pain that he/she usually doesn't understand. It is the *"what if we don't change"* pain related to the current state. Very often if we don't change, it could mean the organization will lose its competitive advantage and jobs will be eliminated. Management has to surface "what-if" pain so that individuals can make a fair decision about how much resistance they are going to apply to the change. As an SST member, you need to look at the individuals who will be impacted by your proposed improvement and answer the following three questions for them:

- What's in it for him or her?
- Why is the change necessary?
- Why is it important to the organization?

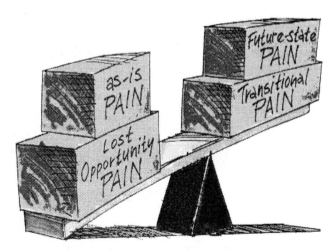

FIGURE 11.23 Pain management

Resistance is normal, so it should come as no surprise to the SST. In fact, the team should be concerned if there is no resistance because that often means that the affected people have just given up and will not cooperate when you need their support and/or their acceptance of the change. If the affected people will not accept the required changes, even the very best Six Sigma program will fail.

Your change management plan has to create a *burning platform* that will cause the individual to move from the current state, through the transitional period, to the future state. This change management plan should be part of your project plan.

NOTE

For more information on organizational change management, we suggest you read *Change Management Excellence* by Dr. H. James Harrington (Paton Press, 2006).

Once the organizational change management plan has been integrated into the project plan, the updated project pan should be reviewed and approved by the Executive Team. This approval allows the project to enter into Phase III Piloting.

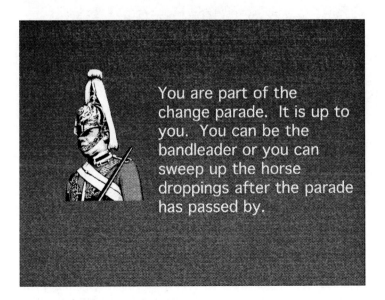

You are part of the change parade. It is up to you. You can be the bandleader or you can sweep up the horse droppings after the parade has passed by.

PHASE III—PILOTING

"Pilot because, as a wise man once said, 'The best-laid plans of mice and men often go astray.'"

—H. James Harrington

The Piloting Phase is subdivided into five activities:

- Activity 1: Define
- Activity 2: Measure
- Activity 3: Analyze
- Activity 4: Improve or Design
- Activity 5: Control or Verify

Hopefully you have recognized these activities as DMAIC or DMADV approaches to the Six Sigma Improvement Strategy that we have already discussed earlier in this book.

Note that some of the tasks usually done during the Define activity have already been completed in Phase II Planning. The SST has been formed, and initial training has been completed. The SST has been assigned, and a project plan has been prepared and approved by the Executive Team.

This is the most interesting and challenging part of the Six Sigma process. We liken it to a "Who Done It?" story, only with Six Sigma it is "What Caused it?" story. Too often, the organization tries to turn Six Sigma activities into "Who Done It Activities." This is absolutely the wrong way to operate. There is enough blame for everyone, so there is no need to waste time defining "Who Did It?" It is always better to spend your effort in defining "Why It Happened" and how the processes can be changed to keep it from recurring.

The crime has already been committed: There are too many errors, too many customer complaints, it takes too long to do it, or it costs too much. These are the crimes that Six Sigma has been designed to solve and return the criminal (the process) back to a productive member of society.

Well, the call is out. Sherlock Holmes, with his black cape and his trusty magnifying glass, has been replaced with an electronic microscope that can see all the way down to 3.4 defects per million and beyond. Along with him are his trusted friends, "The Watson Green Family of Process, Problem and Analyst, Laboratory Technicians, and IT Specialists." Together there is no crime so complex that they cannot solve. The first job this team has is to get to the crime scene and start to collect clues that can be analyzed and put together to solve the puzzle.

Just like the Sherlock Holmes story on TV, which lasts 60 minutes minus time for the commercials, the Six Sigma project should be time-boxed in to a three-month maximum, minus the time to do the team's regular work assignments. Unlike the detective story that ends with the detective bringing the suspects and interested parties together at the scene of crime and revealing the culprit along with the explanation that proves the culprit caused the crime, the SST has to go further to define the cause, which is often hard. But creating a permanent fix that prevents the problem from recurring is the real challenge. It is like the detective having the responsibility for defining the rehabilitation of the criminal, and then having to justify the return on investment for the rehabilitation process.

Often Green and Black Belts become part of long-term research projects that last for one, two, or even three years, but these are not real Six Sigma projects. Sure, the skills that these Black and Green Belts have often are very valuable in these research projects and should be used.

It is not our intent to take you back through how to use DMAIC and DMAV methodologies; that would be redundant. But based upon our experience and other studies, the following are the most useful SST tools:

- Process Mapping
- Root Cause Analysis
- Cause and Effect Analysis
- Process Redesign
- Benchmarking
- Failure Mode and Effects Analysis (FMEA)
- Lean
- Process Capability
- Project Management
- Brainstorming
- Workflow Analysis
- Trend Analysis
- Design of Experiments (DOE)
- Error Proofing
- Standardization

The DMAIC cycle has 12 toll gates designed into it. They should be followed to be sure you come up with the best answer (see Figure 11.24).

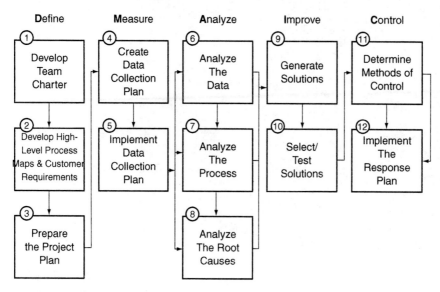

FIGURE 11.24 Six Sigma tollgates

Just one word of caution from a dear departed friend of ours, Dr. Kaoru Ishikawa, the man who made quality happen in Japan:

> "It is true that statistical methods are effective, but we overemphasize their importance. As a result, people on the Executive Team fear or dislike quality control as something very difficult. We overeducated people by giving them sophisticated methods where at that stage simple methods would have sufficed."
>
> —Kaoru Ishikawa, *What Is Total Quality Control: The Japanese Way*
> (Prentice Hall, 1985)

At the end of the improvement or design activities, the SST has defined its preferred solution to take advantage of the opportunity, along with an estimated cost to implement the solution and the projected savings as a result of this implementation. This information should be presented to the Executive Team for its approval. Often, the Executive Team will accept these results, if they are well-presented and supported by sound reasoning, as proof that the Six Sigma approach is good for the organization. In other cases, they will hold off approving the Six Sigma approach until the solutions have been implemented and the results are well-documented.

In Executive Team case, the Executive Team will be required, at some point in time, to take a position to define if the pilot was successful or unsuccessful and to make a decision about what the organization's future involvement in the Six Sigma initiative will be.

If you did a good job in conducting the pilot and had selected opportunities that had real potential, the Executive Team will not only approve the project to continue in Phase IV (Implementation), but it will be excited about reaping the additional benefits from entering into the project very fast. For purposes of this book, we will assume that the Executive Team is anxious to continue the Six Sigma initiative. We will also assume that more than 60 percent of people were able to pass the Six Sigma Green Belt exam and were certified as Green Belts.

PHASE IV—IMPLEMENTING THE SIX SIGMA SYSTEM

"Six Sigma has forever changed GE Everyone…is a true believer in Six Sigma, the way this company now works."

—Jack F. Welch, former GE Chairman

Phase IV Implementation is divided into seven activities:

- Activity 1: Organizing
- Activity 2: Defining the Six Sigma Roles
- Activity 3: Training the Six Sigma Team
- Activity 4: Selecting the Six Sigma Projects
- Activity 5: Forming the SST's
- Activity 6: Executing the Six Sigma Projects
- Activity 7: Internalizing the Six Sigma Culture

Activity 1—Organizing

"I don't give a damn if we get a little bureaucracy as long as we get the results. If it bothers you, yell at it. Kick it. Scream at it. Break it!"

—Jack Welch, former GE Chairman

Now that the decision has been made to implement the Six Sigma initiative within the organization, its time to establish the Six Sigma organizational structure. Although we will be talking about a special Six Sigma organizational structure, we must be careful it is not a stand-alone structure. It should be an integrated part of the total organization. The people who make up this

Six Sigma structure will report into the normal organization structure. (For example: a Black Belt, who is working on accounting problems, will report to the Accounting Manager.)

> "Six Sigma System is about creating a culture that demands perfection...and gives employees tools to enable them to pinpoint performance gaps and make the necessary improvements."
>
> —William S. Slovropoulos, Dow President and CEO

A Six Sigma system is designed to increase profits and customer satisfaction. It is an organized, documented, and understood approach to eliminate root causes of errors throughout the organization by reducing variation and developing streamline processes that are more effective and efficient. The Six Sigma organizational structure is the key part of the Six Sigma System. Figure 11.25 shows a typical Six Sigma structure.

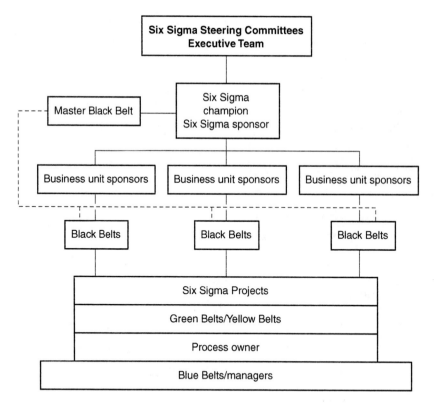

FIGURE 11.25 Six Sigma structure

Figure 11.26 is a top-level Six Sigma organizational structure for one of the HCPs we have worked with. You will note that, due to the organizational structure and the size of the operation, they divided the Six Sigma initiative into to four different parts. All four initiatives are brought together and coordinated by the SS (Six Sigma) Steering Committee.

```
┌─────────────────────────────────┐
│        SS Steering              │
│        Committee                │
│                                 │
│         Surgeon                 │
│        Cardiologists            │
│         Internist               │
│        ED physician             │
│      Hospital-based MD          │
│       Administration            │
│       Quality review            │
│     Finance/contracting         │
│          Nursing                │
│  Ancillary department manager   │
│      Six Sigma Champion         │
│        Consultants              │
└─────────────────────────────────┘

┌─────────────────────────────────┐
│      Business Unit Sponsors     │
└─────────────────────────────────┘
```

```
┌──────────────────────────┐     ┌──────────────────────────┐
│   Intensive Cardiology    │     │   Heart Surgery Protocol  │
│    Protocol Committee     │     │      Flow Committee       │
│                           │     │                           │
│      Cardiologist(s)      │     │        Surgeons           │
│         Surgeon           │     │       Cardiologists       │
│       Internist or GP     │     │      Anesthesiologist     │
│        ED physician       │     │    Critical care nursing  │
│  PITCA unit nursing manager│    │     Telemetry nursing     │
│    Other nursing manager  │     │    Respiratory therapy    │
│        Laboratory         │     │        Laboratory         │
│         Pharmacy          │     │         Pharmacy          │
│      Master Black Belt    │     │        OR nursing         │
│        Consultant         │     │    Cardiac rehabilitation │
│                           │     │     Patient education     │
│                           │     │     Master Black Belt     │
│                           │     │        Consultant         │
└──────────────────────────┘     └──────────────────────────┘
```

```
┌──────────────────────────┐     ┌──────────────────────────┐
│    Cath Lab Committee     │     │       OR Committee        │
│                           │     │                           │
│      Cardiologists        │     │        Surgeons           │
│        Cath lab           │     │      Anesthesiologist     │
│      Central supply       │     │        OR nursing         │
│        Black Belt         │     │      Central supply       │
│        Consultant         │     │        Black Belt         │
│                           │     │        Consultant         │
└──────────────────────────┘     └──────────────────────────┘
```

FIGURE 11.26 Six Sigma HCP organizational structure

Activity 2—Defining the Six Sigma Roles

Each level of management and every employee plays an important role in the Six Sigma System. Each is dependent on each other, and each role adds value to the Six Sigma System.

The Executive Team/Six Sigma Steering Committee

"The company cannot buy its way into quality—it must be led into quality by top management."

—Dr. W. Edwards Deming, *Out of Crisis* (1986)

The Executive Team sets the direction and priorities for the organization. As a result, it must be the owner of the Six Sigma System. It is responsible for managing the system to ensure that it is operating effectively. It needs to be the role model by including Six Sigma thinking into the way it functions. It is responsible for developing the organization's strategic plan that will be the basis for selecting the Six Sigma projects. It needs to understand the Six Sigma System well enough to be able to justify redirecting resources from other day-to-day, business-as-usual work to attack the waste that is causing less-than-perfect performance.

The Executive Team will appoint the Six Sigma Champion and Black Belts. It will also conduct periodic reviews of the Six Sigma System's progress and make the required adjustments when the system is not as effective as it should be.

"In fact, not only did Nasser (Ford's CEO, Jacques Nasser) go through the Six Sigma training, but he also regularly champions Six Sigma projects."

—Louise Goeser, Vice President of Quality, Ford Motor Company

Figure 11.27 shows a typical Six Sigma infrastructure.

Six Sigma Champion/Six Sigma Sponsor

The *Six Sigma Champion* is the Six Sigma Project Manager. He/she is responsible for developing and implementing the Six Sigma System. The Six Sigma Champion ensures that all functions are supporting the Six Sigma System by providing the properly skilled people for the required time and maintaining the Six Sigma activities as a high priority within the function. The Six Sigma Champion will also ensure that there are adequate funds in the annual budget to cover the cost of the Six Sigma process. Management must realize that they cannot assign employees to the Six Sigma activities without removing at least a portion of the workload they previously had. Expecting employees to do Six Sigma projects, in addition to what they were doing, is the major cause for Six Sigma and TQM failures around the world. A Green Belt will be expected to spend between 20 to 60 percent of his/her time working on the assigned projects during the problem-solving and implementation cycle.

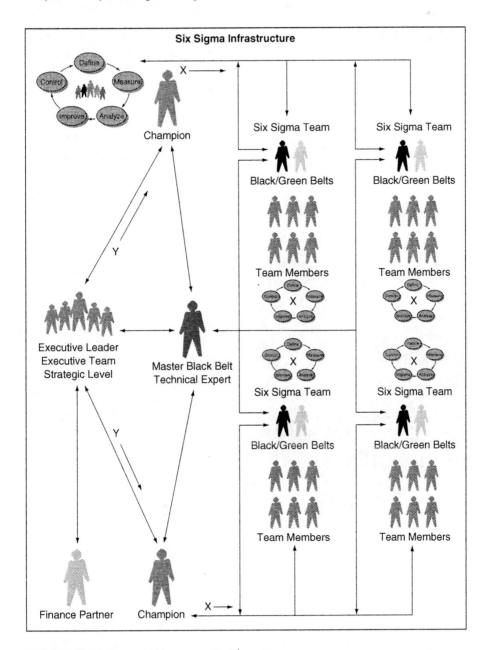

FIGURE 11.27 Six Sigma HCP organizational structure

The Six Sigma Champion will work with the Executive Team to define the improvement opportunities that are necessary for supporting the strategic plan. The Six Sigma Champion will set the goals and expectations for the Six Sigma Team and approve all projects before they are started. The Six Sigma Champion normally is a senior vice president of the organization. Often during the startup phase of the Six Sigma System, a consultant is assigned to this position due to the amount of time and sophisticated problem-solving experience that is required to justify and organize the first year's Six Sigma activities.

> "Effective delegation is perhaps the best indicator of effective management simply because it is so basic to both personal and organizational growth."
>
> —Steven Covey

Business Unit Sponsor (BUS)

Often Business Unit Sponsors' (division, function, and sector) people will be assigned to the Six Sigma process. The *BUS* provides a local view of the problems that are affecting the business unit's performance and how the business unit needs to react in order to support the strategic plan. He/she is often held accountable for the success of the Six Sigma System in the business unit. The BUS is responsible for ensuring that the business unit provides the required Six Sigma resources. He/she also provides input into the Six Sigma Champion related to the business unit's priority improvement needs. The BUS is typically a business unit executive.

Master Black Belt (MBB)

One Master Black Belt for every 15 to 20 Black Belts is the standard practice. A MBB is a highly-skilled Project Manager who should be Project Management Institute Certified. MBBs are the heart of the organization's Six Sigma process. The MBB must be a higher-skilled and more-experienced individual than a Black Belt. This person should be an experienced teacher and mentor who has the wisdom gained from experience in using the Six Sigma tools. The MBB is responsible for

- Certifying Black Belts and Green Belts
- Training Black Belts
- Developing new approaches
- Communicating best practices
- Taking action on projects for which the Black Belt is having problems in defining the root causes and implementing the change
- Conducting long-term Six Sigma projects
- Identifying Six Sigma opportunities
- Reviewing and approving Black and Green Belt project justifications and project plans

Typically, an MBB will interface with 15 to 20 Black Belts to provide mentoring and development service in support of their problem-solving knowledge.

Most organizations, when they start a Six Sigma process, do not have people who possess the experience to take on the role of an MBB even when they have completed the four-week Black Belt training program and the two-week Master Black Belt training. Training alone does not provide the required experience that is needed to function as an MBB. As a result, organizations normally hire a consultant to serve as the Master Black Belt for the first 6 to 12 months, and then they select one of their Black Belts who has performed the best, to gain the additional Master Black Belt training and experience for the following years.

Black Belts (BB)

"Black Belts are the work horses of the Six Sigma System."

—H. James Harrington

One Black Belt for every 100 employees is the standard practice. *Black Belts* are highly skilled individuals who are effective problem-solvers and have a very good understanding of the most frequently used statistical tools that are required to support the Six Sigma System. Their number-one priority is to define and develop the right people to coordinate and lead the Six Sigma projects (Green Belts). Candidates for Black Belts should be experienced professionals who are already highly respected throughout the organization. They should have experience as a change agent and be very creative. Black Belts should generate a minimum of $1 million in savings per year as a result of their direct activities.

Black Belts are not coaches. They are specialists who support the Green Belts. They may be used as SST leaders of complex and important projects. They do manage the projects that they are assigned to lead. The position of Black Belt is a full-time job; he/she is assigned to train, lead, and support the Six Sigma problem-solving teams. They serve as internal consultants and instructors. They normally will work with four to six problem-solving teams at a time. The Black Belt assignment usually lasts for two years. It is recommended that the organization have one Black Belt for every 100 employees. A typical Black Belt spends his/her time as follows:

25 percent	Running projects that he/she is assigned to lead
20 percent	Helping Green Belts who are assigned to lead projects
20 percent	Teaching either formally or informally
25 percent	Doing analytical work
10 percent	Defining additional projects

The Black Belt must be skilled in five areas:

- Project Management
- Leadership
- Analytical thinking
- Adult Learning
- Organizational Change Management

Based upon our experience, most of the Six Sigma Black Belt training has been directed at analytical skills. Even the selection of the Black Belts is based upon their analytical interests. This is all wrong. Traits to look for in selecting a Black Belt are

- Trusted leader
- Self-starter
- Good listener
- Excellent communicator
- Politically savvy
- Has a detailed knowledge of the business
- Highly respected
- Understands processes
- Customer-focused
- Passionate
- Excellent planner
- Holds to schedules

- Motivating
- Gets projects done on schedule and at cost
- Understands the organization's strategy
- Excellent negotiation skills
- Embraces change

Black Belts should be specialists and not have coaches. It is incredibly important to build a cadre of highly skilled Six Sigma Black Belts. However, they must not be placed in charge of the management of the improvement process. Black Belts are sometimes responsible for managing individual projects, but not directing the overall improvement process; that should be the job of management. Don't just keep management engaged in the process—keep them in charge of the process.[12]

Green Belt (GB)

Being a Green Belt is a part-time job. A *Green Belt* is assigned to manage a project or work as a member of an SST by the Six Sigma Champion and his/her manager. Sometimes a Green Belt is the manager of the area that is most involved in the problem, although we prefer that it is a highly skilled professional who has a detailed understanding of the area that is involved in the problem. Green Belts should be people who could be candidates for future Black Belt assignments, if they excel in the way they manage the project on which they are assigned to work.

The primary responsibility for the Green Belt is to form the project's SST and manage (coordinate) its activities during the entire product cycle. The Black Belt will support the Green Belt by providing Just-In-Time training to the project team when the Green Belt feels it is necessary. Green Belts are also expected to identify other Six Sigma opportunities and bring them to management's attention.

Yellow Belts (YB)

Yellow Belts are the people who have served on an SST and completed one successful cycle. They will have a practical understanding of some of the basic problem-solving tools and the DMAIC. They are usually classified as the Yellow Belts when management accepts the project and the SST is dismantled. During the project, they will work part-time on the project and still remain responsible for a reduced quantity of their normal work assignments.

Process Owner

All major cross-functional processes should have a process owner assigned to them. This is not a full time job. The *Process Owner* is the individual appointed by management to be responsible for ensuring that the total process is both effective and efficient. This is a key concept that must be understood to make the process management strategy work. Conventional-functional management has worked well for a number of years, and it is probably the best type of organization, but it has its shortcomings. Functional competition, although healthy in some cases, can be self-defeating because it puts all the functions in competition for limited resources. Frequently, the organization that puts on the best show gets the most resources, but it may not have the biggest need. In other cases, resources are allocated to part of a critical process by one function, but interfacing functions have different priorities and, as a result, only minor improvements are made.

What needs to be done is to stop looking at the business as "many large functions" and start looking at it as "many business processes that flow across functions." (Figure 11.28 shows a view of how the process manager looks at processes). This allows the organization to select the process it wants to improve, obtaining the maximum return on its investment. It is very evident that the process is the important element, and that the process owner plays a critical role in making the total process mesh together. The process owner concept provides a means by which functional objectives can be met without losing sight of the larger business objective.

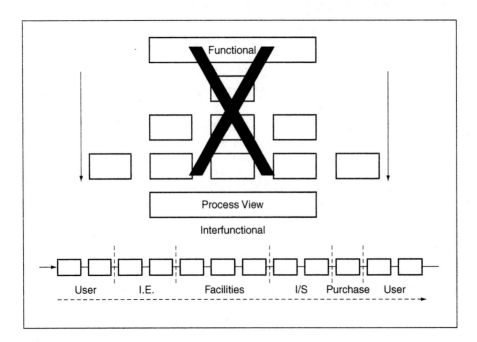

FIGURE 11.28 Business Process Management

The Process Owner must be able to anticipate business changes and their impact on the process. The owner must be at a high enough level to understand what direction new business will take and how it will impact the process.

Blue Belts

"Blue Belts keep the Six Sigma culture alive in the organization year after year."

—H. James Harrington

The Blue Belts are the normal population that may never be assigned to an SST, but need to be part of the Six Sigma culture. They need to be able to apply Six Sigma concepts to their day-to-day activities. They will receive two to three days of training covering the following subjects:

- How teams function
- What the Six Sigma processes are about
- How Six Sigma applies to them
- How to define who their customers are
- The seven basic problem-solving tools
- How to flowchart their process
- Area Activity Analysis

Activity 3—Training the Six Sigma Team

"No company can escape the need to re-skill its people, reshape its product portfolio, redesign its processes, and redirect its resources...The real issue is whether transformation happens belatedly—in a crisis atmosphere—or with foresight—in a calm and considered atmosphere...whether transformation is spasmodic and brutal or continuous and peaceful."

—Hamel and Prahalad, *Competing for the Future*

One of the basic Six Sigma beliefs is that the employees are an investment and not a cost. The accountants classify equipment and buildings as investment, but they treat their employees as a cost. Management requires the oil to be changed regularly in their cars and trucks because it costs less to maintain them than burn out their motors.

They require their measurement equipment to be re-calibrated, but when it comes to maintaining our most valuable assets (our people), managers are misers. Training of all our employees is required maintenance if they are going to perform at the Six Sigma level. Effective training is one of the most important investments that organizations can make. The Six Sigma System is based upon providing the organization's employees and management with many new skills that makes the total organization more competitive and profitable. Without good training, the Six Sigma System will fail. The following are the typical training program timelines for the various Six Sigma assignments:

- Executive Training: 16 hours
- Sponsor/Champion Training: 5 days
- Master Black Belt Training: 5 days
- Black Belt Training: 20 days

- Green Belt Training: 10 days
- Yellow Belt Training: 3 days
- Blue Belt Training: 2 to 3 days

Six Sigma Executive Training

"If it isn't important to the executives, it isn't important to the organization."

—H. James Harrington

The objective of these two eight-hour-day classes is to prepare the Executive Team to understand and participate in the Six Sigma System. It is very important that the executives understand and can talk the Six Sigma language. They must have, at a minimum, a basic working knowledge of the Six Sigma methodology, concepts, and tools in order to ask the correct questions and get relevant answers to their questions. It is recommended that the first class be held during Phase I. This first training session should answer questions such as

- What are the Six Sigma theory and methods?
- What is the history of Six Sigma?
- What is "Six Sigma Thinking"?
- What are the Six Sigma roles and responsibilities?
- Why should we spend our efforts doing Six Sigma?
- How is this different than TQM and ISO 9000?
- What is the difference between 3 Sigma and 6 Sigma, and why is it important?
- What are the basics of the DMAIC approach, and what are its major tools?
- How will it be applied in my area?
- How will we manage the change it will bring?
- What is the implementation strategy?
- How will benchmarking be used?
- Will it work on business processes as well as manufacturing activities?
- What lessons can we learn from other organizations?
- What will it cost and how much will it save?
- Who will do it and how much of our time is required?

Implementing a successful Total Six Sigma program requires a change in the corporate culture that starts with Executive Management. During these two eight-hour sessions for executives the following subjects will be discussed:

- Organizational Values
- Maximizing Customer Satisfaction
- Increasing Quality Levels
- Business Measures (KPIs)
- Six Sigma Business Strategy
- Organizational Six Sigma
- Business Measurements
- Process Capability
- Critical Roles and Responsibilities
- Overview of Six Sigma Tools
- Six Sigma Deployment
- Implementation Strategy
- Measuring Success
- The Executive's Role in Six Sigma Systems
- Defining and Improving Executive Processes
- How to Select People for the Six Sigma Program
- Basic Six Sigma Tools
- Selection of Six Sigma Projects

The second eight-hour class should be held after the pilot is complete and the Executive Team has made the decision to implement a Six Sigma system. During this class, the executives will work on developing a solution to one of the executive improvement opportunities that was identified during the first class. They will also select the projects that will be assigned to SST as well as naming the individuals (Black Belts) who will lead these projects.

> "The executives need the training more than anyone else, because in most cases they need to make the biggest change."
>
> —H. James Harrington

Six Sigma Sponsors/Champion

The Six Sigma Sponsor/Champion plays a key role in the Six Sigma System. This person is responsible for developing and implementing the Six Sigma System, and provides the interface on the day-to-day Six Sigma operations to the CEO. He/she is ultimately responsible and accountable for the success of the projects sponsored. That places a great deal of pressure on this person to identify the best possible opportunities and to push for very creative solution to these opportunities.

The Six Sigma Sponsor/Champions should attend the Six Sigma Executive Training. In addition, they should attend a five-day class. The Six Sigma Champion/Sponsor course includes quantitative analysis and data manipulation exercises and should only be considered for participants who are comfortable with such activities. A typical course would include the following subjects:

- Overview
  - Overview of Six Sigma
  - Why Six Sigma?
  - Random variation
  - Data collection
  - Basic data analysis
  - How to deploy Six Sigma
  - Basic Six Sigma tools
  - Problem-solving approaches
  - Process mapping
- Project Management
  - Return on investment (ROI)
  - Risk management.
  - Project planning
  - Organizational change management
- DMAIC: Define
  - Voice of the Customer
  - Project definitions
  - Project financials
  - Matrices and deliverables
  - Project scheduling
  - Change management
- DMAIC: Measure
  - Process definition
  - Poor-quality cost
  - Process matrices
  - Establishing process baseline
  - Control charts for variables and attributes
  - Analyzing sources of variation

- DMAIC: Analyze
  - Lean thinking
  - Sampling
  - Hypothesis testing
  - Linear regression
  - Multiple linear regression
  - DOE Introduction
  - Design Selection
- DMAIC: Improve
  - Tools
  - Models
  - Transformations
  - Response surface
- DMAIC: Control
  - Tools
  - Serial correlation
  - Multivariate control charts
  - Design for Six Sigma
  - Control plan
  - Process characterization and capability
  - Project guidelines and selection
  - Deploying Six Sigma
  - System for management
  - Business planning
  - Balance scorecard
  - Strategic planning
  - KPIs
  - Leading Six Sigma
  - Process scorekeeping
  - Process management
  - Process redesign
  - Process reengineering
  - Fast Action Improvement Teams (FAST)

- Area activity analysis
- Interpreting data
- Developing business cases
- DMADV

Master Black Belt Training

"The Master Black Belt is the guru of the organization. He/she knows all, sees all and can do all."

—H. James Harrington

The MBB training is the ultimate class for Six Sigma professionals. It is a one-week training program directed toward those professionals who are Six Sigma Corporate Leaders. (The prerequisite is Green Belt Training and Black Belt Training.) The program focuses on applying Six Sigma to the entire organizational model, and when striving for organizational excellence, each Six Sigma role must contribute to the total effort every day and in a different way.

The Master Black Belt Certification program targets those professionals who will oversee the corporate Six Sigma effort in various organizational "Domains of Influence."

The powerful tools, techniques, and software that are used in this course allow those individuals who attend the course to provide immediate value to their company.

Points of interest include the following:

- Lessons learned analysis
- Advanced leadership skills
- Advanced topics, tools, and applications:
  - ANOVA
  - DOE
  - Confidence intervals
  - Continuous data
  - Control charts
  - Correlation analysis
  - Discrete data
  - Gage R&R
  - Hypothesis testing
  - Measurements
  - Metrics
  - Multicollinearity

- Multiple regression
- Probability distribution
- GFD
- Sampling
- Serial correlation
- Taguchi methods
- Tools analysis
- Transformations
- TRIZ
- Advanced facilitation skills
- Advanced topics in technology
- Advanced project management skills
- Advanced Lean tools and techniques

Course Outline

Day One

I. Introduction and Overview

- Introduction
- Course Overview
- Minitab or QI Macros Overview (package provided with course materials)
- Minitab or QI Macros Overview and Exercises

II. Advanced Leadership Skills

- Getting the Most from a Position of Leadership Without Direct Authority
- Leadership Techniques—Achieving Results and Why Leaders Fail
- Leadership and Personality Analysis—How to Use That Information to Influence
- Consulting Leadership—Important Elements and Why They Have Been So Successful
- A Tactical Leadership Approach—The Identification and Elimination of Roadblocks
- Understanding Organizational Models and the Associated Impact on Process Leadership
- Executive Leadership, Expectations on MBBs and Alignment for the Greatest Gain
- Cost Reduction Leadership—Delivering the $$ That the CEOs Have Come to Expect

- Value Chain Leadership and How to Use It for Customer and Internal Innovation
- Organizational Excellence Leadership—What It Is and How to Achieve It
- Technical Leadership—Harnessing Technology to Reduce Defects and Reduce Cycle Time
- Knowledge Management Leadership, System Integration, and Data Intelligence
- Root Cause Analysis Leadership—Making Change Last
- Thinking "Out of the Box"—Skills or Process Leadership
- Project Selection Leadership—Moving the Big Ys on the Corporate Radar Screen
- Performance Leadership—How to Put the Right Equations Together for Total Optimization
- Change Agent Leadership—Know Who Can and Can't Change Corporate Culture
- Metrics Leadership—The Best Metrics, and How Many Metrics Are Too Many
- Collection and Analysis of Metrics for the Entire Business—Packaging Content Counts
- Team Leadership—How to Make Team Output Greater Than the Sum of Its Parts
- Benchmarking Leadership—The Best and the Worst Cases and How to Apply the Best
- What Is Lean Leadership and How Do You Best Approach Tough Decisions
- Review the Most Fruitful Areas for MBB focus
- Internal Tools to Best Enable MBB Success
- Advanced Leadership Case Study

Day Two

III. Advanced Concepts, Topics, and Tools

- DOE Revisited
- Advanced Business Examples
- Advanced Topics in Quality Function Deployment
- Advanced Business Examples
- Advanced Topics in Total Six Sigma
- Advanced Business Examples
- Advanced Case Study with Minitab or QI Macros

IV. Advanced Facilitation Skills

- What Makes a Great Facilitator?
- When to Facilitate
- How to Facilitate
- What Should the Results Look Like from a Great Facilitation Session?
- Advanced Facilitation Tools and Techniques
- Advanced Business Examples
- Exercises

Day Three

V. Advanced Concepts, Topics, and Tools

- Full-Factorial Designs
- Advanced Business Examples
- Fractional Designs
- Advanced Business Examples
- Advanced Topics in Discrete Data Analysis
- Advanced Business Examples
- Control Charts Revisited
- Advanced Business Examples
- Advanced Case Studies with Minitab

VI. Advanced Technical Skills

- 15 Ways Technology is Transforming Corporate Strategy and Processes
- Data Warehousing
- Creating Centers of Excellence
- Business-to-Business Internet Marketing and Sales
- Building a Successful Extranet
- E-Commerce Leadership and How to Create a Portfolio of Transactional Processes
- Customer Relationship Management Tools and Techniques
- Supply Chain Management Tools and Techniques
- Business Online
- Leading Digital Change

- Making the Most of Digital Value
- Area Activity Analysis
- Seamless Organizational Processes
- Advanced Business Examples
- Exercises

Day Four

VII. Advanced Concepts, Topics, and Tools

- Advanced Transformation Topics
- Advanced Business Examples
- Advanced EWMA Topics
- Advanced Business Examples
- Advanced Case Studies with Minitab

VIII. Advanced Project Management Skills

- DMAIC Advanced Project Topics
- DFSS Advanced Project Topics
- BPMS Advanced Project Topics
- Tools and Techniques to Manage Multiple Six Sigma Projects
- Multi-tasking
- Coaching—Professional Teams Have Coaches, So Why Is a 50 Percent Season a Success?
- Mentoring—The Areas that Black Belts Request the Most
- Escalation Policies and Pulling the Plug on Bad Projects
- Communications Planning
- Complete Project Management Process Review—Inputs and Outputs
- Software Development Models and When to Use Each
- How DMAIC Maps to the Project Management Life Cycle and System Development Life Cycle (SDLC)
- The CMM (SEI) Model—What It Is and What the Levels of Certification Are
- Risk Analysis Models—Contingency and Disaster Recovery Planning
- DMAIC Project Template (best practices)
- DFSS Project Template (best practices)

- Quality Management and Variance Analysis for Project Managers
- Advanced Business Examples
- Exercises

Day Five

IX. Advanced Concepts, Topics, and Tools

- Multiple Regression Analysis and Forecasting Models/Advanced Business Examples
- Taguchi Concepts
- Advanced Business Examples
- TRIZ
- Advanced Business Examples
- Advanced Case Studies with Minitab or QI Macros

X. Master Black Belt Certification Exam

- Certification Exam
- Final Certification Assessment

Black Belt Training

Six Sigma initiatives should be customer-focused and project-driven. Research shows, however, that even the most efficient Six Sigma organizations launch process improvement projects without aligning deliverables with "Customer Critical to Quality Requirements" (CTQs), focus too much on statistical packages that are not completely understood by Project Managers, and many projects fail because of a distinct lack of project management skills. This four-week course covers the critical aspects of how to align customer CTQs and analyze data results with "easy-to-use" Microsoft Excel packages, and also covers the most important aspects of leading projects in a Six Sigma environment.

The Black Belt Certification program targets those professionals who will implement projects in a Six Sigma environment. The average cost to train a Black Belt is between $30,000 and $40,000.

The powerful tools, techniques, and software which are used in this course will allow those individuals who attend the course to provide immediate value to their operation.

This four-week training program is directed toward those professionals who will lead Six Sigma Projects (pre-requisite is Green Belt Training). The classes are typically held for five days and then the attendees go back to their organization for three weeks to apply what they learned. The total program covers four months.

Points of interest include the following:

- Enterprise Deployment
- Focusing on the Customer
- Business Process Improvement
- Project Management Topics
- Define—Complete Review
  - House of Quality
  - Quality Function Deployment
  - Probability Distributions
  - Measure—Complete Review
  - Sampling Techniques
  - Analyze—Complete Review
  - ANalysis Of VAriance between groups (ANOVA)
  - DOE
  - Simple Regression
  - Improve—Complete Analysis
  - Hypothesis Testing
  - Control—Complete Analysis
  - Control Charts
  - Close Out—Complete Analysis
  - Introduction to "Lean" Thinking

Course Outline

I. Enterprise-Wide Deployment

- Why Companies Initiate Six Sigma
- How Companies Initiate the Six Sigma Effort
- The Evolution of Six Sigma
- Six Sigma as a Gauge for Corporate Success
- Six Sigma Roles and Responsibilities
- Six Sigma Deployment Models
- Poor Quality Cost
- Introduction to DMAIC and DMADV

- Six Sigma Implementation Methodology Five Absolutes
- Preparing Leaders to Launch and Guide the Six Sigma Effort
- Green Belt, Black Belt, and Master Black Belt
- Political Challenges
- Healthcare Industry—Six Sigma Case Study

II. Process Improvement

- What Is Process Improvement?
- What Does Process Improvement Have to Do with Six Sigma?
- Business Processes and Six Sigma
- Process Flow Structures
- Process Disruption in Large Organizations
- Process Measures of Capability
- Process Mapping
- Process Tools and Techniques
- Processes in Virtual Organizations
- Suppliers Inputs Process Outputs Customer (SIPOC)
- Case Study

III. Project Management

- The Project Management Life Cycle
- Project Management Process Analysis
- Roles and Responsibilities Reviews
- Project Management Variance Analysis
- Earned Value and How to Use It Successfully
- Project Initiation Analysis and Six Sigma
- Project Planning Analysis and Six Sigma
- Project Implementation Analysis and Six Sigma
- Project Control Analysis and Six Sigma
- Project Closeout Analysis and Six Sigma
- Risk Analysis and the WBS
- Contingency Planning
- DMAIC Project Template Review

- Reengineering Project Template Review
- Case Study

IV. Define

- Define Model
- Tools and Concepts
- Process Mapping
- Voice of the Customer
- SIPOC
- Kano Model
- CTQ Matrix
- Quality Function Deployment

V. Measure (Laptop Required)

- Measure Model
- Discrete and Continuous Data
- Definition of Defect Opportunity
- Calculating Process Sigma
- Descriptive Statistics
- Measures of Central Tendency
- Measures of Dispersion
- Run Charts
- Sampling Techniques
- Data Collection Approach
- Introduction of Statistical Software

VI. Analyze (Laptop Required)

- Analyze Model
- Application of Discrete Data
- Chi Square Test
- Binomial Distribution
- ANOVA
- Poisson's Distribution

- Sampling approaches
- Uni-Variate and Bi-Variate Analysis
- Hypothesis Testing
- T-Tests
- Relevant Tools and Concepts Using Control Charts
  - Pareto Analysis
  - Cause and Effect
  - Root Cause Analysis
  - Affinity Diagrams
  - Regression Analysis

VII.   Improve

- Relevant Tools and Concepts
- Design of Experiments
  - Introduction
  - Terminology
  - Planning and Organizing Experiments
  - Randomized and Randomized Block Designs
  - Full Factorial Experiments
  - Fractional Factorial Experiments
  - Taguchi Robustness Concepts
  - FMEA Risk Model

VIII.   Control

- Control Model
- Control Analysis
- Control Charts
  - Control Charts for Variable Data
  - Control Charts for Attributes Data
  - Interpreting Data

IX. Project Closeout

- Closeout Model
- Post Process Audits

X. Design for Six Sigma (DFSS)

- DFSS Explained
- When to Use DFSS
- DFSS Process
- Paradigm Analysis
- Idealized Design
- Prototype

XI. Green Belt Training

- Adult Learning Methods
- Preparing to Teach Potential Green Belts
- Five-day Green Belt Training Course Materials and Schedule
- Developing Exercises

CERTIFICATION EXAM (Black Belt)

- Certification Exam—120 minutes
- Final Certification Assessment

Green Belt Training

"They call them Green Belts because they save lots of greenbacks (dollars)."

—H. James Harrington

Global competition, cost-cutting, outsourcing, customer turnover, changing technology, global competition, and a challenging economy have battered many companies to the brink of bankruptcy. Time waits for no one, and only those organizations best adapted to these changing conditions survive in today's tough business environment. From the optimization of operational efficiencies to shorter cycle time to value-added customer partnerships, the philosophy and application of Six Sigma best practices are optimizing the very nature and culture of successful businesses around the world. Green Belts, too, have the opportunity to significantly contribute to the success of the company.

The Green Belt Certification training is targeted to those professionals who operate at the team member level. These critical professionals, who make the greatest contribution toward the successful outcome of process improvement projects, will find extreme value in the course. The powerful tools, techniques, and software that are used in this course will allow those individuals who attend the course to provide immediate value to their operation.

The ten days of instruction are typically spread throughout a one-month period to provide time for participants to apply what they learn and receive guidance and project mentoring from course instructors at no additional charge. This is a two-week training program; this course is designed for anyone who will be directly involved with Six Sigma Project as a Team Member. The average cost to train a Green Belt is $7,500.

We will not discuss the details of the Green Belt class because we covered it earlier in this chapter.

Yellow Belt Training

The Yellow Belts (sometimes called *White Belts)* are individuals who have received fundamental Six Sigma training. They often help to solve problems by inputting their personal experience and expertise to work on an SST. They also often help collect data that is used by the SST. This training allows them to solve the day-to-day problems they face. The Yellow Belt training is a three-day class that covers the following:

- What the Six Sigma process is about
- How does Six Sigma apply to them
- Six Sigma goals and metrics
- Six Sigma teams
- How to be a part of an SST
- Six Sigma implementation and management
- Creating customer-driven organizations
- Selecting and tracking Six Sigma projects
- How the Six Sigma System works
- Simple Six Sigma tools
- Fast action solution teams (FAST)
- Area Activity Analysis (AAA)

The course is designed to provide a broad understanding of the Six Sigma improvement methodology, concepts, and language, along with a complete toolbox of basic process improvement methods applied within the Six Sigma System, including basic statistical process control charts. Individuals who have completed the Blue Belt training only need one day of training to bring them up to the Yellow Belt level.

Blue Belt Training

"Organizations that don't use Blue Belts usually stop their Six Sigma projects without changing the organization's culture."

—H. James Harrington

The Blue Belts improvement effort is directed at continuously improving the work that goes on in their assigned natural work team. Management looks to them to improve their output between 5 to 15 percent each year by working smarter, not harder. This requires them to be well trained in basic problem analysis and solving tools. They take a two- to three-day class that covers the following topics:

- How teams function
- What the Six Sigma processes are about
- How Six Sigma applies to them
- How to define who their customers are
- The seven basic problem-solving tools
- How to flowchart their process
- Area Activity Analysis
- How to be more creative
- Simple statistics

Training—The Starting Point

"I hear, I forget
I see, I remember
I do, I understand."

    —*Chinese Proverb*

Training is just the beginning of the learning and using process. There is a long road to travel from the time you complete a Six Sigma class until you have mastered what you were presented. Bloom's Taxonomy[13] points out that there are six levels of learning and using: Benjamin Bloom created this taxonomy for categorizing the level of abstraction of questions that commonly occur in educational settings. The taxonomy provides a useful structure in which to categorize test questions, since professors will characteristically ask questions within particular levels, and if you can determine the levels of questions that will appear on your exams, you will be able to study using appropriate strategies.

1. **Remember**. The ability to remember what was presented (recognition, recall, or rote knowledge). Hopefully the training brings you up to this level.

2. **Understanding**. The ability to read and interpret data, reports, graphs, tables, and so on.

3. **Apply**. The ability to apply what you have learned to the assigned tasks.

4. **Analyze**. The ability to break down information into its constituent parts and recognize the relationships in complex scenarios.

5. **Evaluate**. The ability to make sound judgment calls related to the information you have selected to generate new ideas and solutions and to develop value propositions.

6. **Create**. The ability to look at the different parts and different situations to see patterns and/or structures and put them together in a way that has never been done before.

It takes time, effort, and experience to move from Level 1 to Level 6. Each time a Green or Black Belt cycles through a project, he/she becomes closer to becoming a Level-6 performer.

Activity 4—Selecting the Six Sigma Projects

"The best time to stop a poor project is before you begin it."

—H. James Harrington

"Right now, there is little true focus on that (preventing disease rather than treating illness). There's a bit of lip service to it, and there's a lot of talk about anti-smoking and fitness and keeping your weight down."

—Michael Porter, Professor, Harvard Business Review

Now is an excellent time to look at what the HCP is doing and where it wants to go. The HCP of the future must offer the best quality at the lowest cost and that only the sickest patients will require hospital care. This means that the HCP must look at the services they provide from a strategic marketing perspective. The buying power or influence has shifted; the customer has become elusive. Who is the HCP customer—the patient, the employee, the employee's family, the healthcare plan member, the insurer, and/or the physician? Which one is the HCP customer? Or maybe they all are? At least the healthcare system has to be value-added to each of them.

The following will help the HCP accomplish this task and identify major improvement opportunities:

- Define the impact of managed-care penetration on the hospital:
  - Identify how many hospital patients and potential patients belong to capitated health plans.
  - Estimate the penetration of managed-care patients over the next three to five years.

- Estimate the impact of managed-care revenue on the hospital's total revenue stream over the next three to five years.

- Identify the cost structure required to cover operating costs and achieve targeted margins.

- Compare the required cost structure to the hospital's current cost structure to show the need for dramatic change.

- Define patient-population-change trends over the next five years, considering the aging patient population. (For example, the number of acute-care beds occupied each day has dropped 25 to 30 percent in most competitive HCP markets. At about $1,000/day for an acute-care bed, that is a lot of money.)

- Analyze competitor's business trends and estimate their impact on the HCP.

- Define the HCP core capabilities and competencies.

- Identify best practices and best-practices trends in the industries.

- Profile the potential customer base.

- Profile other stakeholders.

- Define new and/or improved services that are needed.

- Define and evaluate major processes.

- Define probable market scenarios (for example, an HMO decides not to approve the HCP for services).

This type of analysis should lead to a five-year improvement plan that will identify many improvement opportunities over a number of years. It is also a good time to define who the stakeholders are and what they will expect from the HCP system. Performance measurements and targets need to be established. They are called *Key Performance Indicators* (KPIs), and should relate to the stakeholder expectations, which typically are the following:

- **Patients**. Trust and belief that they are getting the best professional and personal care.

- **Health Plan Provider**. Low cost with effective results/total value-added activities. No unjustified activities. Follow standard procedure.

- **PCPs (Primary Care Physicians)**. Effective access to patient records and participation in patient planning and monitoring.

- **Specialists**. Instantaneous response to patient test requests.

The Group Health Corporation of Puget Sound, Seattle, Washington, when they were developing their business goals and operations, defined their changing environment as shown in Table 11.3.

TABLE 11.3 Group Health Corporation Changing Environment

	From	**To**
Market Position	The only major managed care provider	One of many managed care providers
Customers	Focus on individual members	Focus on multiple customers
	Comprehensiveness and quality as primary values	Price, quality, and choice are all important
Delivery model	Exclusively staff model	Mixed model with 700 provider contracts and 50 percent of providers in external delivery system—all to support
Products	Single product	Multiple products
	Product uniformity	Demand for flexibility and choice
Competition	Small, weak competitors	Strong, agile competitors
	Local plans with HMO options	National plans
Regulatory environment	Stable	Uncertain
	Few mandated benefits	Comprehensive mandated benefit package under healthcare reform

"Those little cards inserted with bills or set on table tops are not designed to elicit an accurate measure of the customer's experience with that company. They'll give some tepid information on the level of customer satisfaction, but they are not a useful complaint system."

—James G. Shaw, CEO, Shaw Resources

During the first Executive Team training session, the executives agreed on a set of guidelines that would be used to qualify projects as Six Sigma projects. Typical guidelines require

- The solution should have a significant impact upon the external customer's perception of the organization and/or satisfaction.
- The solution should result in a minimum savings of $200,000.
- The solution was not one that was being already addressed.
- The solution will be implemented within 90 days from the start of the project.
- The solution had a significant impact upon the business performance/processes.
- The impact of the solution can be measured and documented.

"The measurements or indicators you select should best represent the factors that lead to improved healthcare outcomes; improved customer, operational, and financial performance; and healthier communities. A comprehensive set of measures or indicators tied to patient/customer and/or organizational performance requirements represents a clear basis of aligning all processes with your organization's goals."[14]

—Harry S. Hertz

"In fact, one and a half points of customer satisfaction drive about one point more loyalty. In North America alone, that translates into more than $2 billion in incremental revenue and roughly $100 million in profit."[15]

—Louise Goeser, Ford's Vice President of Quality

Process Maturity Grid

In Phase I (Activity 3), a list of the major core processes were developed. Now is the time to evaluate each of these processes, using the *Process Maturity Grid*. The grid has six levels, with Level 6 being the lowest level (unknown status). Level 2 (error-free) is the Six Sigma Level. Level 1 should be the target that every organization should be striving to reach. This Maturity Grid was developed by Ernst & Young in 1989 and has been used to define process maturity every since. It can be used to measure your progress to improve your process. We do not recommend that all your processes reach the Level 1 development state, but at least all of your major processes should be at that level.

"Too few organizations understand how good their processes can be since they have no measure of how good they can be."

—H. James Harrington

Introduction to the Process Maturity Grid

Qualification usually is a one-time event because it is designed to validate that the process can perform to its designed specification. But today, organizations that wish to excel have expanded this concept to evaluate the maturity of their business processes. (For example, the software industry has agreed to a five-level process development maturity grid.) We like to use a six-level maturity grid for all business processes (see Table 11.4).

TABLE 11.4 Six Levels of the Process Maturity Grid

Level	Status	Description
6	Unknown	Process status has not been determined.
5	Understood	Process design is understood and operates according to prescribed documentation.
4	Effective	Process is systematically measured, streamlining has started, and end-customer expectations are met.
3	Efficient	Process is streamlined and is more efficient.
2	Error-free	Process is highly effective (error-free) and efficient.
1	World-class	Process is world-class and continues to improve.

To determine whether the process has evolved to the next level, eight major change areas are addressed:

- End-Customer Related Measurements
- Process Measurements and/or Performance
- Supplier Performance
- Documentation
- Training
- Benchmarking
- Process Adaptability
- Continuous Improvement

For each level, a set of requirements has been established. The requirements are more stringent as you move up in levels. Until the process is evaluated, it is considered to be at Level 6. Figure 11.29 shows the six levels versus eight items. As the color gets darker, the requirements become closer to world class.

"Don't make the mistake of trying to run when you are still trying to walk."

—H. James Harrington

Requirements to Be Qualified at Level 5 Qualification Level 5 signifies that the process design is understood by the SST and is operating to the prescribed documentation.

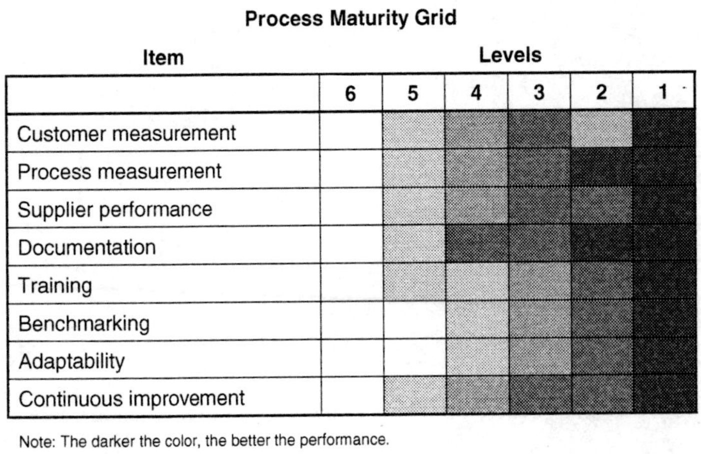

Process Maturity Grid

Item	6	5	4	3	2	1
Customer measurement						
Process measurement						
Supplier performance						
Documentation						
Training						
Benchmarking						
Adaptability						
Continuous improvement						

Note: The darker the color, the better the performance.

FIGURE 11.29 Six levels versus eight items

All processes are classified as Level 6 until sufficient data has been collected to determine their true status. Normally, processes move from a qualification Level 6 to a qualification Level 5. To be qualified at any level, all the criteria in each of the eight major change areas (for example, supplier performance, process measurements, and/or performance) must be met or exceeded. Those for Level 5 are

- End-Customer Related Measurements
  - Measurements reflect the end-customer's view of the process.
  - End-customer requirements are documented.
  - End-customer feedback system is established.
  - End-customer effectiveness charts are posted and updated.
- Process Measurements and/or Performance
  - Overall effectiveness and efficiency are measured and posted where they can be seen by employees.
  - Effectiveness and efficiency targets are set.
  - Process operational and/or control weaknesses are evaluated and meet minimum requirements.
- Supplier Performance
  - All suppliers are identified.
- Documentation

- Process Is Defined and Flowcharted
  - Flowchart accuracy is verified.
  - Documentation is followed.
  - SST members and process owners are named.
  - SST mission is documented.
  - Process boundaries are defined.
- Training
  - SST is trained in the basic tools and the fundamental BPI tools.
  - In-process training needs are evaluated and documented.
  - Resources are assigned to support training needs.
- Benchmarking
  - Not required.
- Process Adaptability
  - Not required.
- Continuous Improvement
  - Basics of BPI are in place.
  - All major exposures are identified, and action plans are in place.
  - A detailed plan to improve the process to the Level 4 is agreed to and funded.

Requirements to Be Qualified at Level 4　When a process evolves to qualification Level 4, it is called an *effective process*. Processes qualified at Level 4 have a systematic measurement system in place that ensures end-customer expectations are met. The process has started to be streamlined.

To be qualified at Level 4, the process must be able to meet all the requirements for the qualification Level 5, plus the following requirements:

- End-Customer Related Measurements
  - End-customer requirements are met.
  - End-customer expectations are documented.
- Process Measurements and/or Performance
  - Overall effectiveness targets are met, and challenge targets are established by the SST.
  - Poor-quality cost measurements are developed.
  - Some internal efficiency measurements are established.
  - Internal effectiveness measurements and targets are 50 percent complete and posted.

- Overall process cycle time and cost are defined.
- No significant effectiveness, efficiency, or control exposures exist.
- Substantial improvement activities are underway.
- Supplier Performance
  - Meetings are held with critical suppliers, and agreed-to input requirements are documented.
  - All critical suppliers meet input requirements.
- Documentation
  - Process is flowcharted, and documents are updated.
  - Overall process is fully documented.
  - Documentation of sub-processes starts.
  - Readability is evaluated.
- Training
  - In-process job training procedures are developed for all critical activities.
  - People are assigned to conduct job and process training.
  - SST is trained in statistical process control.
- Benchmarking
  - Plan exists to benchmark end-customer requirements.
- Process Adaptability
  - Data is collected that identifies problems with present process adaptability.
- Continuous Improvement
  - Process is operational, and control weaknesses are assessed and deemed containable.
  - A plan for improving the process to Level 3 is prepared, approved, and funded.
  - The process philosophy accepts that people make mistakes, provided everyone works relentlessly to find and remove causes of errors.

Requirements to Be Qualified at Level 3 When a process evolves to qualification Level 3, it is called an *efficient process*. Processes qualified at Level 3 have completed the streamlining activities, and there has been a significant improvement in the efficiency of the process.

To be qualified at Level 3, the process must be able to meet all the requirements for qualification Levels 5 and 4, plus the following:

- End-Customer Related Measurements
  - End-customer expectations are met.
  - Challenge targets are set by the SST.

- Process Measurements and/or Performance
  - There is a significant improvement in Poor Quality Cost (PQC).
  - Internal effectiveness and efficiency measurements are in place and are posted, with targets set by the affected areas.
  - There is a significant reduction in cycle time, and in the amount of bureaucracy.
  - Overall efficiency targets are met.
  - Most measurements show an improvement trend.
  - Key process control points are identified.
  - Tangible, measurable results are realized.
- Supplier Performance
  - Meetings are held with all suppliers, and agreed-to input requirements are documented.
  - All critical suppliers meet input requirements.
- Documentation
  - Sub-processes are documented.
  - Training requirements are documented.
  - Software controls are in place.
  - The readability level of all documents is at a grade level less than the minimum education of the people using them.
  - Employees understand their job descriptions.
- Training
  - All people performing critical jobs are trained in the new procedures, including job-related training.
  - In-process job training procedures are developed for all activities.
  - Plans are in place to train all employees, who are part of the process, in team methods and problem-solving tools.
  - SST understands one or more of the BPI 10 sophisticated tools.
  - All employees in the process receive training on the total process operation.
- Benchmarking
  - End-customer requirements are benchmarked.
  - Plan exists to benchmark critical activities.
  - Plan exists to benchmark the process.

- Process Adaptability
  - Employees are trained to distinguish how far they can deviate from the established procedures to meet a customer's special needs.
  - Future process change requirements are projected.
  - A proactive internal and external customer complaint system is established.
  - The end-customer reviews the process change plan and agrees that it meets his or her needs over the strategic period.
- Continuous Improvement
  - A plan to improve the process to the Level 2 is developed, approved, and funded.

Requirements to Be Qualified at Level 2 When a process has evolved to qualification Level 2, it is called an *error-free process*. Processes qualified at Level 2 are highly effective and efficient. Both external and internal customer expectations are measured and met. Rarely is there a problem within the process. Schedules are always met, and stress levels are low.

To be qualified at Level 2, the process must be able to meet all the requirements for the previous qualification levels, plus the following requirements:

- End-Customer Related Measurements
  - End-customer expectations are updated.
  - Performance for the last six months never fell below end-customer expectations.
  - The trend lines show continuous improvement.
  - World-class targets are established.
  - End-customers are invited to regular performance reviews.
  - End-customer desires are understood.
- Process Measurements/Performance
  - All measurements show an improvement.
  - Benchmark targets are defined for external customers and critical in-process activities.
  - In-process control charts are implemented as appropriate and the process is under statistical control.
  - Feedback systems are in place close to the point where the work is being done.
  - Most measurements are made by the person doing the job.
  - There is tangible and measurable improvement in the in-process measurements.
  - No operational inefficiencies are anticipated.
  - An independent audit plan is in place and working.
  - The process is error-free.

- Supplier Performance
  - All supplier inputs meet requirements for the last three months.
  - Regular meetings are held to ensure that suppliers understand the changing needs and expectations of the process.
- Documentation
  - Change level controls are in place.
  - Documents are systematically updated.
- Training
  - All employees in the process are trained and scheduled for refresher courses.
  - Employee evaluation of their training process is complete, and the training meets all employee requirements.
  - Team and problem-solving courses are complete. Employees are meeting regularly to solve problems.
- Benchmarking
  - Process is benchmarked, and targets are assigned.
  - SST understands the keys to the benchmark organization's performance.
- Process Adaptability
  - Employees are empowered to provide the required emergency help to their customers, and are measured accordingly.
  - Resources are committed to satisfy future customer needs.
  - Process adaptability complaints are significantly reduced.
- Continuous Improvement
  - The process philosophy evolves to the point at which errors are unacceptable.
  - Everyone works relentlessly to prevent errors from occurring, even once.
  - Surveys of the employees show that the process is easier to use.
  - Plans to improve the process to Level 1 are prepared, approved, and funded.
  - The process measurement trendline indicates that the process has improved at an annual rate of at least 10 percent in 75 percent of the measurements, and there are no negative trends.

Requirements to Be Qualified ay Level 1 Qualification Level 1 is the highest qualification level. It indicates that the process is one of the ten best processes of its kind in the world, or it is in the top 10 percent of like processes, whichever has the smallest population.

Processes that reach qualification Level 1 are called *world-class processes*. Processes qualified at Level 1 have proved that they are among the best in the world. These processes are often benchmark target processes for other organizations. As a rule, few processes in an organization ever get this good. Processes that reach Level 1 truly are world-class, and continue to improve so they keep their world-class process status.

To be qualified at Level 1, the process must be able to meet all the requirements for the previous qualification levels, plus the following:

- End-Customer Related Measurements
  - End-customer expectation targets are regularly updated, and always exceeded.
  - World-class measurements are met for a minimum of three consecutive months.
  - Many of the end-customer desires are met.
- Process Measurements and/or Performance
  - All measurements exceed those of the benchmark organization for three months.
  - Effectiveness measurements indicate that the process is error-free for all the end-customers and in-process control points.
- Supplier Performance
  - All suppliers meet process expectations.
  - All suppliers meet process requirements for a minimum of six months.
- Documentation
  - All documents meet world-class standards for the process being improved.
- Training
  - Employees are regularly surveyed to define additional training needs, and new training programs are implemented based on these surveys.
- Benchmarking
  - Ongoing benchmarking plan is implemented.
- Process Adaptability
  - In the last six months, no customers complained that the process did not meet their needs.
  - Present process handles the exceptions better than the benchmark organization's process.
- Continuous Improvement
  - All process measurement trend lines indicate that the process is improving at an annual rate of at least 15 percent.
  - An independent audit verifies world-class status.
  - Plans are approved and in place to become even better.

It is important to note that the goal for all Level 1 processes is to go beyond world-class to become the *best-of-breed process*. Although some processes become "best-of-breed" for short periods of time, it is very difficult to stay number 1. It requires a great deal of work and creativity, but the personal satisfaction is well worth it.

For more information related to process maturity grids, read Dr. Harrington's book, *Business Process Improvement* (McGraw-Hill, 1991).

Making the Selection

"Measure twice, cut once."

—The Carpenter's Rule

An initial list of Six Sigma opportunities was developed by the executive committee during Phase I that was not addressed in the Pilot Phase. This provides the start for the potential Six Sigma project list. During Phase II and III, the Six Sigma Champion Black Belt and pilot teams should be instructed to search out and turn in any other Six Sigma opportunities that they run across. These are added to the potential Six Sigma project list. An opportunity must have the following supporting data:

- Definition of the opportunity
- The benefits to the organization if the opportunity is taken advantage of
- An estimate of the dollar savings
- A definition of what parts of the organization will be affected and how will they be affected

Often ideas are submitted to the Six Sigma Champion that had not been thoroughly evaluated and quantified. In many cases, the Six Sigma Champion or the Black Belt will need to collect additional required data. The Six Sigma Champion should personally be able to support the input data before it is submitted to the Executive Team.

The initial selection of Six Sigma projects will be made at the second Executive Team training class. Each executive will be instructed to bring to the class one or two of their projects that they would like to have an SST work on. These inputs will be added to the potential Six Sigma project list.

Now the first inclination is to ask the question, "Why not do all of them right away? After all, each one will add at least $200,000 to the bottom line." That's a very good point, but if you did all of them at once, probably it would have a major impact upon your ability to meet your commitments to your present customers. That is why you need to slow down and consider how many resources you can afford to devote to the Six Sigma System.

The first decision that the Executive Team needs to make is, "Will Black Belts be assigned full-time as the Six Sigma best practices recommends?" Remember BBs should be very proficient people who have a good future with the organization. It is a major decision to take these high-potential individuals and pull them out of the normal workflow for one or two years. It is also a major career decision for the individual.

We suggest that you start this activity by selecting three to five full-time Black Belts that will be assigned to one to three projects. Too often, the Black Belts are selected because they have some specific skills needed to solve a specific problem. This is a bad practice. The Black Belt should be a person that can effectively manage many projects at the same time, not someone who can solve a specific problem. Select them because they are people you want to develop for future higher-level management assignments. By selecting an individual, you are in effect putting him/her on the fast track to the top.

The next step is for the Six Sigma Champion to lead the Executive Team through a prioritization process similar to the one defined in Phase I. The objective of this prioritization process is to identify one to three projects that will be assigned to each of the designated future Black Belts. For each of these assigned projects, the Executive Team should clearly document what it considers acceptable results from the project and the project time frame to complete the project. After the Black Belts are trained and the initial projects are well underway, the Six Sigma Champion can assign additional projects to them.

There will be a continuous flow of requests for Six Sigma projects coming in from the various managers throughout the HCP as the various departments gain better understanding of the Six Sigma process. This means that the potential Six Sigma project list will need to be prioritized from time to time and, as the Six Sigma System grows and gains momentum, you will want to add many more Black and Green Belts. (The normal ratio is for 1 Black Belt to every 100 HCP employees, and 1 Green Belt for 20 HCP employees. This means if the HCP has 2,000 employees, you will end up with 20 Black Belts and 100 Green Belts by the end of the first year.)

The Executive Team should set high-improvement objectives for each project and each Black Belt. Jack Welch, when he was chairman of GE, was willing to ask the organization to make improvements at seemingly impossible levels and rates. This is what Dr. W. Edwards Deming called "Arbitrary Number Goals" and "Cheerleading." But, it worked for GE and it can work for your organization. Sometimes you need a cheerleader to keep you trying to do your very best.

Activity 5—Forming the SSTs

"Successful companies achieve average savings of $400,000 to $600,000 per 'Black Belt' project and add millions of dollars to the bottom line."[16]

—Steven A. Zinkgraf, Author

The Executive Team should identify the Black Belts and assign projects to them. If the selected Black Belts were part of the Pilot Phase and have been certified as Green Belts, you have a good start to move ahead rapidly to provide them with the skills required to perform as a Black Belt. All of a sudden managers want their star people to become Black Belts because they want them working on their pet projects. In addition, many employees see the Black Belt assignment as a very positive career move. As a result, you will have two types of Black Belt candidates:

- Certified Green Belts
- Employees with no Six Sigma training

Let's look closely at these two types of candidates.

The Black Belt Candidates Who Are Certified Green Belts

These Black Belt candidates were good performers during the Pilot Phase and passed the Green Belt examination. In this case, the potential Black Belts can attend a five-day class to prepare them to manage the SSTs that will provide them with enough skills to get through the Define and Measurement phases of the Six Sigma process. Thirty days later, they should take another five-day class to provide them with the information they need to get through the Analyze, Improve, and Control phases. With this approach, the candidates can bring data related to the project that they are assigned to and work on it during this second five-day training program. At the end of their first project, they should attend a three-day class to exchange experience and to provide them with additional detailed tools and approaches. At the end of the three-day class, they will be given a two-hour examination. Those who pass the examination will be certified as Black Belts.

Black Belt Candidates with No Six Sigma Training

In this case, the candidate has not worked on a Six Sigma project, and it will be important for him/her to get trained very fast. We suggest that this individual take the Green Belt training with the other SST members for one week and then take the first week of the Black Belt training. Two weeks later, he/she should take the second week of the Black Belt training. The third week of the Black Belt training will follow about two weeks later. At the end of the first project, the candidate should attend a five-day Black Belt training program that will end with the Black Belt exam. The following is a timeline for this training:

- Week I: Green Belt Training with SST
- Week II: First Week of Black Belt Training
- Week V: Second Week of Black Belt Training
- Week VIII: Third Week of Black Belt Training
- Week XII: Fourth Week of Black Belt Training and Exam

The Master Black Belt or the Six Sigma consultant should work closely with these types of Black Belt candidates during the first project.

What If the Candidate Fails the Black Belt Exam?

"The wisest of the wise may err."

—Aeschylus

This represents a very difficult decision for the Executive Team. If the Black Belt candidate is dropped from the Six Sigma initiative and put back into his/her old assignment, it is very embarrassing for everyone. On the other hand, you cannot afford to have a poorly-skilled individual assigned full time to the Black Belt activities. Based upon our experience and the results of other Six Sigma certification exams, it is not unusual for only 70 percent of the candidates to pass the Black Belt exam the first time.

We recommend the following to our clients when a Black Belt candidate fails to pass the exam:

- Determine if the candidate just barely failed (for example, their grade was 65 and the passing grade is 70) but the project results were acceptable. In this case, we let them conduct another project and repeat the fourth week of the Black Belt training and re-take the exam.

- For individuals whose grades were below 60, we recommend that input be collected from the Six Sigma Champion, the Master Black Belt, and the individual's instructor to determine if they feel that the individual had been really trying and was capable of succeeding. If there is common agreement that the individual tried and is capable and the results of the project he/she is working on were satisfactory, we would suggest that you give the individual another three months to complete one or more projects. After this time, the candidate should then repeat the fourth week of Black Belt training and re-take the exam. Throughout this probationary cycle, the Master Black Belt should work closely with the individual. Of course, the individual should be informed that failure to pass the test on the second try would mean that he/she will be re-assigned.

NOTE

Some organizations that believe the Six Sigma System has an excellent chance of being adopted by their organization will set aside
three to four Black Belts to go through a conventional four-month
Black Belt training program in parallel with the Pilot Phase. This
allows them to have a group of trained Black Belts on hand when
they enter the Implementation Phase.

Activity 6—Executing the Projects

"Great works are not performed by strength, but by perseverance."

—Samuel Johnson

Now that Black Belts or Black Belt candidates have been prepared to form SSTs, the real benefit from the Six Sigma System is close to being realized. The procedures that the Black Belt or Black Belt candidates should go through to form a SST and the SST's activities during the project were discussed in the Pilot Phase of this chapter so they will not be repeated here.

When to Use DMAIC and DMADV

DMAIC is used under the following conditions:

- A process exists.
- Customer needs can be met by changing the existing process.
- The project is part of an on-going continuous improvement activity.
- Only a single process needs to be changed.
- A single customer performance requirement needs to change.
- Competitor's performance is stable.
- Customer's purchase behavior is stable.
- Technology is stable.

Examples of DMAIC problem-solving methods:

- Reduce the cycle time to process a patent.
- Reduce the number of customer complaints about incorrect records.
- Increase the number of prompts on the customer service system.
- Reduce the number of errors in sales' leads lists.
- Improve search time for critical information.

DMADV is used under the following conditions:

- No process exists.
- Existing processes have reached the limits of its capability.
- Project is of strategic importance.
- Multiple processes need to be changed.
- Multiple customer performance requirements need to be addressed.
- Competitor's performance is dramatically improving.
- Customer's behaviors are changing.
- Technology is evolving.

Examples of procedures that the DMADV development method is designed to address:

- Add a new service.
- Reduce the total number of customer complaints.
- Create a multiple-source lead tracking system.
- Create a real-time access to live help.

Activity 7—Internalizing the Six Sigma Culture

"Changing the culture of an institute is a slow process, and one that is best not
rushed. If the effects of TQM are to be lasting, people have to want to be on board."

—Edward Salis

Six Sigma is not just SSTs attacking major problems throughout the organization. It's
about a new culture that requires everyone doing near-perfect work all the time. It looks impressive to have a team work on a problem for three months and save $200,000 dollars, but it is often
better to have 5,000 small problems solved that saved $1,000 each. Yes, this small savings adds
up to real big profits fast. The organization needs to get everyone thinking Six Sigma and Lean.
If a process has 800 activities in it with an average of three failure opportunities in each activity,
that's 2,400 different failure opportunities that need to be analyzed and improved to the Six
Sigma level. Of course, that is an impractical and impossible task if you are assigning an SST to
each opportunity. If the SST spends three months on each failure opportunity, that would require
600 years just to do one process. Of course, this is ridiculous. It is the individuals doing the work
every day that brings a Six Sigma culture into the organization. This can only be accomplished
when each natural work team understands its processes and is committed to supplying the internal and external customers of these processes with Six Sigma level output. A *Natural Work Team
(NWT)*, sometimes called a Natural Work Group (NWG), is any group of people who are
assigned to work together and report to the same manager or supervisor.

Each natural work team and each individual in that natural work team needs to understand
that he/she has a customer for their output; that customer maybe the person who is sitting beside
them, the person that is across the room, the person that's in the next building, or maybe an external customer to the organization. These customers all have needs and expectations of the inputs
they receive. All excellent organizations realize that they need to listen to the voice of both the
internal and external customer if they are going to survive. This applies to every nurse, doctor,
nurse's aid, lab technician, accountant, manager, and janitor. The real Six Sigma challenge is
how you get each member of the HCP performing at the Six Sigma level. It is even difficult to
define the number of failure opportunities at the individual levels. First, think about how many
failure opportunities a manager has each day—a hundred, a thousand, ten thousand, and a hundred thousand? How many error opportunities does a doctor, nurse, accountant, x-ray technician,
and so on, have? And is it even worth while calculating all the potential error opportunities and
measuring them? Many HCPs believe that the concept of error opportunities is legitimate, and
taking the time to establish an accurate measurement of the number of error opportunities per
individual is not cost-effective nor value added.

Making Your NWTs Hum

"In essence, a team that is just starting out is not really a team, even though everyone might call it one…Don't fool yourself."

—Richard S. Wellins, William C. Byham, and Jeanne M. Wilson

The NWT is the engine that drives the organization. Only by educating, empowering, and continuously communicating with the NWT can any organization perform at an acceptable level. Of course, the organization is made up of individuals, each with different personalities and needs that must be managed. But success comes not from each individual doing his or her own thing, but from individuals working together to create outputs that are greater than the sum of the outputs of the single individuals.

> "The face-to-face group is as significant a unit of organization as the individual. The two are not antithetical. In a genuinely effective group, the individual finds some of his deepest satisfaction."
>
> —Douglas McGregor, Author

Internal and External Supplier/Customer Relationships

Defining customer/supplier relationships is only one part of making an area function effectively. There are many other factors that also must be considered. For example,

- What is the area responsible for?
- How is the area measured?
- What is acceptable performance?
- How does the area fit into the total organization?
- How well do the area's employees understand their roles and the ways they can contribute?
- What are the important activities that the area performs from top management's standpoint?

> "Area Activity Analysis (AAA) is the only effective and systematic way to make the internal- and external-customer relationship work."
>
> —H. James Harrington

It is important to note that all these questions pivot around the activities that the area is involved in. It is for this reason that the Area Activity Analysis (AAA) methodology broadened its perspective to go beyond the customer/supplier partnership concept to embrace a complete business view of the area.

> "Groups become teams through **disciplined action**."
>
> —John R. Katzenbach and Douglas K. Smith, Authors

We believe it is important to get everyone thinking about striving to perform at 3.4 errors per million opportunities, but it is often impractical to put these measurements in place. At the individual level it is often better to use the *Error-Free Criteria*. The Error Free approach measures the duration between errors and sets the objective of increasing the duration between errors. This becomes a very personal measurement system where the individual can set personal goals per their own desires. If the present error-free duration is 10 hours for an individual, he/she can set, as an objective, to improve to 15 hours, then to 25 hours, then to 50 hours, and so on. This allows each individual to always be striving for improved measurable performance improvement. At the natural work team level, we have found AAA as the most effective approach to establishing the internal and external supplier customer relationships and measurements. We will discuss this approach parting the next part of this chapter.

But before we go any further, let's discuss what we mean by customer/supplier relationships as they relate to internal and external customers. Basically, a customer/supplier relationship can develop in one of two different ways:

- An individual or organization can determine that it needs something that it does not want to create itself. As a result, it looks for some other source (supplier) that will supply the item or service at a quality level, cost, and delivery schedule that represents value to the individual or organization. We will call this organization the *customer*.

- An individual or organization develops an output that it believes will be of value to others. Then the individual or organization looks for customers that will consider the output as being valuable to them (for example, the Internet, VCR, and so on). We will call this organization the *supplier*.

Although both these situations reflect real life, we will use the first one to discuss how the customer/supplier relationships develop. We feel that after reading this explanation, the reader will be able to apply the concept to the second situation.

"A customer's assessment of the quality of any organization is based on the best that customer has seen. The customer does not know what is technically or organizationally feasible."

—David Hutchins

The customer defines a need (requirement) for an input and begins looking for some source that can fulfill this need (see Figure 11.30).

FIGURE 11.30 Search for a potential source

To find a source for this input, the customer needs to define the performance parameters related to the required input, when the input needs to be delivered, how good the input needs to perform, and how much the individual or organization is willing to pay for the item or service. Usually, all of this data is communicated to potential sources of the item or service with the exception of how much the customer is willing to pay for the item or service. Once the potential source of the input receives the potential customer's information (requirements), it is evaluated to determine if the source has the capabilities of providing the input to the customer in keeping with the customer's performance, quality, and delivery requirements. If there is a near match, the potential source will contact the customer and discuss how their differences can be resolved. Once these requirement issues have been resolved, the potential source will determine how much it will cost them to provide the input to the customer and add to this cost their profit margin, so that a total compensation requirement can be defined. These compensation requirements are then communicated to the customer. Through the negotiation process, a closure of all outstanding issues between the customer and the potential source is reached (see Figure 11.31). It is important to note that at this point the potential source is not a supplier because the customer often is negotiating with other potential sources to provide the same product or service.

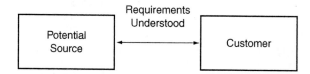

FIGURE 11.31 Complete definition of the potential source's and customer's requirements

If the potential source represents the best-value option to the customer, the customer will agree to accept the input as long as it is in compliance with the negotiated requirements. The customer also agrees to compensate the potential source for the item or service as negotiated. With an external customer, this act often takes the form of a purchase order. Once the potential source agrees to the provisions defined by the customer, it enters into a contract (formal or informal, verbal or written) to provide the input to the customer that meets the requirements in return for the agreed to compensation. At this point in the process, the potential source becomes the supplier (see Figure 11.32).

FIGURE 11.32 Agreed-to requirements that both the supplier and customer are committed to provide

"The customer deserves to receive exactly what we have promised to produce—a clean room, a hot cup of coffee, a nonporous casting, a trip to the moon on gossamer wings."

—Philip Crosby

> **NOTE**
>
> It is important to note that the agreed-to requirements include both the customer requirements and the supplier requirements for compensation.

Now that an agreed-to requirement package has been developed, it is up to both parties to live up to their part of the agreement. The supplier provides the input to the customer, and the customer evaluates the input to determine if it meets the defined requirements. The customer then provides feedback to the supplier related to the performance of the input compared to the agreed-to requirements. This feedback should include both positive and negative data. If the input meets the customer requirements, the customer's feedback that documents positive performance often takes the form of paying the supplier the compensation that was agreed to. We suggest that even if the customer requirements are met, it is a good idea to provide positive feedback to the supplier and suggest ways that the supplier can improve future inputs. All too often, the customer pays the bill but is still not happy with the supplier's output. This represents a major problem with the customer, not the supplier. The suppliers have every right to believe that they are doing a good job if the only feedback they receive from the customer is positive (paying their bills). In the case where the input does not meet the customer requirements, the deviation should be defined so that the supplier can correct the problem. Often, the supplier's compensation is tied into the correction of these problems (see Figure 11.33).

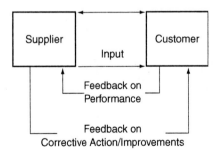

FIGURE 11.33 The complete Supplier/Customer Model

You will note that in Figure 11.33 there is a corrective action/improvement feedback flow from the supplier to the customer. This information flow provides the customer with assurance that past problems will be corrected and/or that continuous improvement is scheduled related to the supplier's output.

What did we learn from this analysis? There are two key points:

- A customer/supplier relationship cannot exist unless the requirements of both parties are understood and agreed to. Too often, customers expect input from suppliers without understanding their requirements and/or capabilities. On the other hand, too many suppliers provide output without defining their potential customer's requirements and obtaining a common, agreed to understanding of both party's requirements.
- Both the customer and the supplier have obligations to provide input to each other. The supplier is obligated to provide the item or service and define future performance improvements. The customer has an obligation to provide compensation to the supplier for its outputs and feedback on how well the outputs perform in the customer's environment.

The customer/supplier process has a domino effect. Usually, when a supplier is defined, that supplier requires input from other sources in order to generate the input to its customer. As a result, most organizations become both a customer and a supplier (see Figure 11.34).

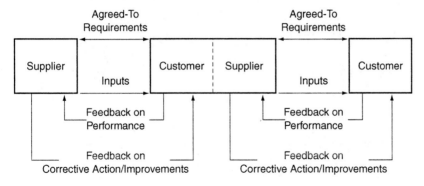

FIGURE 11.34 The Cascading Customer/Supplier Model

Although the procedures related to internal customer/supplier partnerships are less stringent and have been simplified because the internal customer does not pay for the services that are provided, the concepts are equally valid. Too often, we set different standards for internal suppliers than we have for external suppliers. As a result, many of the internal suppliers provide inputs that are far less valuable than it costs to produce the inputs. This often results in runaway costs and added bureaucracy.

Area Activity Analysis (AAA)

With AAA, we will show you how to apply the customer/supplier model to the internal organization, thereby improving quality and reducing cost and cycle time of the services and items delivered both within and outside of the organization.

"Area Activity Analysis is the best approach to developing a true performance culture."

—H. James Harrington

Area Activity Analysis is one of the few, if not only, improvement tools that is specific to an individual NWT and focuses on the internal and external customer/supplier. It's based on a model that has a supplier providing input into an area (organization) that adds value to produce an output that a customer needs. This tool works best with organizations that are well along with their overall improvement effort. It is used to understand how a natural work group fits into the overall picture and to establish the natural work team's measurements.

A Natural Work Team (NWT) or a Natural Work Group (NWG) is defined as a group of people who are assigned to work together and report to the same manager or supervisor. AAA projects are implemented by NWTs.

AAA is known as "The People's Improvement Tool." Why? Because this is the one tool that helps the individual within a particular work area to identify what he/she does for the organization and assists in determining the area's improvement opportunities.

The AAA methodology has been divided into seven different phases (see Table 11.5) to make it simple for an NWT to implement the concept. Each of these phases contains a set of steps that will progressively lead the NWT through the methodology.

TABLE 11.5 AAA Implementation Approach

Phase	Number of Steps
Phase I—Preparation for AAA	5
Phase II—Develop the Area's Mission Statement	6
Phase III—Define the Area's Major Activities	8
Phase IV—Develop Customer Relationships	7
Phase V—Analyze the Activity's Efficiency	6
Phase VI—Develop Supplier Partnerships	5
Phase VII—Performance Improvement	8
Total	**45**

We will briefly describe each of the seven phases of AAA. Implementing these seven phases will bring about a major improvement in the organization's measurement systems, increase understanding and cooperation, and lead to reduced cost and improved quality throughout the organization.

Phase I—Preparation for AAA AAA is most effective when it precedes other initiatives that are taking place such as Six Sigma, Continuous Improvement, team problem solving, Total Quality Management, Reengineering, or new IT systems. It is also best to implement the AAA methodology throughout the organization. This does not mean that it will not work if other improvement activities are underway or of it is only used by one area within the total organization. In the preparation phase, the good and bad considerations related to implementing AAA within an organization should be evaluated. A decision is made whether or not to use AAA within the organization. If the decision is made to use AAA, an implementation strategy is developed and approved by management. Phase I is divided into five steps:

1. Analyze the environment.
2. Form an AAA project team.
3. Define the implementation process.
4. Involve upper management.
5. Communicate AAA objectives.

Phase II—Develop the Area's Mission Statement A *mission statement* is used to document the reasons for the organization's or area's existence. It is usually prepared prior to the organization or area being formed, and is seldom changed. Normally, it is changed only when the organization or area decides to pursue new or different set of activities. For the AAA methodology, a mission statement is a short paragraph, no more than two or three sentences, that defines what the area's role and its relationships with the rest of the organization and/or the external customer.

Every area should have a mission statement that defines why it was created. It is used to provide the area manager and the area employees with guidance related to the activities on which the area should expend its resources. Standard good business practice calls for the area's mission statement to be prepared before an area is formed. The mission statement should be reviewed each time there is a change to the organization's structure or a change to the area's responsibilities. It should also be reviewed about every four years, even if the organization's structure has remained unchanged, to be sure that the mission statement reflects the current activities that are performed within the area.

A *service policy* is a short statement that defines how the area will interface with its customers and suppliers.

During Phase II, the AAA team will review and update the area's mission statement. If a mission statement does not exist, the AAA team will prepare a mission statement. In all cases, any change to the mission statement must be approved by management before it is finalized. Phase II is divided into six steps:

1. Obtain present mission statement.
2. Develop preliminary area mission statement/NWT manager.
3. Develop preliminary area mission statement/each employee.
4. Develop a consensus draft area mission statement.
5. Finalize area mission statement.
6. Develop the area's service policy.

Phase III—Define the Area's Major Activities During this phase, the AAA team will define the activities that are performed within the area. For each major activity (activities that account for more than 10 percent of the area's resources), the AAA team will define its output and the customers who receive that output. An activity champion is also assigned to each activity. Phase III is divided into eight steps:

1. Identify major activities for each individual.
2. Combine into broad activity categories.
3. Develop percentage of time expended.
4. Identify major activities.
5. Compare list to area mission statement.
6. Align activities with mission.
7. Approve of the area's mission statement and major activities.
8. Assign activity champions.

Phase IV—Develop Customer Relationships During this phase, the AAA team will meet with the customers who are receiving the outputs from the major activities conducted by the area to

- Define customer's requirements.
- Define the supplier's requirements.
- Develop how compliance to the requirements will be measured.
- Define acceptable performance levels (performance standards).
- Define the customer feedback process.

Phase IV is divided into seven steps:

1. Select critical activity.
2. Identify customer(s) for each output.
3. Define customer requirements.
4. Define measurements.
5. Review with customer.
6. Define feedback procedure.
7. Reconcile customer requirements with mission and activities.

Phase V—Analyze the Activity's Efficiency For each major activity, the team will define and understand the tasks that make up the activity. This is accomplished by analyzing each major activity for its value-added content. This can be accomplished by flowcharting the activity, and collecting efficiency information related to each task and the total activity. Typical information that would be collected is

- Cycle time
- Processing time
- Cost
- Rework rates
- Items processed per time period

Using this information, the AAA team will establish efficiency measurements (sometimes called *Key Performance Indicators*) and performance targets for each efficiency measurement. Phase V is subdivided into six steps:

1. Define efficiency measurements.
2. Understand the current activity.
3. Define data reporting systems.
4. Define performance requirements.
5. Approve performance standards.
6. Establish a performance board.

Phase VI—Develop Supplier Partnership Using the flowcharts generated in Phase V, the AAA team identifies the supplier that provides input into the major activities. This phase uses the same approach discussed in Phase IV, but turns the customer-supplier relationship around. In this phase, the area is told to view itself in the role of the customer. Their interfaces are called *internal* or *external suppliers*. The area then meets with their suppliers to develop agreed-to requirements. As a result of these negotiations, a supplier specification is prepared that includes a measurement system, performance standard, and feedback system for each input. This completes the customer-supplier chain for the area, as shown in Figure 11.35.

The supplier is an organization that provides a product (input) to the customer (source: ISO 8402).

The internal supplier refers to areas within an organizational structure that provide input into other areas within the same organizational structure. The external supplier refers to suppliers that are not part of the customer's organizational structure.

Phase VI is divided into five steps:

1. Identify suppliers.
2. Define requirements.
3. Define measurements and performance standards.
4. Define feedback procedure.
5. Obtain supplier agreement.

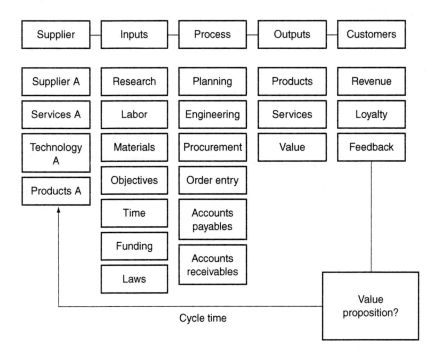

FIGURE 11.35 Detailed Process Model

Phase VII—Performance Improvement

"It is only when management supports, in both word and deed, the goal of continuous improvement that it will begin to see increases in both quality and productivity."

—Donald Wheeler and David Chambers

This is the continuous improvement phase that should always come after an activity has been defined and the related measurements are put in place. It may be a full Six Sigma, TQM, or just a reengineering activity. It could be a minimum program of error correction and cost reduction or a full-blown Six Sigma project.

During Phase VII, the NWT will enter into the problem-solving and error-prevention mode of operation. The measurement system should now be used to set challenge improvement targets. The NWT should now be trained to solve problems and take advantage of improvement opportunities.

All the members of the natural work team should be trained in the following (note: these are your Blue Belts):

- Six Sigma principles
- What 3.4 errors per million opportunities means
- What error-free performance means and how to measure duration between errors
- Plan-Do-Check-Act and/or DMAIC
- Basic problem-solving tools:
  - Brainstorming
  - Check sheets
  - Graphs
  - Nominal Group Technique
  - Force Field Analysis
  - Cause-and-effect diagrams
- Flow charting
- Team operating ground rules and team-building methods

The individual efficiency and effectiveness measurements will be combined into a single performance index for the area. Typically, the area's key measurement graphs will be posted and updated regularly.

"The hunger for performance is far more important to team success than team-building exercises, special incentives, or team leaders with ideal profiles."

—Katzenbach and Smith, in *The Wisdom of Teams: Creating the High-Performance Organization*, Harper Business, 1994.

We further suggest that a 4-by-5-foot area performance board be set up in a very visible part of the area with the following posted on it:

- The area mission statement
- The area performance report
- Improvement plans and their associated measurement charts
- An up-to-date picture of the NWT
- A list of the area's customers
- Letters from customers (both positive and negative)
- A list of the people who make up the NWT, their dates of hire, and their birthdays
- Board posting procedure

We recommend that the area's manager encourage the NWT members to post improvement ideas and suggestions for any measurement on this board in a section of the board called "New Ideas." This eliminates the need to wait for a meeting to get actions started on good ideas. The manager in the area should review the posted ideas at least once a day and move them from the "new idea" part of the board to the "ideas in progress" part of the board (see Figure 11.36).

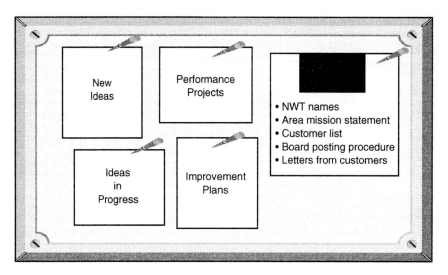

FIGURE 11.36 Performance board

"Visual reminders get attention and results. You need them to keep you focused."

—H. James Harrington

We cannot overemphasize the need to keep the performance board up-to-date. Nothing telegraphs management's lack of interest in performance improvement more than an outdated performance board. I have seen performance boards with reports on them that are six months old. We like to see a statement on the board that defines when the board is updated. For example: "New reports and graphs will be posted each Tuesday that reflect the previous week's performance." If for some reason the new reports and graphs cannot be posted on schedule, an explanation of why the graphs and reports are not available and a new target date for their availability should be posted on the performance board.

We find it is good business practice to write a short document that defines what can and cannot be posted on the performance board. Some organizations will allow personal items to be posted, such as postcards from NWT members who are on vacation. We do not recommend this practice because it is hard to control. First the manager posts a postcard from an employee, then someone posts a birthday card, then someone else puts up a notice that she has a car for sale. We find it is best to clearly define what can be put on the performance board, who can put it up, where they can put it, and when it will be taken down. This type of procedure needs to be defined for each different area of the board.

During Phase VII, management should show their appreciation to NWTs and individuals who expended exceptional error during the AAA project or implemented major improvements.

Phase VII is divided into eight steps:

1. Set up the reporting systems.
2. Identify the activities to be improved.
3. Install temporary protection, if needed.
4. Identify measurements or tasks to be improved.
5. Find best-value solutions.
6. Implement solutions.
7. Remove temporary protection, if installed.
8. Prevent the problem from recurring.

Six Sigma Communications

Throughout the Six Sigma initiative, the Six Sigma Champion and Executive Team should be releasing a series of news items holding meetings and personally selling the Six Sigma concepts of near error-free performance. The results of the SST activity should be highlighted on the organization's website and newsletter. This ongoing communication flow should highlight the culture and behavior changes that the organization is undergoing. It should also be used to give liberal credit to the people who are bringing about these changes, especially at the employee level. Many organizations post pictures of the SST members and the results of their activities on the bulletin boards around the organization. It is important not to just promote the SST activities, as this is just a small part of the total transformation the organization goes through. The communication system needs to focus upon how the individual behavior patterns and performance objectives need to change in order to keep up with the Six Sigma standards. A detailed communication plan should be prepared that provides monthly reinforcement of the importance of everyone improving their performance to near perfection.

The Executive Team Six Sigma Culture

The culture change starts with the Executive Team. We are never surprised when we go into an organization and find that the most and biggest problem set on the top floor in the executive boardroom. If the Executive Team does not change, the rest of the organization will not change. To help the Executive Team change at General Electric, Jack Welch tied the 10,000 top manager's bonus system into the Six Sigma program. GE executive bonus system runs between 20 to 70 percent of the manager's base salary plus additional stock options. As much as 40 percent of the bonus was based upon how well the managers implement Six Sigma in their related areas.[16] The single most cost-effective and fastest way to transform an organization is by transforming the Executive Team. Who has the biggest impact upon the employee's involvement in the improvement process by management levels follows:

- Top Management: 50 percent
- Middle Management: 26 percent
- First Line Managers: 19 percent

The key to embedding a Six Sigma culture within an organization is to change the behavioral patterns of the Executive Team. Our data indicates that the average executive makes between 50 to 80 behavior errors per week, and at the Six Sigma level we want our assembly workers to make no more than one error every three months. It's almost as though we pay people more if they will make more errors.

Dr. Joseph M. Juran has long stated that 80 to 85 percent of all problems are caused by management. Donald Stratton, Manager of Quality at AT&T Network Systems, reported the following findings in a *Quality Progress* article:[17]

- 82 percent of the problems analyzed were classified as common cause. These are process problems owned by management.
- 18 percent of the problems analyzed were classified as common cause. These are problems that were caused by people, machinery, or tools. Only a small portion of these problems can be solved by employee teams.
- Of the 82 percent management controlled:
  - 60 percent of the corrections could be implemented by first- and second-level management
  - 20 percent could be implemented by middle management
  - 20 percent could only be implemented by top management

It is easy to see that the major problems within organizations throughout the world are the processes that management is responsible for modifying and controlling. Unfortunately, all the talk in the world and the desire to do something good does not get it done. The employees cannot correct the problems that management has created. Only management's personal involvement in the improvement process will bring about the required changes.

Top Management Culture Change

"The culture of the organization changes only to the degree that the top management behavior changes."

—H. James Harrington

Top management are all for change, as long as it is someone else who changes. The number one improvement rule is: Top management must change first.

Why should top management change? Aren't they already successful? Look at all the money they are making. In truth, more than 99 percent of top managers have a lot of opportunity to improve. In fact, none of us are perfect and most of us have many opportunities to improve our own personal behavior patterns.

To prepare their personal performance indicators, top managers need to define what they do. I don't mean things like "motivate employees" or "manage R&D." These are their assignments. Examples of what management does include the following:

- Attend meetings
- Read and answer mail
- Answer telephone calls
- Make decisions
- Delegate work
- Chair meetings

Once top management has completed a personal list of what they do, they need to define behavioral patterns related to these activities that could be improved:

- Start meetings on time.
- Do not attend meetings that can be delegated to employees.
- Return all telephone calls within eight hours.
- Don't set items aside that can be done quickly.
- Always show up on time for meetings.
- Read all new mail each day.
- Don't use overnight mail if the project can be finished earlier and sent by regular mail.
- Talk to three customers each day.
- Make a minimum of three one-hour tours of the employee work areas each week.
- Read five technical articles each week.
- Have the office organized so well that there is no need to search for lost or misfiled items.
- Have a clean desk at the end of the day.
- Stop doing things that can be delegated.
- Stop using bad language in the workplace.
- Arrive at work on time.
- Have an agenda in each attendee's hands before any meeting is held.

They then should select a maximum of eight of these behavioral patterns that they want to improve. Each selected behavioral pattern should be recorded on a card similar in size to an airplane ticket, which can be carried easily in a purse or a coat pocket. Each time the executive does not behave as defined, he or she has made an error, and a check mark should be placed behind the appropriate behavioral pattern. Once a week, the total number of check marks should be counted and plotted on a run chart. We recommend that each executive set an improvement target of 10 percent of the first month's average error rate. When this target is reached, it is time to add eight more behavioral patterns to the list and start over again. In organizations where top managers have a high degree of confidence and credibility, each top manager is encouraged to post his or her personal performance run chart in his or her office, demonstrating to their fellow workers that top management accepts the fact that they personally need to change and improve. (Figure 11.37 is an example of a CEO behavioral error-rate chart.) Eventually this same approach will be used by all managers and employees to measure their personal improvement.

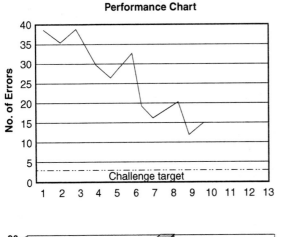

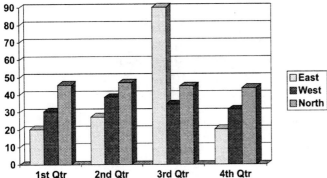

FIGURE 11.37 Executive behavioral performance chart

"Employees listen to your tongue with interest but they believe in the way that the tongue in your shoes go."

—H. James Harrington

Executive Values

Each executive is also encouraged to define his or her personal set of values that govern their behavior at work and in their personal life. These values seldom mirror images of the organization's values or principles because they reflect the total person. We encourage every top manager to post these value statements in a very visible place in their office and/or conference room. Sharing these personal values with their fellow managers and employees and posting then where they can influence the executive's behavior has a major positive influence on the individual and the organization. Don't be afraid to let your employees know you are human.

John D. Rockefeller had 11 management creeds (principles) that he posted and tried to live by. A sample of these are

- "I believe in the supreme worth of the individual and in his right to life, liberty, and pursuit of happiness."
- "I believe in the dignity of labor, whether with head or hand; that the world owes no man a living, but that it owes every man an opportunity to make a living."
- "I believe in the sacredness of a promise, that a man's word should be as good as his bond; that character—not wealth or power or position—is of supreme worth."
- "I believe that every right implies a responsibility; every opportunity, an obligation; every possession, a duty."

Dr. H. James Harrington has selected the document entitled "The Man I Want to Be." The following is just a sample statement. The total document can be found in Appendix B.

"A man who would be concerned with how he could help me instead of himself, who would give me loyalty instead of demanding of me, who would think of himself as my assistant, instead of my boss, who would think it was his job to help me do my job better."

Six Sigma Suggestion Programs

"There is nothing more fragile or precious to an individual than his or her idea."

—H. James Harrington

A *suggestion system* is one of the best ways to provide your employees with a way to continuously improve and get recognition for their activities. World-class organizations are receiving an average of two suggestions per month per employees; 90 percent of them are implemented.

How does the suggestion process work? National Cash Register Company developed the concept back in 1896. The value of the suggestion program is that it offers the person closest to the work activity the opportunity to suggest improvements. This results in more effective utilization of assets, increased productivity, waste reduction, lower product costs, and improved quality. As Paul Petermann, then manager of Field Suggestions at IBM, put it, "Ideas are the life-blood of the company, and the suggestion plan is a way of getting these ideas marketed."

The formal suggestion process requires that employees document their ideas for improvement and submit them to a central suggestion department that is responsible for coordinating and evaluating the ideas and reporting back to the employee. The suggestion department reviews each suggestion and chooses an area within the organization that is best suited to evaluate the suggestion. The evaluation studies the recommended changes to determine if they will provide overall improvement in quality, cost, or productivity. If the suggestion is accepted by the evaluation area, the evaluator will determine what tangible savings will result from implementing the idea.

Paul Revere Insurance Company employees submitted 20,000 suggestions during the first three years of their improvement process. The suggestions were a major contributor to the organization's improved performance:

- Income up 200 percent with no additional staff
- The organization moved from number 2 to number 1 in the insurance field

Frank K. Sonnenberg, in his article "It's a Great Idea, B…" wrote, "A new idea, like a human being, has a life cycle. It is born. If properly nurtured, it grows. When it matures, it becomes a productive member of society." He points out that at 3M, some people claim that the company's 11th commandment is, "Thou shalt not kill an idea."[18]

The following is a quotation from Toyota's Creative Suggestion System manual:

"The system came to Toyota from the United States back in 1951 when Toyota was still a newcomer in the automobile industry. Two Toyota officials traveled to the United States to study modern management methods, and at Ford Motor Company they saw a suggestion system being used that inspired them to try a similar system in Toyota."

Starting with this very modest introduction, the Japanese, in a very methodical way, expanded this application and used it much the same way they did statistical process control and Total Quality Control. Starting from a zero base line, they expanded the idea to the point that today it is the most effective employee involvement tool used in Japan, surpassing even the Quality Circle movement. In a study done by the Japanese Suggestion Association, they reported, "As viewed from the relationship with small group activities, which is the nucleus of suggestion activities, 50 times as many suggestions are made for every solution of one problem by one circle." Dr. Kaoru Ishikawa, the father of the Japanese quality process and the Quality Circle concept, stated, "In Japan, only 10 percent of the quality improvements come from teams. The remaining 90 percent come from individual suggestions."[19]

Now let's compare Japan's and the United States suggestion programs:

Activity	Japan	U.S.
Suggestions per eligible employee	32.4%	.11%
Percent of workers participating	72.0%	9.0%
Percent of suggestions adopted	87.0%	32.0%
Average award value	$2.50	$492.00
Average net savings per suggestion	$129.00	$7,103.00
Yearly net savings per employee	$3,792.00	$276.00

Now this data may be interpreted that the U.S. goes after the big, important problems and the Japanese workers focus on the insignificant problems. But look at the bottom line. The average eligible Japanese worker saves the organization more than $3,500 per year over the savings generated per American worker.

Getting Ideas Flowing

"Creativity is thinking up new things. Innovation is doing new things."

—Theodore Levitt

For the average organization, it is easy to embrace the concept of tapping the hidden powers of the employees' ideas. The problem is, how do you do it? How do you keep your credibility with the employees if they start turning in ideas and swamp the process? A good way to tap into this reservoir of ideas and not open the floodgates is to hold an "idea week." In this approach, management announces to the employees that a specific week will be set aside to see how many improvement ideas can be generated. For example, "The week of January 16 to 21 will be set aside to see how many ideas can be turned in that will improve the safety and quality or reduce costs."

Idea Sharing

"I believe the real differences between success and failure in a corporation can very often be traced to the question of how well the organization brings out the great energies and talents of its people."

—Thomas Watson, Jr.

An important part of developing a creative environment within an organization is the open sharing of the ideas that are generated. Many organizations accomplish this by maintaining a list of new and creative ideas that is made available to the entire organization. Often this data is stored in a computer database that can be sorted in many different ways, providing a valuable database to help solve future problems.

3M has made use of "innovation fairs" to exhibit new ideas. Employees from product engineering, marketing, production, and other departments attend these fairs to gain new ideas and to discuss the ideas that are being exhibited with their creators.

To keep the Six Sigma System operating, we find that focusing your suggestion system on small suggestions that the employees can implement themselves is the most effective approach.

"The never-ending task of self improvement."

—Ralph Waldo Emerson

There are a lot of small improvement opportunities related to each job, and the person who is doing the job is the best person to identify and implement these ideas. For example, an operator put her work into a pail and when it was full, carried it to the next operator. Her suggestion was to put wheels on the pail so she could just push it with her foot to the next operator. When the next operator removed the parts, she could just kick it back to the other operator. No big deal, but it saved two people time and effort, resulting in increased productivity.

These ideas are documented on a very simple form and approved or rejected by the individual managers. This approach is working in Japan and the U.S. For example, Dana Corporation received an average of 38 ideas per person with 82 percent of them implemented.[20] For more information about this approach to suggestion systems, read *The Idea Generator* by Bunji Tozawa and Norman Bodek.

Rewards and Recognition to Support Six Sigma

"Performance will matter to the individual if rewards are dependent upon performance."

—Edward M. Baker

The rewards and recognition system needs to be changed or the organization's culture will not accept the Six Sigma System. If your measurement and reward systems remain the same, then you cannot expect to get different results.

The complexity of today's environment and the sophistication of today's employees make it necessary to carefully design a reward process that provides the management team with many ways to say thank you to each employee, because the things that are valued by one individual may have no impact upon another. In addition, the reward process needs to be closely aligned with the organization's personality. The reward process that functioned well in the 1990s is probably inadequate today because the personalities of most organizations have undergone major changes. The influx of women and various minority groups has had a major impact on the way the reward process needs to be structured.

In today's environment, men's attitudes have changed. The male population is aging, and men are often not the sole breadwinner for the family, causing them to be less financially driven. Because of this, it is easy to see, for example, why time-and-a-half pay is no longer a satisfactory reward for giving up a Saturday for many employees. It is for these reasons that we need to take a fresh look at our reward processes to upgrade them so that they meet the needs of today's organizations and their aggressive goals.

Vince Lombardi said, "Winning isn't everything. It's the only thing." This is true for many people, but for others it is enough to help someone else win. At the Olympics, only one man stood on the top platform to receive the gold medal for cross-country skiing, but without the many people standing along the route to give him water, he would not have won. To these "little people" (and there are a lot more of us little people than there are gold medal winners), often recognition is simply having someone else acknowledge your worth. Recognition is something everyone wants, needs, and strives to obtain. Studies have shown that people classify recognition as one of the things they value most.

Ingredients of an Organization's Reward Process

A good reward process has eight major objectives:

- To provide recognition to employees who make unusual contributions to the organization and stimulate additional effort for further improvement.

- To show the organization's appreciation for superior performance.

- To ensure the maximum benefits from the reward process by an effective communication system that highlights the individuals who were recognized.

- To provide many ways to recognize employees for their efforts and stimulate management creativity in the reward process.

- To ensure that management understands the variation enhances the impact of the reward process.

- To improve morale through the proper use of rewards.

- To reinforce behavioral patterns that management would like to see continued.

- To ensure that the employees recognized are perceived as earning the recognition by their fellow employees.

Why does recognition matter? George Blomgren, president of Organizational Psychologists, puts it this way, "Recognition lets people see themselves in a winning identity role. There's a universal need for recognition, and most people are starved for it."[21]

Definition: *Reward* is something given or offered for a special service or to compensate for extra effort expended.

"Everyone hears 'thank you' in a different way. You need to find the right way to reward each individual."

—H. James Harrington

Rewards can be subdivided into the following categories:

- **Compensation**. To financially reimburse for service (s) provided.
- **Award**. To bestow a gift for performance or quality.
- **Recognition**. To show appreciation for behaving in a desired way.

After the organization has provided the employee with a paycheck and health coverage, what more can or should the organization do for the employee? Management is obligated to do more than just eliminate their financial worries. Employees excel when they are happy, satisfied, and feel that someone else appreciates the efforts they are putting forth. A tangible and intangible reward process can go a long way to fulfilling these needs when properly used.

Research has proven that when management rewards employees for adopting desired behaviors, they work harder and provide better customer service. The benchmark service organizations are more likely to have well-defined and well-used approaches for telling their employees that they are important individuals. Individuals in the world-class organizations who go beyond expectations are held up as customer heroes and role models for the rest of the organization. This provides a continually more aggressive customer performance standard for the total organization.

Key Reward Rules

The reward process needs to be designed, taking into consideration the following points:

- Organization's culture
- Desired behavioral patterns
- Employee priorities
- Behavior/reward timing relationships
- Ease of use

The reward process must be designed to be compatible with the culture and personality of the organization. Things that may be very desirable in one organization can be quite inappropriate in another.

Cut the bureaucracy out of your reward process as much as possible. Give management general guidelines, and eliminate the checks and balances in all but the most significant rewards. For example, an individual should not be given more than three minor awards each year, and no more than 10 percent of the employees should receive major contribution awards each year. Be sure that the employees are not given special awards for just doing their jobs.

Give the manager the power to give the reward and process the paperwork later. Major rewards should be processed through a rewards board to be sure that required standards are met, but there should be a long list of rewards that the manager can give to the employee on the spot— for example: dinners for two, movie tickets, theater tickets, or $50 merchandise certificates.

Types of Rewards

Everyone hears "thank you" in different ways. The reward process must take these different needs into account. Some people want money, some want a pat on the back, others want to get exposure to upper management, while still others want to look good in front of their peers.

American Express has one awards program that it calls "Great Performer Award Luncheon." Typical activities that won employees invitations to these luncheons were

- One American Express employee bailed a French tourist out of jail in Columbus, Georgia

- Another took food and blankets to travelers stranded at Kennedy Airport

Are these unusual performances for employees to take up on their own? Yes, but that's what we need if we want to have empowered employees and a truly world-class organization.

It's easy to see that the reward process is only limited by the creativity of your people and the individuals who design the process. The National Science Foundation study made this point: "The key to having workers who are both satisfied and productive is motivation; that is, arousing and maintaining the will to work effectively—having workers who are productive not because they are coerced, but because they are committed."

To help structure a reward process, let's divide the rewards into the following categories:

- Financial Compensation
  - Salary
  - Commissions
  - Piecework
  - Organizational bonuses
  - Team bonuses
  - Gain-sharing
  - Goal-sharing
  - Stock options
  - Stock purchase plans
  - Benefit programs
- Monetary Awards
  - Suggestion awards
  - Patent awards
  - Contribution awards
  - Best-in-category awards (example: best salesperson, or employee of the year)
  - Special awards (example: president's award)

- Group/Team rewards
- Public Personal recognition
- Private Personal recognition
- Peer rewards
- Customer rewards
- Organizational awards

Basically, the following media are used individually or in combination to produce desired behavior.

- Money
- Merchandise
- Plaques/trophies
- Published communications
- Verbal communication
- Special privileges

A well-designed reward process will use all six, because each has its own advantages and disadvantages. One of the biggest mistakes management makes is to use the same motivating factors for all employees. People are moved by different things because we all want different things. The reward process needs to be designed to meet the following basic classifications of needs:

- Money
- Status (ego)
- Security
- Respect

The Leapfrog Group has developed a Web-based compendium of incentive and reward programs aimed at improving healthcare in both inpatient and outpatient settings. The compendium provides details on both financial and public recognition programs initiated mainly by health plans, purchasers, or purchasing coalitions and aimed at hospitals, physicians, health plans, and consumers. Freely available on the Leapfrog Group website at http://www.leapfroggroup.org/rewards_compendium, the summary allows users to sort by location and program target, and search the programs using a built-in keyword search function, such as one related to quality and safety practices. The compendium has been supported by the Commonwealth Fund and the Robert Wood Johnson Foundation.[22]

CONCLUSION

"Things have gotten bad enough and people have tried all the simple things, and they haven't worked. I think most people are now stepping back and saying, 'My God, we've got to rethink this whole system.'"

—Michael Porter, professor, Harvard Business School

If you have implemented the recommended processes, you will have a very effective and profitable system in place that should grow your market share and improve your customer satisfaction level. But this is not the end of the Six Sigma initiative; it is just the beginning. As the Six Sigma process matures, it will continue to gain momentum. First, no one wants anything to do with it. Then all of a sudden everyone wanted to be part of it. Starting slow and getting at least 10 percent of the organization behind the Six Sigma initiative is key in the start-off phase. Once the results are documented, there will be no question in anyone's mind that this is the right thing for the HCP. As you implement your Six Sigma initiative, there are some things you need to look out for:

- Don't label all the ideas as new ones.
- Don't select small aspects of a larger concept.
- Don't streamline without process redesign.
- Don't do process change without the cultural change.
- Don't redesign without fundamentally re-thinking the way you are doing business.
- Don't think that the change process is not going to affect you personally.
- Don't make Six Sigma separate from the normal business structure of the HCP.
- Don't make Six Sigma a problem-solving initiative. It should be a strategic initiative that sets new culture and behavioral patterns.
- Don't measure your Six Sigma by dollars saved alone; a much more meaningful measure is lives saved.

The Six Sigma program should result in establishing a very extensive set of KPIs (Key Performance Indicators) for the HCP. Some typical high-level, general KPIs are

- Patient satisfaction
- Employee satisfaction
- External doctor satisfaction
- Turn-over rates
- Ratio of management and staff to patient
- Percentage of medical records completed within 30 days

- Percentage of billing arrears
- Percentage of multi-skilled employees
- Percentage of staff cross-trained, admittance cycle time, outpatient wait time
- Operating cost ration to dollars collected
- Collections to full-time equivalent (FTE)
- Percentage increase in collections fiscal year 2006-2007
- Percentage of insured inpatient stays billed
- Percentage of insured outpatient visits billed
- Average claims generate by FTE for insured outpatient visits billed
- Average claims for insured outpatient visits billed
- Average age of insurance claims outstanding

Specific sub-process measures are

- Number of calls attempted
- Number of calls connected
- Number of demographic changes
- Number of next-of-kin changes
- Number of employment changes
- Number of insurances identified or changed
- Number of billable insurances of total identified
- Dollar amount billed: inpatient
- Dollar amount billed: outpatient
- Preregistration (monthly)
- Dollar amount collected: inpatient
- Dollar amount collected: outpatient

These KPIs should be a direct result of the AAA process where each natural work team's processes are analyzed to define efficiency and effectiveness measurements. The result is a balance scorecard for the HCP that is extremely robust and reflects real business needs and measurements. These measurement systems should cover all the major healthcare systems including HCP governance, resource management, patient acquisition, health maintenance, health restoration, and continuous learning.

"No one has ever reached the point that there is no room for improvement"

—Dr. H. James Harrington

ENDNOTES

1   Porter, Annette Wilkerson. Six Sigma takes root at North Carolina Baptist Hospital. *Visions*, Fall/Winter, 2005.

2   Jones, Milton M. Jr., "Six Sigma...at a Bank?" *Six Sigma Forum Magazine*, February 2006.

3   Miller, Kurt. "Beyond Traditional Reengineering." *Redesigning Healthcare Delivery*, by Peter Boland. 210. Berkeley CA. Boland Healthcare, Inc. 1996

4   Dusharme, Dirk. Healthcare quality increases. *Quality Digest*, December 2005.

5   Ibid.

6   Smith, Laura. Healthcare report cards unreliable. *Quality Digest*, April 2006.

7   Levinson, William A. Taking the QMS cure. *Quality Digest*, December 2005.

8   Hackle, John. The agency for healthcare research and quality. *Quality Progress Editor*, August 2005.

9   McGee, Marianne Kolbasuk. Brailer gets vote of confidence. *IT Magazine*, May 31, 2004.

10 Revere, L., K. Black, and A. Hug. Integrating Six Sigma and CQI for improving patient care. *The TQM Magazine* 16: 2, 105-113, 2004.

11 Goel, Parveen S.; Gupta, Praveen; Jain, Rajeev; and Tyagi, Rajesh K. *Six Sigma for Transactions and Service*. New York: McGraw-Hill. 2004.

12 Brassard, Michael and Diane Ritter. *Sailing Through Six Sigma*. Marietta, Ga. Brassard & Ritter, LLC. 2001.

13 Bloom, Benjamin S. *Taxonomy of Educational Objectives*. Allyn and Bacon, Boston, MA. Copyright (c) 1984 by Pearson Education. Adapted by permission from the publisher.

14 Hertz, Harry S. *Healthcare Criteria for Performance Excellence*. Gaithersburg, MD: Baldrige National Quality Program. 2004.

15 Paton, Scott M. No small change: Making quality Job 1 again. *Quality Digest*, September 2001.

16 Brassard, Michael and Diane Ritter. *Sailing Through Six Sigma*. Marietta, Ga. Brassard & Ritter, LLC. 2001.

17 Harrington, H. James and Harrington, James S. *Total Improvement Management*. New York: McGraw-Hill. 1995.

18 Ibid.

19 Ibid.

20 Goel, Parveen S.; Gupta, Praveen; Jain, Rajeev; and Tyagi, Rajesh K. *Six Sigma for Transactions and Service*. New York: McGraw-Hill. 2004.

21 Harrington, H. James and Harrington, James S. *Total Improvement Management*. New York: McGraw-Hill. 1995.

22 Hackle, John. Leapfrog Group provides incentive program summary. Quality Progress, November 2004.

LEAN SIX SIGMA IN HEALTHCARE

SECTIONS

The Lean Process
Case Study 1: Combining Lean and Six Sigma to Improve Throughput
    in the Emergency Department at St. John Health
Case Study 2: Expanding CT Capacity at North Shore University Hospital
Endnotes

Six Sigma in healthcare is becoming a prerequisite for improving quality. Inattention to efficiency in healthcare, however, has led to built-in procedural wastes in the system that must also be addressed. Lean principles have been used successfully in manufacturing, services, and even healthcare facilities successfully. While Six Sigma helps healthcare organizations pay attention to errors and reduce risks associated with patient safety, a combination of Lean with Six Sigma helps organizations to streamline operations and achieve better patient satisfaction.

One of the simplest and most common examples to illustrate the benefits of Lean in a private practice or a healthcare facility is patient waiting time. Many times patients feel they get sicker while waiting for their time with the physician. Here the issue may be to streamline and synchronize processes rather than reduce the error rate. In case of emergency or intensive care facilities, streamlining operations will allow health professionals to attend to more patients and—depending on underlying issues—may not require the rigor of Six Sigma to reduce errors. Thus, using the appropriate approach to improve either effectiveness or efficiency will provide maximum improvement in achieving overall healthcare excellence.

Lean thinking was being practiced in manufacturing in the 1980s in the U.S. and Japan. Lean principles were first deployed by Ford while standardizing parts production and assembly operations. In the U.S., Lean used to be called *JIT*, or *Just-In-Time* (JIT) manufacturing, which was implemented successfully in parts distribution by delivering customer-ordered parts when needed and where needed. However, implementing Lean in manufacturing operations impacts the entire supply chain, which makes it difficult to achieve "'ideal" results. When implementing JIT principles, the focus shifted from producing to a forecast to producing to the customer order. This thinking was also called *Pull system* (build to order) versus the *Push system* (forecast). One can see that in healthcare operations (because of the nature of the business), the Pull system makes more sense, rather than planning to "push" a certain number of patients through the healthcare system. The old system focuses on its internal strategy and objectives before looking at the customer versus the new system that focuses on the customer in order to achieve its strategy and objectives.

One of the challenges people in the healthcare industry face is to adapt the same techniques that have been successful in the manufacturing industry. Of course, the same argument can be made for Six Sigma implementation as well. Instead of being a challenge, it must be viewed as an opportunity to expand use of the known and mastered tools to a new industry. Yes, there are differences at the surface between healthcare and other industries at both the input and the output level. As an activity, however, there may be many similarities; but at the process framework level there are a few differences. The 4-P model of process management illustrated in Figure 12.1 shows that each process includes some things to do to "prepare," which include getting supplies, tools, patients, and skilled employees. The "perform" level includes activities at surgery or physical examination stations. For either of these processes, there is an expected outcome. In other words, the eventual outcome is a "healthy" patient. If the patient is not healthy, the physician prescribes remedies to help. Similar analysis can be performed in clinical, administrative, and executive processes. Interestingly, healthcare operations today are managed like a business, where there is a CEO and CFO similar to any manufacturing business. Thus, we must see any function in a healthcare facility as a process, which helps us appreciate the value of various known Lean or Six Sigma tools.

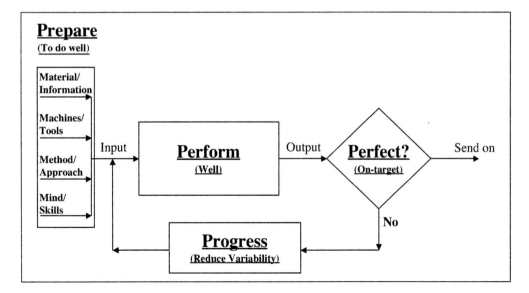

FIGURE 12.1 4-Ps of process management (Gupta. *Quality Progress,* July 2007)

THE LEAN PROCESS

Quality improvement begins with housekeeping, given the house is there and rooms are habitable. Similarly, Lean begins with a concept of identifying activities necessary to add value to the intended outcome, be it patient safety or the patient examination. Then one makes sure that these value-added activities are performed efficiently and effectively. To ensure efficiency of an activity, the concept of Lean thinking looks into establishing controls at the input level to minimize waste. Once the waste is removed, the flow is built in to the activity so the rhythm is synchronized with the expected outcome to minimize excessive activities. Establishing the rhythm requires balancing demand and supply. To manage demand, customer needs are understood better, and to manage supply, JIT deliveries are expected. Typically, demand is difficult to control, and supply can be mandated at some extra cost. However, benefits outweigh the cost. Thus, supply and demand are balanced to some practical level, and sustained. Various tools are used to map, streamline, improve, balance, and sustain the Lean principle in order to have a shortest, straightest, and simplest flow of information, material, or patients.

Lean Six Sigma

Having leaned the process, performance may still be unacceptable due to poor design and execution, which leads to inconsistencies. Lean can cause waste with an erroneous process design; however, poor product design or execution can cost lives. Thus, Six Sigma typically is used to reduce the error rate and process variability, and Lean is used to reduce the waste or nonvalue-added activities. The two goals are interrelated, however—excessive waste can lead to a high error rate, and a high error rate can lead to excessive waste. Thus, applying Lean and Six Sigma principles concurrently may assist in addressing both the error rate and waste in the system.

Lean principles have helped organizations improve in terms of cycle time (~50%), work in process inventory (~50%), productivity, lead time (~50%), throughput, and space requirements (~30%). Regardless of the size of an organization, significant and unprecedented gains and improvements are typical to any successful Lean initiative. According to the report "Going Lean in Healthcare" published by the Institute of Healthcare Improvement, 175 Lean projects at Virginia Mason Medical Center have resulted in the following significant improvements: [1]

- 53% reduced inventory
- 36% improved productivity rate
- 41% reduced floor space
- 65% reduced lead time
- 44% reduced people effort
- 72% reduced distance traveled by product
- 82% decrease in set-up time

One can see that applying Lean helped the healthcare organization reduce waste. Two key Lean tools that result in immediate savings and improvement are *Value Stream Mapping* and *5S's*. Value Stream Mapping helps identify waste in the system. The 5S's stand for the following:

- **Sort** to keep the unnecessary out
- **Simplify** to organize the necessary with clearly marked visuals
- **Sweep** to clean the area or remove the clutter
- **Standardize** best practices
- **Sustain** by continually redefining the new status quo

The 5S's are directed at value-generating processes to achieve the desired performance. According to a project completed at the Nebraska Medical Center,[2] by applying Value Stream Mapping and the 5S's they were able to reduce 20 minutes inpatient "time to bed after bed assignment" and realized a savings of more than $300,000.

Principles of Lean Thinking

The currently known "Lean" principles have been attributed significantly to the *Toyota Production System* (TPS), which is a system to do "right" things in the "right" way to minimize waste. Employees play a critical role in implementing Lean principles, which gives peace of mind to workers in knowing that the outcome of Lean does not mean automatic layoffs. Instead, it means redeployment of excess capacity to support growth, improvement, and housekeeping. This implies that any Lean initiative must be supported by concurrent sales activities. Lean is meant to be implemented in growing times rather than in times of cost-cutting. Lean is an improvement tool, not a cost-cutting tool. One of the troubling issues with current implementations is that in some instances Lean's success is measured in terms of headcount reduction, or *right-sizing*. As a result, expected job loss leads to change resistance, and thus marginal performance of Lean initiatives.

Lean is intended to be a waste-free operation irrespective of being a manufacturing or service operation. *Waste-free production* means producing what is needed, when it is needed, and at a specific rate of production in response to the customer demand, rather than using maximum capacity to build to a hypothetical forecast. Thus, one of the objectives of Lean implementation is to design a system that can be in rhythm with the customer demand or patient traffic. *Rhythm* implies minimal wait time in medical facilities through design of operations considering available resources and known constraints. Lean minimizes changes, abnormalities, or fluctuations in the flow of material or patients; it also minimizes the use of wrong tools or equipment, ensures visibility of operations and deviations, immediately remedies unacceptable activities or outcomes, and emphasizes planned and leveled workload.

Lean, when combined with Six Sigma, overcomes disruptions during implementation and speeds up the Six Sigma implementation. An ideal and sustainable implementation of Lean on its own is impossible, similar to achieving the ideal Six Sigma level performance for a healthcare facility. The practical combination of Lean and Six Sigma leads to significant reduction in material waste, streamlines process, and reduces errors to virtual perfection.

Table 12.1 highlights differences between Lean and Six Sigma in order to exploit their combination. For example, Lean normally starts in an area headed by the area manager, whereas Six Sigma is normally launched with an organization-wise commitment. While implementing Lean Six Sigma, one could decide to involve the organization by committing to Lean Six Sigma throughout for minimizing resistance and practicing Lean Six Sigma locally for ease of control. At a personal level, Lean requires a commitment to challenge the current system, while Six Sigma requires commitment to strive toward perfection.

TABLE 12.1 Lean and Six Sigma Differences

Lean	Six Sigma
Lean can be considered a prerequisite for Six Sigma	Six Sigma builds on Lean operations
Implemented for efficiency and reduce wasted activities	Implemented for effectiveness, and reduces waste in an activity
Driven by middle management	Driven by leadership
Supports the target of achieving virtual perfection	Provides targets for virtual perfection
Synchronizes the resources utilization with the patient flow	Synchronizes skills with the patient illness for improvement
Requires personal commitment to challenge current processes	Requires passionate and inspirational commitment from CEO to create awareness for virtual perfection
Impacts selected processes for speed and value	Impacts all aspects of business products and processes
Lean has been thought of as "thinking" or "principles"	Six Sigma has been called "DNA," "Culture," "Philosophy," "Thinking," and "Standard of Excellence"
Provides tools to sustain Six Sigma better	Six Sigma can be achieved without Lean

Table 12.2 lists several aspects of thinking for Lean and Six Sigma. For example, the management thinking for Lean implies speed and flow, while for Six Sigma it's quality and time. If we combine Lean and Six Sigma, one can think in terms of quality and flow, which will minimize time and speed up the process. In the case of a patient visiting a medical facility, it becomes important that the patient receives due attention at the earliest possibility in a predetermined flow. Due to flow, if there is a known waiting time, the patient can plan for the waiting time and not be disturbed. If one were implementing Lean alone, the solution could lead to very fast process in a flow, but a dissatisfied patient due to lack of attention from a physician. If one were implementing Six Sigma alone, the patient will have a great visit, but the medical facility may not be able to keep up with a required number of patients in order to be a financially viable organization.

TABLE 12.2 Six Sigma and Lean Organization Thinking

Thinking Aspects	Lean	Six Sigma	Lean Six Sigma
Management	Speed and Flow	Quality and time	Quality and flow
Goal Setting	On Demand	Reach out and innovative	On demand and innovative
Control	Local	Distributed	Hybrid
Problems	Elimination	Prevention	Elimination
Focus	Customer Value	Virtual perfection	Perfection in customer value
Outlook	Longer Term	Long-term	Reasonably long-term
Organization	Autonomy	Learning	Learning autonomy
Training	Natural	As necessary	Natural and necessary

Similarly, Table 12.2 looks into goal-setting, control, problems, focus, outlook, organization, and training aspects of Lean and Six Sigma. The Lean Six Sigma combines strengths of both Lean and Six Sigma to maximize value of the improvement effort.

Lean Tools

Similar to Six Sigma, Lean uses several tools, but not as many as Six Sigma methodology. The list of Lean tools include

- Value Stream Mapping (VSM)
- Cycle Muda (waste)
- TAKT (time allowed per unit by demand) time
- 5S (sort, simplify, sweep, standardize, sustain)
- Kaizen
- Visual Manufacturing
- Kanban
- TPM

VSM is a process of mapping operations in an area, and evaluating each operation for its value contribution to the end product and impact on quality. If the process does not add value, it is considered a total waste and a good candidate for elimination. If a process step adds value, it is evaluated for waste elimination. Once non-value-added steps are identified and addressed, the new future state process map is designed to create maximum value with minimum waste. The objective with VSM is to come up with the shortest, streamlined, and shallowest (without any bureaucratic practices to accumulate outcomes) process flow. Figure 12.2 outlines steps to perform VSM. While evaluating VSM, a total cycle time is determined based on its components. There are five components of cycle time: Wait Time, Move Time, Queue Time, Run Time, and Inspection Time. Normally, if a process is performed well, only the runtime is considered to be value-added, and it is about 5 to 10 percent of the total cycle time. In other words, about 90 percent of the cycle time is wasted. If a patient only spends five minutes with the physician, and it takes him about three hours for the visit, there is a significant waste of the customer's valuable time. The three hours starts from the time patient arrives in the medical facility and ends at the time the patient leaves the facility. (Some may include the time the patient leaves his home to the time the patient returns.)

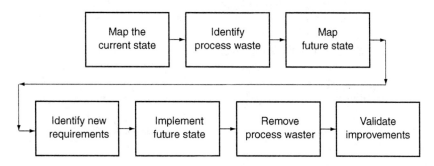

FIGURE 12.2 Value Stream Map

Muda is a term of waste in operations. There are seven wastes:

- **Overproduction**. Having excess capacity or extra services to take care of patients
- **Inventory**. Having too many supplies in the facility
- **Extra processing steps**. Scheduling too many tests
- **Motion**. Actual patient move time, and how many yards patient has to walk around to get to the physician
- **Defects**. Errors, mistakes, wrong prescriptions, overlooked tests, or a scissors left inside the patient after completing the surgery
- **Waiting**. The time patient waits for receiving services
- **Transportation**. How long it takes the patient to get to and from the facility

One can identify right away his or her own experience with a variety of these wastes while using or perhaps providing healthcare services.

TAKT is the time available for each patient. For example, if a physician normally examines 60 patients in a day in an eight-hour shift, the physician has about eight minutes per patient (8 hours × 60 minutes / 60 patients = 8 minutes). In other words, the objective ideally becomes to synchronize various processes and activities such that physician can see a patient well within 8 minutes. In this case, the physician has been considered the most critical resource, or the bottleneck operation. In the case of a surgeon, TAKT time will be equal to the time available for each surgery to meet the customer demand.

When the operation is streamlined, waste is eliminated, TAKT is determined, and the 5S and visual factory concepts are applied. In the case of 5S, the goal is to declutter and organize the area, and make it user-friendly to minimize opportunities for error by not wasting time looking for things. The visual factory concepts address the issue of making your tools and information visible and easily available to ensure realization of intended results in a planned time—in other words, making the right tool at the right place at the right time available for use.

Having streamlined the operations and minimized the waste, it is time to create the necessary rhythm. In order to create the rhythm, the first thing is to ensure that supplies are maintained at the required level. TAKT time allows the planning to schedule such that a certain level of inventory is maintained. Interestingly, healthcare facilities already have a "batch" size of one, thus managing inventory to deal with one patient at a time should lead to minimal inventory of supplies. The system to maintain desired inventory of supplies is called *Kanban*. A stocking method can standardize quantities with a card attached to each item. The card identifies the necessary quantity to maintain, and initiates a trigger for replenishing the supply once consumed to a predetermined level. Kanban simply implies a "card" system consisting of visual and physical inventory management rather than a complex computer-based inventory management system that accumulates excessive inventory, thus causing waste. *TPM* brings maintenance into focus as a necessary and vitally important part of the business.

One can see that while implementing Lean across an organization, collaboration may be required from the entire supply chain. This requirement leads many organizations to benefit from its local and limited implementation, which normally is confined to using the VSM and 5S methods to organize the workplace.

Table 12.3 shows how various Lean tools can be accommodated in the DMAIC methodology to maximize benefits of the combined approach.

TABLE 12.3 Integrating Six Sigma and Lean

Six Sigma	Applicable Lean Tools	Benefits of Integrating Lean and Six Sigma
D	VSM, Muda, 5S	Problem clarity and improved customer perspective
M	VSM, TPM	Sources of non-value activity
A	VSM, TPM	Better cause-and-effect relationships in process and product characteristics
I	VSM, 5S, TPM	Efficient process flow design with capable processes
C	5S, Muda, TPM	Highly efficient and effective workplace, and sustained customer focus

Gupta. Six Sigma Performance Handbook, 2004.

The following sections are case studies that demonstrate the use of various Lean and Six Sigma tools concurrently, or in an integrated approach.

CASE STUDY 1: COMBINING LEAN AND SIX SIGMA TO IMPROVE THROUGHPUT IN THE EMERGENCY DEPARTMENT AT ST. JOHN HEALTH

Located in southeast Michigan, St. John Health (SJH) provides extensive services through a system comprised of 9 hospitals and more than 125 medical facilities. Its vision is to "provide the highest quality patient care experience each time, every time (www.stjohn.org).

Initiatives such as Six Sigma and Lean help to support this vision by providing a structured approach to performance improvement. Initially, 14 people were trained as Six Sigma Black Belts, and 12 are currently serving in this role. St. John Health has completed 43 DMAIC projects, increasingly incorporating elements of Lean for rapid improvement. More than 35 Kaizens have been completed across SJH since December 2005. The process and measurement skills acquired through Six Sigma at St. John Health have been instrumental in effectively adapting Lean techniques.

Some of the Lean Six Sigma successes at St. John Health include

- SJHMC reduced time it takes to deliver CT/radiology results to ED clinicians by an average of 50 percent.

- Daily rounds are improving service to patients in progressive care at SJHMC—the average LOS has decreased by 30 percent.

- Moving patients efficiently to the right bed the first time creates better patient experiences and better work environment for staff. Turnaround times have improved by 88 percent.

- St. John-Providence ED patients are spending less time waiting for an inpatient bed—wait time has decreased by 50 percent.

- Visual cues are helping to better manage patients in observation status at St. John-Providence—the average LOS has decreased by 31 percent.

- Hours from St. John-Providence ED arrival to inpatient bed *maintained the same* from 1st Qtr FY'06 to 1st Qtr FY'07, while ED visits have *increased* by 1.4 percent.

- While Press Ganey patient satisfaction scores increased from a top box of 52.5 percent to 58.9 percent, hours from triage to discharge *decreased* 9.7 percent.

"The use of Six Sigma and Lean tools is becoming the way we work across St. John Health," says Todd Sperl. "With a disciplined approach, we are also beginning to see the long-term, sustained improvements that will help us to consistently provide the highest quality patient care experience in all we do."

Six Sigma Organization at St. John Health

Six Sigma and Lean are part of St. John's Operational Excellence initiative launched in the Fall of 2003, which represents a systematic approach to process and quality improvement (see Figure 12.3) There is an innovative and steadily improving infrastructure in place to provide leadership, ensure accountability, prioritize projects, manage the selection and training of participants, and measure and monitor results. For 2006, the initiative had a positive financial impact of $8.5 million on the fiscal year budget.

"As we have gained experience using Six Sigma, Lean, and change management, the team has become more comfortable picking up the right tool at the right time," says Todd Sperl, Master Black Belt with St. John Health. "I absolutely see the value to having a full toolkit. Some hospitals are only using Lean, but we think that's a dangerous route. Without a built-in control phase, the success rates can suffer. St. John has a 100 percent success rate because Black Belts are able to ensure the project is on track and determine statistical considerations, such as the existence of special cause variation and so on."

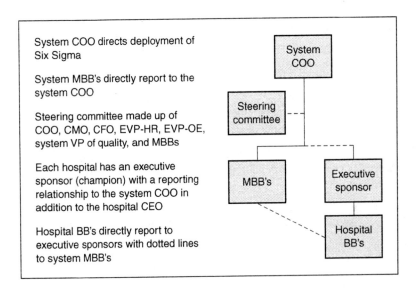

FIGURE 12.3 Six Sigma organization at St. John's

According to Sperl, St. John's goals are to link to the organization's strategic initiatives, identify value streams and waste, and then structure and rank opportunities for rapid improvement. One of the initiatives successfully completed by the team at St. John Health-Providence Hospital was a project to improve patient throughput in the emergency department, which required the use of Lean to support the Six Sigma process.

As the project began, the wait time for a patient to see a physician in the hospital's emergency department could range from 11 minutes to 4 hours. With more than 60,000 patients visiting the Providence ED on an annual basis, the variability and delays represented a significant opportunity for improvement.

Gathering the voice of the customer (VOC) led the hospital's Lean Six Sigma team to set the Upper Specification Limit at 60 minutes for patients to be seen in the ED. The hospital also had a goal to reduce the LWBS rate (patients leaving without being seen) from 2.4 percent to below 1 percent. The existing process averaged 64 minutes, but with a 39-minute standard deviation, and only 67 percent of the patients were actually seen within the 60-minute specification limit. The team initially set a goal to increase the number of patients seen within 60 minutes to 80 percent.

Findings from the Analyze Phase

Analysis indicated that issues such as bed availability, higher census, and the need for x-rays all contributed to longer waiting times for patients. Furthermore, lower acuity patients treated in express care also waited longer to see a physician—making the term "express" somewhat of a misnomer. Using historical Design of Experiments (DOE), the team verified that 94 percent of the variation in waiting to see a physician was driven by bed availability, radiology, and express care (see Figure 12.4).

Results for Historical DOE (Design of Experiment)
Door to Doctor Time

Factorial Fit: D2D Express Care, X-Ray, Bed Open

Estimated effects and coefficients for D2D (coded units)

Term	Effect	Coef	SE Coef	T	P
Constant		87.34	2.547	34.30	0.000
Express care	35.56	17.78	2.547	6.98	0.000
X-Ray	36.06	18.03	2.547	7.08	0.000
Bed open	−37.81	−18.91	2.547	−7.42	0.000
Express care * X-Ray	33.69	16.84	2.547	6.61	0.000
Express Care * Bed open	32.56	16.28	2.547	6.39	0.000
X-Ray * Bed open	14.06	7.03	2.547	2.76	0.025
Express Care * X-Ray * Bed open	5.19	2.59	2.547	1.02	0.338

$S = 10.1865$ R-Sq = 96.87%   R-Sq(adj) = 94.12%

Analysis of variance for D2D (coded units)

Source	DF	Seq SS	Adj SS	Adj MS	F	P
Main effects	3	15979.9	15979.9	5326.6	51.33	0.000
2-way interactions	3	9571.7	9571.7	3190.6	30.75	0.000
3-way interactions	1	107.6	107.6	107.6	1.04	0.338
Residual error	8	830.1	830.1	103.8		
Pure error	8	830.1	830.1	103.8		
Total	15	26489.4				

FIGURE 12.4 Results for historical DOE door-to-doctor time factorial fit: D2D express care, x-ray, bed open

Solutions Emerge

With participation from key stakeholders, the team held a Work-Out to address radiology turnaround time for emergency patients. Through this process, they quickly developed and implemented staffing adjustments and other solutions.

Use of the Priority/Payoff Matrix demonstrated that focusing on express care presented the greatest potential for change with the least amount of difficulty. Because it was under the control of the ED leadership, the lion's share of improvement for this initial project would come from this area. Data analysis showed that it took nearly twice as long to see a physician in express care as it did in the balance of the department.

Lean became the method of choice in this area. Data collection had already helped to identify problems with flow during the Six Sigma project, so the team met for four hours in a mini-Kaizen (instead of the typical weeklong event) to work through the issues.

According to Sperl, combining methods and learning when and where to use various tools has been very beneficial for the team. "We discovered that the appropriate use of Lean and Six Sigma helps us to achieve greater efficiency within a shorter amount of time," he says.

The VSM shown in Figure 12.5 illustrates various "flows" or traffic patterns within the ED. Various bottlenecks have been flagged to help the team analyze the current situation and identify any potential opportunities to streamline the department using Lean techniques.

One of the Lean techniques used was *5S Red Tag* (Sort, Standardize, Simplify, Sweep, Sustain) to identify and eliminate waste throughout the express care area of the ED. The team physically walked the process of moving from quick registration to express care, and rapidly moved supplies and workstations (where possible) to facilitate the flow of the patient. Red tags were used for those changes that could not be immediately addressed, and the changes were accomplished within 24 hours.

Uncovering the use of antiquated fax machines in express care helped to identify a barrier in communication. As so often happens in healthcare, the hospital staff had been unaware that a problem existed because they had developed workarounds to the issue.

Ben Miles, St. John Health Black Belt on this project, noted the benefit of using Lean to quickly uncover and address factors that might be involved. "The mini-Kaizen helped our staff to recognize the delays and customer satisfaction challenges caused by these everyday problems and empower them to make changes," he says.

By leveraging both Six Sigma and Lean methods within the ED, the team was able to realize the following accomplishments (see Figures 12.6 and 12.7):

- Mean reduced by 25 minutes (38 percent)
- Standard deviation reduced by 17 minutes (38 percent)
- Range reduced by 46 percent
- Z-score improved by 0.44 Sigma
- DPMO reduced by 158,333
- Flow improved with elimination of non-value-added process steps
- Standards created to sustain change
- Financial impact equaled more than $1.2 million

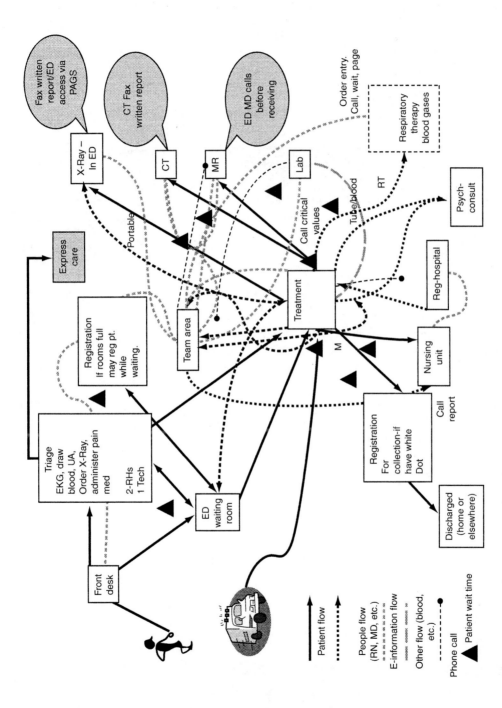

FIGURE 12.5 Emergency department spaghetti diagram

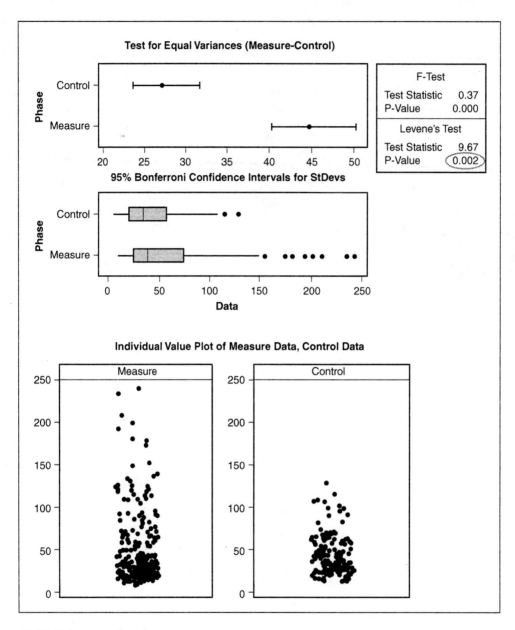

FIGURE 12.6 Statistical results

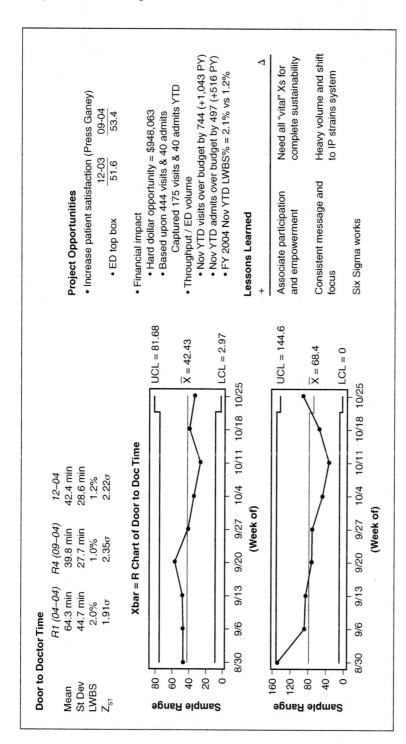

Door to Doctor Time

	R1 (04–04)	R4 (09–04)	12–04
Mean	64.3 min	39.8 min	42.4 min
St Dev	44.7 min	27.7 min	28.6 min
LWBS	2.0%	1.0%	1.2%
Z_{ST}	1.91σ	2.35σ	2.22σ

Xbar = R Chart of Door to Doc Time

UCL = 81.68
$\bar{X}$ = 42.43
LCL = 2.97

(Week of)

UCL = 144.6
$\bar{X}$ = 68.4
LCL = 0

(Week of)

Project Opportunities

- Increase patient satisfaction (Press Ganey)

  - ED top box

12-03	09-04
51.6	53.4

- Financial impact
  - Hard dollar opportunity = $948,063
  - Based upon 444 visits & 40 admits
    Captured 175 visits & 40 admits YTD
- Throughput / ED volume
  - Nov YTD visits over budget by 744 (+1,043 PY)
  - Nov YTD admits over budget by 497 (+516 PY)
  - FY 2004 Nov YTD LWBS% = 2.1% vs 1.2%

Lessons Learned

+	Δ
Associate participation and empowerment	Need all "vital" Xs for complete sustainability
Consistent message and focus	Heavy volume and shift to IP strains system
Six Sigma works	

FIGURE 12.7 Results

"The change has been profound on my initial contact with the patient," says Dr. Steven McGraw, ED physician. "Instead of apologizing for the delay in greeting a patient and defusing his/her frustrations, I can now more readily move ahead with treatment."

The Operational Excellence Team at St. John Health includes:

- James Tucci, MD, Chief Medical Officer
- Judy Avie, VP of Performance Improvement and Care Design
- Todd Sperl, Master Black Belt
- Diane Radloff, President, Providence
- Maria Strom, CNO, SJMH
- Dr. Ernie Yoder, Physician, Providence
- Chris Palazollo, VP Finance, SJHMC
- Brendon Weil, Black Belt, SJHMC
- Mary Naber, Worklife Service Leader
- Ben Miles, Black Belt

CASE STUDY 2: EXPANDING CT CAPACITY AT NORTH SHORE UNIVERSITY HOSPITAL

One of the most prevalent challenges in healthcare involves the ability to move patients efficiently through the system without lengthy delays and bottlenecks along the way. The dilemma can take many forms across the healthcare enterprise, and may relate to issues such as throughput, turnaround time, length of stay, patient flow, or capacity constraints. Lean and Six Sigma have proven useful in many healthcare facilities to pinpoint and address the underlying causes that drive lack of capacity.

Identifying opportunities to improve throughput in radiology can help providers optimize performance and better meet the needs of patients and physicians. At North Shore University Hospital (NSUH), a project team applied its Lean Six Sigma skills to reduce delays and increase throughput in CT procedures. NSUH is located in Manhasset, New York, and is part of the North Shore-Long Island Jewish Health System (NSLIJ). Launching an effort to improve CT capacity would align with the health system's Strategic Performance Dashboard dials of Service Excellence, Quality, and Operational Performance.

Focusing on both inpatient and outpatient CT scanners, the cross-functional project team was comprised of physician, technical, managerial, transport, and secretarial staff from the radiology department as well as Six Sigma experts from NSLIJ's Center for Learning and Innovation. Through data collection, leadership support, and a four-day Kaizen event, the team identified three primary target areas:

- Workspace
- Workflow
- Scheduling

Voice of the Customer (VOC) data indicated that the expectation for turnaround time for a routine CT scan was several hours. Looking at current data, however, the team found that turnaround averaged 20.7 hours, with wide variance—anywhere between 8 and 34 hours. They began to evaluate daily patient throughput on the two CT scanners, Monday–Friday (8AM–12PM), with the goal to increase average daily patient throughput by 20 percent (increase patient volume from 45 to 54 patients daily). The anticipated benefits to the organization were to decrease length of stay, reduce scheduling delays, and raise patient and physician satisfaction.

By analyzing baseline data and information from key stakeholders, the team found that the methods used to prepare and deliver oral contrast media were too time-consuming, and that the manual or handwritten inpatient schedule had no visibility to nursing units or the CT reception desk. This situation contributed to a number of problems: excessive phone calls to the technologist control rooms, lack of transporter availability, and a slow pre-transport process. Furthermore, CT technicians and transporters often traveled long distances to obtain order requisition and transport notice forms, and the work environment had become so cluttered that it left the lead tech without any designated workspace.

To resolve these issues, the team used a combination of Six Sigma for process improvement and Lean to reduce or eliminate waste. They led a four-day Kaizen event, which included preparatory work to define the scope of the project, the collection of baseline data, and the formation of a charter to clarify expectations among participants.

The Measure phase began on the first day of the Kaizen event. The team created a detailed value stream map of the CT process, beginning at the point the test is ordered to completion of the test on the CT scanner. Group activities included classification of Value-Added (VA) activities, Business Non-Value Added (BNVA), and Non-Value Added (NVA) activities. Leveraging Lean concepts, the team identified seven forms of waste within the process: Transportation, Inventory, Motion, Waiting, Overproduction, Overprocessing, and Defects/Rework.

The team developed a cause and effect diagram to identify the key drivers to CT throughput (see Figure 12.8), and baseline data collected prior to the Kaizen was added to the process map. Measurement system analysis using a gage R/R confirmed the accuracy of the data, and key metrics were tracked including the number of patients scanned, staff travel distance, and reasons for cancellations.

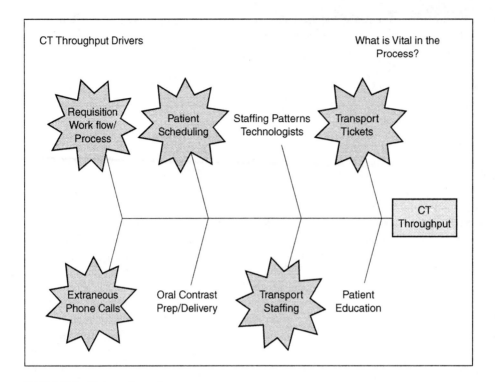

FIGURE 12.8 CT throughput drivers

On day two of the Kaizen event, it was time to begin brainstorming solutions. Through a collaborative effort built on the 5S method, a number of changes were implemented to create a more positive and orderly work environment, including designating workspace for the CT lead technologist, adding wall-mounted shelves with file holders, and creating a computer station for technical staff (see Figure 12.9).

Travel time presents another opportunity to apply Lean techniques, and use of a spaghetti diagram can help to visualize the issues. Prior to the Kaizen, data indicated the average CT technologist traveled 6,480 feet per day to the requisition printer—or 324 miles per year of non-value added activity. The transporter logged 432 feet per day (or 21.6 miles per year) of non-value added travel going to and from the transport notification printer.

Scheduling was another area of concern. A handwritten schedule was constantly being revised to meet departmental needs, and there was a lack of scheduling visibility for clerical staff and nursing units. This led to CT technologists receiving approximately 75 calls per day, taking time away from their value-added job of scanning patients.

Operation	Problem	Actions Taken	Results
Work Environment	• Cluttered workspace in CT Room A. • No designated work space for CT Lead Tech.	• Coordinated some of the 5S activities yielding positive changes to work environment. • Kaizen team collaborated with Engineering, Environmental Services and IS to complete projects. • Cleaned and re-organized the area.	• Created designated work space for CT Lead Tech including new computer, wall-mounted shelves and file holders. • Relocated RMS computer for optimal use by tech staff • Clean, functional work area.

Before Kaizen   **After Kaizen**

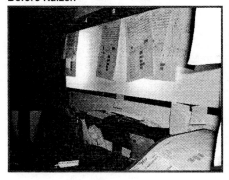

FIGURE 12.9 Kaizen impact on workspace

On the third day, the team try-stormed potential solutions for workflow and scheduling issues. To reduce CT technician and transporter travel time, the team routed both the requisitions and transport tickets to one designated, centrally located printer. This cut out 300 miles of non-value added travel time per year, improved communication between the CT technical staff and transporters, and reduced traffic in the main radiology department hallway (see Figure 12.10).

Operation	Problem	Actions Taken	Results
Workflow / travel distance	• Average CT tech travel distance to requisition printer = 6,480 feet / day (324 miles per year!) • Average Transporter travel distance to trasport notice printer = 432 feet / day (21.6 miles per year!)	• Obtained one printer capable of printing the two types of forms (requisitions & transport notice) • Relocated printer to a more central location (for techs & transporters) in Room B	• Eliminated need to travel down hallway multiple times during the shift, substantially reducing distances traveled by techs & transporters (>300 miles per year). • Improved work flow with less hallway traffic

Before Kaizen   **After Kaizen**

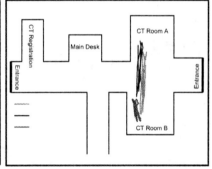

FIGURE 12.10 Kaizen impact on workflow

Further improvements to the department were made through

- Constructing and reorganizing the reception area
- Reassigning oral contrast preparation to the evening shift
- Delivering morning contrast incorporated into first transporter run for inpatients
- Implementing a new schedule in a Microsoft Excel format (see Figure 12.11)
- Developing a process for faxing schedules to floors and providing access through Microsoft Outlook for the CT department and unit secretaries

Operation	Problem	Actions Taken	Results
Scheduling (Rooms A and B)	• Manual scheduling process (hand written) revised continuously in attempt to meet demand. • No schedule visibility for CT clerical staff and hospital nursing units.	• Implemented new schedule (Excel format) with an additional 15 scan slots. • Trailed schedule changes; instituted process for faxing of schedule to floors and transfer to Outlook to provide visibility within and outside the CT Department.	• Created 15 new slots/daily with better utilization of scanners around special procedures • Implemented "pull" scheduling process resulting in increased throughput and improved TAT • Modified patient procedure types served by each scanner to facilitate optimal patient flow

Before Kaizen   **After Kaizen**

FIGURE 12.11 Kaizen impact on scheduling

The team implemented a "pull" process for scheduling, so that as a scan was completed, the next patient was advanced regardless of time. STAT orders were inserted in the schedule and after completion the next patient moved forward. The team felt nursing unit access to scheduling would reduce the daily cancellations caused by improper patient prep or patient unavailability, and minimize calls to technical staff. Another schedule change involved designating the 8AM slot for outpatients and the 8:15AM slot for inpatients. Data showed that although the number of inpatients scanned on Mondays increased, total CT patient volume was statistically higher between Tuesday through Thursday when the department scheduled outpatient procedures (see Figure 12.12). Modifying patient procedure types optimized patient flow through both scanners. A balanced scorecard tool allowed the team to add ten additional outpatient slots to Mondays, generating additional revenue, and a WWW plan (Who What When) insured actions items were assigned with deliverable dates.

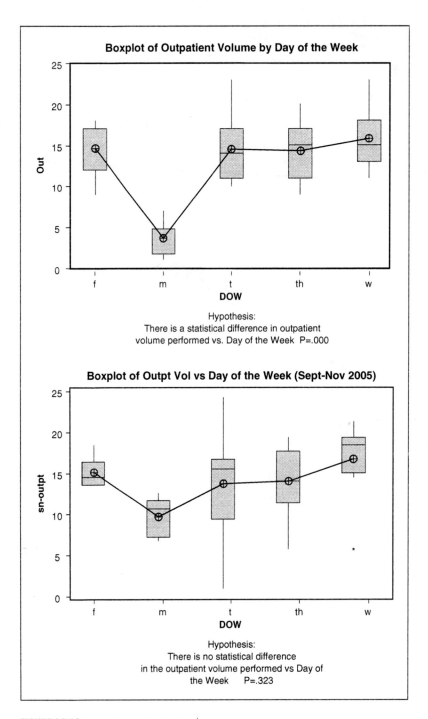

FIGURE 12.12 Impact on outpatient volume

On day 4, the team piloted the improvements and found a 33 percent increase in CT patient throughput on the two CT scanners. Feedback indicated the nurses appreciated email access to the CT schedule and felt it improved workflow. Strategies were developed to implement and sustain changes across the hospital. I-MR control charts were utilized to track daily patient volume (see Figure 12.13) and process charts monitored turnaround time. At the 30-day report-out, the number of patients scanned daily had increased from an average of 45 per day with a standard deviation of 7 per day to 51 patients per day with a standard deviation of 4. Each patient has an average of 1.4 procedures. The increased patient capacity yielded approximately 200 additional inpatient procedures per month and an additional 60 outpatient procedures per month (see Figures 12.14 and 12.15). Turnaround time for inpatient CT scans decreased from 20.7 hours to 11 hours (see Figure 12.16). Procedure cancellations due to improper patient prep decreased from 30.6 percent to 22.7 percent.

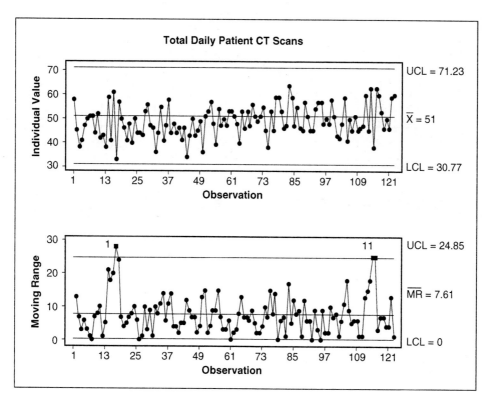

FIGURE 12.13 Variability in total daily patient CT scans

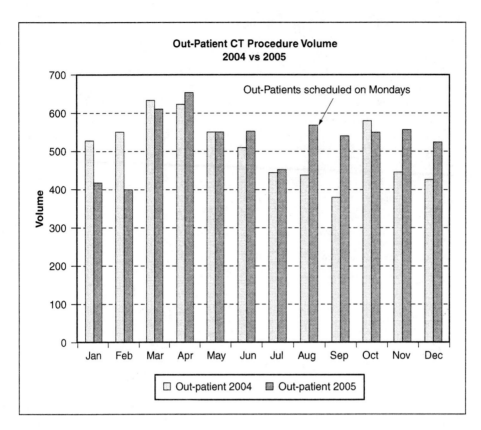

FIGURE 12.14 Out-patient CT procedure volume

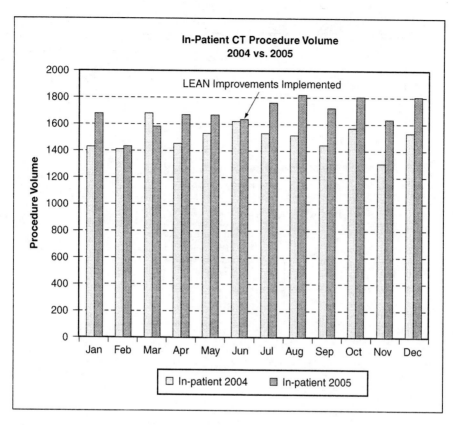

FIGURE 12.15 In-patient CT procedure volume

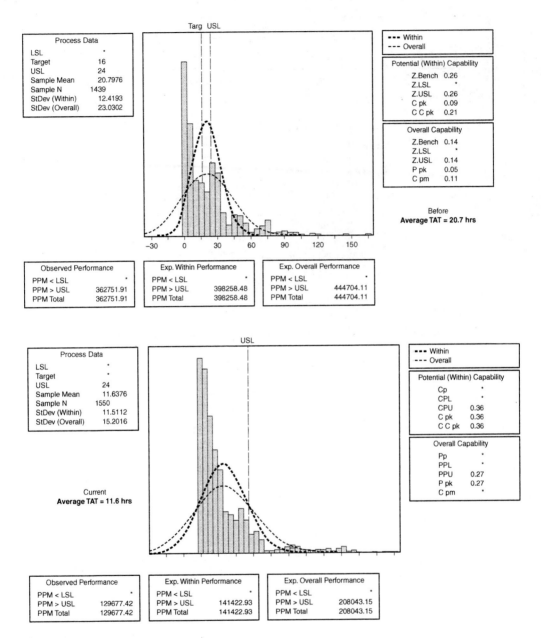

FIGURE 12.16 CT inpatient turnaround time

In terms of organizational results, the radiology department was able to increase capacity without additional staff while decreasing turnaround time (see Table 12.4). Additional outpatient CT procedures increased revenue to the radiology department by approximately $400 per procedure. For inpatients, length of stay decreased on units with high radiology usage. Employee satisfaction was higher as a result of the project, and though it was doing more scans per day, radiology staff said it felt their jobs were less stressful. In-house calls to CT techs decreased, enabling radiology staff to spend more time performing patient scans and less time on non-valued added tasks such as answering the phone and adjusting the schedule.

TABLE 12.4 CT Scan Volume at North Shore University Hospital

	Oct 04	Nov 04	Dec 04	Jan 05	Feb 05	Mar 05	Apr 05	May 05	June 05	Jul 05
Inpatient	1585	1311	1539	1696	1444	1599	1681	1680	1667	1781
Outpatient	576	449	422	415	398	609	655	592	777	644

	Aug* 05	Sept 05	Oct 05	Nov 05	Dec 05	Jan 06
Inpatient	1846	1757	1843	1681	1835	1730
Outpatient	806	732	706	798	699	828

*Italic indicates post implementation of process improvements.

NOTE

This project was a finalist in two categories for The 2006 Global Six Sigma Awards:

- Best Achievement of Six Sigma in Healthcare
- Best Achievement of Integrating Lean and Six Sigma

ENDNOTES

1. Whitepaper. *Going Lean in Healthcare*. Cambridge, MA: Institute for Healthcare Improvement, 2005 (http://www.ihi.org/IHI/Results/WhitePapers/GoingLeaninHealth-Care.htm).

2. Normal, Gary, Phil Kaczmarksi and Carolyn Pexton "Integrating Six Sigma with Lean & Work-Out in Healthcare," Six Sigma Healthcare, www.healthcare.isixsigma.com/library/content/c031126a.asp.

THE ROAD AHEAD

SECTIONS

"Is Six Sigma good enough? Not in healthcare, it isn't. We are talking about lives, not dollars. 3.4 deaths per million opportunities is just a starting point."

—H. James Harrington

Although the figures may paint a gloomy picture, things are getting better. In some ways, repairing healthcare quality practices is a lot like an alcoholic looking for help. The hardest part of any transformation is recognizing that one is needed. When the alcoholic arrives at his/her first AA meeting, the transformation has started. Fortunately, the transformation has begun for improving healthcare quality. During the past 10–15 years, the healthcare problem has been identified and brought to the attention of the practitioners and the general public. Many healthcare providers have come a long way down the road to excellence, using Total Quality Management (TQM), and now they are embracing a Six Sigma approach to healthcare processes and practices. Do we still need further improvement? The answer has to be "yes." By far, the majority of healthcare professionals are dedicated, hard-working individuals who are trying to do perfect work in an imperfect world. There are relatively few critical errors being made today, but if even one is made, it often results in a death. Each healthcare provider (HCP) has thousands of error opportunities each day and errors may or may not be avoided. Some of these errors have no long-term impact, some of them cause the patient to require additional treatment and cost, and a few result in the patient dying.

Installing a Six Sigma culture of less than 3.4 errors per million opportunities is a good next step, but when that milestone is reached, the HCP needs to strive for even higher standards because even one accidental death is one too many. We need to be operating at the one error-per-billion opportunity level. If you are manufacturing computers and have a 3.4 errors-per-million opportunities, this may be good enough because these errors cause an inconvenience only to the customer, but that is not good enough when you are taking a person's life in your hands.

DOES THE HEALTHCARE INDUSTRY NEED SIX SIGMA?

"You are safer flying in an airplane than in your local hospital."

—H. James Harrington

There is no other industry in the world that is more in need of Six Sigma than the healthcare industry. About 2 percent of the people who are admitted will experience an adverse drug effect, resulting in increased length of stay and a $4,700 increase in related-cost. Errors account for at least 2.5 percent of the total HCP budget. The Center for Disease Control and Prevention estimates that more than 2 million patients per year acquire an infection while in a U.S. hospital for other conditions. About 88,000 people die as a direct or indirect result of these infections. These HCP-acquired infections alone cost the U.S. an additional $5 billion in healthcare cost per year. Jefod M. Loeb, Ph.D., executive vice president, Division of Research for the Joint Commission on Accreditation of Healthcare Organizations (JCAHO), stated, "With the possible exception of anesthesia care, most of healthcare operates at a level of about 3.8 Sigma—which roughly equates to 6,210 defects/million opportunities."[1]

> "The costs of poor quality care for employees are at least $1,800 per employee per year for healthcare coverage. The estimated direct cost of poor-quality care averaged between $344 billion to $698 billion—or about $1,200 to $2,500 for every American."
>
> —Brian J. Swayne, author

An HCP's cost of poor quality is estimated to be as high as 30 to 50 percent of the total amount paid for healthcare. The cost of medical malpractice insurance premiums is directly impacted by medical errors. Up to 85 percent of the medical errors are preventable by a good quality management system. Research shows that a vast majority of the medical errors are system, rather than human, errors.[2]

What Is the Problem?

"The road to hell is paved with good intentions, and the road to managerial and organizational ruin is paved with decisions that have not been implemented—or worse, still, that have been implemented half-heartedly."

—Everard and Morris

The Committee on the Quality of Healthcare in America (QHCA), as reported by the Institute on Medicine (IOM), summarized the current state of healthcare delivery systems as

- In need of fundamental change
- Harms too frequently
- Routinely fails to deliver its potential benefits
- Frequently delivers care which is not based on the best knowledge
- Has quality problems (everywhere)
- Has not just a gap, but a "chasm" in terms of quality
- Does not make best use of its resources
- Has waste present
- Cannot achieve higher quality by further stressing the current system

The focus of the IOM "chasm" report is on how the system can be redesigned to innovate and improve care. It presented an "agenda" for redesigning the twenty-first century healthcare systems.[3] Donald M. Berwick, M.D., CEO of the Institute for Healthcare Improvement and clinical professor of pediatrics and healthcare policy at Harvard Medical School, wrote that 100,000 needless deaths could be prevented every year by known improvements in the following six areas:[4]

- Respiratory pneumonia
- IV/catheter infections
- Surgical-site infections
- Increased response to early warning signals
- Make heart-attack care absolutely reliable
- Medication errors

It is estimated that for the use of beta blockers (used to treat high blood pressure, irregular heartbeats, and congestive heart failure) the sigma rating is as low as 1 Sigma. That is an error rate of 691,500 errors per million opportunities. For identifying and treating depression, the sigma rating is about 2 Sigma or 308,538 errors per million opportunities. The estimated sigma rating for antibiotic misuse is 3 Sigma or 66,800 errors per million opportunities.[5]

The industrialized world is faced with a major healthcare problem that is four-fold as follows (see Figure 13.1):

- Aging population
- Healthcare worker shortage
- Healthcare costs growing at a double-digit rate
- Healthcare costs are reducing the U.S. product's competitiveness

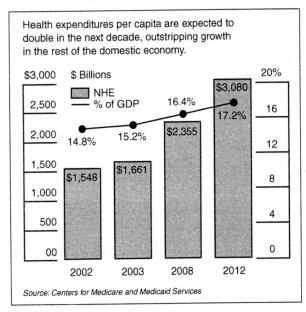

FIGURE 13.1   Projected national health expenditures and percent of GDP.

We estimate that liability coverage and defensive medicine account for more than $100 billion per year of the medical cost. Thirty-one cents of every healthcare dollar is spent on administrative cost. More than 70 percent of the remaining costs go to treating chronic diseases. Improved programs to prevent and better manage chronic disease is a must.

General Motors in North America alone spends about $5 billion per year in healthcare. This cost is the largest purchased component of the vehicle. Is it any wonder that they are closing plants in the U.S. and moving them to India, Canada, and Russia? The U.S. automotive industry is spending billions each year on healthcare. A reduction of only 1 percent would save millions annually.

The Government's Problem with Healthcare

The government is facing a major challenge in paying its part of the healthcare cost, because the tax base is declining as a result of the aging population. Healthcare costs are increasing the cost of U.S. products to the point we are not competitive with products that are produced in other parts of the world. Healthcare costs run over 16 percent of the U.S. GNP compared to other countries' 8 to 10 percent.

As spending in healthcare rises, public programs like Medicare and Medicaid will pay an increasing part of the cost from 45.6 percent in 2003 to 49 percent by 2014. This will have a big impact on the government budget that can only be offset by tax increases. President George W. Bush's 2006 budget proposed cutting $40 billion from the federal share of Medicaid over the next 10 years by cracking down on state accounting methods. Healthcare costs for public programs are already causing budget problems at the state level. Texas Governor Rick Perry stated that his state and others may need to declare bankruptcy unless they get additional money from the federal government to cover Medicaid costs. Today, there are 44 million Americans who have no medical coverage, which is driving up costs for other payers, mostly government and business.

The Economic and Social Research Institute reported that within a three-year period, the U.S. government spent $410 million to recover $5.2 billion in Medicare-related fraud settlements and judgment.[6]

Something must be done now. Six Sigma systems will not solve the total problem, but it can go along way to reduce the waste that will provide a good start to turning the problem around.

Example of Government Action

"It is common sense to take a method and try it. If it fails, admit it frankly and try another. But above all, try something."

—Franklin D. Roosevelt

The Federal Office of Personnel Management now requires preferred provider organization and fee-for-service plans to input quality performance measurement in HEDIS (Health Plan Employer Data and Information Set) database. This will provide 8 million federal employees, dependents, and retirees with data that will allow them to make better decisions related to their HCP. The National Committee for Quality Assurance, in its 2005 State of Healthcare Quality Report, estimated that between 2007 and 2012, reported data will have improved blood pressure control by 15 percentage points, saving 8,600 to 15,000 lives each year.[7]

The State of Pennsylvania has taken action to pay to improve quality in its state healthcare system. According to legislation passed, "There is a 20 percent discount in each premium for a healthcare provider that implements, to the satisfaction of the Department of Health, a total quality management healthcare system approved by the Department of Health."[8]

The International Organization for Standardization (ISO) revised ISO IWA 1:2005, "Guidelines for Process Improvements in Health Services Organizations," in 2005. It focuses on assisting HCPs in implementing a quality management system. It translates quality terminology and situations into a language that the healthcare professional can easily understand.

Another ISO document that the HCP needs to know how to use is ISO/TC 22004:2005, Food Safety Management Systems—Guidance on the Application of ISO 22000:2005. It gives good advice for organizations in the food supply chain.

Six Sigma Is Part of the Answer

What if you could not fail? What if everyone within your HCP brought his/her creativity and intelligence to continually improve work each day? This would ensure that your HCP is the accepted healthcare leader in your area. That is what Six Sigma will help you accomplish.

There was a time when Six Sigma was a new concept in the healthcare arena. It sounded good, but so did a lot of other things that did not work. Today that is not the case. Today, Six Sigma is a proven methodology for which many HCPs take advantage of its rewards. It is no longer a competitive advantage to install a Six Sigma initiative, but it is a very significant competitive disadvantage if you do not already have a Six Sigma System in place. We are often asked by our clients how long will they need to plan on running the Six Sigma initiative at their HCP organization. We asked them to tell us how many accidental deaths they want to cause in the next 10-year period. How many patients do they want to become infected with a disease/condition that they did not have when they entered the hospital or office? How many of the staff do they want to become infected as a result of coming in contact with their patients? Most of our clients respond "none," and with that they set their own cut-off date. Six Sigma started as 3.4 errors per million opportunities, but that does not mean that the organization should stop improving when it reaches that level.

I can remember back in the old days when we used to buy items at a 2 percent Average Outgoing Quality Level (AOQL). On one occasion we ordered 2,000 needles. The supplier sent the order in two boxes; one box had 1,960 needles labeled as good, the other box had 40 needles labeled as bad. He also sent in a note stating that he had to bend the 40 needles to make them bad but the next time he would like to just send in all good needles, and if we still needed 2 percent bad needles he would need to increase the price to take care of the additional operations.

Poor-Quality Cost and Six Sigma

"Defects are not free. Somebody makes them and gets paid for making them."

—W. Edwards Deming

Poor-quality cost measures the cost that the HCP incurs because it is not doing everything right the first time. The following provides the reader with an example of how poor-quality cost changes as the process variation is reduced:[9]

- 3 Sigma: 25 to 40 percent of gross
- 4 Sigma: 15 to 25 percent of gross
- 5 Sigma: 5 to 15 percent of gross
- 6 Sigma: less than 1 percent of gross

The direct parts of poor-quality cost are

- Prevention cost
- Appraisal cost
- Internal error cost
- External error cost

As an organization increases the money spent on prevention and appraisal cost, the internal- and external-error cost decreases. As the Sigma level of the preventive and appraisal processes increases, the related cost decreases (see Figure 13.2).

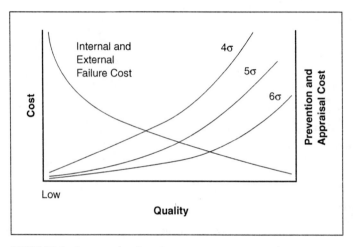

FIGURE 13.2 Impact of reduced error rates on poor-quality cost.

To get the total direct poor-quality cost, you add the internal and external failure costs to the prevention and appraisal cost.

Customer Loyalty—Customers/Patients for Life

It costs 10 to 15 times more to get a new customer than to keep a current customer. Do you know how much a current customer is worth? The following are typical examples:

- One hospital patient is worth $800,000.
- One doctor's office patient is worth $60,000.
- A new insurance policyholder becomes profitable in three years.
- In the credit card business, the breakeven point is six years.
- A loyal pizza eater is worth $8,000.

- A Cadillac owner is worth $332,000.
- The tennis player's tennis ball expense is worth $3,200.
- A grocery store customer is worth $50,000.

To provide the best and least expensive services today, the HCP needs to look at and consider the total community's healthcare facilities (see Figure 13.3).

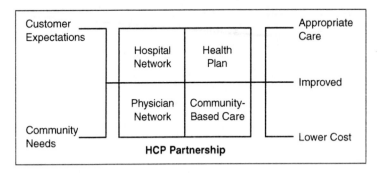

FIGURE 13.3 Community care model

Some Six Sigma Results

"Six Sigma is unabashedly focused on three targets: lowering cost, increasing productivity, and realizing more profit out of operations."

—Michael Brassard and Diane Ritter, authors

"It would be a mistake to think that Six Sigma is about quality in the traditional sense. Quality, defined traditionally as conformance to internal requirements, has little to do with Six Sigma. Six Sigma is about helping the organization make more money..."

—Thomas Pyzdek

Table 13.1 shows what some major companies have achieved from using Six Sigma.

TABLE 13.1 What Others Have Achieved

Company	Year	Savings
Motorola	1986–2001	$16 billion
Bechtel	2001–present	$1 billion
Honeywell	1998–2000	$$1.8 billion
Ford Motor Company	2000–2002	$1 billion
General Electric	More than five years	$12 billion

- **General Electric**

  - Rail car project: Reduced repair time, increased revenues by 11 percent; redesigned the leasing process, increased revenues by 13 percent.

  - Aircraft engine imports for Canadian customer project: Reduced order delays; increased operating margin to 16.7 percent.

  - GE Capital Services project: Reduced defects and improved customer satisfaction; resulted in increased earnings per share of 14 percent.

- **Allied Signal, Inc.** Increased productivity: Increased operating margin to 13.1 percent from 12 percent; saved more than $2 billion in direct cost.

- **Polaroid Corporation**. Improved quality and profit margins on a product-by-product basis. The result was a 6 percent improvement to the gross profits.

- **ABB Asea Brown Boveri Group**. Applied Six Sigma to its power transformer facility which resulted in decreased measurement error by 7 percent and no-load loss by 2 percent. The savings per average plant was $750,000.[10]

Jill M. Considine, the CEO of Depository Trust and Clearing Corporation (DTC) was named the 2005 Six Sigma CEO of the Year. One of her Six Sigma teams streamlined the bond redemption process that resulted in more than $1.4 million savings per year and increased customer satisfaction related to the process from 73 percent to 90 percent. By the end of the first half of 2006, DTC completed 145 Six Sigma projects, saving more than $17 million (an average savings of more than $117,200 per project). As of mid-2006, it had 14 Black Belts and 69 Green Belts.[11]

James O. Pearson, Vice President of EMC Corp., led the Six Sigma movement within EMC. He was named the Six Sigma Vice President of the Year. In 2005, the Six Sigma process at EMC resulted in $95 million of additional benefits. EMC conducted 586 projects for an average return on investment that was greater than $157,000 per project. The average Black Belt saved $357,000 during a 12-month period. More than 5,000 employees completed their Six Sigma Advocate training class.[12]

Cooper-Standard Automotive's Global Fluid Systems division, located in Auburn Hills, Michigan, focused on using Design for Six Sigma (DFSS) process to deliver a cost-effective water valve design while generating increased sales for the company. The result was a savings of $883,200 annually and more than $2 million in additional annual revenue.[13]

The first Black Belt project of TD Bank Financial Group, headquartered in Toronto, Canada, resulted in $1.6 million in savings. The project focused on improving the call-center processes.[14]

Lonmin PLC of South Africa, a platinum group metals mining and refining company, implemented Six Sigma in 2004 by training 24 Black Belts, 184 Green Belts, and 850 Yellow Belts. In 2005, it completed 81 projects, many of these focused on safety, health, and environment. The 2005 savings were $34 million in sustainable realized benefits ($87 million annualized).[15]

Customer-driven Six Sigma saved Ford $300 million. Ford has 2,300 Black Belts and more than 6,000 Green Belts. Ford purchased a license from the Six Sigma Academy for Six Sigma training for $6 million. In the first year, Six Sigma projects added $52 million to the bottom line, and the company gained a 2-point increase in customer satisfaction the following year. Ford has completed more than 4,000 Six Sigma projects.[16]

SOME SIX SIGMA HEALTHCARE RESULTS AND LESSONS LEARNED

There are numerous examples of how HCP's have applied Six Sigma concepts to improve their total organization performance. Here are just a few:

- Santa Rosa Memorial Hospital in one year went from $8 million lost to $10 million profit. Santa Rosa's processes allowed them to have a Lean staff not in nursing but in the support auxiliary staff.[17]

- Stanford University Medical Center in Palo Alto, California, began an "Operational Improvement" program.[18] The goal was to decrease the annual operating budget by $26 million the first year and another $18 million the second year. It cut the budget by $44 million and increased revenue by another $10 million. These savings resulted from improvements such as redesigning the cardiac monitoring system so that the hospital could eliminate the need for the RNs to watch the patients 24 hours per day, which saved $900,000 per year and freed up 13 RNs to do other patient-related work.

- St Joseph's Hospital, Carondelet Healthcare Services' in Tucson, Arizona, improvement activities saved $1.2 million per year; $400,000 of it was the result of putting in a redesigned "unit-based care team" approach. This team, led by an RN clinical manager, included practical nurses, patient-care technicians, and patient-care associates who handle the "hotel-management" functions.[19]

- Legacy Emanuel Hospital and Health Center in Portland, Oregon, reduced variation in patient flow processes by standardizing the work flow and reducing 350 operating unit-specific procedures to 63 system-wide procedures that were cross-functional. They also standardized billing and collection processes, moving them to one site which saved $350,000 per year and eliminated almost 15 jobs.[20]

- Robert Wood Johnson University Hospital (RWJUH) of Hamilton, New Jersey, provides healthcare services to 350,000 people per year. The hospital won the 2004 Malcolm Baldrige Quality Award. The following list incorporates just some of their improvements:

  - RWJUH's 15/30 program, which guarantees that patients will see a nurse within 15 minutes and a doctor within 30 minutes of entering the emergency room, has improved patient satisfaction from 85 percent in 2001 to 90 percent in 2004. From 1999 to 2003, ER patient volume doubled.

  - Inpatient satisfaction with nursing and nursing courtesy improved from 70 percent in 1999 to more than 90 percent in 2004.

- Employee satisfaction with benefits rose from nearly 30 percent in 1995 to slightly greater than 90 percent in 1999 to 100 percent in 2003, and satisfaction with employee participation in decisions increased from 40 percent in 1999 to 90 percent in 2003.

- Charleston Area Medical Center in Charleston, West Virginia, redesigned the supply chain management for surgical supplies. The result was a reduction in inventory levels, saving the center about $2 million per year.

- Scottsdale Healthcare in Scottsdale, Arizona, focused on the overcrowded condition in the Emergency Department. The result was faster transfer of patients from ED to a normal hospital bed.

- Mount Carmel Health for Central Ohio, looked at the plan reimbursement and the Medicare choice paper flow processes. The result was reduced error rates, saving $857,000 per year.

- Presbyterian Hospital in New York invested $8 million to implement Six Sigma. After the first year of the program (2004), the hospital recorded $47 million increase to the bottom line, all directly related to the Six Sigma project.[21]

- Three hospitals and a regional business office of Christus Schumpert Health System (CSHS), located in Northern Louisiana, set up a team to apply Lean Six Sigma to the healthcare system. At the time the team was formed, CSHS was in the red by an average of $8 million per year. In a three-year period (from February 2003 to February 2006), its net operating margin improved from –0.2 percent to +1.5 percent CSHS reduced the uncollectible accounts from $8.1 million in 2003 to $4.3 million in 2006. The projected annual savings is $5.7 million per year.[22]

- The St. Charles Medical Center in Bend, Oregon, focused on changing the way it used their resources related to orthopedic and neurosurgery.[23] Table 13.2 defines how resources were deployed before the improvement process started and where they were deployed at the end of the first round of improvements. The target is their future goal.

TABLE 13.2 St. Charles Medical Center in Bend, Oregon, Changes in Their Resources Related to Orthopedic and Neurosurgery and Their Future Targets

	Before	**After**	**Target**
Direct patient care	24 percent	31 percent	43 percent
Scheduling and coordinating	19 percent	8 percent	10 percent
Documentation	29 percent	19 percent	17 percent
Patient support	14 percent	21 percent	16 percent
Other	14 percent	21 percent	14 percent

- One mid-sized hospital focused on using Lean Six Sigma in medication administration. They defined the process as

  - Supplier selection

  - Purchasing

  - Storing

  - Ordering

  - Dispensing

  - Delivering medication

  - Outcome monitoring

  The results were as follows:

  - Errors reduced from 213 per month to 96—a 55 percent reduction

  - Total error rates reduced from 0.33 percent to 0.14 percent in five months

  - Labor cost reduced by $1.32 million per year

  - Much improved employee morale and better relationship between nurses and pharmacists[24]

- McLeod Regional Medical Center in Florence, South Carolina, cut the death rate among its heart-attack patients from 10 percent (the U.S. average) to about 4 percent, just by developing and using improved processes related to the use of aspirin and beta blockers on arrival and stint or clot buster promptly after admission.[25]

- Dominican Hospital in Santa Cruz, California, went for more than a year without one ventilator-associated pneumonia (VAP) infection.[26]

- John Hopkins University in Baltimore, Maryland, reported that 70 hospitals cut their central-line infections in half, saving $165 million per year. Johns Hopkins altered its processes related to washing hands, changing bandages, and being sure that catheters were removed as soon as possible.[27]

- By changing its processes related to giving the right antibiotics on time, enforcing strict hand washing, and avoiding sharing the surgery site before the operation allowed Mercy Health Center in Oklahoma City to process 1,200 consecutive patients without a wound infection.[28]

- North Shore-Long Island Jewish Hospital System in New Hyde Park, New York, trained 24 Black Belts, 70 Green Belts, and 2 Master Black Belts. It also completed 60 projects. One of the projects focused on the laboratory process. The process improved from 3.9 Sigma to 4.5 Sigma. Productivity improved by 43 percent, resulting in a cost reduction of $339,000.[29]

"Almost all quality improvements come via simplification of design, manufacturing, layout, processes and procedures."

—Tom Peters

- Decatur Memorial Hospital in Decatur, Illinois, implemented a Six Sigma system and installed a patient technology software package. The project focused on the medication process errors, which originally consisted of 132 steps. As a result of implementing the Six Sigma system, it was able to eliminate 42 of these steps. Moreover, the time to dispense and administer the drugs to the patients was reduced from 186 minutes to 104 minutes. Medication errors also dropped by 70 percent. All of this was accomplished in only 10 months.[30]

- The Red Cross Hospital in Beverwijk, Holland, implemented a Six Sigma system. One of the Six Sigma projects focused on reducing the number of mistakes in invoicing. At the start, 9 percent of the invoices were returned for mistakes. The process was changed, and now it is down to 1 percent. This resulted in a $200,000 per year savings. It also improved the temporary agencies invoicing process, resulting in a one-time refund of $35,000 and a yearly savings of $75,000.[31]

HOSPITAL PERFORMANCE

"If the HCP systems we are using don't improve soon, 'It's time to give up the free enterprise HCP system and follow the international best practices systems (government-controlled system).'"

—H. James Harrington

Maybe your HCP doesn't need to install a Six Sigma system. It is a lot of work and costs a lot to get started. Maybe the people who work on your problem already have the skills that Six Sigma brings to the table. So why do anything new? To see what new skills Six Sigma brings to your HCP, evaluate the people who solve your problems and improve your processes against the Six Sigma tools listed in Appendix D "Total Six Sigma Tools Self-Evaluation Form."

In 2005, the Leapfrog Group surveyed more than 1,000 hospitals. The following are its findings:

- Eight out of 10 have implemented procedures to avoid wrong site surgeries.
- Seven out of 10 require a pharmacist to review all medication orders before medication is given to patients.

- Seven out of 10 do not have an explicit protocol to ensure adequate nursing staff or a policy to check with patients to ensure they understand the risks of their procedures.

- Six out of 10 lack procedures for preventing patient malnutrition.

- Five out of 10 do not have procedures to prevent bed sores.

- Four out of 10 lack policies requiring workers to wash their hands with disinfectant before and after seeing a patient.

The survey collected data on hospitals' progress toward implementing practices in four categories: computerized physician order entry, ICU physician staff, evidence-based hospital referral, and the Leapfrog Quality Index of 27 safe practices.[32]

There is a great deal of regional differences in HCPs. Ashish Jha, assistant professor at Harvard School of Public Health, with the aid of the Hospital Quality Alliance of 3,558 hospitals, examined quality indicators in different hospitals and cities. Jha stated, "Hospitals scoring high for one medical condition did not necessarily score high in the other condition." Table 13.3 shows the result of this study. The higher the CHF score, the better the performance.[33]

TABLE 13.3 Rankings of Quality Care Among the 40 Largest Hospital-Referral Regions

Hospital-Referral Region	CHF Score (percent)	Number of Hospitals
Top-Ranked		
Boston, MA	89	39
Detroit, MI	88	14
Baltimore, MD	87	21
Camden, N.J.	87	21
Cleveland, OH	86	24
Bottom-Ranked		
San Diego, CA	77	22
Nashville, TN	76	37
Orlando, FL	74	22
Little Rock, AR	69	28
Lexington, KY	68	30

"Some countries that are spending 50 percent of what the U.S. is spending on healthcare are providing better services and results."

—H. James Harrington

The U.S. is spending a higher percentage of its GNP on healthcare than any other country, and yet it is far from providing the best service and results. Countries like Canada are rated better than the U.S. because its HCP cost a lot less to provide the services. In 1995, the American

Customer Satisfaction Index was published for the first time by the University of Michigan for hospitals in the U.S. Customer satisfaction for hospitals was rated 74 out of a possible 100. In the nine years that followed, the average rating was 70.6, a 3.4 percent decrease in customer satisfaction. You have to ask yourself, "Why is hospital customer satisfaction getting worse? Why is the hotel industry doing better than we are doing with less skilled employees? Even the federal government is doing a better job than the hospitals are doing?"

Typical industries with higher customer satisfaction indices than hospitals include[34]

- Hotel industry
- Automobile industry
- Beer industry
- Pet food industry
- Banking industry
- Travel industry
- U.S. Postal Service
- Federal government

Typical industries that have a lower customer satisfaction index than hospitals include

- Healthcare insurance industry
- Local government
- Airline industry
- Cable industry
- Cell phone industry

If we do not do something soon in the U.S. to make a major performance improvement in the healthcare system, we will have to follow the lead of the benchmark countries and do away with our present free enterprise approach to healthcare.

> "CEOs were asked to gauge current healthcare costs. The top 10 percent of respondents cited costs exceeding $9,000 per employee per year, with some spending more than $15,000."
>
> —Chief Executive Way, June 2006

LESSONS LEARNED

> "At the 4 Sigma level, the special cause variation defect rate is often higher than the common cause variation."
>
> —H. James Harrington

Throughout the years, we have seen some big successes and some big failures when HCPs have implemented performance improvement projects, including TQM and Six Sigma. The following is a list of some things we have learned or some things you need to consider as Six Sigma is implemented in your organization:

- If top management isn't behind it, don't do it.
- Shared institutional and professional beliefs, goals, and values are required for the Six Sigma program to be successful.
- The Six Sigma system will be a fad if the culture of the organization does not change while it is being implemented.
- The Black, Green, and Yellow Belt activities are only 50 percent of a Six Sigma system. It's the Blue Belts who change the culture.
- There is a need to develop a multi-disciplinary thinking and culture in patient care.
- The interests and roles of all the stakeholders must be fully considered and viewed from the stakeholders' perspective (for example, the entrenched physician-patient relationship).
- A team-oriented approach to patient care will decrease the autonomy of all the HCP employees. This is sometimes hard for some employees to accept. It is particularly true of physicians, who are fearful about decreasing their authority and autonomy.
- Don't try to do Six Sigma without a budget that covers all its costs.
- A significant number of the staff of physicians must be part of the Six Sigma planning process.
- Six Sigma is not a statistical system; it is a culture-change system. Thinking statistically is part of it, but the main focus is on the total elimination of waste, along with a culture change that everyone and everything can be improved.
- The use of electronic medical recorders can result in big savings through less paperwork, fewer redundant tests, better adherence to preferred drug lists, and communication errors. John Halamka, CIO at Care Group Health Systems in Boston, estimates that putting as statewide E-record system would cost about $1 billion. Blue Cross Blue Shield of Massachusetts is backing a $50 million project to wire one community with electronic medical records as a pilot.

"A lot of studies say the use of IT has the potential to transform the healthcare industry. But bottom line, unless as an industry we work collaboratively to make this happen, it will happen at an excruciatingly slow pace, like it has so far."

—Carl Ascenzo, CIO, Blue Cross Blue Shield of Massachusetts[35]

- Kaiser Permanente has set aside $3.2 billion to spend over an 11-year period to install healthcare records into electronic form. This came after major failures with an earlier system it developed with IBM's help.

- Nurses are more likely than doctors to report medical errors. In a study conducted by Tufts New England Medical Center in Boston in 2006, out of 26 U.S. hospitals it found that of the 92,500 errors reported, RNs made almost 50 percent of the reports while physicians made less than 2 percent.

- Don't think of Six Sigma as something new; it is based upon the current TQM/CQI programs. The tools are all the same. Six Sigma has just set a new standard of performance and given the quality engineers a new title: "Black Belt." It has provided many more people with the quality engineering tools and set them aside to do problem-solving and prevention.

- Today Six Sigma has become ill-defined and confusing. It has become too complicated as each author, consultant, and organization has included its products into the Six Sigma system. The body of knowledge for Black Belts includes many tools that they will never use. (See Appendix C "The Six Sigma Body of Knowledge.") The result is that it takes far too long to train them and, once trained, they are not trained well enough on the tools that they will really be using.

- Don't think that a Six Sigma process will result in only 3.4 errors per million opportunities. That is not true. It only means that it will be 3.4 *common* errors per million opportunities. The special-cause errors often increase it to more than 900 errors per million opportunities.

"Mediocrity is the result when fear of failure permeates an organization."

—William Scherkenbach

SIX SIGMA AND THE NATIONAL QUALITY AWARDS

"Problems breed problems, and the lack of disciplined method of openly attacking them breeds more problems."

—Philip Crosby, quality consultant

Too many HCPs are measuring their progress and results in dollars saved. We believe that the measurement system used in the Malcolm Baldrige National Quality Program (see Figure 13.4) provides a much better way to measure your progress. It provides a point score of 0 to 1,000 points in the areas included in Table 13.4.

TABLE 13.4   The Malcolm Baldrige National Quality Program Maximum Point Scores by Category

Area	Maximum Points
Leadership	120
Strategic Planning	85
Focus on Patient, Other Customers, and Market	85
Measurement, Analysis, and Knowledge Management	90
Staff Focus	85
Process Management	85
Organizational Performance Results	450

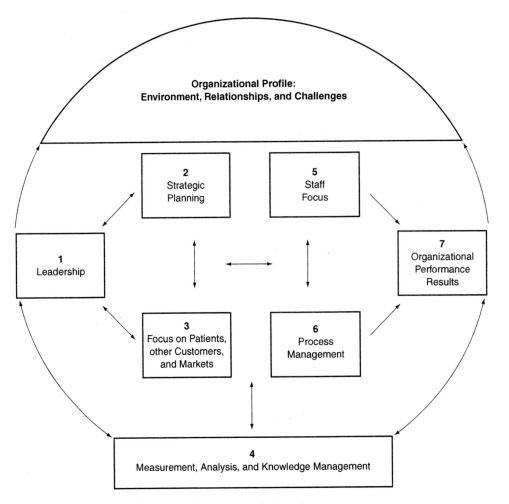

FIGURE 13.4   Malcolm Baldrige Healthcare Model for Excellence

"Everyone takes pride in working for an organization that others rate as the best."

—H. James Harrington

WHY DO SOME SIX SIGMA SYSTEMS FAIL?

"It is not the methodology that is bad; it is the way it is used or, to be more correct, **misused**."

—H. James Harrington

Not All Six Sigma systems are successful. Our data indicates that there are as many or more failures than there are successes. One of the basic improvement rules is: "Learn from every failure." That doesn't mean that you have to make all the failures to learn from them yourself. Let's look at some of the common reasons for failures and learn from other people's mistakes:

- **Lack of resources**. A Six Sigma program costs money—a lot more than the cost of training a few Black Belts and Green Belts. The Six Sigma program needs to have a budget that covers the cost of every person who will be working on the projects.

- **Lack of top management participation**. Six Sigma is a cultural change, not just solving a few problems. Top management needs to change its behavioral patterns if the culture within the organization is going to change. If top management can't find time to attend the executive training sessions, the Six Sigma system is doomed for failure.

- **It only applies to manufacturing**. Too many organizations only apply Six Sigma concepts to the manufacturing part of their organization and do not apply it to the service sector. The truth of the matter is that much of the reported Six Sigma savings come from improvements in the support and service processes. Limiting Six Sigma to manufacturing cuts the potential savings by 80 percent.

"The lack of initial Six Sigma emphasis in the non-manufacturing areas was a mistake that cost Motorola $5 billion over a four-year period."

—Bob Galvin, former CEO of Motorola

- **Poor project management**. Time after time, the individual Six Sigma projects take longer and cost more than they should. Sometimes the Six Sigma project runs so long that the team members change and the project is not completed. This results in a negative impact upon the bottom line. With the number of Six Sigma projects that are going on at the same time, the portfolio of projects must be managed and tracked by management.

- **Poor project selection**. Too many projects that are assigned to a Six Sigma team do not have the potential for justifying the Six Sigma effort. Only Six Sigma projects that have the potential of a 10-to-1 return on investment should ever be started.

- **Limiting Six Sigma to Black Belts and Green Belts**. A Six Sigma program must involve everyone within the organization. Too many organizations limit the Six Sigma system to the trained Black and Green Belts. The Black Belts are the high-stepping band majors that lead the band, and the Green Belts are the baton twirlers who just precede the band. The ones who make the music, however, are the Blue Belts who do the continuous improvement activities that result in 5 to 15 percent reduction in the total cost of doing business year after year after year.

- **No culture change**. Too many people believe that Six Sigma is just another fad. They can wait it out and not change any of their behavioral patterns. To reinforce that there is *no need* for change, the management team doesn't change the rewards and recognition system. If you don't change your rewards and recognition system, you will not change the results you get.

- **Selecting the wrong people**. Too many organizations feel that they cannot afford to put their best people into training to become Black Belts, so they assign people who are surplussed or relatively unimportant in the day-to-day organizational operations. This is a sure way to waste organizational funds and to ensure that the Six Sigma system will fail.

- **Shallow thinking**. Too often Six Sigma is looked upon as a quality program that is owned by the quality assurance organization. The organization functional units need to think about the needs of the total organization, not just their part. This goes for the Six Sigma project team also. Sometimes other projects should take priority over Six Sigma programs, and sometimes the Six Sigma program should have priority. Often a CRM (Customer Relations Management) software system can do more to improve customer satisfaction than the Six Sigma program itself. It is absolutely essential that you make Six Sigma part of the organization's system, not keep it as a separate part of the organization. We need to break down the silo thinking and look at the organization as a group of processes that flows across different functional boundaries.

- **Focus on problem-solving, not on prevention**. Six Sigma provides your organization with some very effective problem-solving tools, but that is not its real objective. The objective of your improvement system must be to prevent problems. Unfortunately, the financial group gives little credit to the cost avoidance, and management is primarily interested in cost reduction. Every problem you have is a sign that you did a poor job earlier. An unwritten rule at IBM was "To get ahead, you create a problem that you can solve and then solve it, as this is the best way to get promoted." A really successful Six Sigma system is one to which there are no problems of great enough magnitude to assign Green Belts or Black Belts.

Too Many Black Belts

"A really great organization does not need Black Belts."

—H. James Harrington

As the HCP's Black Belts maintain a sustained attack on the improvement opportunities, the opportunities that will save the organization large amounts of money become fewer and fewer. In some cases, they reach the point of no major problems to be identified. When this level of improvement is reached, there is no need to have Black Belts assigned full-time. Certainly, they are not required at the same ratio to the total population that was necessary when the HCP had many improvement opportunities. Re-assigning the Black Belts back to normal work assignments is not detrimental if the HCP culture has undergone the required transformation. In these cases, the natural work teams have picked up the Six Sigma culture and kept it intact by focusing on continuous improvement. At the same time, the Black Belts and Green Belts who are re-assigned to the normal population will bring back with them the skills that they were using in their previous assignment, allowing them to apply these skills to their normal job assignment. This will help their fellow workers assimilate these new skills.

HARRINGTON'S WHEEL OF FORTUNE

"Every organization must improve. When it stops improving, it is not standing still but slipping backward, because the competition is improving."

—Dr. H. James Harrington

The Six Sigma concepts in themselves will help any organization improve, but for the best, long-lasting results, these concepts must be supported by a complete improvement process that involves all facets of the organization (see Figure 13.5).

As you look at the wheel of fortune, you will note that the outer ring that holds the wheel together consists of management leading a process of unending change directed at continuous improvement. The wheel focuses this change process on making the organization more effective and efficient (the hub of the wheel). The spokes of the wheel make up the principles that are required to bring about continuous improvement.

- **Customer focus**. Customer focus is at the top of the wheel because it is the most important principle. Understanding customer needs and expectations is essential to staying in business. Your organization needs to be so close to customers that you can realize their present and future needs even before they recognize them on their own.

"Running a company by profit alone is like driving a car by looking in the rearview mirror. It tells you where you've been, not where you are going."

—Rafael Aguayo

FIGURE 13.5 Harrington's Wheel of Fortune.

- **Planning.** Excellence does not happen by accident. It requires a well thought-out, well communicated plan that is embraced by everyone. This plan must be based on a shared vision of how the organization will function and how the quality of work will improve, while providing output to the external customer that surpasses his or her expectations.

- **Trust.** Management must trust the employees before it can earn the trust of the employees. To excel, both parties have to trust each other. Employees will never willingly identify and eliminate waste until they trust management enough to be sure their own jobs will not be eliminated as a result of their suggested improvements.

- **Standardized Processes.** Real improvement occurs when everyone is performing an activity in the same way so that the results are predictable. When different people approach the same task in many different ways, the results are difficult to control or improve. Standardization is a key step in the improvement cycle.

- **Process Focus.** As we strive to continuously improve, we need to focus our efforts on improving the process, not on who caused the problem. The improvement process must define what went wrong with the process that allowed the problem to occur so that the process can be changed to prevent the problem from ever recurring. Variation within the organization's processes must be almost eliminated.

- **Total Participation**. No one in the organization is immune from the continuous improvement process. All people have a responsibility to improve the way they are working and to help the team they are part of be better. The time when employees were hired for their physical abilities alone is gone. We need the ideas and cooperation of all the team members if we are to excel. Everyone must be involved and be actively encouraged to participate in the improvement process.

- **Training**. Would you consider not putting oil in your car or not maintaining the equipment in your laboratories? The answer has to be no. Your most valuable asset is your people. Training is the maintenance of your human resources. Training is an investment in the future of your organization. Training is not costly—it is ignorance that is costly. Organizations are undergoing rapid change in the way they operate and the way people think, talk, and act. This change process must be supported by an aggressive training program that reinforces these changes and provides growth opportunities for your employees.

- **"Us" Relationships**. All members of the organization need to realize that they are part of the total organization. All individuals have customers to whom they provide output and suppliers who provide input to them. Our success, our growth, and our rewards are based on how well the total organization performs. Everyone has to stop thinking about *my* job, *those* people, and *management versus employees*. It can no longer be a *we* and *them* type of operation. The organization is *us*. Working together, we can make it better, make it grow, and make it prosper; as the organization prospers, all of *us* will prosper.

- **Statistical Thinking**. We can no longer run our complex business by our best guess. We need hard data. We need to know our options. We need to know the probability of success. Our businesses are too complex, and the difference between success and failure is too small. We can no longer continue to fly by the "seat of our plants." Sure, there will always be some judgment involved in many final decisions, but we should be able to quantify the risks involved in these judgment decisions.

- **Rewards**. Rewards and recognition are an essential part of improvement process. They reinforce desired behavior and visually demonstrate management appreciation of a job well done. To accomplish the desired result, a comprehensive reward and recognition system needs to be developed, one that allows management the latitude to be creative. Everyone hears thank-you in a different way. In addition, the reward must be based on the magnitude of the contribution. You need both team and individual rewards. At times, a simple thank-you is appropriate; on other occasions, financial reward is more appropriate. Take, for example, an employee who has worked hard for the last three months and has come up with an idea that saved the organization

$1 million. Her manager, in an effort to reward the employee, walks up to her, shakes her hand, and says, "That was an outstanding job. Keep up the good work, Jane. "Jane replies, "Thanks, boss, I will try." But what Jane is really thinking is, "I saved the organization $1 million, and all I get is a thank-you?! That's the last time I am going to knock myself out for this organization." There is a time for a pat on the back, and a time for a pat on the wallet.

PUTTING IT ALL TOGETHER

"Good, better, best! The best will always out do the rest."

—H. James Harrington

Henry Ford, Sr., was a man of the future. More than 80 years ago, he wrote, "The same kind of management which permits a factory to give the fullest service will permit a hospital to give the fullest service, and at a price so low as to be within the reach of everyone."[36]

In going around Harrington's Wheel of Fortune, we end up at Customer Focus, and quite appropriately so, because we can never get far away from the customer. As John A. Young, past president of Hewlett-Packard, put it, "Satisfying customers is the only reason we are in business." Harold A. Poling, past president of Ford Motor Company, stated, "Continuous improvement in everything that is done is what it will take to continue to satisfy the customer."

We are frequently asked, "What is the difference between Total Quality Control (TQC), Total Quality Management (TQM), Six Sigma, and Total Improvement Management (TIM)?" Table 13.5 shows a comparison of these major tools.

TABLE 13.5   Comparison Between TQC, TQM, Six Sigma, and TIM Tools/Approaches*

Harrington Institute, Inc.				
Tool or Approach	**TQC**	**TQM**	**Six Sigma**	**TIM**
Design of Experiments	X	X	X	X
Design Review	X	X		X
Problem-Solving Approach	PDCA	PDCA	DMAIC/DMADV	Many
Process Controls	X	X	X	X
Supplier Controls	X	X		X
Control Charts	X	X	X	X
Cpk Level	1.4	1.4	1.5	1.4
Quality Cost	X	X		X

Harrington Institute, Inc.				
Tool or Approach	**TQC**	**TQM**	**Six Sigma**	**TIM**
Product Directed	X			
Total Organization Director		X	X	X
Change Management		X		X
Quality Function Deployment (QFD)		X	X	X
Business Process Improvement		X		X
Teams		X	X	X
Total Involvement		X		X
Reliability Analysis		X		X
Process Qualification	X	X		X
Business Planning		X		X
Quality Policy		X		X
Quality Reporting Systems	X	X		X
Root Cause Analysis	X	X	X	X
Top Management Involvement		X	X	X
CRM				X
Knowledge Management				X
Quality Performance Level	Zero Defects (ZD)	Error-free	3.4/M	Error-free
Balanced Scorecard				X
Rewards and Recognition		X		X
Organization Transformation				X
ISO 9000/14000				X
National Quality Awards				X
Cycle Time Reduction		X		X
Lean		X	—	X
Quality Engineering	X	X		X
Special Problem-Solvers	X		X	
Continuous Improvement		X		X

(continued)

TABLE 13.5 (Continued)

Harrington Institute, Inc.				
Tool or Approach	**TQC**	**TQM**	**Six Sigma**	**TIM**
Primary Measure of Success				
• Reduced variation			X	
• Improved customer satisfaction		X		
• Reduced cost			X	X
• Reduced quality cost	X	X		
• Reduced defect level	X			
• Improve stakeholders satisfaction				X
Project Management				X
Corporate Governance				X
Primary Focus				
• Customer		X		
• Investor/management	X		X	
• Stakeholders				X
Quality Training for All		X		X
Quality Training for Specialists	X	X	X	X
Concurrent Engineering	X	X		X

*Prepared by Harrington Institute Inc.

We hope you have (or will soon have) started your organization on its improvement journey. It is a long journey with no end, a race with no finish line. Some people never start down this long road because they see no end. Others start jogging down the road and stop under a shady tree, never to reenter the race. Others get up everyday, get back on the road, and make real progress. These are the people who make a difference. They make difference to themselves, their families, their organizations, and their countries. Please join us in our long run for continuous improvement!

Good Enough

With "good enough" ships have been wrecked,
The forward march of armies checked,
Great buildings burned and fortunes lost;
Nor can the world compute the cost
In life and money it has paid
Because at "good enough" we stayed.

Who stops at "good enough" shall find
Success has left them far behind
With "good enough" the shirkers stop
In every factory and shop;
With "good enough" the failures rest
And lose to those who give their best;
With "good enough" the car breaks down
And those of high renown fall down.
My son, remember, and be wise
In "good enough" disaster lies.
My son, beware of "good enough"

It isn't made of sterling stuff;
It's something anyone can do,
It marked the many from the few,
It has no merit to the eye,
It is something anyone can buy,
Its name is but a sham and bluff.
For it is never "good enough."
There is no "good enough" that's short
Of what you can do and ought.
The flaw which may escape the eye
And temporarily get by,
Shall weaken underneath the strain
And wreck the ship or car or train,
For this is true of men and stuff—
Only the best is "good enough."

—Unknown Author

"It is always the last song that gets the most applause."

—H. James Harrington

ENDNOTES

1. Loeb, J. M. 2004. "Patient safety: An accreditor's perspective." *Healthcare Division Newsletter*, Spring.

2. Swayne, Brian J. 2003. "First aid for healthcare." *Quality Digest*, December.

3. Reid, Ralph D. and Marvin M. Christensen. 2002. "Using IWAI to span the healthcare quality chasm." *American Society for Quality Conference*, September 2002.

4. Berwick, Donald M. 2005. "Six keys to safer hospitals." *Newsweek*, December 12.

5. Revere, L., K. Black, and A. Hug. 2004. "Integrating Six Sigma and CQI for improving patient care." *The TQM Magazine* 16: 2, 105-113.

6. Serota, Scott P. 2005. "Fighting the battle against healthcare fraud." *Chief Executive Magazine*, June.

7. Dusharme, Dirk. 2006. "Federal agency requires health quality reporting." *Quality Digest*, March.

8. Levinson, William A. 2005. "Taking the TMS cure." *Quality Digest*, December.

9. Harry, Mikel, and Richard Schroeder. 1999. "Six Sigma: The Breakthrough Management Strategy Revolutionizing the World's Top Corporations." New York, NY: Doubleday Random House.

10. Revere, L., K. Black, and A. Hug. 2004. "Integrating Six Sigma and CQI for improving patient care." *The TQM Magazine* 16: 2, 105-113.

11. Bajaj, Vijaj. 2006. Speech given at the Global Six Sigma Awards held at the Venetian Resort Hotel and Casino. Las Vegas, NV, June 28.

12. Ibid.

13. Ibid.

14. Ibid.

15. Ibid.

16. Paton, Scott M. 2001. "No small change: Making quality Job 1 again." *Quality Digest*, September.

17. Hite, Roger and Dominican Santa Cruz Hospital. 1996. "Catholic Healthcare West: Documenting operational improvement." *Redesigning Healthcare Delivery*, Peter Boland, 331. Berkeley, CA: Boland Healthcare, Inc.

18. Southwich, K. 1993. "Multi-Year Restructuring Changes Stick at Stanford University Medical Center." *Strategies for Healthcare Excellence* 6:1.

19. Curran, C.R. and D. K. Houghton. 1995. "Renewing the Catholic healthcare ministry." St. Louis: Catholic Health Association.

20. Besecker, Walter J., Carol A. Craft, and Melissa McCanna. 1996. "Redesigning cost recover programs." Berkeley, CA: Boland Healthcare, Inc.

21. Bajaj, Vijaj. 2006. Speech given at the Global Six Sigma Awards held at the Venetian Resort Hotel and Casino. Las Vegas, NV, June 28.

22. Ibid.

23. Martin, Rick. 1996. St. Charles Medical Center: Streamlining hospital operations. Berkeley, CA: Boland Healthcare, Inc.

24. Esimai, Grace. 2005. "'Lean Six Sigma Reduces Medication Errors." *Quality Progress*, April.

25. Berwick, Donald M. 2005. "Six Keys to Safer Hospitals." *Newsweek*, December 12.

26. Ibid.

27. Ibid.

28. Ibid.

29. Riebling, Nancy B., Susan Condon and Daniel Gopen. 2004. "Toward error free lab work." *Six Sigma Forum magazine, ASQ*, November.

30. Dusharme, Dirk. 2006. "Six Sigma helps Illinois hospital." *Quality Digest*, August.

31. Bajaj, Vijaj. 2006. Speech given at the Global Six Sigma Awards held at the Venetian Resort Hotel and Casino. Las Vegas, NV, June 28.

32. Dusharme, Dirk. 2005. "Leapfrog Group releases hospital quality and safety survey." *ASQ Quality Progress*, January.

33. Smith, Laura. 2005. "Regional differences in hospital quality." *Quality Digest*, September.

34. Fornell, Claes, and Donald Cook. 2005. *The American Customer Satisfaction Index at Ten Years*. Ann Arbor, MI: University of Michigan Press.

35. McGee, M.K. 2004. "E-Health records get $50M shot in the arm." *Information Week*, July12.

36. Ford, Henry and Samuel Crowther. 1922. *My Life and Work*. Doubleday Page and Co.

PART V

APPENDIXES

PMBOK Tools and Techniques

Some of the more commonly used Project Management tools and technique (as recommended by the Project Management Institute and others) are listed in the following table. Evaluate yourself to determine your Project Management maturity level. For each one, check off your present level:

❑ Do not know it

❑ Know it but have not used it

❑ Used it

❑ Mastered

If you would like a more information on these or other improvement tools, contact the Harrington Institute web site: www.harrington-institute.com.

	Don't Know It	Know It, but Haven't Used It	Used It	Mastered It
1. Arrow diagramming method (ADM)				
2. Benchmarking				
3. Benefit/cost analysis				
4. Bidders conferences				
5. Bottom-up estimating				
6. Change control system				
7. Configuration management				
8. Checklists				
9. Communications skills				

(continued)

	Don't Know It	Know It, but Haven't Used It	Used It	Mastered It
10. Computerized tools				
11. Conditional diagramming methods				
12. Contingency planning				
13. Contract change control system				
14. Contract type selection				
15. Control Charts				
16. Control negotiation				
17. Cost change control system				
18. Cost estimating tools and techniques				
19. Decision trees				
20. Decomposition				
21. Design of Experiments				
22. Duration compression				
23. Earned value analysis				
24. Expected monetary value				
25. Expert judgment				
26. Flowcharting				
27. Human resource practices				
28. Information distribution tolls and techniques				
29. Independent estimates				
30. Information distribution systems				
31. Information retrieval systems				
32. Interviewing techniques				
33. Make-or-buy analysis				
34. Mathematical analysis				
35. Negotiating techniques				
36. Network templates				
37. Organizational procedures development				
38. Organizational theory				

	Don't Know It	Know It, but Haven't Used It	Used It	Mastered It
39. Parametric modeling				
40. Pareto Diagrams				
41. Payment system analysis				
42. Performance measurement analysis				
43. Performance reporting tools and techniques				
44. Performance reviews				
45. Pre-assignment technique				
46. Precedence diagramming method (PDM)				
47. Procurement audits				
48. Product analysis				
49. Product skills and knowledge				
50. Project Management information system (PMIS)				
51. Project Management information system organizational procedures				
52. Project Management software				
53. Project Management training				
54. Project Planning methodology				
55. Project selection methods				
56. Quality Audits				
57. Quality planning tools and techniques				
58. Resource leveling heuristics				
59. Reward and recognition systems				
60. Schedule change control system				
61. Scope change control system				
62. Screening system				
63. Simulation modeling				
64. Stakeholder analysis				
65. Stakeholder skills and knowledge				

(continued)

	Don't Know It	Know It, but Haven't Used It	Used It	Mastered It
66. Statistical sampling				
67. Statistical sums				
68. Status review meetings				
69. Team-building activities				
70. Trend analysis				
71. Variance analysis				
72. Weighting system				
73. Work authorization system				
74. Work Breakdown Structure templates				
75. Workarounds approaches				
Total				
Times Weight	0	1	2	3
Point Score				
Sum of Point Scores				

Using the sum of the individual point scores, the following is your Project Manager maturity level:

Excellent Project Manager	175–225
Acceptable Project Manager	125–174
Acceptable Project Team Member	100–124
Unacceptable Project Manager	50–100
Unacceptable Project Team Member	0–50

All Project Managers who have a point score below 125 need Project Manager training.

The Six Sigma Body of Knowledge

The following is a list of the Six Sigma Body of Knowledge. Under the columns marked Green, Black, or Master belt, the following symbols are used:

- **A** means they are almost *always used*. At least 90% of the projects will use these tools. (The related belt must be trained on how to use these tools or already have been trained in the use of these tools.)
- **O** means *often used*. It is used in more than 50% of the projects. (The related belt should be trained on how to use these tools or already have been trained on these tools.)
- **S** means *sometimes used*. It is used in 49% to 25% of the projects. (The related belt should know what they are used for and know where to go to get more information on how to use them.)
- **I** means *infrequently used to never used*. It is used in less than 24% of the projects. (These tools are nice to know but not required and not part of the belt's training or certification test.)

	SIX SIGMA BELTS		
BODY OF KNOWLEDGE	**Green**	**Black**	**Master**
5 S's	O	O	O
Acceptance Decisions	I	S	S
Activity Network Diagrams	S	S	S
Affinity Diagrams	S	O	O
Area Activity Analysis (AAA)	S	I	I
Automation	I	S	S

(continued)

	SIX SIGMA BELTS		
BODY OF KNOWLEDGE	**Green**	**Black**	**Master**
Axiomatic Design	I	S	S
Bar Charts/Graphs	A	A	A
Benchmarking	S	O	O
Bessel Function	I	S	O
Binomial Distribution	O	O	O
Bivariate Distribution	I	S	O
Box plots	S	O	O
Brainstorming	A	A	A
Bureaucracy Elimination	S	O	O
Business Case Development	A	O	O
Business Process Improvement	S	O	O
Calibration	O	O	O
Cause-and-Effect (Fishbone) Diagrams	O	O	O
Cause-and-Effect Matrix	O	O	O
Central Limit Theorem	O	O	O
Chi-Square Distribution	O	O	O
Coefficient of Contingency ©	I	S	S
Collecting Data	A	A	A
Communication Techniques	O	O	A
Confidence Interval for the Mean/ Proportion/Variance	O	O	O
Conflict Resolution	O	O	O
Continuous Flow Manufacturing (CFM)	S	O	O
Control Charts			
X bar -R Charts	O	O	O
Run Charts	O	O	O
MX bar-MR Charts	S	O	O
X-MR Charts	S	O	O
X bar-S Charts	S	O	O
Median Charts	I	S	O
Short Run Charts	S	S	O
p Charts	O	O	O
np Charts	O	O	O
r charts	S	O	O
u charts	S	O	O
Cusum Control Charts	I	S	S
Correlation Coefficient	O	O	O
Cp	O	O	O
Cpk	O	O	O
CQFA (Cost, Quality, Features, and Availability)	S	S	O

	SIX SIGMA BELTS		
BODY OF KNOWLEDGE	**Green**	**Black**	**Master**
Critical-to-Quality (CTQ)	A	A	A
Critical Path Method	O	O	O
Culture Roadblocks	I	O	O
Cumulative Distribution Function	S	O	O
Current State Mapping	O	O	O
Customer Requirements	A	A	A
Customer Surveys	S	O	O
Cycle-Time Analysis	S	O	O
Design for Maintainability and Availability	I	S	S
Design for Six Sigma (DFSS)	I	S	O
Design for X (DFX)	I	S	O
Design of Experiments (DOE)			
Three Factor, Three Level Experiment	I	O	O
Randomized Block Plans	I	S	O
Latin Square Designs	I	O	O
Graeco-Latin Designs	I	S	O
Full Factorial Designs	I	O	O
Plackett-Burman Designs	I	S	O
Taguchi Designs	I	O	O
Taguchi's Robust Concepts	I	S	O
Mixture Designs	I	S	O
Simplex-Lattice Designs	I	S	O
Steepest Ascent/Descent	I	S	S
Central Composite Designs	I	S	S
Response Surface Design	I	S	O
EVOP Evolutionary Operations	I	I	S
DMADV (Define, Measure, Analyze, Design, Verify)	S	O	O
DMAIC (Define, Measure, Analyze, Improve, Control)	O	O	O
Effort/Impact Analysis	I	O	O
Equipment Certification	S	S	S
Error Proofing	O	O	O
Exponential Distribution	I	O	O
External and Internal Customers	O	O	O
F Distribution	I	S	S
Facilitation of Teams	I	O	O
Factorial Experiments	I	S	O
Failure Mode and Effect Analysis (FMEA)	O	O	O
Fast-Action-Solution Team (FAST)	O	O	S

(continued)

	SIX SIGMA BELTS		
BODY OF KNOWLEDGE	**Green**	**Black**	**Master**
First-time Yield (FTY) or Rolled Through Yield (RTY)	O	O	O
Five Whys (5Ws)	O	O	O
Flow Charts	O	O	O
Focus Groups	S	O	O
Force Field Analysis	O	O	O
Frequency Distribution	O	O	O
Future State Mapping	O	O	O
Gantt Charts	O	O	O
Gaussian Curves	I	S	S
General Surveys	O	O	O
Histograms	O	O	O
History of Quality	S	S	S
Hypergeometric Distribution	I	S	O
Hypothesis Testing			
Fundamental Concepts	S	O	O
Point and Interval Estimation	I	S	O
Tests for Means, Variances, and Proportions	I	O	O
Paired Comparison Tests	I	O	O
Analysis of Variance	O	O	O
Contingency Tables	S	O	O
Nonparametric Tests	S	O	O
Interrelationship Diagraphs (ID)	S	O	O
Interviewing Techniques	O	O	O
IT Applications	S	O	O
Just-in-Time	I	S	S
Kaizen Blitz	I	I	I
Kanban	S	S	S
Kano Model	S	O	O
Kendall Coefficient of Concordance	I	I	S
Knowledge Management	I	S	O
Key Performance Indicators (KPIs)	O	O	O
Kruskal-Wallis One-Way Analysis	I	S	S
Lean Thinking	S	O	O
Levene Test	I	S	S
Lognormal Distribution	I	S	S
Loss Function	S	O	O
Management Theory History	I	S	O
Mann-Whitney U Test	I	S	S
Market Segmentation	S	S	O

BODY OF KNOWLEDGE	SIX SIGMA BELTS		
	Green	**Black**	**Master**
Matrix Diagrams	O	O	O
Measure of Dispersion	O	O	O
Measurement Error	O	O	O
Measurement Systems Analysis (MSA)	S	O	O
Measurement Tools	O	O	O
Method of Least Squares	O	O	O
Mood's Median Test	I	S	S
Motivating the Work Force	S	O	O
Mulit-Vari Analysis	S	O	O
Multiple Linear Regression	S	O	O
Negotiation Techniques	O	O	O
Nominal Group Technique	O	O	O
Normal Distribution	O	O	O
Normal Probability Plots	S	O	O
Null Hypothesis	S	O	O
Opportunity Cyle (Protection, Analysis, Correction, Measurement, Prevent)	S	S	S
Project Management	A	A	A
Organizational Change Management	O	O	O
Organizational Culture Diagnosis	S	O	O
Pareto Diagrams	A	A	A
Pattern and Trend Analysis	I	S	S
Plan-Do-Check-Act (PDCA)	S	S	S
Plan-Understand-Streamline-Implement Continuous Improvement (PUSIC)	S	O	O
Poisson Distribution	S	O	O
Poka-Yoke	S	S	S
Poor-Quality Cost	S	S	O
Portfolio Project Management	I	S	O
Prioritization Matrices	O	O	O
Probability Concepts	O	O	O
Probability Density Function	I	S	O
Probability Plots	O	O	O
Process Capability Studies	O	O	O
Process Decision Program Charts (PDPC)	S	O	O
Process Elements	O	O	O
Process Failpoints Matrix	S	S	S
Process Mapping	O	O	O

(continued)

	SIX SIGMA BELTS		
BODY OF KNOWLEDGE	Green	Black	Master
Process Performance Matrix	S	O	O
Process Redesign	S	O	O
Program Evaluation and Review Technique (PERT)	I	S	S
Poisson Series	I	S	O
Project Charter	A	A	A
Project Decision Analysis	I	S	O
Project Financial Benefits Analysis	A	A	A
Project Selection Matrix	I	S	A
Pugh Concept Selection	I	I	I
QFD (Quality Function Deployment)	S	O	O
Qualitative Factor	O	O	O
Quantitative Factor	O	O	O
Reengineering	I	S	O
Regression Analysis	S	O	O
Reliability Analysis	I	S	O
Response Surface Methodology (RSM)	I	S	S
Rewards and Recognition	S	O	O
Risk Analysis	A	A	A
Risk Assessment	A	A	A
Robust Design Approach	S	O	O
Root Cause Analysis	A	A	A
Rotation Patterns	I	S	O
Run Charts	O	O	O
Sampling	O	O	O
SCAMPER	S	S	S
Scatter Diagrams	O	O	O
Seven Basic tools	O	O	O
Sigma	O	O	O
Sigma Conversion Table	O	O	O
Signal-to-Noise Ratio	I	S	O
Simple Language	S	O	O
Simple Linear Regression	S	O	O
Simplification Approaches	O	O	O
Simulation Modeling	I	S	O
Single Minute Exchange of Die (SMED)	I	S	O
Six Sigma Metrics	I	S	O
Spearman Rank Correlation Coefficient	I	S	O
Stakeholders	O	O	O
Statistical Process Control	O	O	O

BODY OF KNOWLEDGE	SIX SIGMA BELTS		
	Green	**Black**	**Master**
Statistical Tolerance	S	S	O
Stem and Leaf Plots	I	S	O
Strengths, Weaknesses, Opportunities and Threats Analysis (SWOT analysis)	S	O	O
Structural Roadblocks	S	O	O
Student's T Distribution	I	S	O
Supplier Controls	S	O	O
Supplier, Inputs, Process, Outputs, Customers (SIPOC) Diagrams	O	O	O
Systematic Design	S	S	O
Takt Time	S	S	O
Team Building	O	O	O
Team Management	A	A	A
Theory of Constraints	S	S	O
Through Put Yield (TPY)	I	S	S
Tollgates	O	A	A
Total Productive Maintenance (TPM)	S	S	O
Tree Diagrams	O	O	O
TRIZ	I	I	I
Types of Data	O	O	O
Types of Teams	I	S	O
Value/Non-Value Added Activities	S	O	O
Value Stream Analysis (Mapping)	S	O	O
Variance (o?, s?)	I	O	O
Variation Analysis			
Rational Subgroups	S	O	O
Sources of Variability	S	O	O
Randomness Testing	S	O	O
Pre-control Techniques	I	S	O
Exponentially Weighted Moving Average (EWMA)	I	S	S
Moving Average	S	O	O
Visual Factory/Visual Office	S	O	O
Voice of the Customer (VOC)	A	A	A
Voice of the Supplier (VOS)	O	O	O
Weibull Distribution	I	O	O
Wilcoxon-Mann-Whitney Rank Sum Test	I	S	S
Work Breakdown Structure	O	O	O
Work Standard	I	S	O
Z Value	I	S	O

TOTAL SIX SIGMA TOOLS SELF-EVALUATION FORM

THE 20 QUESTION SIX SIGMA STATUS CHECKLIST

Prepared by Dr. Frank Voehl, Greg Brue, and the Allied Signal Design Team

The following 20 questions were developed back in the 1990s when we were doing high-level Six Sigma consulting work with the Allied Signal leadership team. They have proven to be an excellent guide to assessing the sustained performance of any organization's Six Sigma initiative. By routinely examining and reinforcing the mission with this 20 Question Checklist, clients can help minimize the potential for slipping or slacking in companywide projects. The key is to keep asking and keep answering these fundamentally important questions in order to keep the Six Sigma initiative on track:

1. Do you think the Six Sigma process is self-sustaining in your group?
2. What is the status of your Master Black Belts?
3. What is the status of your Green Belts?
4. How many reviews do your senior executives attend?
5. What are the dropout rates?
6. How many projects are officially completed?
7. How many Black Belts are ready for certification?
8. Have the Finance and HR Departments been an active part of the process?
9. Have you and the involved departments agreed on the guidelines that define true savings?
10. Do you currently have a manual system for tracking the backlog list of Black Belt projects by plant?

11. Do you have the next set of Black Belts identified and is upper management supportive?

12. Do you think you are focusing on implementing project completions?

13. Are you attempting to change the program or staying with the Black Belts' focus?

14. Should you stop doing Six Sigma? Why?

15. What is the status report you are giving to senior management?

16. Are the controllers signing off on your projects? Are they aware of the savings?

17. If you were to spot-check the controllers, what defect rate would you find? (In other words, how many do not know about the savings achieved by the projects?)

18. What database are you going to use through the life of tracking your Six Sigma projects?

19. What is the status of the Black Belt incentive program discussed at the beginning of the Six Sigma initiative?

20. What are the consequences for champions not helping and driving Black Belts?

All these questions are highly relevant and thought-provoking. And all the answers must be true and backed up by proof, not assumptions, to keep the momentum going. The last question is directed at the CEO and Senior Managers. They need to honestly examine whether or not they are removing barriers and supporting Black Belts in their efforts to achieve financial results. If not, they need to take the necessary steps to do so. Because Black Belts and project teams see management as the motivating force, they are the initiators of the culture change required to identify and remove defects!

STUDENT CHECK LIST

Please indicate your level of knowledge and/or proficiency related to each of the following items:

	Don't Know It	Know but Haven't Used It	Used It	Mastered It
Affinity Diagrams				
ANOVA				
Application of Discrete Data				
Benchmarking				
Binomial Distribution				
Business Process Improvement				
Calculating Process Sigma				
Cause and Effect				
Chi Square Test				
Contingency Planning				
Control Charts				
Control Charts for Attributes Data				
Control Charts for Variables Data				
CTQ Matrix				
Data Collection Approach				
Descriptive Statistics				
DFSS				
Discrete and Continuous Data				
DMADV				
DMAIC				
Earned Value and How to Use it successfully				
FMEA				
Fractional Factorial Experiments				
Full Factorial Experiments				
Hypothesis Testing				

	Don't Know It	Know but Haven't Used It	Used It	Mastered It
Introduction of QI Macros Software				
Kano Model				
Measure Model				
Measures of Central Tendency				
Measures of Dispersion				
Pareto Analysis				
Poisson's Distribution				
Poor Quality Cost				
Process Flow Structures				
Process Mapping				
Project Closeout Analysis				
Project Control Analysis				
Project Management Variance Analysis				
Quality Function Deployment				
Randomized and Randomized Block Diagrams				
Redesign				
Reengineering				
Regression Analysis				
Risk Analysis				
Root Cause Analysis				
Run Charts				
Sampling Approaches				
Sampling Techniques				
SIPOC				
Six Sigma Deployment Models				
Six Sigma Implementation Methodology 5 Absolutes				
Taguchi Robustness Concepts				

	Don't Know It	Know but Haven't Used It	Used It	Mastered It
The Project Management Life Cycle				
TRIZ				
T-Tests				
UniVariate and BiVariate Analysis				
Voice of the Customer				
Work Breakdown Structure (WBS)				

STUDENT NAME _____

DATE _____

ADDITIONAL RESOURCES

If you'd like to learn more about Lean and Six Sigma in healthcare, we've included a list of additional resources you might find helpful.

ASSOCIATIONS AND WEB SITES

Asia Pacific Quality Organization. www.apqo.org/

ASQ Six Sigma Forum. www.asq.org/sixsigma/

International Society of Six Sigma Professionals. www.isssp.com

ISixSigma Healthcare Portal. www.healthcare.isixsigma.com

QualityDigest. www.qualitydigest.com/sixsigma/

Six Sigma.US. www.6sigma.us/

Six Sigma Zone. www.sixsigmazone.com

BOOKS

Area Activity Analysis—Aligning Work Activities and Measurements to Enhance Business Performance (CD-ROM). H. James Harrington, Glen D. Hoffherr, Robert P. Reid, Jr., McGraw-Hill, 1998.

Business Process Improvement. H. James Harrington, McGraw-Hill, 1991.

Change Management Excellence: The Art of Excelling in Change Management. H. James Harrington, Paton Press, 2006.

Design for Six Sigma for Green Belts and Champions: Applications for Service Operations—Foundations, Tools, DMADV, Cases, and Certification. Howard S. Gitlow, David M. Levine, Edward A.Popovich, Prentice Hall, 2006.

High Performance Benchmarking: 20 Steps to Success. H. James Harrington, McGraw-Hill, 1995.

Leading Six Sigma: A Step-by-Step Guide Based on Experience with GE and Other Six Sigma Companies. Ronald Snee, Roger Hoerl, FT Press, 2002.

Lean Six Sigma: Combining Six Sigma Quality with Lean Production Speed. Michael L. George, McGraw-Hill, 2002.

Lean Six Sigma for Service: How to Use Lean Speed and Six Sigma Quality to Improve Services and Transactions. Michael L. George, McGraw-Hill, 2003.

Lean Thinking: Banish Waste and Create Wealth in Your Corporation, Revised and Updated. James Womack, Daniel Jones, Simon & Schuster, 1996.

Performance Improvement Methods: Fighting the War on Waste. H. James Harrington, Kenneth Lomax, McGraw-Hill, 1999.

Process Management Excellence: The Art of Excelling in Process Management. H. James Harrington, Paton Press, 2006.

Six Sigma Beyond the Factory Floor: Deployment Strategies for Financial Services, Health Care, and the Rest of the Real Economy. Ronald Snee, Roger Hoerl, Prentice Hall, 2004.

Six Sigma Business Scorecard, 2nd Edition. Praveen Gupta, McGraw-Hill, 2006.

Six Sigma for Green Belts and Champions: Foundations, DMAIC, Tools, Cases, and Certification. Howard S. Gitlow, David M. Levine, Prentice Hall, 2004.

The Six Sigma Handbook: The Complete Guide for Greenbelts, Blackbelts, and Managers at All Levels, Revised and Expanded Edition. Thomas Pyzdek, McGraw-Hill, 2003.

The Six Sigma Performance Handbook: A Statistical Guide to Optimizing Results. Praveen Gupta, McGraw-Hill, 2004.

The Six Sigma Way: How GE, Motorola, and Other Top Companies are Honing Their Performance. Peter Pande, Robert Neuman, Roland Cavanaugh, McGraw-Hill, 2000.

Stat Free Six Sigma. Praveen Gupta, Arvin Sri, BookSurge, 2007.

Statistics for Six Sigma Green Belts with Minitab and JMP. David M. Levine, Prentice Hall, 2006.

What is Six Sigma? Peter Pande and Larry Holpp, McGraw-Hill, 2001.

The Man I Want To Be!

A man who would be concerned with how he could help me instead of himself, who would give me loyalty instead of demanding of me, who would think of himself as my assistant, instead of my boss, who would think it was his job to help me do my job better.

A man whose pride was peculiar because his pride was in his people. A man who could walk around the organization and say, "Yes, it was well done but not by me. I just happen to be lucky enough to have the best team in the whole organization." That is where his pride lies. Anything worthwhile that comes out of the department, his team did. If something goes wrong, he feels that maybe he was not on the ball. Maybe he had not directed or guided or taught or led his team properly. He will take the blame for anything that goes wrong.

A man who never made a promise he didn't intend to keep, merely to slough me off. I would pick a man who might say, "Gee, I'm so busy, Jim, I just don't know if I'll ever get done. But let's not wait until tomorrow when it is more convenient for me. Let's sit down right now and go at it. Now is the time."

A man who knew that I was not a genius. If I come to him with an idea, I don't want him to give me that objective stuff. I don't want him to say, "You have a suggestion. Here is the form. Fill it out. Stick it in the box and three months later if it is any good we will give you an award for it."

I want him to get excited about my brain child. I want him to treat my brain child carefully, because it is the most wonderful idea in the world at the moment. I gave birth to this child of mine. I want him to treat it tenderly, especially tenderly if it is a feeble-minded brain child. The man who is going to get an award doesn't have to worry. It is I. If I don't get one, I will feel low. I want my boss to pick me up and encourage me.

A man who would handle every grievance right now, not like the fellow who has a 40-room mansion, but no garbage pails, and who says, "We just kick it around until it gets lost."

A man who in many ways reminded me of my father whom I loved dearly. But who had the knack if I stepped out of line, of lowering the boom so fast I didn't know what struck me until too late. But who if he thought I had been pushed around, would fight for me every step of the way up the line, even to the president of the company and the chairman of the board if necessary, to see that I got a fair shake and a square break.

—by Dr. J. L. Rosenstein
Modified by Dr. H. James Harrington, CEO, Harrington Institute

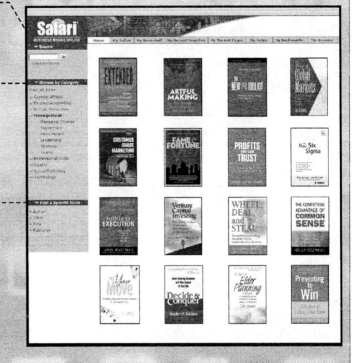

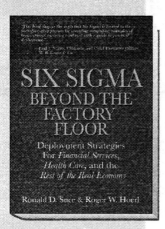

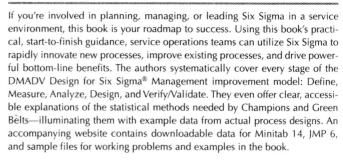